History of British Intelligence

Britannia and the Bear

History of British Intelligence

ISSN 1756–5685

Series Editor
Peter Martland

With the recent opening of government archives to public scrutiny, it is at last possible to study the vital role that intelligence has played in forming and executing policy in modern history. This new series aims to be the leading forum for work in the area. Proposals are welcomed, and should be sent in the first instance to the publisher at the address below.

Boydell and Brewer Ltd, PO Box 9, Woodbridge, Suffolk, IP12 3DF, UK

Previous volumes in this series:

British Spies and Irish Rebels: British Intelligence and Ireland, 1916–1945,
Paul McMahon, 2008
Available in hardback and paperback editions

The Spy Who Came In From the Co-op: Melita Norwood and the Ending of Cold War Espionage, David Burke, 2008
Available in hardback and paperback editions

The Lawn Road Flats: Spies, Writers and Artists, David Burke, 2014

Britannia and the Bear: The Anglo-Russian Intelligence Wars, 1917–1929,
Victor Madeira, 2014

The Secret War Between the Wars: MI5 in the 1920s and 1930s,
Kevin Quinlan, 2014

Britannia and the Bear

The Anglo-Russian Intelligence Wars
1917–1929

Victor Madeira

THE BOYDELL PRESS

First published 2014
The Boydell Press, Woodbridge
Paperback edition 2016

ISBN 978–1–84383–895–1 hardback
ISBN 978–1–78327–153–5 paperback

The Boydell Press is an imprint of Boydell & Brewer Ltd
PO Box 9, Woodbridge, Suffolk IP12 3DF, UK
and of Boydell & Brewer Inc.
668 Mt Hope Avenue, Rochester, NY 14620–2731, USA
website: www.boydellandbrewer.com

A CIP catalogue record for this book is available
from the British Library

The publisher has no responsibility for the continued existence or accuracy
of URLs for external or third-party internet websites referred to in this book,
and does not guarantee that any content on such websites is,
or will remain, accurate or appropriate

This publication is printed on acid-free paper

Contents

Illustrations

Tables

To my parents and Elaine –
For showing me the way.

Foreword

For over half a century after the Bolshevik Revolution the term 'subversion', though commonly used around Whitehall, was never officially defined. Even the Security Service (MI5), though it had the lead role in counter-subversion for most of this period, was reluctant to attempt a definition. In 1971, the Director General (DG) of MI5, Sir Martin Furnival Jones, told the Conservative Home Secretary, Reginald Maudling, that he had 'always refrained from trying to define subversion'. In the following year, however, the future DG, John Jones, then head of MI5 F Branch (counter-subversion), at last rose to the challenge, defining devised subversion as 'activities threatening the safety or well-being of the State and intended to undermine or overthrow Parliamentary democracy by political, industrial or violent means'. This definition was officially, though inconspicuously, adopted by Harold Wilson's Labour government in 1975, and reaffirmed by the Jim Callaghan government three years later.

Victor Madeira's pioneering study of 'Anglo-Russian Intelligence Wars' during the twelve years after the Bolshevik Revolution provides a persuasive and vivid analysis of the period during which fears of Soviet-inspired subversion in Britain were at their peak. Even the usually non-alarmist British Prime Minister, David Lloyd George, declared in March 1919: 'The whole of Europe is filled with the spirit of revolution.' At various times subversion was believed to threaten to undermine the loyalty not merely of the British working class but also of the police, civil service and armed forces.

Dr Madeira is the first to integrate successfully the early history of British counter-subversion with the development of the British intelligence services which provided secret evidence of Soviet subversion. Some senior ministers were so alarmed by the intelligence they received that they were willing to compromise secret sources and methods in order to make it public. As Prime Minister during the Second World War, Winston Churchill attached enormous importance to protecting the Ultra secret – the success of British codebreakers in decrypting German communications – for fear that its revelation would do serious damage to the war effort. Twenty years earlier, however, he was willing to reveal what was then Britain's most important intelligence source, the signals intelligence (SIGINT) derived from breaking Soviet ciphers. In 1920 Churchill was 'convinced that the danger to the state which has been wrought by the intrigues of [Russian] revolutionaries and the disastrous effect which will be produced on their plans by the exposure of their methods outweighs all other considerations'. In 1927, in order to justify breaking diplomatic relations with the Soviet Union, the Prime Minister, Stanley Baldwin, the Foreign Secretary, Austen Chamberlain, and the Home Secretary, Joynson-Hicks, all revealed to the Commons the contents of decrypted Soviet telegrams. Moscow responded by adopting the virtually unbreakable 'one-time pad' for its diplomatic and intelligence communications. The operational head of GCCS (the predecessor of today's SIGINT agency GCHQ), Alastair Denniston, wrote bitterly that the consequence of this orgy of governmental indiscretion had been 'to compromise our work beyond question'.

Britannia and the Bear also adds much to our knowledge of how much Soviet intelligence discovered about British counter-subversion. Arguably the greatest success of the OGPU (forerunner of the KGB) during the 1920s was to penetrate the Special Branch of the Metropolitan Police, which then had the lead role in monitoring civil subversion. The discovery of this penetration by MI5, then responsible only for counter-subversion in the armed forces and counter-espionage, enabled it in 1931 to gain the lead intelligence role in all aspects of counter-subversion – a turning point in British intelligence history.

Like all pioneering works, *Britannia and the Bear* points the way to further research. The degree of concern about subversion felt by Labour as well as Conservative governments during the Cold War has been widely underestimated. None of the excellent studies of Clement Attlee's post-Second World War Labour government mentions that Attlee, at his own request, had more one-on-one meetings with the DG of MI5 than any other twentieth-century British Prime Minister (probably more indeed than all other Prime Ministers combined). Attlee instructed MI5 to inform him personally whenever it had 'positive information that a Member of Parliament was a member of a subversive organisation'. He was deeply concerned that some Labour backbenchers were secret communists. As late as 1961, his successor as Labour leader, Hugh Gaitskell, in agreement with George Brown, the deputy leader, and the future Foreign Secretary Patrick Gordon Walker, Gaitskell's closest associates within the shadow cabinet, gave MI5 a handwritten list on House of Commons notepaper of sixteen Labour MPs who, they believed 'were in effect members of the CPGB pretending to be Labour members or men under Communist Party direction', as well as the names of nine 'possible' crypto-communists on Labour benches. Unwilling to become embroiled in internal Labour Party politics and anxious 'to do nothing which could be represented as partaking of a party political nature', MI5 decided not to investigate any of the MPs on the list.

Following the revelations of *Britannia and the Bear* on the twelve years after the Bolshevik Revolution, there is now a clear need for a similar volume on the early Cold War.

Christopher Andrew
Emeritus Professor of Modern and Contemporary History,
University of Cambridge
Convenor of Cambridge Intelligence Seminar

Preface

The news headlines tell the story...

At home, after costly and unpopular foreign wars, ordinary Britons turn on career politicians they see as out of touch with the public they supposedly represent. These wars, many believe, solved nothing. If anything, Britain now faces greater threats. Financial crises and political scandals involving the honours system only deepen the anti-Establishment mood of already disaffected (and by now poorer) voters.

Labour Party membership grows but concern deepens about many of the new joiners – they are not interested in Labour's broadly Socialist outlook. These are 'hard' Left, their sole aim to infiltrate and eventually seize the Party – body and soul – regardless of real-world consequences. Some opponents call these new members 'entryists' while others prefer the term 'Trotskyites', but the finer ideological differences are lost on the average voter. Another word for these 'hard' Leftists is 'Communists' but the term rarely makes the headlines.

Meanwhile a Conservative Party until recently divided appears to have temporarily made peace with itself. Led by a seasoned and plain-speaking Prime Minister, the Conservatives seem to be in the ascendant. And the new Prime Minister clearly wants to seize the political centre-ground, traditionally dominated by the 'soft' Left (the Liberals – now reduced to Parliamentary near-irrelevance following years of Coalition Government with the Conservatives – and the bulk of a Labour Party in growing disarray). At times, there seems to be no credible official opposition.

Abroad, after years of stagnation under increasingly out-of-touch rulers, Russia's charismatic new leader reverts to exporting anti-Western ideology while seeking to reclaim lost national pride and influence. A tiny circle of politicians seeks to achieve this by any means necessary: corruption; subversion (including the use of pro-Moscow agents of influence in Western political, financial and media circles); espionage; propaganda; promises of trade; calls to fight 'common enemies'; and outright war when needed.

Parts of Ukraine, the Baltics and Poland, along with slices of Georgia and other Caucasus nations, are firmly in Moscow's sights. But after years of costly and unpopular war, made worse by financial crises, Europe has severely cut its defence and security spending. As a result, Western leaders are unable to do much, even if they really wanted to. The British, by virtue of their outsize influence in European and world affairs, are the 'Anglo-Saxon' liberal enemy that must be sidelined and weakened where possible. Russia does this either by exploiting national, class and economic divisions in the United Kingdom, or by creating them where none exists through subversion and propaganda.

Sound familiar?

What may surprise readers is that the above is not about the present but actually describes what Britain faced near the end of the First World War and well into the 1920s. Disturbingly, though, this description does also apply to the UK and the West today. But our societies, policy-makers and national security communities face two additional related issues.

One is an overall decline in awareness of the past and the other is a rising tide of information (much of it irrelevant) that obscures a true understanding of events. For these reasons, Western commentators have called Russian actions in Crimea/Ukraine since 2013–14 'a new kind of war'. It is not. At its core, this hazy mix of political, covert, economic and other activity – things like espionage, provocation and propaganda – is actually only the latest chapter in a 100-year-old playbook the Bolsheviks called "active measures".

Though modernised to exploit the speed and reach of twenty-first-century mass and social media, this playbook retains its basic aim: *to influence behaviour*, enabling the Soviet-era intelligence, security and military men ruling Russia today to manipulate opponents. Active measures seem new to us now only because the West, which never fully came to grips with this challenge between 1917 and 1991, allowed its Russia expertise to die away after the Cold War and forgot vital lessons along the way.

Events in Ukraine show clear continuity from Bolshevik days, with adaptation along the way to benefit from technological and other developments over the past century. And this is set to continue. Russia's military doctrine to 2020 favours a shift from destruction to influence; from eradication of opponents to their inner decay; from conventional battlegrounds to information, psychological and perception wars; and from physical conflict to that in the human consciousness.

Modern Russian influence operations can be directly traced to Soviet "special propaganda", first taught in the early 1940s. Along the way, the Soviets perfected the concept of "reflexive control": essentially making opponents act as desired without them ever being aware of Moscow's hidden hand. Eventually, Soviet military doctrine saw victory as social revolution in enemy territories – just what east Ukraine and Crimea have experienced since 2014.

Moscow strategically exploits the volume and speed of modern communications to create alternative but quickly-shifting realities, causing uncertainty and stopping debate. This flood of conflicting information eventually overwhelms opponents' ability to make sense of it. By paralysing their decision-making, Russia gains the initiative. Ultimately, the goal remains what it has always been: winning the war for human minds.

Russia continues to exploit a range of new and longstanding ties across the European continent, to widen any cracks in solidarity. And since the 2007–08 financial crisis there have been plenty: northern Europe vs southern Europe; creditors vs debtors; and western nations ('old' Europe) vs eastern ('new' Europe). Moscow's campaign has benefited from residual Cold War ties between Russian intelligence and elements of the European Left.

Bullets cannot kill ideas. What the illegal annexation of Crimea has reminded us of is that, when used properly, the subversion of ideas and values makes victory possible without firing a single shot. Speaking after the Cold War, Oleg D. Kalugin – a former Major-General in Soviet intelligence and head of foreign counter-intelligence in the late 1970s – stressed that active measures were a tradition and not something new:

[Active measures are] the heart and soul of Soviet intelligence.... Not intelligence collection, but subversion: active measures to weaken the West, to drive wedges in the Western community alliances of all sorts – particularly NATO – to sow discord among allies, to weaken the United States in the eyes of ... Europe, Asia, Africa, Latin America, and thus to prepare ground in case ... war really occurs.*

V. P. M.
September 2016

---

* Cable News Network (CNN), 'Inside the KGB', *Cold War* series, January 1998.

Acknowledgements

I am particularly indebted to Dr Boris Volodarsky, Dr Ivo Juurvee, Will Fripp and Dr David Burke for their invaluable insights into Russian and Western intelligence, past and present.

Years ago, a Russian colleague started me on a fascinating journey; along the way, the Vetterlein family and Professor T. W. Körner have been equally kind and supportive. I am grateful to them all.

Russia's current political climate increasingly resembles that of the 1920s, when the security organs looked to isolate and control ordinary citizens by proscribing their interaction with the outside world. My only concern is the well-being of those who encouraged and advised me over time. I do not mention them here but they know who they are.

Elsewhere, sincere thanks to: Anna Abelmann; Professor Richard Aldrich; Professor Christopher Andrew; the late Dr Tennent H. Bagley; Dr Nick Barratt; Dr Jim Beach; Gill Bennett; the Cellan-Jones family; Christopher Donnelly; Chris Ellmers; the late Professor John Erickson; John Gallehawk; Richard Gibb; Professor Lord (Peter) Hennessy; R. A. J. Jansari; the late Professor Keith Jeffery; Eleanor Joyner; Dr David Kahn; Dr Zdzisław Jan Kapera; Professor Amy W. Knight; the late Dr Raymond Leonard; Lockie MacPherson; the late Dr Michael Parrish; Dr Michael Roi; Professor Robert Spence; Anthony Struthers; John Taylor; Michelle Van Cleave; Professor Dr Michael Wala; Major Warren W. Williams, Ph.D., US Army Special Forces (Ret.); and former intelligence officials who must remain anonymous.

The Bibliography and endnotes list archives consulted. For permission to quote from their material, my thanks to: the British Library Board; the Syndics of the Cambridge University Library; the Churchill Archives Centre, Cambridge, regarding The Papers of Lord (Maurice) and Lady (Adeline) Hankey, as well as Peter Headlam-Morley regarding The Papers of Sir James and Lady Agnes Headlam-Morley held there; the Curtis Brown Group Ltd (material reproduced with permission of Curtis Brown, London, on behalf of the Estate of Sir Winston Churchill; copyright © Winston S. Churchill); the Imperial War Museum in London and Dr Suzan Simpson regarding The Papers of Major-General Sir Vernon Kell KBE; the Metropolitan Police Authority; the National Maritime Museum; the Parliamentary Archives; the Special Collections Centre, University of Aberdeen; the Keeper of The National Archives,

Kew (copyright material from the Ramsay MacDonald papers is reproduced by permission of the granddaughter of the late Malcolm MacDonald); the Master and Fellows of Trinity College, Cambridge, and Brian Pollitt and Milton Gendel regarding the Maurice Dobb and Edwin Montagu collections, respectively, held there; and the Wiltshire and Swindon Archives. Quotations of Crown Copyright material in The National Archives and elsewhere are by permission of the Comptroller of Her Majesty's Stationery Office.

Overseas, I would like to thank staff at the French Army Historical Service (Vincennes), and the Foreign Policy Archive of the Russian Federation and the Russian State Archive of Socio-Political History (both in Moscow) for their professionalism and efficiency.

Excerpts from Victor Madeira, 'Moscow's Interwar Infiltration of British Intelligence, 1919–1929', *The Historical Journal* 46:4 (2003), 915–33, © 2003 Cambridge University Press, are reprinted with permission. Excerpts from Victor Madeira, '"Because I don't trust him, we are friends": Signals Intelligence and the Reluctant Anglo-Soviet Embrace, 1917–24', *Intelligence and National Security* 19:1 (2004), 29–51, and Victor Madeira, '"No Wishful Thinking Allowed": Secret Service Committee and Intelligence Reform in Great Britain, 1919–23', *Intelligence and National Security* 18:1 (2003), 1–20, are reprinted with permission (www.tandfonline.com).

For permission to reproduce illustrations, I am grateful to: the Syndics of the Cambridge University Library; Corbis Images (© Hulton-Deutsch Collection/CORBIS); Mageslayer99, Creative Commons (CC BY 3.0); the International Institute of Social History, Amsterdam; Bassano and Walter Stoneman (© National Portrait Gallery, London); the Keeper of The National Archives, Kew; and the Vetterlein family. I have made every reasonable effort to trace copyright holders of illustrations and unpublished documents used here; apologies to anyone whose copyright may have been unwittingly infringed.

Many others have been of great help but I would particularly like to acknowledge: Ash Birch Ruffell for early work on the cover design; Steve Ovens (Bletchley Park); Jovita Callueng (British Library); Don Manning, Lynda Unchern and Dr Patrick Zutshi (Cambridge University Library); Linda Nicol (Cambridge University Press); Francesca Alves (Churchill Archives Centre); Nicholas Malherbe and Yuliya Stuart (Corbis Images); Richard Pike (Curtis Brown); Yvonne Oliver and Anthony Richards (Imperial War Museum); Gerben van der Meulen, Co van Rooijen and Guusje Varkevisser (International Institute of Social History); Camilla O'Hare (Metropolitan Police Authority); Mike Bevan and Graham Thompson (National Maritime Museum); Alexandra Ault and Matthew Bailey (National Portrait Gallery); Dr Mari Takayanagi (Parliamentary Archives); Lisa Dowdeswell (Society of Authors); Michelle Whittaker (Taylor & Francis Group); Paul Johnson and Tim Padfield (The National Archives); Jonathan Smith (Trinity College Library); Michelle Gait (University of Aberdeen); Kathleen Fagan (University of Glasgow); Ruth Cavender (War Memorials Trust); and Claire Skinner (Wiltshire and Swindon Archives).

To the Boydell & Brewer team – my editors (Drs Megan Milan, Peter Martland and Michael Middeke), Nick Bingham, Rohais Haughton, Catherine Larner, Simon Loxley, Rosie Pearce, Bruce Phillips, Anna Robinette, Lena Waller and their technical wizards – thank you for making this project happen.

A portion of any royalties earned from the sale of this book will go to charity.

I alone am responsible for any omissions or errors; readers' comments or corrections are welcome.

V. P. M.

September 2016

Abbreviations

2ᵉ Bureau	Military intelligence section, Army General Staff (France: 1871–1940)
IV Upravlenie	IV Directorate, Army General Staff (USSR: 1926–34)
ABCR	Association of British Creditors of Russia
AI4	Signals intelligence branch, Air Ministry Air Intelligence Directorate
ARCOS	All-Russian Cooperative Society
AVP RF	Foreign Policy Archive of the Russian Federation, Moscow
BBC	British Broadcasting Company/Corporation
BEU	British Empire Union
BP	Secret Intelligence Service agent identifier: Reval (present-day Tallinn); Bletchley Park
BWL	British Workers' League
"C"	Chief, Secret Intelligence Service
CB	Companion, The Most Honourable Order of the Bath
CBE	Commander, The Most Excellent Order of the British Empire
CIA	Central Intelligence Agency (USA: 1947–)
CID	Committee of Imperial Defence; Criminal Investigation Department, London Metropolitan Police
Cmd	Parliamentary Command Paper
CMG	Companion, The Most Distinguished Order of St Michael and St George
COMINT	Communications intelligence (see Glossary)
Comintern	Third Communist International (Russia, USSR: 1919–43)
COMSEC	Communications security
CPGB	Communist Party of Great Britain
CX	Secret Intelligence Service reports
DBFP	*Documents on British Foreign Policy*
DMI	Director(ate) of Military Intelligence, War Office
DNI	Director of Naval Intelligence, Naval Intelligence Division, Admiralty
FF	French franc
FO	Foreign Office
FR	Secret Intelligence Service agent identifier: Riga
FSB	Federal Security Service (Russian Federation: 1995–)
FY	Financial year

GCCS	Government Code and Cipher School (1919–46)
GCHQ	Government Communications Headquarters (1946–)
GDP	Gross Domestic Product
GPU	State Political Directorate (Russia, USSR: 1922–23)
GRU	Main Intelligence Directorate, Army General Staff (USSR, Russian Federation: 1942, 1945–46, 1953–2011/16? Now GU?)
HMS	Her/His Majesty's Ship
HUMINT	Human intelligence
IIB	Industrial Intelligence Bureau
IJIC	*International Journal of Intelligence and Counter-intelligence*
INO	Foreign Section, *(V)Cheka* and successors (Russia, USSR: 1920–41; later First Chief Directorate of the Committee for State Security)
INS	*Intelligence and National Security*
IP	Intelligence and Police (Club)
IPI	Indian Political Intelligence (1909–47)
ISC	Intelligence and Security Committee/Coordinator
ISK	Illicit Signals Knox
ISOS	Illicit Signals Oliver Strachey
IWM	Imperial War Museum
JAFO	Japanese Forces Section, Bletchley Park
JIC	Joint Intelligence Committee
KBE	Knight Commander, The Most Excellent Order of the British Empire
KCB	Knight Commander, The Most Honourable Order of the Bath
KCMG	Knight Commander, The Most Distinguished Order of St Michael and St George
KGB	Committee for State Security (USSR: 1954–91)
KIM	Young Communist International
KRO	Counter-intelligence Section, *(V)Cheka* and successors (Russia, USSR: 1922–91; later Second Chief Directorate of the Committee for State Security and Directorate K of the Committee's First Chief Directorate)
Luftwaffe	German Air Force
MI1$_{(b)}$	Code-breaking bureau, War Office (1914–18)
MI1$_{(c)}$	Secret Intelligence Service (1916–21; see SIS)
MI5	Security Service (1916–29/31, but still commonly used)
MI6	See SIS
MI(B)	Military Intelligence (B)
MID	Ministry of Foreign Affairs (Russia: pre-1917 Bolshevik Revolution; Russian Federation: post-1991)

MP	Member of Parliament
NATO	North Atlantic Treaty Organisation (1949–)
NEP	New Economic Policy
NID	Naval Intelligence Division, Admiralty
NKID	People's Commissariat for Foreign Affairs (Russia, USSR: 1917–46)
NMM	National Minority Movement
NSA	National Security Agency (USA: 1952–)
NUPPO	National Union of Police and Prison Officers
OBE	Officer, The Most Excellent Order of the British Empire
ODNB	*Oxford Dictionary of National Biography*
OGPU	Combined State Political Directorate (USSR: 1923–34)
Okhrana	Department for Defence of Public Security and Order (Russia: 1881–1917; see Glossary)
OMS	International Liaison Service, Third Communist International; Organisation for the Maintenance of Supplies
OSA	Official Secrets Act
OTP	One-time-pad (see Glossary)
P	Secret Intelligence Service agent identifier: Petrograd (present-day St Petersburg)
PCO	Passport Control Officer/Organisation
PID	Political Intelligence Department, Foreign Office (1918–20)
PMS2	Section 2, Parliamentary Military Secretary Department (1916–17)
PRO	Public Record Office, London (The National Archives since 2003)
Profintern	Red International of Labour Unions
RAF	Royal Air Force
Razvedupr	Intelligence Directorate, Army General Staff (Russia, USSR: 1921–22, 1924–26)
Registrupr	Registration Directorate, Army Field Staff (Russia: 1918–21; see Glossary)
Rezident	Head of Russian/Soviet intelligence station (*rezidentura*)
RGASPI	Russian State Archive of Socio-Political History, Moscow
RN	Royal Navy
RNVR	Royal Naval Volunteer Reserve
ROSTA	Russian Telegraph Agency
RPI	Retail Price Index
RR	Russian rouble
RU	See *Razvedupr*
SIGINT	Signals intelligence (see Glossary)
SIS	Secret Intelligence Service (1921–)

SIV	Single Intelligence Vote
SNK	See *Sovnarkom*
Sovnarkom	Council of People's Commissars (Russia, USSR: 1917–46)
Spetsotdel	Special Section (Russia, USSR: 1921–36)
ST	Secret Intelligence Service agent identifier: Helsingfors (present-day Helsinki); initially for Stockholm, Sweden
STO	Supply and Transport Organisation
SVR	Foreign Intelligence Service (Russian Federation: 1991–)
TASS	Telegraph Agency of the Soviet Union
THJ	*The Historical Journal*
TNA	The National Archives, London
Tsentrsoyuz	All-Russian Central Union of Consumers' Societies
TUC	Trades Union Congress
UK	United Kingdom
UKIC	UK intelligence community
USA	United States of America
USSR	Union of Soviet Socialist Republics (1922–91)
(V)Cheka	(All-Russian) Extraordinary Commission for Combating Counter-Revolution and Sabotage (Russia: 1917–22; see Glossary)
VTsIK	All-Russian Central Executive Committee
VTsSPS	All-Russian Central Council of Trade Unions
WSA	Wiltshire and Swindon Archives, Chippenham
YCL	Young Communist League

Glossary

COMINT (See Abbreviations). 'Technical information and intelligence derived from foreign communications by other than the intended recipients.'[1]

Currency In this book, currency exchanges for wages use the historical standard of living based on the RPI, while those for budget or expenditure calculations use the economic cost of share of GDP, as in www.measuringworth.com.

Intelligence In this book, intelligence is insight or knowledge derived from the assessment of both covert (HUMINT and SIGINT; see below) and overt reporting (e.g. media).

Okhrana (See Abbreviations). Created in 1881, though foreign operations by predecessors dated back to the mid-1820s. *Okhrana* tradecraft was so effective that the *Cheka* adopted virtually all of it.

O. S. After the Bolshevik Revolution, Russia switched from the Julian to the Gregorian calendar at midnight on 31 January 1918. The next day became 14 February (i.e. Julian equalled Gregorian minus thirteen days). Events in Russia up to 31 January 1918 followed the Julian calendar and had the suffix (o. s.), for "old style".

OTP A one-time-pad is an encryption method that uses a randomly generated key only once, known only to the sender and receiver of a message. Re-using the key makes the message vulnerable to decryption.

Registrupr (See also '*Registrupr*', '*Razvedupr*', '*IV Upravlenie*' and 'GRU' in Abbreviations). The Registration Directorate, in place from November 1918 to February 1921, was the first incarnation of the GRU.[2]

SIGINT (See Abbreviations). '1. A category of intelligence comprising either individually or in combination all communications intelligence [COMINT; see above], electronic intelligence, and foreign instrumentation [SIGINT], however transmitted.

---

[1] US Department of Defense, *Joint Publication 1–02: Dictionary of Military and Associated Terms* (2013), p. 53, www.dtic.mil.

[2] V. M. Lurie and V. Ia. Kochik, *GRU: Dela i Lyudi* [Affairs and People] (Sankt Peterburg, 2002), p. 6.

2. Intelligence derived from communications, electronic, and foreign instrumentation signals.'[3]

(V)Cheka   (See also '*(V)Cheka*', 'INO', 'GPU', 'KRO', 'OGPU' and 'KGB' in Abbreviations). Established on 20 December 1917 and better known as *Cheka*, this was the first Bolshevik secret police; its foreign intelligence section (INO) was created on 20 December 1920. Many officers in the FSB and SVR, the main post-Soviet successors to the KGB, still call themselves *Chekisty*.

On 2 February 1922, the Politburo abolished the *(V)Cheka* and ordered a GPU statute. The VTsIK Presidium adopted the resolution abolishing the *(V)Cheka*, transferring it into the GPU on 6 February. After GPU Order no. 247 of 11 June 1923, a reorganisation commission was set up.

On 2 November, the VTsIK Presidium adopted a resolution to reorganise the GPU into the OGPU under *Sovnarkom*. On the 15th, the Presidium adopted the 'Statute of the OGPU and its Organs', formalised by OGPU Order no. 486 of 21 November 1923. The name did not change until 1934.

[3]   US Department of Defense, *Joint*, p. 263.

Heads of Agency (1917–29)

GCCS[1]

Commander Alexander Guthrie Alastair Denniston, CMG, CBE, RNVR
(1919–42)

Home Section, Secret Service Bureau
(later MI5, Security Service)

Major-General Sir Vernon George Waldegrave Kell, KBE, CB
(1909–40)

Special Branch
CID, London Metropolitan Police[2]

Sir Basil Home Thomson, KCB
(1913–21)

Major-General Sir Borlase Elward Wyndham Childs, KCMG, KBE, CB
(1921–28)

Hon. Sir Frank Trevor Roger Bigham, KBE, CB
(1928–31)

Foreign Section, Secret Service Bureau
(later $MI1_{(c)}$, SIS/MI6)

Captain Sir Mansfield George Smith Cumming, KCMG, CB, RN
(1909–23)

Admiral Sir Hugh Francis Paget Sinclair, KCB, RN
(1923–39)

---

[1] In September 1923, GCCS was formally subordinated to SIS, making Hugh Sinclair the School's director. Alastair Denniston continued overseeing daily operations.

[2] From May 1919 to November 1921, Basil Thomson headed a new agency (Home Office Directorate of Intelligence), essentially a Special Branch independent from CID.

Introduction

> Insanity: doing the same thing over and over again, and
> expecting different results.   Albert Einstein

BETWEEN October 1917 and October 1929, Great Britain[1] and Bolshevik Russia fought the "first" Cold War.[2] Like the better-known one later on, this was above all a struggle between security and intelligence services – and not just those on opposing sides. Those early 'dances in deep shadows',[3] between the imperial superpowers of the time, earned British intelligence officers the grudging respect (and enmity) of their Russian counterparts, who to this day still privately regard Britons as their toughest opponents. This illustrates the need for historical perspective in understanding the cultural-strategic mind-sets of rival powers like Russia, where State needs already outweighed individual rights centuries before Communism appeared.

Even before Vladimir V. Putin's appointment as Prime Minister in August 1999, but certainly since then, he and other *siloviki* (a dominant but divided faction consisting mainly of Soviet-era intelligence and military officers)[4] have revived *Chekist*[5] myths. This process has increasingly centred on what was ultimately the main concern for communist security organs: foreign subversion, however defined, of State institutions and ideology.[6]

With warnings from the past so loudly echoing in the present, this book explores three related themes. First is the exploitation of intelligence by factions in British government to advance particular policies toward Moscow. In this context, intelligence means the information as well as the people (and institutions) providing it. The second is the influence of intelligence (in both these senses) in shaping those factional views of Bolshevik subversion. The final theme is the gap between Russian "realities" of subversion and British official perceptions of it, especially at times of diplomatic tension. Underlying these themes was a vital question that had exercised Britain's finest legal minds for centuries but remained unanswered in the twelve years under review. What is subversion?

A blend of old fears and new conditioned Bolshevik perceptions of Western subversion. From the days of Kievan Rus eleven centuries ago, Russia's twin terrors have been foreign invasion and internal unrest – particularly if they are simultaneous.[7] To this mindset shaped by climate, geography and history, Bolshevism added an element of its own: a refinement of the Russian radical tradition of *konspiratsya*.[8] For Vladimir I. Lenin's followers this became an indispensable survival tactic, honed in clandestinity while trying to outwit the *Okhrana* (the Tsarist secret police renowned for its use of *agents provocateurs* against opposition groups).[9] The fearful Bolsheviks embraced secrecy as a norm, compulsively seeking security through a 'never-ending search for enemies'[10] – a reflex reinforced by Western support for the counter-revolutionary Whites. To overcome this alliance the Reds deployed a range of "legal" and "illegal" subversive measures,[11] the full sophistication of which the West did not recognise for years. Ideologically motivated, amply funded and often ruthless in execution, this decades-long campaign was at times a one-sided affair. With the West's insistent refusal to learn from the past (and given Russia's current rulers), why does it keep deluding itself that much has changed?[12]

The end of the Union of Soviet Socialist Republics (USSR)[13] on 26 December 1991 – what in 2005 President Putin reportedly called 'the greatest geopolitical catastrophe' of the twentieth century[14] – was a unique opportunity. The West could have created a modern-day Marshall Plan to help a chaotic post-Soviet Russia to integrate into the new international system. Though requiring vigilance given the collapse of central authority in an empire with a formidable unconventional arsenal, such foresight could have drawn Russia much closer to the West.

What followed instead was a Grand Strategic blunder borne partly out of unnecessary triumphalism and self-congratulation, the consequences of which are visible today concerning issues like weapons proliferation, Ukraine and transnational organised crime. After the Soviet collapse, some in the United States (USA) set the tone by declaring 'the end of history'.[15] At the same time, the remaining superpower and its allies sought large peace dividends from military and intelligence budgets,[16] dismissed a weakened Russia as diplomatically inconsequential and hastily tried reforming the country's shattered economy. In the early 1990s, this much-needed but hated economic "shock therapy" caused most Russians (including some *siloviki*) untold hardship, reinforcing their perceptions that the West's main concern was opening up local markets to foreign businesses. Nobody would argue Moscow badly needed help with institutional reforms by 1991. However, the manner in which Westerners sometimes acted and the tone of some of their advice needlessly made a proud – and by now fearful – people feel like beggars.

Even a scrap of historical perspective would have underscored just how short-sighted some Western actions were, which along with the 1998 financial crisis ultimately contributed to a backlash that smothered Russia's version of emerging democracy. Having lost everything overnight and now struggling just to survive, ordinary Russians resented how Western influence (perceived and actual) bankrupted and demeaned them during the tumultuous Yeltsin years. The *siloviki* exploited this bitterness and desire for a return to stability. Bent on restoring national pride and status, preferably if coinciding with personal advancement, they have thrived under Putin, supplanted the oligarchs and become the State,[17] seizing the spoils along the way. Despite cosmetic reforms, the old Committee for State Security (KGB) has survived, morphing into an entity with an even more insular and aggressive mindset now that so much personal wealth and power are at stake. The West forgot bitter lessons identified over seventy-four long years fighting Communism. But why?

To answer this question is to gain insight into East–West rivalry not just during the (second) Cold War but also in an increasingly unstable twenty-first century. Culture, upbringing and age shape perception. More importantly, individuals from diverse cultures can attribute different historical interpretations to the same generic narrative. The implication is therefore that some historical patterns unnecessarily repeat themselves because people – and the organisations they belong to – fail to learn lessons identified that could prevent painful and costly errors.

Early Bolshevik Russia, like that of early post-Soviet years, was chaotic. On both occasions, there was deep unease about Western intentions. In both instances Russians, though of two minds about the security and intelligence organs, ultimately regarded them and the military as arguably the only institutions that could still protect the country from foreign hostility. Both times, security and intelligence men had a tight hold on the nation within a decade. The difference is that while in communist days the organs served the Party and the State, today the *siloviki* are the State. These men proudly embody and uphold traditions dating back to the early days of Soviet (and increasingly Tsarist) intelligence to legitimise their position. Identifying precedents set in the first decade of Bolshevik relations with the West thus seemed a valuable way 'to think the present historically'.[18]

Taking the long view of British fears of communist subversion from 1917 to 1991 underscores the importance of learning about the first Cold War to understand the second – and perhaps even help avoid a third. The 1926 General Strike, the gradual introduction of positive (or developed) vetting between 1947 and 1951 by the British Government, Prime Minister Harold

Wilson's response to striking seamen in 1966 and Prime Minister Margaret Thatcher's handling of the 1984–85 miners' walkout help to put Anglo-Soviet relations in perspective.

The Second World War changed British official thinking on communist subversion. Western advances in atomic weaponry forced Whitehall to consider positive vetting[19] from 1947 because espionage had finally become a greater worry than ideological subversion. In September 1945, a defecting military intelligence (GRU) cipher clerk in Canada had exposed Soviet spying on wartime allies,[20] but Western politicians should have seen this not as a new practice but as the continuation of an old one.[21]

Conversely, for seventy-four years British anxieties about Communism displayed much continuity. The greatest fear was Moscow's influence (perceived or actual) on trade unions. Not only did successive Cabinets feel unions could paralyse the country and bring down governments through strikes[22] but the Soviets did at times fund industrial action in Britain. Contingency planning by Whitehall was quickly in place,[23] and preparations for the 1984–85 miners' walkout were remarkably similar to those for the 1926 General Strike. Another element of continuity was official willingness to defy strikers regardless of political party in power. Thatcher's Conservatives were just as determined to face down miners in 1984–85 over pit closures as Wilson's Labour had been to confront seamen in 1966 over pay.

Continuity in British official thinking about subversion manifested itself in two other, related ways. One was the lasting, self-admitted inability of the intelligence "community"[24] to cope with pervasive Soviet activities. The other was that the community therefore redefined over time what constituted loyalty, above all for a small number of intellectuals and civil servants who held sensitive posts but supported Communism.[25] Constant 'vigilance for signs of disloyalty and intrigue' often created 'a distorted picture',[26] further straining Anglo-Russian ties.

Most Western works on Russian foreign intelligence regard the 1934 recruitment of Harold "Kim" Philby as the start of serious targeting of Whitehall.[27] Despite relying primarily on exfiltrated Russian intelligence officers and records for content, however, these books barely address the importance of the seventeen years after the Bolshevik Revolution.[28] For Moscow would have found it far harder to recruit agents like the Cambridge Five had there been as much of a Soviet "intelligence vacuum" in Britain as key works seem to imply by their omissions.[29] In the 1930s, Soviet penetration agents ("moles") succeeded to the extent they did thanks largely to Whitehall's difficulty in recognising the scope of Russian clandestine groundwork laid beforehand in Britain. In exploring this groundwork, this book complements pioneering research on some of Moscow's greatest intelligence successes against London.[30]

Russian historiography of foreign intelligence is more problematic, largely because of a tradition of 'cynical bias' dating back to the 1920s, when Joseph V. Stalin started rewriting history.[31] Since 1991, dozens of works have appeared, mainly by former or serving intelligence officers usually writing sanitised memoirs or historical accounts. In a process similar to what happens in Britain and elsewhere, Russian security and intelligence organs vet manuscripts but especially those referring to still-classified records or events. However, modern Russian agencies retain the old Soviet practice of distorting perception through selective information releases,[32] unfortunately undermining the reliability of many works despite their authors' creditable efforts.[33] A good example was a history of the GRU, arguably Russia's most secretive and effective human intelligence (HUMINT) service. The work discussed espionage in Germany and the USA but not in Britain, a prime target in the interwar period.[34]

This book draws on sixty-three collections from fifteen British, Russian and French archives, with many of the documents published here for the first time in nearly a century. They transform our understanding of Anglo-Russian intelligence history, showing, for instance, that the Cambridge Five were not the first long-term Soviet sources in the British Foreign Office and intelligence community, as previously thought. The earliest known penetration occurred around 1919, when the Five were not yet teenagers.

By the Armistice, Victorian and Edwardian mindsets shaped the responses of men like Winston Churchill (Munitions Minister), Lord Curzon (Leader of the House of Lords), Walter Long (First Lord of the Admiralty) and General Henry Wilson (Chief of the Imperial General Staff) to reports on the spread of the Bolshevik "cancer". When Stanley Baldwin twice led the Conservative Party to power in 1923–24 – first after helping topple Prime Minister David Lloyd George and the Coalition Liberals, and then after Labour's first spell in office – Churchill's and Curzon's anti-Bolshevism had even fewer constraints. Nevertheless, views depended on who held what ministerial or Civil Service post. Lloyd George[35] felt a no-nonsense but consistently engaging approach toward Moscow could contain subversion.[36] However, Churchill, Curzon and Long – for the Bolsheviks, the true opponents in Cabinet of Anglo-Soviet ties[37] – likened subversion to a real infection[38] that would ravage the British Empire if not confronted.

Linkages between the home and war fronts further shaped official views. Attitudes formed initially by the First World War changed as a longer-term perspective on Bolshevism became possible. Because many politicians and officials genuinely believed in a communist threat, they encouraged a "Red Scare" in Britain following the October 1917 Revolution. Hardline intelligence officials in particular, some of them now responsible for reporting on subversion, stoked initial fears. This book concentrates on four agencies: the London Metropolitan Police Special Branch, MI5, the Government Code and Cipher School (GCCS) and MI1$_{(c)}$ (later known as SIS and MI6);[39] and key individuals overseeing both intelligence work against Moscow and British intelligence reforms from 1917 to 1929.

Britain's self-delusion about potential commercial opportunities with the USSR was a defining feature of bilateral relations from 1917 to 1991,[40] and one that continues to colour Anglo-Russian ties to this day. Yet when British politicians employed intelligence wisely,[41] it crucially allowed them to understand threats to the State better and (re-)direct scarce resources to counter them. Fear that Bolshevism threatened social order and imperial interests prompted some politicians and officials to press for intelligence reform at the end of the war. Afterwards, the symbiotic relationship between anti-communist politicians and security officials made them (and Britain, in the longer term) victims of their shorter-term success in preventing revolution.

By concentrating on symptoms of popular discontent more to do with postwar socio-economic conditions and State policies than foreign interference, these men helped blind government to the graver danger of Bolshevik penetration. This book argues that early distortions by British political and intelligence diehards of a nevertheless real overt subversive threat subsequently undermined evidence of Bolshevik covert subversion (both current and planned). Ultimately, Soviet intelligence practices and successes in the 1920s paved the way for even more damaging penetrations in the 1930s.

PART I

First Symptoms

This country has to protect itself against a new and insidious menace. ... Not all of our enemies work in the light of day. Those ... most dangerous to our public security and peace today are doing evil work in the dark. ... They ... evade our laws, while ... working secretly to destroy those laws by force. ... At the same time they appeal to these same laws for their personal protection. ... In this free land of ours in recent years we have been permitting the growth of the most sinister organisation for evil the world has yet seen. An organisation with ... one object and one only: the forcible destruction, at first by secret methods and then by open methods, of our liberty, our constitution, our laws, our religion, and our heritage. ... These men intend that we shall be subjected to the tyranny of a powerful alien body which has never enjoyed our freedom or any freedom; which hates all who have enjoyed this freedom, and is determined that we shall enjoy it no longer. ... The time has come when we must say ... : 'Come to our free country and learn to be free, but you must behave yourselves properly while ... here.' ... These men ... are out for their own power: absolute power to control the liberty of every [Briton]. ... These attempts to *subvert and dominate* our democratic system are being made by ... extremists. ... We must ... excise this social cancer before it does fatal mischief.[1] [my italics]

---

[1] 'Security Intelligence Policy & Organisation: Notes by Holt-Wilson (1920 Onwards)', piece 44 (Notes on British Public Security Legislation for Protection against Seditious & Revolutionary Incitements to Public Violence, 1933), pp. 3–7, TNA KV 4/416–/417. Note the similarities with language used nowadays to describe Islamicists in Britain.

CHAPTER 1

The Committee

The Rise of "Barbarism" ~ The 1918 Police Strike ~
The Secret Service Committee

> The only proper motto, which ought to hang over every
> intelligence office, is 'no wishful thinking allowed here'.
> E. W. B. Gill[1]

> Everyone who is not a Tory is either a German, a Sinn
> Féiner or a Bolshevist.   Reginald "Blinker" Hall[2]

> It is a great mistake to reduce your enemy to a demon.
> It leaves you at a distinct disadvantage when you are
> attempting to outwit him.   *Starik*, in *The Company*[3]

MAURICE Dobb, the Cambridge economics don and communist,[4] described the October Revolution as ranking in world history 'more prominently than even the French Revolution': to some it was 'the dawn of a new era' but to others 'the first stirring of the Great Red Dragon of the Apocalypse'.[5] However, the impact of the revolution on Anglo-Russian relations must be gauged within the context of the First World War, of which historian A. J. P. Taylor wrote 'smoothed the way for democracy – one of the few things to be said in its favour'.[6]

This chapter examines how the war affected British society and culture, helping to identify and understand what influenced official perceptions of subversion between 1917 and 1929. The war unsettled even those charged with preserving order, the usually conservative police forces.[7] The first symptoms of unrest, in the form of a London police strike in August 1918, led to a reorganisation of British security and intelligence the following year[8] to stop the Bolshevik "cancer" spreading.

By November 1917, the main agencies tackling Bolshevik subversion on British shores were the Special Branch of the London Metropolitan Police's Criminal

Investigation Department (CID) and MI5,[9] later known as the Security Service. Most foreign intelligence came via MI1$_{(c)}$ (later the Secret Intelligence Service, SIS, and later still MI6)[10] and, from November 1919 on, GCCS. Both Special Branch and MI5 expanded during the war. Special Branch grew from 114 staff to 700 between the outbreak of war on 4 August 1914 and the Armistice on 11 November 1918. In this time, MI5 grew from nine officers, three detectives and seven clerks to 844 personnel.[11] Special Branch and MI5 initially concentrated on preventing German sabotage and espionage. By 1916–17, however, concern shifted to Pacifism and potential domestic unrest. For MI5, the Armistice brought operational difficulties caused not only by sharp reductions in budget and staff,[12] but also having to share the monitoring of communist activities with Special Branch.

By mid-1919, MI5 had lost all its wartime duties except counter-espionage in Britain and counter-subversion in the military, while Special Branch tackled all civilian revolutionary activity. After October 1917, MI5 set up a section to combat Bolshevik espionage but not the Communist International (Comintern);[13] it remained Special Branch's responsibility except when targeting the military. As Christopher Andrew has noted, 'MI5 viewed Comintern's commitment to military subversion with peculiar horror and almost continuous concern.'[14]

Events soon confirmed British concerns about Bolshevik intentions. On 23 November 1917, Lenin urged Asians to imitate Russians in bringing down oppressive regimes (i.e. European colonial powers). Not three weeks later, the Council of People's Commissars (*Sovnarkom*, or SNK) allocated two million gold roubles to spread revolution 'in all countries, regardless of whether they are at war with Russia, in alliance … or neutral.'[15] This is important in understanding London's reactions. Moscow never intended revolution to occur in one country alone; the goal was to spread it worldwide. However, from the point of view of the pre-eminent imperial power at the time, Communism sought to topple every British institution. No matter one's perspective of Britain – one that stood for monarchy, aristocracy and empire or one that stood for democracy and free enterprise – Moscow seemed hostile to it.[16]

Historian John Ferris has remarked that British postwar power was due not so much to actual economic and military strength (which had declined) but instead to reputation in ruling circles abroad.[17] Historically, Britain's tendency 'to intervene in Europe and her willingness to associate herself with Continental powers' had reflected its prestige. When 'commitment to Europe was greatest … reputation was highest, particularly as victory was the adjunct of effort.'[18] Though victorious and relatively untouched physically compared to continental allies and enemies alike, Britain nevertheless endured great hardship during the war. This eroded traditional British values and institutions by compressing 'half a century of political evolution into just four years'.[19] The working classes, having taken the brunt of the conflict, now aspired to a better life.[20] The postwar expansion of suffrage, empowering overnight 'millions of untrained and inexperienced voters ... with no Party traditions, all alike affected by the restlessness' of the time, further raised expectations.[21]

Many wondered if the re-emergence of a Labour Party 'newly committed to Socialism', backed by 'stronger and more militant trade unions' and generating 'one of the most vigorous and sustained propaganda[s] ... that has ever appeared in this country',[22] meant the revolutionary upheaval disfiguring Russia would also happen in Britain. In the early 1920s, rising British unemployment triggered successive crises.[23] Renewed industrial strife and 'the "poison" of class politics' embraced by a newly enfranchised but impatient mass electorate diminished prospects of a speedy postwar recovery.[24] Concern therefore increased in parts of society and government following calls for workers to 'turn the lessons of the War against their upper-class masters'.[25] To many Britons, their country too showed symptoms of the cancer ravaging Russia. Sir Basil Thomson,[26] the Metropolitan Police Assistant Commissioner responsible for Special Branch from 1913 to 1921, was a key advocate in official circles of Bolshevism as an illness.

Three common elements in the lives of leading officials and politicians shed light on why they equated Communism with disease: social changes caused by the war and its aftermath; the Victorian and Edwardian mores of these men's social environment; and the ideological conditioning most of them experienced as youths. This last point is particularly significant since a disproportionate number of key individuals in interwar Anglo-Russian relations were alumni of elite institutions like the public schools Eton and Harrow, and Oxford and Cambridge Universities.[27] Middle-class hostility toward the working classes over postwar unemployment and social unrest should thus be one prism through which to view postwar anti-socialism.

By 1916–17, German spy scares[28] gave way to concerns over Pacifism and potential domestic unrest. The Entente's inability to break the deadlock on the Western Front prompted conservative politicians to accuse British pacifists of conspiring with Germany to undermine national war efforts. Irish Unionist Member of Parliament (MP) Sir Edward Carson,[29] for example, asked the War Cabinet to scrutinise pacifist funding. Basil Thomson did this, finding nothing unusual. However, his language was so ambiguous that Cabinet ordered the production of fortnightly (later weekly) reports on the pacifist-revolutionary

1 Sir Basil Thomson, Home Office Director of Intelligence (1919–21). The *bête noire* of both MI5 and the British Left, he warned Cabinet in 1920 that Moscow sought to infiltrate British government via universities.

threat.[30] Thomson and his successor Sir Wyndham Childs[31] watched leftist extremists whose rhetoric only reinforced Special Branch prejudice; that is, intolerance of any type of radicalism.[32]

By war's end, thanks largely to the intelligence community, much of Cabinet viewed citizens (especially the labour movement) mainly in terms of capacity for treachery. The Liberal-Conservative Coalition Government scrutinised and classified 'individuals according to secret definitions of threat and loyalty'. Thus, encouraged by conservative politicians, the community narrowed 'the definition of patriotism'[33] to smear labour groups. The hope was that Lloyd George[34] would adopt harsher policies given the apparent connection between industrial unrest and Bolshevik subversion.

Such turmoil shocked the middle and upper classes. Late Victorians and Edwardians believed crime and social violence were declining, perceiving them as 'the hallmark not of the plebeian [masses] ... but rather of a pathological minority'.[35] With the Armistice, however, many Britons feared this minority was larger than believed. Immediate concerns focused on the perceived brutalisation of daily life, illustrated by aggressive ex-servicemen and fears 'the barbarism of war had left an indelible mark on British society'.[36] Thus, 'perceptions of what constituted legitimate popular involvement in public life' changed.[37]

Like most of his colleagues at the top of government and the Civil Service, Basil Thomson was the product of a Victorian public school upbringing.[38] The third son of Archbishop of York William Thomson and Zoë Thomson[39] (both on good terms with Queen Victoria), Basil studied at Eton and Oxford. One contemporary of his at those institutions was future Foreign Secretary Lord Curzon. A respectable, though not stellar, career saw Thomson serve as a magistrate in Tonga, governor of several prisons, Head of Special Branch and finally, from May 1919, as Home Office Director of Intelligence. His experiences shaped his views and precocious experiences in Tonga, for example, heightened Thomson's imperial pride. As prison governor he was close to the criminal element, believing he understood its psychology and that of the working classes, from where most criminals came.[40]

Thomson's desire to please and succeed had deeper roots. He adored his mother Zoë[41] but was mainly the product of paternal influences and expectations. Reading about William Thomson, one easily identifies traits his son later exhibited:

His character ... was peculiarly mixed ... pompous yet humble ... a man of action yet a sentimental.... [He had] a sense of inferiority from which he never [recovered]. It made him over-sensitive to criticism and over-pugnacious in controversy.... But at heart he was shy and unsure of himself.[42]

An 1871 article in *Vanity Fair* stated the Archbishop was 'equally at home in Low Church and in High Society' and while he 'insists upon the natural depravity of the human race, he has a profound respect for human dignities'.[43]

Before the age of twenty, Basil Thomson already considered himself a disappointment to his father – an understandable though perhaps extreme reaction, since perceived failings were not his fault. Heart trouble at Eton and early on at Oxford[44] prevented him from living up fully to a growing reputation as a rower. Frequent depression led Thomson to America in 1882 to train as a farmer and rancher without having finished his degree at New College (not unusual at the time).[45] He felt he had failed to measure up to his siblings' achievements:

My eldest brother had been a success both at Eton and at New College [academically and as a rower]; my second had won mathematical prizes and passed high into [Royal Military Academy] Woolwich; he had just won distinction ... in the Zulu Campaign, where he had shared a tent with the Prince Imperial. He had been selected ... as one of the astronomers for the transit of Venus ... and here was I, at the age when careers are embarked upon, with no qualifications except facility in learning languages and no prospective career. I was a disappointment, but my father made no complaint.[46]

Harsh thoughts for a young man, no doubt, but heartfelt nevertheless.

Leading public schools shaped how Thomson and his contemporaries in government subsequently saw Communism. These institutions looked to develop 'a chapel-centred moral life reinforced by compulsory participation in team games'.[47] Games were undeniably the 'wheel around which moral values turned', the pre-eminent instrument for shaping character. Through this 'games ethic', pupils received the basic tools of imperial rule: 'courage, endurance, assertion, control and self-control'. The main objective, historian James Mangan has written, was to create a 'universal Tom Brown: loyal, brave, truthful, a gentleman and, if at all possible, a Christian'. Once the Empire became critical to Britain's economy and status in the 1860s,[48] public schools bred enthusiasm for the imperial vision primarily for commercial, security and reputational reasons.[49]

Top public school headmasters were influential in shaping this ideology in the mid to late nineteenth century. They believed governing India was the 'greatest and most interesting' of British political achievements, with traditions nurtured in the 'schools of the privileged' resulting in the 'acquisition, maintenance and development' of empire. Relying on games, these traditions injected new chivalrous concepts into the imperial vision and encouraged the development of qualities necessary for the success of future imperialists.[50] One headmaster urged students to be truthful, courageous, reverential and set

honesty above cleverness, manliness above refinement, character above attainments, moral and physical perfection above ... possessions.... [H]e looked for a new generation of men not characterised by literary accomplishment or ... culture, but disciplined and strong.... The don ... was ... more noxious ... in a Regiment than even in a school.[51]

Another headmaster argued:

The ... purpose ... was not to produce classicists and mathematicians, but ... administrators, generals, philanthropists, and statesmen.... 'Englishmen are not superior ... in brains or industry or science and apparatus of war, but they are superior in the health and temper which games impart'. ... The supreme ruling virtue of Englishmen was "character" – essentially unswerving honesty.... Add ... the Englishman's fear of God and the secrets of superior imperialism are revealed: 'physical strength, promptitude, character, religion'.[52]

His apotheosis concluded:

The boys of today are the statesmen and administrators of tomorrow. In their hands is the future of the ... Empire.... [T]he sport, the pluck, the resolution, and the strength ... that has accomplished their deliverance are ... acquired on the ... fields of the great public schools, and in the games of which they are the habitual scenes.... The self-control, the cooperation, the *esprit de corps* ... are the qualities which win the day in peace or war.... In the history of the British Empire ... England has owed her sovereignty to her sports.[53]

Which elements of the games ethic did Thomson and his contemporaries absorb at public school? One was games' ability to engage mind and body

to serve an ideal by fostering a sense of belonging, shared aims and cama-
raderie. Another element was defining parameters of morality (spiritual and
physical), loyalty and honesty. A third component was avoiding ostentation
and excess, for there were worthier pursuits in life than accumulating possessions. Another strand was suspicion of intellectuals, their presence usually
undermining imperial cohesion[54] (the colonial mindset known as "Blues
[varsity athletes] not Firsts [top scholars]").

The virtues games taught were clearly more desirable than intellectual
attainment, for as Mangan has pointed out, 'clean-limbed men and boys of
British origin *played* against treacherous, hypocritical, lying, cunning, and
well-organised' adversaries [my italics]. Here is a fifth element of the games
ethic: an ingrained sense of exclusivity and superiority over others based not
only on class or ethnicity but also on perceived nobility of purpose and ideals.
To be a colonising Briton bringing light to the farthest reaches of the globe
seemed the most virtuous of callings;[55] public school traditions were therefore
'agents of seduction for an imperial dream of noble service and intoxicating
adventure.'[56] Predictably, Thomson's contemporaries saw espionage, arguably
the most cerebral form of warfare, as the greatest game of all.[57]

He believed much of this, writing in his autobiography that at Eton 'one
was a greater man as Captain of the Boats or of the [cricket] Eleven than as
Captain of the Oppidans [elite intellectuals]. "Saps" [serious students] were
little thought of', the 'real energies' being applied to 'the playing fields or the
river'. Thomson confessed he

> thrilled with pride when the Captain of the Boats ... a far greater
> personage in my estimation than the [Prime Minister], stopped me as
> we were coming out of Chapel and said ... "Will you take an oar?" ...
> the formula ... for conferring a place in the Eton Eight [rowing crew].
> My heart stopped beating: the promotion was ... beyond my dreams.[58]

Lord Dufferin, the prominent Anglo-Irish diplomat and future Viceroy of
India, upon hearing from Lady Thomson her son was now second Captain of
the Boats, reportedly said to young Basil: 'I hope you realise that to whatever
giddy heights you may rise in future life you will never be in such a position
of power and responsibility as ... now.'[59]

Regarding intellectual achievement, Thomson felt that 'in the futility of
the short span of human life', 'great ambition and ... industry' were 'a curse
rather than a blessing'. Family environment also shaped these attitudes for
even his father, the strict cleric, was visibly proud of his sons' athleticism:

Basil 'is strong in two things which have the advantage of being wholly useless: music and boating'. In the latter, however, he had 'obtained, as his brother did before him, the best distinction that Eton can give'.[60] Naturally, character traits young Britons developed in public schools were the opposite of those shown by subversive Bolsheviks.[61]

Knowledge about Russian aims after the 1917 Revolution may nowadays make it seem absurd that some issues at the time so concerned security and intelligence officials. Yet since Thomson and many of his contemporaries had grown up believing in the virtuous supremacy of the British, the novelty of Bolshevism in Britain alarmed them. For such men of empire, subversion was but a new poisoned arrow in Russia's old expansionist quiver. To Thomson, Bolshevism's most sinister trait was its internationalism, enabling communists to find 'accomplices and allies' in 'battleships, wireless stations, military barracks, Post Offices, consulates, palatial hotels and mansions'. No high Western official could be certain that among his staff was not at least one 'embittered subordinate ... with a genuine belief in Communism as a cure for all the ills of the world, but more frequently aggrieved' due to 'a natural incapacity which education does not and cannot remedy'.[62]

These views, common in contemporary official circles, showed a fundamental misunderstanding about what motivated many leftists. Though Thomson often offered balanced opinion, he either forgot or ignored genuine grievances over postwar inequality. Many Britons who turned to Communism probably did so not because they were unequipped or too dim to succeed but because they wanted better lives and felt disenfranchised, despite end-of-war promises and electoral reforms. Consciously or otherwise, Thomson and his peers overlooked the point that the great majority of Britons had neither their opportunities nor lineage. These views reflected the Spencerian mindset[63] of the time that only the higher classes were fit to lead. The duty of the working classes was to obey, this passing for patriotism.

In 1955, sociologist Roger Kelsall examined the backgrounds of British administrators in the Home Civil Service. Of all higher civil servants in 1929 (mostly born between 1870 and 1890), 28% of Principal Assistant Secretaries and above had attended a Clarendon school. Of all Secretaries and Deputy Secretaries, 35% had attended one of the twenty best-known public schools, this rising to 74.5% if including lesser-known institutions that could still be classed as public schools. Also in 1929, 63% of all Secretaries and Deputy Secretaries had attended either Oxford (51%) or Cambridge (12%), and nearly 64% of ranks above Assistant Secretary had attended either Oxford (48%) or Cambridge (16%).[64]

Still in 1929, the top five occupations of fathers of civil servants above Assistant Secretary were clergymen/ministers (13%), retail traders (10%), landed gentry (8%), teachers (7.5%) and manufacturers (6%). Compared with a 1% sample of British males aged twenty to sixty-four in the 1951 Census, Kelsall noticed the incidence of higher civil servants above Assistant Secretary whose fathers were in higher administrative, professional or managerial positions was twelve times higher than in the general population. Conversely, representation of civil servants of like ranks in 1939 whose fathers were either semi-skilled or unskilled labourers was less than a tenth of that in the general population.[65]

The above data have serious implications for any examination of how British intelligence officials influenced political perceptions of Bolshevism. Until the Labour Party first came to power in 1924, politicians and senior civil servants had experienced broadly similar social and educational backgrounds. This is crucial, for as a former mandarin put it, 'in such a country as England' different social rank 'between two men who ... transact important business together nearly every day for years is not an insignificant matter'.[66]

Basil Thomson was a curious blend of psychologist and charlatan in his views on workers' susceptibility to communist subversion. He feared an ideology as outwardly attractive as Bolshevism would radicalise (or "infect") a physically and psychologically weakened labour force. An unnamed British colonel in Constantinople wrote:

> No one brought into close contact with the Bolshevik leaders and listening to them ... can avoid sympathy for their principles and for the faith, earnestness, temperance and enthusiasm with which they hold these principles. They preach the simple human doctrine of Christ and the early disciples. They wish to create a new Heaven and a new Earth in which there is no greed, envy, hatred [or] malice.[67]

Thomson, conversely, described Bolshevism as

> a sort of infectious disease, spreading rapidly, but insidiously, until like a cancer it eats away the fabric of society.... A nation attacked by it may, if we may judge from the state of Russia, be reduced to a political and social morass, which may last perhaps for a generation or more, with no hope of reaction; whilst civilisation crumbles away and the country returns to its original barbarism.[68]

Barbarism was a common theme at the time, as historian Jon Lawrence's work on fears of social collapse has shown (see above). In turn, those fears indicated how far a restless population might allow extremists to go before rejecting their aims and methods. Given such fluid popular and official perceptions of what constituted appropriate participation in politics, an answer to an important question begins to take shape. Given all the resources Moscow threw into supporting British leftist groups between 1917 and 1929 (primarily the Communist Party of Great Britain, CPGB, founded in August 1920),[69] why did revolution not happen? The explanations Thomson most often offered, including in various memoirs, were the traditional insularity of British workers[70] and their 'good sense and moderation'.[71]

Yet these were certainly not his views when he launched his career as the Government's authority on revolutionary movements in November 1917. Thomson said pacifist feelings among workers were only a ruse to avoid conscription and 'save their own skins'.[72] While some potential conscripts no doubt saw Pacifism as expedient, Thomson's suggestion that male civilian workers of military age were cowards revealed a lack of appreciation for the real causes of unease; namely uncertainty about job security, their families' futures and how conscription might affect them. Thomson's words were those of someone who neither had experienced the horrors of trench warfare nor would ever need worry about frontline service.

A 19 January 1918 article in the *Daily Herald* – the British socialist newspaper Moscow subsequently funded – entitled 'Peace or the Comb-Out?' criticised the Government over this issue. The piece suggested Cabinet and others who wanted the war to continue should fight it themselves, and argued workers were neither unpatriotic nor cowardly. If Cabinet restated 'war aims in accordance with what is thought worth fighting for by the people who have to do the fighting ... then if Germany still clings to militarism ... British Labour will [not] put any obstacle in the way of providing all the men that can possibly be provided'.[73]

One problem with Thomson's portrayal of the peace movement was that from 1916, authorities not only regarded all resident aliens as probable German spies or saboteurs but increasingly viewed pacifists as part of the same German conspiracy to damage British war efforts. Special Branch rarely, if ever, distinguished between pacifists (those opposing any war) and "pacificists" (those wanting a compromise peace). Government regarded the latter as more dangerous since they included MPs and former military officers. Still, the intelligence community viewed both groups as pacifists, branding them 'potential traitors'.[74]

This definition was problematic. In the critical period from November 1917 to March 1921 when London and Moscow did not have formal bilateral ties,[75]

Cabinet based its policies largely on information from 'a confusing array of diplomatic and other official missions' in Russia, several of them intelligence ones.[76] British foreign intelligence,[77] for much of those three years, informed decision-making but in doing so became a key lens through which politicians viewed revolutionary Russia. Likewise, Bolshevik interaction with Britain in that period was mainly through the Foreign and Trade Commissariats,[78] and intelligence organs. British policy was multifaceted, comprising subversion, sabotage, financial and logistical support for anti-communists, and eventually intervention alongside White Guards and other anti-Red elements.[79]

Domestically, the problem was that Thomson's own preconceptions tainted Special Branch assessments around this time. He therefore failed to make his organisation conform to its role of evaluating information objectively. The fatal flaw in gauging the Bolshevik subversive threat accurately was that middle- and upper-class men believed they knew what the working classes thought and felt. Given the complete class disconnect, official commentary on workers' fears, aspirations and aims was largely inaccurate and alarmist at first.[80]

Many British workers opposing the continuation of war nevertheless felt Russia had let Britain down, reported Thomson, adding they were also 'inclined to distrust anyone who holds up Russian institutions for imitation'.[81] By mid-1918, though, at a critical stage of the war, he was more concerned with the upper classes than with workers regarding Pacifism:

> the worst form ... is the tea party and dinner table tittle-tattle in London. Certain ladies of position, who profess to be [close to] the official world, are busy disseminating this ... poison, and the worst ... is that it ... is founded on despair. Fortunately, their activities are confined, more or less, to their own class, and do not reach the class below.[82]

The class below was of course the middle class, the true foundation of any democracy and safeguard against social unrest. Thomson's reports repeatedly showed his preoccupation with the radicalisation, or "infection", of the middle and working classes.

That was why the Metropolitan Police strike of 30 August 1918 shocked government like 'a bolt from the blue'.[83] Fearful that Britain was coming 'face to face with a Revolution',[84] Prime Minister Lloyd George and his Cabinet had to appease strikers, postponing the reckoning until a second police walkout in July 1919. In the context of contemporary social and industrial unrest, though, the 1918 police strike was a watershed: it contributed directly not only to

British intelligence reforms within five months but also to more damaging developments.

The 1918 strike was the culmination of nearly seventy years of government neglect and outright abuse of police officers, especially in London. The first major unrest over pay happened in 1853 but the London Police Commissioner at the time, Sir Richard Mayne, dismissed virtually all complaints, forcing officers to appeal to outside officials. In July 1890 dozens of officers stunned Londoners by refusing to go on duty, seeking among other things the right to form a union and strike. The Victorians' constant fear was that what Karl Marx called the 'dangerous class, the social scum, that passively rotting mass thrown off by the lowest layers of ... society'[85] would run rampant in the absence of police.[86]

The Metropolitan Police had long been 'underpaid, over-disciplined and over-worked'.[87] Before the war, constables took home £1 7s (2011: £106) a week, receiving only ten shillings (2011: £40) more after twenty years' service. From the start of the war to late 1917 the cost of living went up 76%; in that period, however, police pay rose 20% only. Meanwhile, wages of engineering labourers increased by 113% while those of semi-skilled mechanical engineering fitters rose by 75% (even without overtime). Unlike industrial labourers who could easily double their wages by working extra hours, police officers had no such option despite having lost their only day off due to the war. By 1918, an officer earned a third of a munitions worker's wages. Wartime conditions became so bad that malnourished constables fainted on duty.[88] As a retired senior officer wrote, it was 'hard for many men to keep body and soul together'.[89]

With the war in its final year, police officers nationwide had

> experienced a relative decline not only in pay but, equally crucially, in economic status and prestige *vis-à-vis* other reference groups, particularly in terms of their ... perceptions of themselves as skilled men, i.e., a relative deprivation in social stratification. They claimed that not only were they unable to match the living standards of "equal status" engineers and draughtsmen ... but even ordinary labourers now disparaged them. Seeing themselves as markedly undervalued, they looked to the ... union, as a potential collective bargaining agent, to restore ... pay and prestige.[90]

In September 1913 an unofficial Metropolitan Police union appeared, becoming the National Union of Police and Prison Officers (NUPPO) in 1914.[91] Membership spread to forces nationwide but since officers could not join trade unions, NUPPO membership remained clandestine (and small) until 1918. Support surged that year, however, with officers upset by government indifference to longstanding complaints about poor pay and work conditions. At this time, NUPPO also chose six of its own to serve with the London Trades Council.[92]

One reason why the 1918 strike was so unexpected was the complete disconnect between police leaders and the rank-and-file. Home Secretary Sir George Cave[93] relied mainly on Commissioner Sir Edward Henry for information. However, Henry's superintendents – most of whom he had personally selected – were ignorant of union matters and failed to keep him updated. In early 1918, the Metropolitan Police postponed the publication of new pay rates, not just because the offer included a widows' pension (at Henry's insistence) but also since final calculations were not yet ready. Unfortunately, in intervening months nobody thought of informing the men, leading to increased tension.[94] Even Basil Thomson and Sir Nevil Macready[95] (Henry's successor) criticised the Government: keeping everyone informed would have prevented the 1918 strike.[96]

The 25 August dismissal of Constable Tommy Thiel for NUPPO activities sparked the walkout. On 27 August, union leaders issued an ultimatum: offer us better pay, recognise NUPPO and re-admit Thiel or face a work stoppage by midnight, 29 August. Superintendents kept reassuring the Metropolitan Police leadership the ultimatum was a bluff and that few men would strike. How wrong they were. The estimated number of strikers was 12,000; even worse, the 1200 men of the City of London force joined their Metropolitan colleagues.[97]

After urgent consultations with Cabinet on 30 August, the Prime Minister realised he would have to resolve the matter personally, drawing on every ounce of 'his resources of conciliation and guile'. The next day, he, Cave and Henry received NUPPO representatives including Constables James Marston (Chairman) and Tommy Thiel. The Government agreed to generous pay raises and reinstate Thiel. On union recognition, however, Lloyd George equivocated as only he could, eventually causing NUPPO to collapse. While the Prime Minister believed the delegates voiced the men's wishes and concerns, he argued that in wartime the police were like the military: 'in neither case could the Government recognise a union'. NUPPO leaders assumed the Government would accept unionisation once hostilities ended. On this assumption, which proved costly, NUPPO representatives said Cabinet had accepted a union in principle. On 31 August, the strikers accepted the terms and ended industrial action.[98]

Had Lloyd George not acted this way, the August 1918 events might have had a more serious outcome. The expansion of NUPPO and its ties to bodies like the London Trades Council worried Cabinet, though not as much as the 'potential threat to discipline in the armed forces'.[99] Lloyd George's biographer John Grigg has written that despite 'the inconvenience ... ordinary Londoners felt considerable sympathy for the strikers.... Even soldiers on duty ... tended to treat the "mutineers" with geniality'.[100] Fears of subversion in the military help explain why within five months of the police strike, the Government reorganised and re-tasked its secret machinery to confront Bolshevism. After all, as early as February 1918 a secret memorandum by Home Secretary Cave already noted the 'stream of men in khaki' going into the Victoria Street offices of Maxim M. Litvinov, the revolutionary (and future Soviet Foreign Commissar) at the time living and agitating in London.[101]

The Government Communications Headquarters (GCHQ, the successor to GCCS) and MI5 have released historical files[102] on interwar Anglo-Soviet relations but SIS has not. In 1998 Robin Cook, the Labour Foreign Secretary, reiterated the longstanding policy of SIS files remaining closed both to protect national security, and to reassure past, present and potential sources of perpetual anonymity.[103] This policy did not fundamentally change even for Keith Jeffery and his centenary official history that ended in 1949.

Many have written on the origins and structure of modern British intelligence[104] but few have examined why and how Cabinet restructured it in early 1919 to tackle Bolshevism (one exception being historian Gill Bennett's biography of SIS officer Sir Desmond Morton).[105] This knowledge gap endured because Secret Service Committee proceedings remained classified until 2002.[106] Secret intelligence sources during the war ranged from excellent to poor. Signals intelligence (SIGINT) was decisive at times but otherwise, since nothing yet existed along the lines of the Joint Intelligence Committee (JIC),[107] telling useful from unreliable HUMINT remained challenging. As the conflict dragged on, Cabinet succumbed to that affliction of Imperial Russian governance once memorably termed '*la manie de police*',[108] evidenced by an expanding British security and intelligence community.

The Secret Service Committee first met on 3 February 1919,[109] prompted by a memorandum from Walter Long[110] (one of the Coalition Cabinet hardliners). First Lord of the Admiralty Long wrote that though 'no alarmist', he firmly believed that 'elements of unrest and ... Bolshevism are ... more deepseated than many of us believe'. Vigilance was essential: now more than ever Britain needed a competent civilian secret service 'under a Minister who can bring the facts to ... Cabinet'. So the Committee emerged, comprising Lord

Curzon (Foreign Secretary),[111] Long, Edward Shortt (Home Secretary),[112] Winston Churchill (War Secretary)[113] and Sir Hamar Greenwood (Home Office Parliamentary Under-Secretary of State).[114]

The Committee eventually consisted of officials like the Cabinet Secretary and the Permanent Under-Secretaries of the Home and Foreign Offices, and Treasury, who updated Cabinet on intelligence matters.[115] While civil servants dealt with details, original committee members – mainly politicians – made strategic decisions. Long's note was the force behind the Committee and its support for the creation of a civilian secret service to combat sedition on 1 May 1919: the Directorate of Intelligence, led by Basil Thomson. Curzon asked the agencies to submit summaries of their work ahead of the first meeting, giving historians a useful overview of British security and intelligence at the time.

MI1$_{(c)}$ (or SIS) supplied four main consumers: the Foreign Office, Admiralty, War Office and Air Ministry. From 1914, the agency was structured geographically, with departmental officers on secondment to the Service liaising between it and consumers. By November 1917, however, an important re-shuffle[116] took place to improve efficiency. Now each 'Department of State was directly represented by a section' dealing in issues with which 'the department it represented was concerned'. Being the central secret service suited SIS. The unpalatable option – similar to Germany's wartime system of separate military, naval and political services – was 'most expensive', causing 'overlapping and inter-departmental competition' for top agents.[117]

MI5, responsible for counter-espionage and counter-subversion in the military, said it had a policy of not investigating political or labour unrest except in cases of clear-cut enemy activity.[118] This, of course, gave the agency a wide remit. By 1916–17, for example, MI5 regarded most Russian political émigrés active in the British wartime labour movement as Russo-German-Jews, and therefore scrutinised them.[119]

The Admiralty, in turn, acknowledged that while theoretically the Director of Naval Intelligence (DNI) should have formally requested intelligence on naval matters from the Chief of SIS ("C"), the DNI had been running his own foreign intelligence organisation for this purpose since 1914. For domestic investigations, the DNI relied on Scotland Yard's CID and the Director of Military Intelligence (DMI) at the War Office (to which MI5 had belonged during the war). The DNI had also set up special secret services worldwide, paid for by special funds provided directly to him for this. However, these networks were either already dismantled or in the process. Current collection arrangements troubled the Admiralty, which considered "C" to have insufficient authority.[120]

Predictably, Basil Thomson – eyeing the soon-to-be-created post of civilian intelligence director – wrote the longest entry. In wartime, he stated, Special Branch had cooperated fully with naval and military intelligence, especially on counter-espionage. In late 1917, the Ministry of Munitions had approached Special Branch to establish an agency (Parliamentary Military Secretary Department, no. 2 Section; PMS2) to monitor labour unrest. Officers infiltrated English and Scottish factories posing as munitions inspectors, each organising a network of informants. To curtail Bolshevik infiltration, Thomson received all relevant Foreign Office despatches. His sources included Chief Constables; informants; liaison officers in France, Holland, Italy and Spain; returning prisoners of war; Russian sources; and US Secret Service (a protective security, rather than an intelligence, agency) staff in Paris. Domestic intelligence, Thomson hinted, would soon become critical in light of what he saw as brewing revolutionary unrest. Since Ministry of Munitions funding for existing operations (£12,000 annually; 2011: £3.5 million) ceased at war's end, finding alternatives was imperative if this vital information were to flow uninterrupted.[121]

The Committee set to work, initially convening three times in a month. At the first meeting, Curzon summarised what various departments had said, reminding attendees that despite many wartime accomplishments, coordination had been poor. For some consumers of intelligence, it 'often came too late' to be useful. Curzon hinted that in future, civilian and military intelligence would probably have to exist separately. No matter the final arrangement, Lord Hardinge (Foreign Office Permanent Under-Secretary) insisted his department fund all secret naval and military work abroad. Attendees accepted this; only his department could decide if such operations contravened British foreign policy. He regarded budgetary power even more important in peace than in war for in wartime 'acts are committed ... in neutral countries that would hardly be tolerated in ... peace. Such control is secured by holding the purse-strings.'[122]

The meeting adjourned since differing opinions arose about Long's exact intentions: his note had made no mention of restructuring military intelligence. Furthermore, Curzon was unsure if the First Lord of the Admiralty was suggesting Thomson replace Mansfield Cumming as "C". Lord Lytton, speaking for Long, said one man alone should shoulder their workload.[123]

Proceedings re-convened four days later, this time with Long present.[124] He elaborated on his idea after Curzon informed him the Committee now focused mainly on parts of secret service tackling domestic revolutionary propaganda. Long explained he did not criticise the 'wholly excellent' intelligence-gathering methods in place but rather the lack of departmental action on the information. To him, most mistakes arose from overlap – hence his push for a single head of secret service, subordinate to a single minister with power to act if needed. Thomson naturally agreed: 'one great evil of the present system was ... duplication'.[125]

Cumming, when asked, added little but agreed with Thomson on the dangers of 'parallel organisations' and duplicating 'agents and reports'. He cited examples from Holland where agents had denounced friends to earn money. At present, SIS headquarters staff numbered 180, with more abroad, but "C" agreed cuts were inevitable with war's end. On tackling Bolshevism, Sir Edward Troup (Home Office Permanent Under-Secretary) argued his should be the core department, given the need to centralise this work. He also stressed the lack of anti-Bolshevik propaganda so far. Curzon replied an effective propaganda agency should be part of any restructuring, agreeing to oversee such a scheme for the Committee to consider.[126]

At its third meeting,[127] the Committee established the Directorate of Intelligence. Curzon added the Foreign Office had recently created the Political Intelligence Department (PID), which collected and analysed all material on foreign countries, and conducted propaganda overseas.[128] The man in charge, Assistant Under-Secretary Sir William Tyrrell,[129] worked closely with Thomson. Regarding domestic propaganda, Thomson mentioned private societies formed to prevent the spread of Bolshevism. The Committee made it clear he should have 'a suitable man' under him to organise propaganda and maintain contact with such groups – but oddly, so long as they were not of a political nature. This individual should be an experienced journalist, not need a large staff, work from Fleet Street and answer to Thomson for all propaganda; the Foreign Office would also supply information. There was an 'acute need for regular meetings' between intelligence officials and the press, 'to give them information and guidance on social unrest'.[130]

From the start, Thomson exceeded his mandate to assess domestic revolutionary unrest, examining issues like the impact of subversion on other countries' morale, encroaching on SIS's mandate. More upsetting was his insistence on tackling subversion in the British military, the preserve of MI5 and Vernon Kell. The two men disliked each other. Wartime secrecy had prevented Kell from publicly celebrating MI5 "successes" against German spies[131] with the aid of Special Branch. Scotland Yard's Thomson, however, could and did so with zest, angering Kell. Opposed temperaments – Kell, reserved; Thomson, flamboyant – stoked the rivalry, intensified by overlapping responsibilities regarding subversion.

2 Sir Vernon Kell, founding Director of MI5 (1909–40). He spoke several languages, including Chinese dialects, French, German, Polish and Russian. Kell is the longest-serving head of any British intelligence agency to date, and arguably the ablest linguist to hold such a post.

Personalities also coloured the indifferent rapport the MI5 Director had with some of Thomson's supporters at the time – hardliners like DNIs Admiral Reginald Hall and Commodore Hugh Sinclair, and Chief of the Imperial Staff General Henry Wilson.[132] Despite Kell's staunch anti-Bolshevism, they still regarded the gifted and bookish linguist as 'short-sighted and timorous'.[133] MI5 retained responsibility for counter-espionage but the agency budget decreased by 72% between 1918 and 1921.[134] This was partly a peace dividend[135] but Thomson's inflation of subversive threats to head the intelligence community also played a role. Kell argued against such deep cuts but by early 1919 Cabinet feared revolution far more than espionage.[136]

Thomson had supported Long's calls in October 1918 for a unified civilian secret service, though the Head of Special Branch was well aware Kell would fight to preserve MI5's mandate, even if reduced. Thomson went even further than Long, proposing a civilian head for the entire intelligence community, with the directors of military, naval, foreign and domestic intelligence serving as his deputies. Ministers and officials rejected this ambitious plan but after much bureaucratic wrangling, Thomson got the Directorate of Intelligence. Lavish funding only deepened Kell's resentment of his adversary's 'exclusive responsibility for monitoring ... civil subversion, labour unrest and revolutionary activity'.[137]

Though Thomson paradoxically believed the working classes rejected yet might possibly fall prey to Bolshevism, another reason for his hyperbole was the power struggle with Kell. If no significant civilian unrest existed, the ambitious Thomson could not expand his authority at MI5's expense. Because war and the October Revolution conditioned Cabinet to regard civilian unrest with much greater unease than espionage, Thomson may have felt untouchable, believing exaggeration would cause no harm (especially if his influence grew). He once mocked ambition as 'a curse rather than a blessing', adding that above all, revolutionaries wanted 'exaggerated importance and advertisement'.[138] One wonders if Thomson ever appreciated the irony.

CHAPTER 2

The Mutinies

The 1919 Mutinies & Police Strike ~ The Federated Press
of America ~ The School

> Go to the war, workers, go to the war;
> Heed not the Socialists, but wallow in gore;
> Shoulder your rifle, worker, don't ask what it's for;
> Let your wife and children starve, and go to the war.
>   Chorus of 1918 British street song[1]

> I have seen references to it even in our Secret Service
> reports, which of course do not deal with the better
> classes.   Walter Long[2]

> With the Devil, but for Russia and against the Bolsheviks.
>   Pyotr N. Wrangel[3]

IN months leading up to the July 1919 police strike, James Marston's fortunes
as NUPPO General-Secretary dwindled, coinciding with the rise of his
successor, Sergeant Jack Hayes.[4] The element of surprise that ensured the
success of the 1918 walkout was non-existent a year later; Hayes understood
another successful strike would be impossible and so pushed for a different
approach. Both inside and outside police circles, many saw this as a sign of
moderation. He is of singular interest both as NUPPO leader and, it turned
out, as a talent-spotter, facilities agent and probable agent of influence for
Moscow. In these roles, Hayes enabled the earliest known Bolshevik penetration of the British Government, leading to a scandal in 1929 that changed how
Britain's secret machinery operated.

This chapter investigates the impact of post-Armistice military and police
unrest on British assessments of subversion. Army mutinies, unionisation attempts in the Royal Navy (RN) and another police strike – in addition to growing industrial strife – stoked official fears of revolution. Using
Hayes's activities as a convenient link, this chapter concludes by re-visiting

the 1 November 1919 establishment of GCCS,[5] the peacetime cryptographic successor to the Admiralty's Naval Intelligence Division (NID) 25 (better known as Room 40)[6] and the War Office's MI1[(b)]. At a time when telling subversive capability from intent was vital, the School proved critical; unsurprisingly, it was an early target for Bolshevik intelligence.

In a December 1918 report, only a month after the Armistice ended the war, Basil Thomson stated revolutionary feeling was at its highest ever in Britain. Yet a few lines later, he explained how the suffragette Sylvia Pankhurst[7] acknowledged in an intercepted letter 'the working man's interest in Bolshevism was flagging. ... [W]hat interested [him] were pensions, the cost of living, unemployment, the return of soldiers in time for Christmas.'[8] On the eve of 1919, therefore, workers' concerns could not be described as extreme: job and pension security, and reasonable wages and treatment. However, in a political climate of heightened popular hopes fuelled by electoral promises, many employers chose to ignore such concerns. Inflexibility by the 'Guardians', Thomson warned, would fuel extremism if workers felt without alternatives.[9]

Fears of revolution seemed justified in early 1919 by the eruption into mutiny of long-suppressed discontent within the armed forces. With the Armistice, servicemen felt the hardship they had endured was no longer justifiable. The main triggers for mutinies were the unpopular guidelines governing demobilisation and its persistent postponement for millions of men. As early as mid-1917, senior British officers were already warning politicians of declining morale on the Western Front due to poor food and pay inequalities.[10]

Two related factors affected military discipline late in the war and beyond: the introduction of conscription and the changing social composition of the armed forces (particularly the army). By September 1915, the two million volunteers who had joined since August 1914 could no longer satisfy military requirements.[11] Rather than start conscription and risk upheaval, the Government chose instead to register all males by profession and start a verification system (the Derby Scheme) to identify all men ready to enlist when needed. However, as historian J. M. Winter concluded, by late 1915, not even 25% of able-bodied males would volunteer so conscription became inevitable in January 1916.[12]

The influx in 1916–17 of conscripts previously working in British industrial centres gradually radicalised the armed forces. David Englander has concluded that professional soldiers, drawn almost exclusively from isolated and socially marginal elements of the population, were displaced by an army of uniformed civilians ... from the urban working and lower middle classes.... Hastily-trained and without ... career commitment ... newcomers had absorbed ... rudiments of discipline but failed to acquire a military bearing or the habit of unthinking obedience.... Citizen-soldiers remained susceptible to outside influence: to the courage-sapping influence of family and friends; to the disintegrative effects of ethnic, class, racial, religious and regional loyalties; and to the subtle subversion of trade union, pacifist and other oppositional elements.[13]

These were not professional soldiers and so they expected to go home at war's end.[14] But go they did not, at least not immediately, upsetting long-suffering servicemen and setting the stage for the mutinies.

Table 1. Postwar British Military Strength[15]

	Navy: Officers	Navy: Other Ranks	Navy: Total	Army: Officers	Army: Other Ranks	Army: Total	Air Force: Officers	Air Force: Other Ranks	Air Force: Total
11.11.18	36,243	378,919	415,162	194,500	4,806,500	5,001,000	--	--	293,000
31.12	--	--	--	--	--	4,740,000	--	--	--
31.01.19	--	--	--	--	--	4,001,000	--	--	--
31.03	--	--	--	--	--	2,852,000	--	--	--
15.04	28,043	210,919	238,962	--	--	--	--	--	--
30.06	--	--	--	--	--	2,072,000	--	--	--
15.07	20,243	165,919	186,162	--	--	--	--	--	--
31.10	--	--	--	--	--	--	--	--	58,000
15.11	3000	3000	6000[a]	--	--	--	--	--	--
15.12	--	--	--	--	--	1,001,000	--	--	--

[a] This figure refers only to Navy personnel who had enlisted at the start of the war.

Returning millions of servicemen to civilian life was a complex task needing time but two other factors slowed demobilisation initially. One was that the original plan, based on British industrial and reconstruction requirements, first released from duty those who had actually served the shortest time: industrial workers conscripted between 1916 and 1918. Delays arose because for release men first had to present to (and have approved by) military authorities a written employment offer from their old company.[16] This struck those who enlisted early in the war as unfair. Only when British servicemen mutinied in January 1919 did the Government change its demobilisation criteria, now basing them on age and length of service.[17] The second factor was the policy shift from November 1917 toward military intervention against the Reds. This hardening stance therefore meant Britain needed sufficient troops[18] ready to deploy to Russia.[19] If not enough volunteered, the Government argued, conscription would need extending[20] – and therein lay the problem.

The media stoked resentment further. In the feverish weeks leading up to the 14 December 1918 General Election,[21] mass-circulation newspapers popular with servicemen criticised demobilisation delays and the Government's ill-disguised aim to intervene in Russia.[22] Pent-up frustration exploded. From 11 November 1918 to 11 March 1919, there were over fifty documented mutinies and protests by British servicemen in Britain, France[23] and Russia.[24] Evidence suggests 54,000 men[25] refused to perform their duties due to continuing discharge delays and possible deployment to Russia.

On these two points,[26] at least, the labour movement supported servicemen. In March–April 1919 the National Conference of the Miners Confederation, the National Conference of the Labour Party, the Trades Union Congress (TUC), the Miners Federation, the National Union of Railwaymen and the Transport Workers Federation all passed resolutions calling for an end to conscription and immediate British withdrawal from Russia.[27] Within Cabinet, Prime Minister Lloyd George was one of few who took all this with relative composure.

A 'democratic politician whose power derived from Wales, nonconformity and the people at large, rather than from hereditary wealth and status or from big business,'[28] he had by 1919 a long political record as an arch-pragmatist, much less bound by class-defined ideological constraints than his well-heeled peers in Cabinet. Lloyd George's approach to the "Red Question" demonstrated his understanding of popular moods and mindsets. In his outlook and perceptions of potential or actual Bolshevik subversion (even in the military), he differed from many colleagues.

For anti-communists like Winston Churchill and Henry Wilson, converging aims and demands by labour unions and restless servicemen meant two things. First, without enough volunteers, British plans for large-scale intervention in Russia against the Bolsheviks were doomed. Second, hardliners feared what had happened in Russia in 1917 was now happening in Britain: 'the disintegration of armies'[29] as a potential prelude to revolution. External and internal developments became mutually reinforcing, skewing threat perceptions.

In his discussion of the mutinies, founding CPGB member Andrew Rothstein[30] cited official correspondence on both the unrest and the situation in Russia:

On 16 January [Churchill] wrote ... 'under the present pressure the Army is liquefying fast'. The next day ... Wilson noted ... 'We are sitting on the top of a mine which may go up at any minute.'... By 22 January Wilson [added] 'We dare not give an unpopular order ... discipline is a thing of the past' ... On 27 January [Churchill] wrote to [Lloyd George], saying ... Britain should continue the intervention ... until victory ... 'but unfortunately we have not the power – our orders would not be obeyed, I regret'.[31]

By February 1919, intervention in Russia was a personal crusade for Churchill, causing tension in Cabinet (especially with Lloyd George). The following correspondence illustrates just how inflexible Churchill had become:

[From Lloyd George] Am very alarmed at your second telegram about planning war against the Bolsheviks. The Cabinet have never authorised such a proposal.... [T]he [War Office] reported to ... Cabinet that ... intervention was driving the anti-Bolshevik parties ... into the ranks of the Bolsheviks.... An expensive war of aggression ... is a way to strengthen Bolshevism in Russia and create it at home. We cannot afford the burden ... if we are committed to a war against a continent like Russia, it is the road to bankruptcy, and Bolshevism in these islands. The French are not safe guides in this matter. Their opinion is largely biased by the enormous number of small investors who put their money in Russian loans and who now see no prospect of ever recovering it. I urge you therefore not to pay too much heed to their incitements.... [B]ear in mind the very grave labour position in this country. Were it known that you had gone over to Paris to prepare ... war against the Bolsheviks, it would do more to incense organised labour than anything I can think of; and what is still worse, it would throw into the ranks of the extremists a very large number of thinking people who now abhor their methods.[32]

But Churchill would not relent:

You need not be alarmed about the phrase 'planning war against the Bolsheviks'. We are, as you pointed out at the Cabinet, actually making war on them at the present moment. All that is intended is to assemble possible means and resources for action in a comprehensive form.[33]

Churchill's obsession with a large British deployment shocked even Foreign Secretary Curzon, himself a staunch anti-communist.[34] By autumn 1919, Lloyd George was at wit's end:

My dear Winston.... I have found your mind so obsessed by Russia that I felt I had good ground for the apprehension that your great abilities, energy and courage were not devoted to the reduction of expenditure.... At each interview you promised me your mind to this very important problem. Nevertheless the first communication I have always received from you after ... related to Russia.... I am frankly in despair.... [T]his obsession ... if you will forgive me for saying so, is upsetting your balance.... But as you know that you won't find another responsible person in the whole of the land who will take your view, why waste your energy and usefulness on this vain fretting which completely paralyses you for other work? I have worked with you now for longer than I have probably cooperated with any other man in public life and I think that I have given you tangible proof that I wish you well. It is for that reason that I write frankly to you.[35]

Military unrest affected British policies and policy-makers alike. Yet since the armed forces were a microcosm of civil society, there too discontent spread, as Basil Thomson repeatedly warned. He disapproved of flamboyance by the wealthy, claiming it caused unnecessary resentment. In Liverpool, police agents spoke of bitterness at the lack of alcohol and early closure of public houses at night. Thomson named high prices, scarce housing and the 'foolish and dangerous ostentation of the rich' as three causes of unrest. Only the steadying influences of the Royal Family and sport kept the peace, he argued.[36]

Here were elements of the public school ethos: belief in the positive influence of national institutions and sport, and a dislike of extravagance – especially since it complicated the job of containing the Bolshevik "cancer". Frivolous press reporting also upset Thomson:

[It is] very difficult for working men to reconcile the two facts, that the public debt amounts to thousands of millions and that there has never been a time when there has been so much money in the country as at the present.... Press accounts of the Motor Show and the number of orders given for costly cars are pointed to as proof that working men are not obtaining their fair share.... The foolish paragraphs in newspapers, reporting cases of inflated profits and foolish extravagance, are doing untold harm.

Outside London, the situation was no better. In Leeds,

never before have the miners seen evidence of the wealth ... as during late years with the development of motor cars and the describing of society functions in ... papers. Coupled with this is the experience many ... younger men have had during their travelling whilst in the Army, being stationed in London and other big towns and seeing for themselves the wealth and luxury of the other side of life.[37]

Most worrying for Thomson was the perceived Bolshevik subversion of the middle classes, luring them 'into the arms of the Labour Party'.[38]

By February 1919, at his request, European bankers were already monitoring suspicious money transactions to keep Bolshevik funds out of Britain,[39] a method perfected in wartime against Germany and its allies. The following month, Reconstruction and National Service Minister Sir Auckland Geddes summarised the labour situation:

I find ... widespread stagnation both in trade and industry ... the causes of this are complex. The first and most obvious ... is psychological. Ministers, officials, employers and employed – all are showing the effects of war strain in a certain lassitude.... It is coupled with a sense of impending change. We have heard so much of the new and better Britain that the people await a sign. Employers do not know whether it is to be heralded by confiscation of capital, by nationalisation of the great industries, by a marked increase in income tax, or by the imposition of some new form of taxation. The workers expect ... new houses, less work, more wages, or a combination of all three.[40]

Post-Armistice euphoria soon gave way to apprehension over socio-economic turmoil. Walter Long noted in June 1919 that

unrest is very general. I come across it even in the Navy, where anything of the kind has been ... previously altogether unknown. You find it in all classes of society, and in the most unreasonable form.... The unemployment question is one of the most pressing and most difficult.... The police trouble is an instance of this. The firm action of the Government has broken the agitation for the time; but there is no doubt that the agitators are doing all they can to convince people ... they refuse to believe that there is any such thing as Government – and ... endeavour to persuade ... malcontents in every class.[41]

Agitation within the Metropolitan Police had subsided after the 1918 strike, but only just. Almost as soon as it ended, the NUPPO executive[42] began rallying members in pursuit of formal recognition. Events quickly took on a life of their own, setting up a decisive confrontation between NUPPO and the Government. The July 1919 police strike had two outcomes. One was the virtual end of union activism within British police forces for decades because of the Cabinet's response. The other (and related) outcome was that the 1918–19 strikes and their aftermath politically radicalised British police, enabling Bolshevik intelligence to infiltrate it by exploiting the ideology, resentment and precarious financial situation of some officers. This was the earliest known communist penetration of the British intelligence community and lasted around a decade.

The August 1918 strike forced Metropolitan Police Commissioner Henry to resign. A stern but paternalistic figure who introduced many modern techniques to police work, he nevertheless fell to 'events he could not understand … at a pace he could not appreciate'.[43] Henry's replacement, General Sir Nevil Macready,[44] took the post at Lloyd George's personal request and almost immediately clashed with NUPPO. Throughout his military career Macready had shown he enjoyed a challenge, proving decisive and innovative even (some would say, especially) when those traits ran counter to existing mindsets.[45]

In 1910, however, his name became synonymous with events in and around the Welsh town of Tonypandy, a 'legend of class warfare that endured for generations'.[46] That year, a strike by coal miners in the Rhondda and Aberdare Valleys led to mass rioting that local and external police forces put down violently. The latter included 300 Metropolitan Police officers sent from London by Home Secretary Winston Churchill, backed up by a military contingent on stand-by. Both the police and military detachments were under Macready's direct command.[47] By most accounts, he cared little about the causes of the unrest and detested uncompromising miners and mine owners almost equally.[48]

Macready dealt with the situation impartially and delicately,[49] determined to prevent circulation of inaccurate information that might trigger military action. He therefore put in place a comprehensive intelligence apparatus,[50] and came to appreciate and respect the Metropolitan Police for its work in Wales. Between November 1910 and his September 1918 appointment as Commissioner, Macready performed duties similar to those in the Rhondda three more times, thus establishing his reputation as a soldier who understood police work and got the job done.[51]

Once he took stock of his new organisation, Macready realised that legitimate injustices, and lack of communication between senior and rank-and-file officers, had contributed to the August strike. The result was internal reform,[52] which to the dismay of the NUPPO executive proved a success with the men. This confused Macready's critics, defying their portrayal of him as Lloyd George's 'martinet'[53] or a 'Prussian at the Yard'.[54] These and subsequent reforms greatly contributed to NUPPO's failure to maintain solidarity during the 1919 strike.

The Union's demise arguably began at a 12 September 1918 meeting attended by Home Secretary Sir George Cave, Macready, and NUPPO executives James Marston (Chair) and John Crisp (Secretary). Cave stated the existing ban on Union membership could be lifted provided 'such union does not claim or attempt to interfere with the regulation and discipline of the Service' or 'induce members ... to withhold their services'. Were this condition breached, '[Force] members ... may be called up to sever their connection with such union'. NUPPO accepted this and the Home Office duly announced an agreement that evening.[55]

The four men also discussed one of Macready's earliest proposals: to create a representative board for constables and sergeants through which they and inspectors at each station could elect one man to represent it. Station representatives in each division would in turn elect a divisional representative to serve on the board, which would be 'entirely independent of any outside body'. Marston and Cave signed the agreement; when the first board vote happened on 5 October, all NUPPO executives were elected.[56] In months following Macready's arrival, relations with the executive worsened. Not only had officers welcomed the reforms (undermining NUPPO's role and authority) but the executive also wanted to get rid of Macready and, ultimately, to have their organisation replace the board.

The November 1918 Armistice, ending the war, was a turning point that tested Lloyd George's earlier vagueness about recognising a police union. Moreover, NUPPO members heard of their executive's proposal to appoint Marston as General-Secretary after infighting led Crisp to resign. To Macready's delight, nearly 'every branch in London, and many of those in the provinces ... insisted that no General-Secretary should be appointed, except by ballot of the members'.[57] Marston's executive was now on notice over its high-handed ways.

Nevertheless, by January 1919 the executive still seemed intent on its original plan to appoint Marston. Complaints from Union members nationwide streamed into the magazine *Police Review*: any qualified member should be able to contest elections for executive positions, particularly since London officers currently filled them all.[58] Marston and his executive gradually aligned NUPPO with major trade unions.[59] Partly because of this, the new Home Secretary Edward Shortt appointed the Desborough Committee on 1 March to consider 'whether any and what changes' should be made to recruitment 'for, the conditions of service of, and rates of pay, pensions and allowances' of police in England, Wales and Scotland.[60]

Meanwhile, relations between Macready and NUPPO deteriorated over elections to the representative board. He wanted it based on separate ranks, with constables, sergeants and inspectors appointing representatives of their own grade. Macready kept insisting the Home Office make it clear it would not recognise NUPPO.[61] By March 1919, Jack Hayes – subtler in his rhetoric though no less committed to the goal of union recognition – was on the ascendant. Late that month NUPPO held a three-day delegate conference in London to elect a new twelve-man executive, which for the first time included provincial members. On 25 March, the second conference day, Marston himself nominated Hayes as candidate for General-Secretary, to which he was elected. *Police Review* described his speeches as 'striking ... by their sanity, sincerity, wisdom and force, with an unaffected moderation'.[62]

Within weeks, however, Hayes overplayed his hand. On 26 May, police clashed with 10,000 people attending a National Federation of Discharged Soldiers and Sailors rally. With casualties on both sides, British labour savaged Hayes and NUPPO, claiming 'the police were no friends of the working class'. Desperate not to lose other unions' support in the fight to have his own recognised, Hayes publicly apologised the next day, saying militarism within the police was to blame and calling for closer ties between all unions. In doing so, however, he alienated his own men, many of whom quit NUPPO. Worse, Hayes's apology suggested that were the Union to have a say, police intervention to stop future unrest was not guaranteed.[63]

Sensing a confrontation, Macready issued a clear warning on 30 May:

> [A]ny officer or man ... who fails to report in the ordinary course of duty, or when called upon, will be forthwith dismissed from the force. Such officer or man will under no circumstances be permitted to rejoin ... and dismissal will result in the loss of all service counting towards pension.... Officers and men will ... defend themselves by all legitimate means if interfered with in the execution of their duty.[64]

The battle lines were drawn. The following weeks were rife with rumours about impending walkouts and government responses. In reality, a NUPPO executive still largely composed of London officers had disappointed provincial branches, which sidelined Marston.[65]

Even worse for Hayes, the Desborough findings appeared on 14 July. Aside from proposing nationwide standardisation of police pay, the report outlined the creation of a local representative body for constables, sergeants and inspectors in each force, 'to be elected by each rank separately' but able to act 'together in matters of common interest'. This Police Federation meant officers could not join a union, the penalty for disobeying this being up to two years in prison.[66] Of greater impact was a suggestion that officers receive a pay rise retroactively from 1 April; many received four months' pay (£10; 2011: £376) at once.[67]

NUPPO leaders outside London opposed a strike since many of their rank-and-file refused to join in following pay rises. Still, after Lloyd George rejected a last-minute approach by Marston and Hayes on 30 July, the executive had no choice but to call for industrial action. The call came the next day for a strike to begin at 10.00p.m.;[68] as predicted, disaster ensued. With only £3000 (2011: £113,000) in strike funds, NUPPO appealed for donations. By 6 August, and in contrast to the previous year, only 1156 out of 18,200 Metropolitan officers (6.5%) had walked out; within the City of London force, only 58 out of 970 (6%); in Birmingham 119 out of 1320 (9%); and in Liverpool 954 out of 1874 (51%). Nationwide, 2365 police officers out of 60,000 (4%) and 74 prison officers out of 2000 (4%) walked out. Authorities summarily dismissed all strikers, never reinstating any. On 15 August, the 1919 Police Act came into force: NUPPO ceased to exist as a nationwide body within a month.[69]

A reason why the second strike failed so dramatically was British labour's unwillingness to back up its early promises of support for NUPPO. However, perhaps the best explanation was the Desborough report. In the words of a bitter striker: 'It's marvellous what a ten-pound note will do.'[70] With many former policemen facing an uncertain end to 1919, several eventually found work with the All-Russian Cooperative Society (ARCOS),[71] which oversaw British trade with Bolshevik Russia. Most such officers, one should add, did this simply out of desperation. For a few, however, the Bolshevik connection went much further.

More than a decade before Soviet intelligence recruited "Kim" Philby and the rest of the Cambridge Five in the early 1930s, yet another Trinity College man already worked for Moscow. Known by the cover name "Trilby" (a child-hood nickname), William Norman Ewer[72] in time became a distinguished journalist, called on by institutions as politically diverse as the socialist *Daily Herald* and *Tribune*, the British Broadcasting Corporation (BBC) and *The New York Times*, and the Information Research Department (the secretive Foreign Office unit set up in 1947 to counter Soviet propaganda).[73] Yet few realised

3 William Ewer, the noted journalist best known in interwar years for his *Daily Herald* work. According to Soviet intelligence records, he was also the main source for the OGPU *rezidentura* in London while he was active.

Moscow had supported Ewer financially and logistically for nearly a decade, to organise and oversee espionage networks targeting the British and French Governments.

Starting around 1919, Ewer's group infiltrated several British government departments. Until recently, evidence suggested the Cambridge Five were the first long-term Soviet penetration agents, starting with Donald Maclean in 1935.[74] Hence, MI5 files on Ewer's group offer compelling grounds for re-assessing early Bolshevik efforts to infiltrate British government. Knowing the key players helps to understand the scope of Ewer's organisation, which operated out of a private residence until 1923. That year, the group moved to the London branch of the Federated Press of America,[75] set up in 1920 but used as business cover for Russian intelligence. Ewer later stressed that except for Carl Haessler, the Federated Press director in New York who occasionally helped him with secret work for Moscow, the American parent entity was unaware of the real purpose of the London branch.[76] The main known players were head agent Ewer; his friend and colleague in Paris, George Slocombe; former Metropolitan Police officer Walter Dale, the group's security officer; and Arthur Lakey, the Federated Press manager who in 1928 became an MI5 informant under his new name Albert Allen.

Codenamed HERMAN, Ewer was B-1, the main source for the Russian *rezidentura* (intelligence station) in London while he was active.[77] A CPGB founding member,[78] he first aroused official interest in July 1915 after making a pacifist speech. Ewer had been with the *Daily Herald* since 1912 and, refusing military service, registered as a conscientious objector in 1916. In early 1919, he rejoined the *Daily Herald* full-time. In April, just shy of his thirty-fourth birthday, he became Foreign Editor, remaining so even after falling out with the CPGB in December 1929 over a "deviationist" article he refused to retract.[79] Ewer's deputy in Paris, George Slocombe, also joined the *Daily Herald* in 1912 but fought in the war despite being a pacifist. He spent three years in the Royal Flying Corps (later the RAF), beginning in 1916. In 1919, Slocombe became Chief Foreign Correspondent for the *Herald*.[80]

Walter Dale was one of the strikers dismissed from the Metropolitan Police in August 1919.[81] He and others found work either with local pro-Bolshevik organisations or with the Russians themselves when they opened facilities in Britain. Dale became chief investigator for the Vigilance Detective Agency (which protected the Federated Press group), once even trying to recruit his own brother-in-law, the chauffeur of Major John Wallinger, Head of Indian Political Intelligence (IPI).[82] The final protagonist was Arthur Lakey, a Special Branch sergeant until his discharge for striking in 1919. He subsequently changed his surname to Allen, which was also MI5's codename for him (retained hereafter). Soon after his dismissal, he joined the Federated Press, becoming a manager there while his wife worked at ARCOS. Allen held his post until November 1927 but in mid-1928 turned on the group, selling information to MI5 (including on operations before November 1924, when the Federated Press first drew official attention).[83]

The group's exact origins are unclear but it was evidently a *Cheka*[84] network. While the Federated Press often fronted for the Comintern (itself cover for Bolshevik military and other intelligence organs) and Ewer had contacts in British military establishments,[85] his network gathered intelligence almost exclusively on policy, diplomatic and counter-intelligence[86] matters. Allen insisted the Federated Press kept 'absolutely clear, as far as possible' from collecting military intelligence.[87] A 1927 *Cheka* INO assessment of the London *rezidentura* stated Ewer and his sources provided an average of fifty 'very extensive' counter-intelligence reports a month, which then went to the Foreign Commissariat (NKID), Politburo and occasionally military intelligence (*Registrupr*, later *Razvedupr* and IV Directorate).[88] Allen believed the *Cheka* ran the Federated Press because Ewer worked closely with Nikolai K. Klyshko,[89] officially Secretary of the trade delegation that arrived in London in May 1920 to negotiate a trade agreement. Though not a *Cheka* officer, he was a linchpin of early Bolshevik intelligence work in Britain and one of the most knowledgeable people on Russian operations.[90]

Maxwell Knight, by 1950 a senior MI5 counter-intelligence officer reviewing old files and closing old cases before retiring, questioned Ewer that year, when inquiries into the Federated Press seem to have ended. In their second interview, Ewer said his group's role was to him 'purely counter': to determine British intelligence and counter-intelligence capabilities, as well as countermeasures against Bolshevik and CPGB activities in Britain. With the exception of Slocombe in Paris, he claimed disingenuously, the Federated Press did not spy.[91] Not until visiting Moscow in 1922, he added, did the Bolsheviks ask for his help.[92]

Russian intelligence reportedly first approached Ewer in 1921. In early 1922, he went with Klyshko to Moscow, visiting Vienna that spring to see *rezident* (station chief) Józef Krasny. In mid-June 1923, Ewer again visited Moscow, this time with Andrew Rothstein. On one of these Russia trips – a Soviet source says 1923 – Ewer formally agreed to work for the OGPU. The 1927 INO assessment put motive as 'material assistance [money] and access to information, thanks to which he builds up his [journalistic] career and passes for a clever fellow'.[93]

Though it is unclear when Ewer started working for Moscow even informally, the earliest date in his MI5 file regarding suspected pro-Bolshevik activities is 2 February 1919. He said the "forged *Pravda*" (Truth) incident[94] prompted him to form his group. Various sources suggest forgeries of that Bolshevik newspaper circulated in Britain at different times – 1917, 1919 and 1921. Ewer was likely referring to the last instance, which proved controversial. On 28 February, the *Daily Herald* published a photograph of what seemed to be a *Pravda* but still bearing details of Luton Printers, the British business producing the forgeries. When questioned in Parliament, Home Secretary Shortt said he had no knowledge of this matter but acknowledged Sir Basil Thomson was behind it.[95]

In his MI5 debriefings starting in June 1928, Allen shed light on the early days of the network. Discharged from the Metropolitan Police in August 1919, he worked 'in close touch' with Jack Hayes, NUPPO General-Secretary and head of Vigilance Detective Agency, raising relief funds for other dismissed officers and their families. Ewer had asked Hayes to look for individuals willing to conduct political enquiries 'ostensibly on behalf' of the Labour Party. Hayes introduced Allen, who was hired after disclosing Thomson's involvement in the "forged *Pravda*" affair[96] that triggered Parliamentary questions. Later in 1921, Ewer confided in Allen all work so far had in fact been 'for and on behalf of ... Russian Government'. Soon after, a Max Grinfeld visited Britain (whose brother, Nathan,[97] was reportedly from December 1924 private secretary in Paris to Leonid B. Krasin, the trade representative who became Soviet ambassador there that year; see below). Klyshko introduced Grinfeld to Allen as a member of Russian intelligence. Until returning to Moscow in 1922, said Allen, Max Grinfeld was in touch with the Federated Press, which helped him and Klyshko with intelligence work.[98]

After his admission to Allen in 1921, Ewer asked him if he would carry on. He agreed and Ewer told him to contact Klyshko, on whose orders and at whose expense Allen rented a London apartment, living and working there until 1923. When Klyshko left that year, Allen reported, a Joseph Bittner[99] became the new Russian contact for the group. Given the above, and since Allen was but one of several former policemen at Vigilance Agency and the Federated Press,[100] the inescapable conclusion is that Jack Hayes – a future Labour MP and Party Whip – talent-spotted for Ewer (and Bolshevik intelligence) within British law enforcement.[101]

The Bolshevik "cancer" spread even in those perceived bastions of conformity, Oxford and Cambridge Universities. With considerable alarm, Sir Basil Thomson reported in late 1919 some undergraduates supported the labour movement; even at Oxford, he wrote, 'advocates of revolution are of alien origin'. The group 'belonged to the glib and raw type of young intellectual' always found at university.[102] One again detects views formed during his Eton days. Foreigners as the reason why trouble had arisen at Oxford seemed to dismiss the possibility that a few "real" Britons there may have actually worried about important political issues of the day. Thomson remained dismissive of intellectuals, so noxious to both nation and empire. At this time, Andrew F. Rothstein – son of Theodore A. Rothstein, the Bolshevik agent and later member of the Soviet delegation in London – was a Scholar at Balliol College.[103]

In late November 1919 the GCCS Russian Section, numbering five to seven people[104] and headed by a top Tsarist codebreaker who had fled to Britain the year before, began decrypting higher-grade diplomatic Bolshevik communications. Ernst Constantine Vetterlein deserves special mention, given the significant contribution he (and later his family) made to British national security. Born on 3 April 1873 in St Petersburg, he graduated from its Imperial University in 1894 with excellent marks in Eastern languages (Arabic, Persian and Turkish),[105] starting work at the Russian Foreign Ministry on 25 November 1896.[106]

On 3 May 1897, Vetterlein joined a small unit headed by Vladimir V. Sabanin, an expert on British, American and Romanian codes and ciphers;[107] the team secured Russian diplomatic communications and attacked foreign ones. By March 1903, however, Vetterlein was still only a temporary appointee and therefore ineligible for a pension, this despite an improving performance since joining and being the team's best linguist, having defeated Bavarian, Bulgarian, Danish, French, Persian and Turkish systems. Sabanin appealed to the Ministry's Director of Personnel, praising Vetterlein as 'a highly useful' cryptographer who by 1903 had uncovered Bulgarian, Persian and Turkish keys. Stressing only Vetterlein knew these critical languages, the head of the unit put the performance of his young subordinate in context:

Table 2. Russian Foreign Ministry Cipher Bureau Output: 1899–1902

	1899	1900	1901	1902	Individual total
Sabanin	1117	340	764	954	3175
Naperskiy	490	605	537	532	2164
Mattey	457	503	276	358	1594
Vetterlein	198	167	321	509	1195
Ziegler	64	133	230	357	784
Dolmatov	131	98	78	84	391
Bureau total	2457	1846	2206	2794	9303

If the Ministry could find Dolmatov a consular post, said Sabanin, Vetterlein could take up a permanent slot. He did not disappoint, solving complex Austrian keys six months later.[108]

Vetterlein may have first drawn the attention of British intelligence in August 1909, when he reportedly accompanied Tsar Nicholas II on his last ever visit to Britain.[109] By 1915, Vetterlein was one of nine specialists in the cipher bureau, which now reported directly to the Foreign Minister. However, according to another top Ministry cryptographer at the time, Vladimir I. Krivosh-Nemanjic, only two or three of these men (including Vetterlein) were true experts; the others were staff officers, though experienced ones. The 1915–16 annual report on the bureau's activities highlighted problems in deciphering British and Italian communications due to frequent code changes. Before the war, the report stated, Britain usually switched codes twice a year; now, with the wartime need to secure military and political communications, Britain changed codes up to five times a year. The report commended Vetterlein for work against Persian and French codes, suggesting a 2400-rouble bonus (2011: £13,310) – the highest in the bureau. On 22 February 1916, Baltic Fleet Commander Admiral Viktor A. Kanin praised his 'special assignments of great military significance'. Vetterlein received the Imperial Order of Saint Anna, 2nd Class, and the rank of State Counsellor along with it. Before the October 1917 Revolution, he broke several diplomatic codes, including British.[110]

Vetterlein reportedly had good connections in Britain because his work was 'vital to the English', who did not want the Bolsheviks to learn about and compromise both friendly and enemy (i.e. British) codes.[111] Exfiltrating him was therefore crucial. Some sources suggest Vetterlein and his wife escaped Petrograd (as St Petersburg was renamed in 1914) aboard a Swedish ship during or soon after the revolution.[112] Others state he slipped across the border into Finland and made his way to Britain.[113] Ernst's brother Pavel (Paul) Karlovich did this in August–September 1922,[114] so either Ernst set a precedent or his British colleagues confused the brothers' stories as years passed. Pavel Karlovich's son, Pavel Pavlovich, said his uncle's departure happened 'between the two revolutions' (i.e. February and October 1917); rumour was 'the British sent someone to collect him' because he was 'absolutely vital'.[115]

The chronology of Vetterlein's location became hazy for a time but in March 1918, Captain Wion Egerton (British Naval Attaché in Helsingfors, now Helsinki) cabled DNI Hall:

> FETERLEIN [*sic*] cypher expert to Russian F. O. for 25 years who worked all war with Russian D.?I.D. [Director of Intelligence Division] offers his services and full information of German position square [*sic*] Austrian Military and diplomatic codes. He is highly recommended by many well known to D.I.D. but will need financial aid for himself and wife to reach England.[116]

Ernst and Angelica Vetterlein arrived in Britain on 17–18 May 1918, reportedly at Tilbury in Essex,[117] adding weight to the Swedish ship premise. Britain was the first major power to establish a unified postwar SIGINT agency, which soon paid handsome dividends against the Bolshevik target. Yet as Vetterlein sought to escape Russia, France was equally keen to employ him. However,

 (6,7/17—(6010) 13367/P25 1000 pads 1/18es 754 O & S 112

TELEGRAM.   No. 55

From   N.A. Helsingfors   DATE 9.3.18

To   10.44 am 7th
                                              8.21 am

Allied No.1.

55.   FETERLEIN cypher expert to Russian F.O. for 25
years who worked all war with Russian D.?I.D. offers
his services and full information of German position
square(sic) Austrian Military and diplomatic codes.
He is highly recommended by many well known to D.I.D.
but will need financial aid for himself and wife to
reach England.

D.I.D.2

4 Message from present-day Helsinki informing London that Ernst Vetterlein, the leading Tsarist cryptologist, wanted to work for Britain. Vetterlein and his brother Pavel's expertise gave the country a significant edge in both peace and war for over a quarter of a century.

with wartime British cryptographic successes still fresh on their minds, enthusiastic SIGINT supporters like Churchill realised what an intelligence coup Vetterlein was and London aggressively outbid Paris.[118] Vladimir K. Korostovets, a Tsarist diplomat who became prominent in London émigré circles, offered an explanation in 1928 for Vetterlein's popularity:

[He] was given an intercepted wireless telegram in the German naval cipher and he discovered a complete order with ... details for an advance into the Bays of Riga and Finland, where a demonstration against the Russian Fleet was to take place. This work ... made it possible for our Fleet not only to take ... necessary countermeasures but also to send out a detachment of minelayers.... The German Fleet's diversion miscarried.

During their return home some … ships hit … mines that had been laid, one trawler and some minesweepers sank and also, if I am not mistaken, the cruiser *Magdeburg* [foundered on 26 August 1914].

Six men worked on German naval traffic under Vetterlein and this success was almost certainly part of the wartime work Admiral Kanin later commended. Russia shared *Magdeburg*'s codebooks with the Admiralty's Room 40, enabling subsequent British SIGINT successes against the Imperial German Navy. Once in Britain, from June 1918 to May 1919 Vetterlein solved various codes and ciphers, including Bolshevik, Austrian military and Georgian.[119]

Earl Jellicoe, Grand Fleet commander during the Battle of Jutland, wrote of Vetterlein having 'been appointed or lent for temporary service during the War', although unpaid.[120] This was because his nationality (still Russian) and age (forty-five) made him ineligible for a pension. He began work as a Temporary Assistant at Room 40 on 24 June 1918, a post he held until 16 December 1919. The next day, still listed as Admiralty staff, he became Senior Assistant in the newly formed GCCS, a rank he held until 31 March 1922. On 1 April, Vetterlein formally became Senior Assistant at the Foreign Office, which by now had taken over GCCS.[121]

Illustrating his worth was a letter by GCCS head Commander Alastair Denniston, RNVR, to DNI Hall's successor, Commodore Hugh Sinclair, on the need to retain Room 40 personnel after the war. Denniston listed eighteen men – including talents like Alfred "Dilly" Knox ('a candidate for Senior Assistant') and Leslie Lambert ('The W/T [wireless telegraphy] expert') – yet only Vetterlein was deemed essential.[122] For a year, starting in August 1920, Vetterlein mentored renowned cryptographer John Tiltman on Russian systems. Tiltman later repaid Vetterlein by recruiting his brother Pavel into GCCS in 1935 and helping the nephew, Pavel Pavlovich, into Bletchley Park (BP) in 1942.[123]

Having retired on 3 April 1938 at the compulsory age of sixty-five (although a heart condition was reportedly also a factor), Ernst Vetterlein returned to service in November 1939 after the capture of German Air Force (*Luftwaffe*) codebooks. As a civilian attached to the Air Ministry with the rank of Temporary Senior Assistant, he worked at BP and Wavendon House (the facility near Bletchley housing the Commercial Section)[124] between 1939 and March 1942. From then until late 1943, Vetterlein was at Berkeley Street (the location from March 1942 of the Diplomatic Section, near Piccadilly, London) working on solutions for the Commercial and Air[125] Sections. From late 1943, he also worked at Aldford House (in Park Lane, London), which from March 1942 had housed the Commercial Section and elements of the Diplomatic

Section. Vetterlein was instrumental in breaking the German diplomatic cipher FLORADORA, with which GCCS had struggled since 1919 but finally broke[126] mid-war. Before his death on 9 June 1944 in Surrey, he reportedly translated Russian messages at Ivy Farm, Knockholt Pound, Kent (although this was a Foreign Office intercept site for German teleprinter communications from mid-1942).[127] If Vetterlein was not mistaken for his nephew (posted in southern England late in the war to work on Soviet traffic), these messages may have been part of Project ISCOT, BP's work on Russian non-military codes from June 1943 on.[128]

When established on 1 November 1919, GCCS had twenty-eight clerical and twenty-five cryptological staff, these numbers increasing significantly from 1921 to 1935, when the School had between eighty and ninety-five personnel (thirty of them cryptologists).[129] While cryptological staff numbers only increased by five in fourteen years, clerical staff nearly trebled, most likely because an ever-greater number of customers demanded a growing number of intercepts and decrypts, which had to be organised, distributed and filed.

Of these customers, Churchill and Curzon were the most obsessed with Russia, explaining their passion for SIGINT on the country. Churchill, whose 'Ducal blood ran cold'[130] on hearing of Bolshevik atrocities against Russian aristocrats, was an anti-communist, though one who let Party politics colour his views. In time, he grew aware of the realities of international relations but they barely tempered his ambition – a better explanation for his shifting political allegiances over the years. Curzon too was a committed anti-Bolshevik but mainly because of India where, as Viceroy at the turn of the century, he had been a key player in the Great Game and grown convinced of the mortal danger Russia posed. Unsurprisingly, both Russophobes – whose interest in SIGINT verged on the obsessive – sat on the Secret Service Committee that suggested in early 1919 that 'a peacetime cryptographic unit' unite the 'remnants of Room 40 and MI1$_{(b)}$.'[131]

The USA is nowadays considered the world's first SIGINT hyperpower but Britain was truly its equivalent after the First World War, having 'virtually invented' the field.[132] From November 1919 to January 1924, GCCS eavesdropped on thirty-four nations,[133] a considerable feat since by 1924 the School had just ninety-four staff (twenty-nine of them cryptologists).[134] Still, Britain's near-complete control of and access to global cable networks (terrestrial and submarine, the main communication channels) eased the burden. Given the vastness of the British Empire, regardless of where a cable 'originated or was destined', chances were it would eventually connect to British networks.[135]

The subsequent Russian diplomatic intercepts[136] deserve a few words. Owing either to weeding of records over time or accidental loss, as well as Bolshevik cryptographic security measures, the declassified series in The National Archives is incomplete. From March 1922, the number of messages concerning Russia dropped dramatically.[137] Fortunately, this occurred a full year after the Anglo-Russian Trade Agreement of 16 March 1921, allowing at least a partial tracking of Bolshevik compliance with treaty terms, particularly where subversion was concerned. Even if incomplete, the HW 12 (Russia) series at Kew deserves attention.

After the October Revolution, four factors caused British officials to perceive danger. One was fear of how Bolshevism would affect postwar Britain, so politicians and senior officials worried about connections between worker unrest and communist subversion. Another factor was the novelty of the domestic threat: not since the French Revolution had a regime dedicated itself ideologically, politically and financially to toppling British institutions. This related closely to the third factor: the threat to the "crown jewel" that was India, though British administrators there and in London came to regard Bolshevism as a new variation on an old theme (imperial rivalry with Russia).[138] The final factor was the critical role intelligence – both the community and the information it provided to Cabinet – played unintentionally or otherwise in portraying the scope and nature of the "Red Menace".

These factors, as well as the socio-economic background of British politicians and senior officials (see Chapter 1), ensured government had a predominantly colonial perspective[139] on the Bolshevik issue[140] for much of the period this book covers. The combination distorted efforts to understand some of Moscow's aims and methods. Though in relative terms probably more information reached Cabinet concerning Russia than on any other country, much of this arrived via places like Riga and Helsinki.[141] This was problematic since they were active centres of anti-Bolshevik intrigue and forgery.[142] Consequently, some intelligence reaching Cabinet proved destabilising for two reasons.

First, for several years there was no effective system to grade incoming HUMINT. A basic system did emerge in mid-1922, following an incident involving Foreign Secretary Curzon in which information SIS acquired in Estonia turned out to be forged.[143] Second, the same evidence could produce a range of reactions within government: what Coalition pragmatists such as Lloyd George considered Russian posturing, hardliners like Churchill and

Curzon saw as duplicity. This ideological divide lasted until the Coalition collapsed in October 1922. SIGINT (unambiguous and "cleaner") soon overtook HUMINT (complex, open to manipulation and therefore potentially embarrassing) as the favourite form of intelligence in British government. Bolshevik communications were vulnerable for two related reasons: an unwillingness to introduce sophisticated codes and ciphers developed by Tsarist experts (thus relying on insecure systems) and the defection of talented codebreakers after the revolution.[144]

What all this (should have) told Britain about its own communications security (COMSEC) is another question, addressed below. Russian intercepts from November 1919 to May 1920 showed Asia was Moscow's main concern,[145] above all a possible alliance with Afghanistan and consequent subversion in India. Most messages dealt with logistical and administrative questions, given the tendency of Bolshevik delegations to discuss issues with local authorities independently from Moscow. In these first months, Moscow repeatedly reprimanded its officials for acting without consulting central authorities.[146]

Content about subversion appeared as early as December 1919: 'When sending agents and agitators abroad ... furnish us with ... names ... biographies and the qualifications of the persons you are recommending.' The first clear reference to subversion in India appeared a month later: 'the Afghans undertake to help us send our military experts and agitators to the Indian frontier and ... facilitate our espionage and propaganda'.[147]

As early as January 1920, intercepts showed Moscow wanted a rapid economic recovery. Foreign Commissar Georgi V. Chicherin[148] advised Bolshevik representatives in Tashkent (in present-day Uzbekistan) to abandon plans to provoke war between Britain and Afghanistan lest Russia become involved, preventing it from 're-establishing our economic position'. Earlier that month Moscow had already warned Tashkent not to act alone and commit the Bolsheviks to helping the Afghans against the British, 'in view of a possible [trade] agreement with England'. Any agreement with the Afghans could only be defensive in nature, never offensive.[149]

Reading the HW 12 (Russia) series created a peculiar impression, the tone and wording of some cables suggesting Moscow knew before December 1920 that London could read Bolshevik traffic. John Ferris has written of Moscow's use of radio deception in late December 1920 during the trade negotiations.[150] Yet one should also consider the possibility Russia might have used deception earlier to lead London to commit to trade talks in the first place.

By January 1920, the Kremlin was urging Tashkent to 'organise the interception of English wireless messages' and let Moscow know the content.[151] This suggests Moscow's ability to decrypt British messages (as Vetterlein had done in Tsarist times), possibly by predecessors of the earliest known Bolshevik SIGINT unit, the *Spetsialniy Otdel* (or *Spetsotdel*, Special Section) of the *Cheka*, formed by decree of 28 January 1921 and operational on 5 May.[152] One could argue Russia would be unlikely to reveal such capabilities knowing Britain could decipher its messages. Yet this would be neither the first nor the last time Moscow traded one thing for another of greater value. As Basil Thomson observed, 'the tendency of the Russian Communists is to sacrifice one after another of their original principles'.[153] Whether by choice or necessity, the Bolsheviks would almost certainly have given up their ability to intercept British traffic locally if deception, a central component of communist doctrine,[154] achieved the critical foreign policy goal of a trade agreement with London.

In February 1920, when some British officials still had doubts about (even informal) trade talks with Russia, Chicherin contacted his deputy in Copenhagen, Maxim Litvinov:

> The Afghan mission in Tashkent is secretly working out ... with our (representatives?) a draft ... offensive and defensive alliance, but we ... decided not to bind ourselves in view of [possible] peace with England, in which case we would renounce in Asia a policy hostile to her. We are ... as yet not concluding anything which [*sic*] would bind us.[155]

By suggesting Moscow would effectively give up Asia in exchange for peace and trade, and if the Kremlin knew GCCS was reading Bolshevik traffic (Vetterlein's disappearance was known), then these messages would be an ideal vehicle to nudge Lloyd George's Cabinet toward the negotiations Russia so needed. The sense is almost that Moscow was saying what some in London wanted to hear, namely the Prime Minister and others favouring trade. Russia knew the obstacles Curzon, for one, would pose if threats to India were not at least mitigated.[156]

Is it possible Moscow knew GCCS was reading traffic and so tried to induce London into starting trade negotiations? In the early 1920s, *Cheka* INO agents in London reportedly stole numerous British diplomatic codes and ciphers, which the *rezidentura* forwarded to the *Spetsotdel*. There is no indication of how early in the decade this breach occurred but with those codes, the unit then broke diplomatic traffic to and from the British Mission in Moscow. The *Spetsotdel* also broke White communications whenever possible (including with Britain, presumably) by using any codes and ciphers found on counter-revolutionaries arrested by the *Cheka*.[157]

Given its successes in using HUMINT to enable SIGINT, Moscow naturally feared Western intelligence acquiring plain-text copies of cables. The Bolsheviks were certainly suspicious of COMSEC vulnerabilities well before December 1920, when Mikhail V. Frunze, Red commander on the Southern Front during the civil war, alerted Moscow to this. In March 1920, Chicherin cabled Litvinov that Estonia allegedly could 'decipher our keyed telegrams. In view of the identical system of the cipher please ... ascertain if our enemies [can decipher] our telegrams.' Litvinov replied he had 'no reason' to suspect this but would investigate further.[158]

On 19 August 1920, leading Bolshevik Lev B. Kamenev[159] cabled Chicherin to look for leaks closer by: given 'your announcement ... that deciphering ... telegrams is not easy, attention should be paid to the possibility' of their 'being stolen from the Chancery [sic] at Moscow or Copenhagen.'[160] Chicherin informed Lenin the next day that weak ciphers and the defection of Tsarist codebreakers to the enemy, in his view, raised COMSEC concerns. On 10 September, however, Leonid Krasin – temporarily Kamenev's deputy in London – also wrote to Lenin about suspicions leaks actually came from the NKID cipher bureau. Krasin urged its 'radical cleansing', making it independent of Chicherin and employing only trustworthy staff known personally for at least a decade. Lenin took the issue seriously; in September, the Politburo discussed possible COMSEC improvements, asking War Commissar Leon D. Trotsky to convene a commission on the question. Lenin followed up the matter several times, including with Chicherin on 25 November, urging him to tighten control over ciphers at NKID and legations abroad. More importantly, key representatives like Krasin and Litvinov were to receive maximum-security ciphers for personal use only.[161]

These events raise the issue of cognitive dissonance in Britain regarding its COMSEC. Fragmentary evidence suggests London behaved early in the interwar period much as Berlin did early in the Second World War. On paper, at least, government priorities seemed right:

[C]ipher security is of great national importance. It is paradoxical to concentrate on ... reading ... communications of other Governments without taking every step to prevent the reading of our own ... [;] of the two functions of ... [GCCS] that of our ... cipher security is ... the more important.[162]

In reality, however:

It is unfortunate ... security can only be secured at the expense of the time taken to cipher; but what is the use of ciphering at all if secrecy is not attained? It is interesting ... to compare our methods with those of three of the greatest Powers, who invariably recipher their best cipher, whereas, excepting in the [War Office], it is only resorted to in this country when a cipher is thought to be compromised or in very rare cases for particularly secret messages.[163]

GCCS solved Russian traffic in the 1920s but the notion Moscow may have reciprocated the courtesy has sometimes been met with scepticism. No archival evidence has emerged so far indicating Britain knew of comparable breaches but until Russian primary sources on the topic emerge – a remote prospect – one never knows. The question is how Russia went from having some of the best cipher bureaus in 1917 to being supposedly unable to read enemy traffic. Evidence suggests some staff continuity[164] and familiarity with British cryptographic practices, and while Moscow may have lost key experts, foreign ones of the view their enemy's enemy was their friend helped the Bolsheviks.[165]

They were not the only ones seeking renewed trade; Britain too felt the pain of postwar reconstruction. Board of Trade official (Edward) Frank Wise[166] argued in January 1920 the Russian Civil War and the Allied blockade had stopped vast amounts of Russian goods reaching international markets. Soaring inflation contributed further to the high prices at which Washington sold grain to London. Renewed trade with Russia 'would go further than any other factor to reduce the cost of living', wrote Wise; from our standpoint,

> the longer ... reopening of trade ... is delayed, the more formidable will be German and American competition. At the moment Germany has not got the manufacturing resources to compete effectively, and America has not ... the necessary knowledge of ... export trade and ... Russian markets. Our relative advantage ... [grows] less each month.[167]

Two causes of unrest in Britain, according to Basil Thomson's reports, were high cost of living and concurrent profiteering; resuming trade with Russia increasingly appealed to the Lloyd George government (more so after the September 1919 railway strike).[168] By early 1920, unemployment crept up, reaching 2.6% of the workforce in June that year.[169]

Concern about the potential for widespread labour unrest prompted officials to take precautions. In January 1920, Cabinet Secretary Sir Maurice

Hankey wrote to Lloyd George on how to ensure government continuity in case of civil unrest. One step was protecting government in London with 'thoroughly reliable troops' while another was guarding heavy calibre weapons and ammunition properly ('absolutely vital'). Ensuring enough well trained forces were available in any emergency was essential, so the War Office should organise all this since it could 'put their hand on discreet and trustworthy persons' to act appropriately should the need arise.[170]

Yet revolution in Britain was unlikely by this time. Quoted in a January 1920 Directorate of Intelligence report, an activist stated he was not one to advocate 'a bloody revolution' because 'unfortunately' the British were 'not ripe for taking the law into their own hands'.[171] This is one reason why Moscow never succeeded in creating enough unrest to threaten stability seriously. As bad as the postwar situation was, as difficult as conditions were even in the poorest areas, and as unjust as circumstances may have been in shops and factories, they were nowhere near conditions endured by average Russians under Tsardom. State "repression" in Britain was rarely violent and there certainly was no widespread, deep-seated resentment against government brought on by centuries of corrupt autocratic rule.

Unemployment was not yet the seedbed of serious revolutionary threat Thomson feared. Granted, to dismiss unemployment as only a minor cause of unrest would be unwise but most workers were patriots generally loyal to British institutions. Average working-class men were 'deferential, conservative in outlook, yet resentful of insults and condescension'.[172] Thomson nevertheless viewed ongoing social changes through a security lens. He portrayed the Bolshevik subversive threat as ever-present, calling for harsher legislation in early 1920 – a criticism of Lloyd George's "soft" approach to the issue:

> English opinion appears ... divided between those who fear Bolshevism too much and those who fear it too little. ... It is rather remarkable that ... it is still not illegal ... to advocate the abolition of Parliament and the setting up of Soviet Government, to circulate Bolshevik literature, to accept money from abroad for revolutionary agitation, and to be a secret representative of the Russian Soviet Government, provided that one does not advocate acts of violence or armed rebellion. ... It may be possible to use some of the *unofficial agencies for combating Bolshevism* to expose the conspiracy and turn it into ridicule ... publicity ... is now the only weapon.[173] [my italics]

Unofficial agencies became central to the Government's strategy of constantly scrutinising and containing interwar Communism. These informal networks were either closely connected to, or actually used by, British intelligence as cover; often both. Under the guise of assisting government and employers with contingency plans to face labour unrest, these agencies grew in importance from mid-1917 on, 'encouraged implicitly and explicitly by ... Coalition Government and its Conservative successors'.[174] By early 1920, the key unofficial agencies were National Propaganda, Industrial Information and the Industrial Intelligence Bureau (IIB).[175] The last one arose from a private wartime network set up by ultra-conservative Sir George Makgill[176] and the British Empire Union (BEU).[177]

Former DNI Sir Reginald Hall, who retired in November 1918 and became a Conservative MP for Liverpool, chaired National Propaganda.[178] Created on 26 August 1919, it coordinated anti-socialist work nationwide. The Right felt the need for such an organisation after bitter rivalries since mid-1917 undermined cohesion and effectiveness.[179] Government saw National Propaganda as a

[V]oluntary fund with headquarters in London ... finances being subscribed or guaranteed by commercial firms or eminent private individuals. Central control is vested in an Executive Committee holding monthly meetings ... and administration is carried out through a Management Committee selected from the Executive.... The country is divided into areas, each under a local Area Committee. National Propaganda's ... aim is ... 'the utter annihilation of falsehood by a continuous and universal statement of economic truth'. [S]tated objects ... are to diminish unrest, to correct economic and other misstatement, to impress upon employers and employed the vital necessity for increased production, to combat all activities directed against ... Government, and to ... assist the activities of other non-Party organisations having the like or similar objects. Methods are ... (a) Leaflet distribution at meetings, in workshops and from house to house. (b) Placarding of posters urging increased production. (c) The organisation of meetings at which working men are addressed by, and invited to question, speakers ... trained in modern economic problems. Very little work is attempted through the Press. The last progress report ... shows that [in] the last few months 44 industrial centres have been "worked"; ... 3 million ... leaflets (11 subjects) ... distributed; 341,000 posters (15 subjects) displayed; and 89 well-attended meetings held.... "N.P" specially trains its own speakers. This part of their work is not fully developed, but ... is hoped ... for over 200 weekly in the ... near future. [Regarding] leaflets, 8 new subjects are in hand and it is estimated ... annual ... distribution will [reach] 72 million, all of the "anti-Bolshevism", "increased production" and "harmony between capital and labour" type.[180]

Industrial Information, headed by pioneering "spin doctor" and Lloyd George press officer Sydney Walton,[181] covered the remaining areas:

[F]inanced from an unofficial fund administered by the Whips. The fund, unlike that of "National Publicity" [*sic*], is capital and not on an annual subscription basis.... It stands for Constitutional Government and advocates higher production and anti-Bolshevism. Most ... work is ... through the Press, comparatively little being attempted in the direction of leaflets, speeches and posters, which are covered by "N. P." This organisation began work at the end of last October. Since then, an average circulation of articles exceeding 1000 a week has been issued. Special articles appear in the London press and in trade journals. Galley proofs are sent ... to over 700 provincial papers.... In addition to a staff of about 25 expert economists and journalists, help is secured from practically every eminent person who is in sympathy with the movement and can command any kind of public attention.... Every type of journal is made use of, from "Truth" to the "Family Companion", from the "Pall Mall Gazette" to "Answers", and from the "Organiser" to the "Domestic" journals issued by big firms like Lyons and Harrods for ... employees.... [L]ittle has been attempted or is contemplated in the way of posters, only one having been issued so far.... There is a friendly understanding between "N. P." and "I. I." although they are constituted on different lines and ... would not amalgamate.[182]

Both National Propaganda and Industrial Information 'exercise[d] control and [gave] financial support in return for the use of local machinery'. Unlike most groups they oversaw, National Propaganda and Industrial Information were secret[183] and had close ties to British intelligence.

Established at war's end and led by Sir George Makgill, the IIB was a 'highly secretive and private intelligence agency',[184] arguably one of the most influential in interwar years. The BEU, with Makgill as Secretary, had from April 1915 on set up a network of private agencies across Britain to collect intelligence on German espionage. By 1918, however, he and his industry patrons worried about 'the upsurge of industrial unrest and political militancy' triggered by the Bolshevik Revolution and the Armistice. The existing BEU network was enlarged, reorganised and re-tasked.[185]

As fearful as Makgill was that 'the postwar return to profitability' might be endangered, the Federation of British Industries, and the Coal Owners' and Ship-Owners' Associations funded him 'to acquire intelligence on industrial unrest' caused by 'Communists, Anarchists, various secret societies in [Britain] and overseas, the Irish Republican Army and other "subversive" organisations'.[186] Thus, the IIB was born, and the close working relationship in wartime between Makgill, the BEU and British intelligence intensified in peacetime. Chapter 3 examines how close relations became between government and private agencies in the name of fighting Bolshevik subversion.

Perhaps unsurprisingly, just as better SIGINT on Russia became available in late 1919, Thomson's reports shifted focus from unemployment, strikes and so on to Russia, Communism, and possible ties between British revolutionaries and Moscow. Whether trying to compete with SIGINT or simply complement it,[187] Thomson's portrayal of the labour movement by early 1920 was nevertheless unflattering:

> treated as a hothouse plant for so many years, behaves like other hothouse plants; when suddenly put out into the cold air of criticism its petals curl up.... Many think ... their obligations to their Unions are finished when they have elected their delegate; the rest is his business. The average worker is far more concerned about the cost of living, which includes beer and tobacco, than the question of nationalisation, and if he knew that in the event of nationalisation his responsibilities, which he could not delegate, would be increased, he would quickly change his views.[188]

Even the Labour publication *Forward* seemed to agree: 'the only International presently understood and appreciated by the bulk of the working class, was held a fortnight ago, when England beat Scotland by four goals to none'.[189] In compiling his reports, Thomson relied on a vast network of correspondents. He embellished some reports to support his politicised warnings that Bolshevism was infecting Britain.[190] The situation, he added, would only worsen after trade resumed with Moscow. The snippet below, reportedly from a Welsh porter, illustrates what reached Cabinet as trade negotiations began in May 1920:

> Give the working man lots of drink and you will never hear a word about Revolution except from foreigners and Jews. This is what every Englishman back from the front thinks ... [I] never knew so many people hate foreigners.[191]

5 Ernst Vetterlein and wife Angelica, c. 1927. In 1923, despite grave Foreign Office concerns about Bolshevik reprisals against him, the Home Office kept to protocol and published Vetterlein's address as a requirement of his British naturalisation.

That remark, even if made up, betrayed the fear that Thomson and large segments of British society shared: the symptoms of the alien ideology that was Communism. To many Britons, Lloyd George's negotiations with the Bolsheviks must have seemed like madness. Yet there was method in it. The next chapter examines his views on the need to accommodate Moscow, and why they differed from those many of his ministers held. Hostility towards foreigners reflected concerns about the threat communist internationalism posed to British nationalism, or rather, national identity, symbols and institutions. Thomson's reporting around this time brought out an intriguing paradox. He prided himself on understanding the mentality of the lower classes and criminals, yet even a hint of Bolshevik agitation animated him. One should reiterate the effectiveness of Special Branch and his Directorate of Intelligence: few unions, meetings or protests were beyond reach, as Thomson's detailed accounts showed. His problem was that bureaucratic empire-building and ventures abroad undermined success at home.

This chapter examined the impact of military mutinies, the second police strike, and SIGINT successes on British domestic and foreign policies in 1919–20. Cabinet pragmatism during both crises – compromise with the military, harshness with the police – prevented the escalation of already tense situations. However, the short-term triumph over NUPPO created a longer-term threat: Bolshevik penetration of British security, intelligence and policy circles thanks to a handful of disaffected police officers. They were either ideologically motivated or embittered by the Government's firm response to the 1919 police strike (and often both). Nevertheless, at the strategic level, Britain had the upper hand thanks to GCCS, Ernst Vetterlein and his Russian Section. Much to their dismay, surely, British ministers and senior civil servants bent on de-railing Anglo-Russian negotiations in 1920–21 were blinded by their hatred – and fear – of Bolshevism. The result was a cavalier attitude toward SIGINT and a willingness to give up long-term strategic advantage for short-term political gain.

PART II

Diagnosis

CHAPTER 3

The Agreement

"It's the Economy, Dummy" ~ Conflict within Cabinet ~
The Intercepts

> It is hardly an exaggeration ... that in a few months ... the
> American executive and ... public will ... dictate to this
> country on matters that affect us more dearly than them.
> John Maynard Keynes[1]

> We can ... make sure that in our life and time, the deadly
> disease which has struck down Russia ... not be allowed to
> spring up here and poison us as it is poisoning them.
> Winston Churchill[2]

> The greatest thing of all is a constant chain of hypothesis,
> check and verification, coupled to an infinite capacity for
> taking pains. Anonymous, on codebreaking[3]

A 1909 War Office note commented on the 'wholesale dishonesty' of
Russian officers, whose 'greed for money' made it simple for Britain to
buy secrets. Russia had long absorbed into its society Orientals from newly
conquered territories, so the 'wiles and cunning treachery of the Russian
diplomatists and their secret service agents' were unrivalled.[4] In the context
of the 1917 Revolution, three points emerged from this document.

First, even if one discounts the chaos of the revolution and the ensuing civil
war,[5] the initial fanaticism and "incorruptibility" of the new regime threatened British intelligence gathering because the Reds either drove away or
killed most Imperial staff. A sizeable minority chose to work for the Bolsheviks but revolutionary suspicions proved almost insurmountable. Only when
the new regime recognised it could not survive without these experts were
they allowed (or forced) back into service. Second, the note implied British
espionage was somehow inferior since Britain, despite its empire, was more
homogenous than Russia. The Bolsheviks were threatening because they could

deploy "Orientals" across the British Empire. Third, the note linked diplomacy and espionage, suggesting where the Russian diplomat went so too did his spy. Many British politicians and officials served in the colonies[6] so to their imperial mindset, hardened further by Communism, establishing ties with Moscow seemed dangerous indeed.

This chapter revisits a controversy that split British politics and society soon after the war. Should Britain have ties with Bolshevik Russia, granting it the international recognition so needed for political legitimacy and even survival? Unlike some of his ministers, why did David Lloyd George believe trade could better subdue Bolshevism than force?[7] How did those on either side of the divide advance their views and interests by using intelligence?

Three realities emerged. Economics, then as now, usually trumps ideology and conviction; some British politicians and intelligence officials deliberately sought to de-rail government policies they felt endangered Britain; and Moscow overestimated its ability to sway hearts and minds. One reason Britain blunted overt subversion after the war was timely SIGINT on Kremlin intentions. HUMINT also played a role, but because politicians worried far more about social unrest than espionage at this time (despite emerging threats),[8] Basil Thomson's anti-Bolshevik patrons tried furthering their aims by encouraging his ambition.[9]

Bolshevism among the working classes caused official anxiety but so did subversion in the Civil Service. In May 1920, the Home Affairs Committee advised that to prevent possible trouble, department heads should be able to dismiss summarily any civil servant striking without warning, 'on the ground of desertion of duty'. Fortunately, the report added, pensions had a calming effect. Thoughts of losing or having it reduced 'for infidelity' were usually enough. Still, such measures would only be effective during short walkouts; department heads should otherwise exercise judgement. The report suggested drafting a Bill making it an 'offence for ... Civil Servants to strike without a month's notice'.[10]

This issue had been but one symptom of growing unease in the previous six months. Following a pivotal Lloyd George speech on 8 November 1919,[11] the second anniversary of the Bolshevik Revolution, a battle raged on within and outside Cabinet, both publicly and in private. At stake, believed opposing camps, was nothing less than Britain's very soul and future survival. Lloyd George almost single-handedly[12] took on the anti-communist camp led by Winston Churchill and, to a lesser extent, Lord Curzon and Walter Long. Both sides paradoxically sought the same strategic outcomes: to spur economic growth and hasten postwar recovery, by restoring Britain's position in Russian markets to what it was before November 1917 (and internationally before August 1914). Where opinions differed was over tactics. Whereas Lloyd George believed that even limited trade would more effectively thwart Communism than severing relations or meddling in Russian affairs,[13] the Churchill faction sought instead to restore the old regime, thus also ensuring continuity in a vital trading relationship going back nearly 160 years.[14]

Bolshevik repudiation of Tsarist debts[15] especially outraged hardliners. This raises questions about if, for some of them at least, self-interest[16] and susceptibility to lobbying shaped their actions. One must therefore turn momentarily to the financial and commercial underpinnings of Anglo-Russian (and European) relations up to 1920 to appreciate better why Lloyd George and his opponents acted as they did.

For economic and strategic reasons, French diplomats and bankers were manoeuvring for a Franco-Russian Entente as early as 1880, based mainly on French government and private finance. Not only did both nations have common enemies (Britain and Germany), but French loans and investment were also critical for Russian industrial development. However, chronic instability in French financial markets created doubt as to their ability to withstand large commitments in Russia.[17] From 1890 on, it borrowed heavily to support a vast industrialisation drive, with national debt essentially doubling within two decades.[18] Total foreign investment in Russian firms was by 1890 just under £23 million; by 1900, it was £96.5 million; and £237 million by 1914. That year, Britain accounted for about 23% of total foreign investment in Russia, France leading the way with 33%.[19]

Yet with the exception of British bankers Baring Brothers,[20] serious British financial involvement in Russia on a scale similar to France's only developed later. By January 1899, following volatility in French financial markets, Russia looked more broadly within The City (London's financial centre) and to British government for loans. In under a decade, deepening trilateral financial ties helped revolutionise European diplomacy, as shown by the 1907 Anglo-Russian Entente. Especially after the 1904–05 Russo-Japanese War prompted Russia to seek even more loans to modernise her shattered military, Paris and London worked closely to preserve international financial stability.[21]

From 1904 on, several factors led foreign investors to see Russia as their 'biggest credit risk': humiliation by the Japanese, rising national debt fuelled largely by rearmament, mounting discontent over the Romanovs' harsh and corrupt rule, and perceived political backwardness.[22] Bearer bonds (long favoured by outside investors as a buffer against fluctuations in Russian markets) remained the preferred choice, trading mainly in Paris and London.[23]

With the tarnishing of Russia's image abroad and given the country's dependence on foreign investment, in 1904 alone Russia spent about £131,000 (2011: nearly £14 million) to bribe 'the foreign press, politicians, trade unionists and other opinion leaders' to promote Russian foreign bonds.[24] The strategy worked since St Petersburg continued to find ready lenders, lured by prospects of high returns. Russia's borrowing history shows the country is 'punished only rarely and lightly for failures to honour its external obligations. ... Creditors ... *tend to show more concern for future opportunities than past losses*'[25] [my italics]. By January 1914, Russia owed British and French investors nearly £344 million (£26.5 million and £317.5 million, respectively). They were Russia's main creditors on the eve of the First World War.[26]

Commercial relations in the decades leading up to 1914 also mattered.[27] From 1870 to 1913, despite an overall increase in the absolute value of Anglo-Russian trade, each nation's export share in the other's market declined. One reason was booming Russo-German commerce, dwarfing Anglo-Russian trade.[28] From 1900 to 1913, British exports consisted mainly of cotton (24%), iron and steel (11%), coal (10%) and woollens (6%). By 1913, Europe purchased 35% of British exports; core non-European markets[29] took another 43%. Conversely, Europe that year supplied 40% of British imports, of which 73% was food and raw materials, and 2% fuels.[30]

Self-interest; misunderstanding the nature of modern war and economic interdependencies; a Royal Commission;[31] and political reluctance to endorse Admiralty plans for all-out economic warfare against Germany all contributed to Britain settling for a wartime strategy of "business as usual":

> It rested on the proposition ... the war must involve the minimum amount of disruption to the worldwide ... trade and payments [sustaining] the British economy.... The cost of [any] rising imports [would be] easily met by the earnings from exports together with invisible earnings.... Chancellor of the Exchequer [Lloyd George said] in 1914 ... Britain could pay for five years of war from ... foreign investments [earnings] alone.[32]

There was, however, a flaw in this reasoning: wars rarely go to plan. By December 1914, more than a million Britons had already enlisted. War therefore meant a massive and sudden re-orientation of domestic production to supply a rapidly growing military. British exports and related earnings therefore declined in the first year of war.[33] Simultaneously, spending on imports rose sharply.[34] Making a bad situation worse were reversals of foreign trade and financial flows, one of the war's hallmarks. In 1914, 18% of British imports came from the USA; by 1918 it was 39%. That year, Britain's visible trade deficit with the USA was £489 million (2011: nearly £144.5 billion). London paid for American imports in dollars, purchasing them by liquidating many foreign investments in the USA at a fraction of their original value.[35]

Another core source of invisible earnings,[36] shipping receipts, also declined as war disrupted longstanding trade patterns.[37] Since income from foreign investment was but one component of total annual invisible earnings, Lloyd George was therefore either over-confident or inept as Chancellor of the Exchequer in preparing his 1914 estimates.

Table 3. Selected United Kingdom (UK) Revenue, Deficits & Expenditures: FY 1914/18 (£ million)[38]

	1914	1915	1916	1917	1918
Total Invisible Earnings	315	395	520	575	580
Trade Deficit (Exports minus Imports)	170	368	345	467	784
Annual Military Expenditure (Fighting Services plus Munitions only)	362	981	1350	1599	1622
Total Invisible Earnings as % of Annual Military Expenditure	87	40	39	36	36

At no time during the war were total invisible earnings (let alone earnings from foreign investments on their own, as Lloyd George had stated) enough to cover annual military spending – never mind five years' worth. Taxation funded only 20% of British wartime outlays;[39] credit covered the remainder. Banks either issued loans to the British Government (including the Bank of England by printing money) or received promissory notes, then increasing money supply with those notes as reserves. If loans had been based on actual savings instead of bank credit, much of Britain's wartime inflation from spring 1915 on could have been avoided.[40]

Europe faced enormous challenges by war's end: 'low output, famine imminent, disease rampant, capital and materials in desperately short supply', as well as 'transport systems [that] were completely disorganised, and financial and currency mechanisms ... out of control'.[41] Between August 1914 and November 1918, British national debt grew from £711 million[42] to £6.6 billion[43] (2011: nearly £437.5 billion to £1.95 trillion). By the end of FY 1918/19, Britain had lent almost £1.75 billion to seventeen nations. Two accounted for nearly 58% of the amount: Russia (33%; £568 million) and France (25%; £435 million). Altogether separately, Russia owed France £204.5 million.[44] The British Government borrowed £1.4 billion in wartime – 75% of that from the USA,[45] now overtaking Britain as the global economic and financial powerhouse. Washington's inflexibility as London's main creditor, along with Moscow's refusal to reverse fully[46] its 1918 debt repudiation, added urgency to British postwar reconstruction. Despite Moscow's actions, Washington kept insisting London and Paris fully repay their war loans.[47] To Britain alone, Tsarist Russia had owed nearly £595 million.[48] Yet Britain's difficulties at this time were not all foreign-made; much of the damage was self-inflicted.

Wartime government centralised power, managing the economy, so by 1919 Lloyd George eliminated many controls to restore peacetime normalcy.[49] Import restrictions and other domestic measures to re-orient the economy for war had reduced trade, despite stable foreign demand for imports. As Britain exported less, the USA and Japan expanded market share.[50] By war's end, Britain sought to reassert itself but faced stiff competition. Besides, an estimated 10% of private British assets overseas were sold off in wartime to service a growing trade deficit so a comparable fall in interest earnings pressed Britain even more to improve its balance of trade.[51] Yet London's 'desire to restore ... pre-war arrangements clashed with a reality [differing] greatly from that in 1913'. Britain was now financially weaker (its foreign holdings declining as national debt exploded), and faced competition in former export markets as domestic trade unions grew more powerful and demanding. Still, officials 'sought to restore nineteenth-century policies in a twentieth-century environment'.[52]

This meant keeping British economic specialisation in traditionally strong areas (coal, iron and steel, textiles and shipbuilding), for which postwar demand was weak. The result was chronic oversupply for much of the 1920s, adding to an already difficult situation for exporters due to rising labour costs and worsening exchange rates. Chemical, electrical and mechanical engineering were increasingly the key areas of economic development so staple goods in which Britain traditionally specialised became an ever-smaller share of final expenditures. The old industries' powerful lobbying further slowed critical reforms.[53]

By April 1919, after a few months of mild postwar recession, Britain in particular experienced a short but impressive one-year economic surge, followed by an equally impressive downturn. The boom made prices rise sharply: long-suppressed demand for commodities shot up as many plants were still in a default setting of military production. Orders poured into factories, ensuring a demand for labour and mitigating the massive demobilisation of troops and munitions workers at the time.[54] However, rising demand and suppliers' difficulty meeting it fuelled inflation. Within a year, the postwar shift of human resources from wartime to peacetime footing ended. Production, exports and prices peaked, then started to dip. Unemployment shot up because high wages did not match declining prices, forcing employers to lay off staff.[55] Matters were at their worst in 1921: overall production declined by 18%,[56] and unemployment peaked at nearly 24% during the May coal strike.[57] Postwar reconstruction ceased 'almost overnight', dragging into 1925.[58] Still, despite financial, economic and labour turbulence from mid-1917 to mid-1919, Britain reached pre-war production levels by 1920.[59]

Russia's was an altogether different story.[60] The December 1917 armistice with the Central Powers and subsequent Brest-Litovsk Treaty in February 1918 made the country cede nearly 15.5% and 23.5% of its pre-war territory and population, respectively. Russia also lost a third of its factories, accounting for 20% of pre-war annual industrial output.[61] By 1920, civil war, border disputes and Bolshevik mismanagement[62] had shattered the economy. That year, industrial production was a fifth of 1913 levels,[63] which Russia did not resume until 1926,[64] six years later than Britain. Finished and semi-finished product output in 1921 was 16% and 12% of 1912 values respectively. As a percentage of 1912 levels, output of key finished products by 1921 was: oil (36%), wool (34%), mining (29%), chemicals (21%), metals (10%), food (10%) and cotton (7%).[65] Thus, Moscow's expansionist ideology and continued refusal to honour Tsarist debts was by 1920 not just revolutionary conceit: it was also economic imperative.

The preceding pages put into context the Cabinet rift pitting the Churchill camp against Lloyd George from his 8 November 1919 speech calling intervention in Russia untenable[66] to the signing of the 16 March 1921 trade agreement. Yet trade negotiations only began formally[67] on 31 May 1920, when Britain's postwar boom was turning to bust, and both nations were arguably at their lowest point financially, economically and socially. Both Moscow and London badly needed trade despite assertions to the contrary by diehard anti-Bolsheviks.[68]

Others have covered the negotiations well.[69] Beyond a basic chronology, the main interest here is twofold. How did intelligence on Moscow's actions and intent inform policy in the year leading up to the agreement? And how did opposing camps in Cabinet use this intelligence to further their aims? One can break down the negotiations into three distinct phases. From 31 May to 7 July 1920, despite inevitable differences of opinion, relative civility and formality prevailed. After initial wrangling, by early July Moscow finally agreed to London's four pre-conditions to any agreement.[70]

The second phase, from 8 July to 11 September, was harsher for two reasons (one foreign, one domestic): a Polish attack on Russia in late April under cover of liberating Ukraine, and the inclusion in the Russian delegation in London of two individuals deemed undesirable. Poland achieved quick victories but these were reversed by June. Even with Western help,[71] Poland barely held off ferocious Russian counter-attacks that regained territory between June and mid-August. Bloodied, both sides finally signed an armistice on 12 October.[72]

Domestically, the main reason for clashes (in Cabinet, and between London and Moscow) was the accreditation of Lev Kamenev and Theodore Rothstein in early July to an expanded delegation. They were both experienced propagandists and Rothstein himself had long been Lenin's main clandestine agent in Britain. Moscow's goal in appointing the men was to stir up further opposition in political circles to direct intervention in the ongoing Russo-Polish conflict. On 11 July, Kamenev temporarily replaced Leonid Krasin as Head of Mission, retaining him as his deputy.[73] Kamenev's activities led Cabinet hardliners to press Lloyd George for a response. Historians have often written he expelled Kamenev outright but in fact, the Russian was Moscow-bound anyway. He left on 11 September,[74] effectively ending the second phase.

The final stage, from 12 September 1920 to 16 March 1921,[75] saw 'a sort of three-sided tug-of-war' between Lloyd George, Curzon and Churchill. The Prime Minister's twin strategy was not to ignore the debt and reparation issues outright, but keep engaging Moscow. Curzon occupied a middling[76] ground: his view was Russia critically needed trade with Britain, giving London an advantage on issues like Eastern subversion (India and Persia[77]), debt and the return of British citizens still in Russia. Under popular pressure, the Foreign Secretary finally convinced Cabinet that repatriating all Britons should be the price of resuming negotiations.[78] Churchill still opposed any dealings with the Kremlin and did his best to de-rail negotiations, aided by the mercurial Walter Long[79] (First Lord of the Admiralty) and Austen Chamberlain[80] (Chancellor of the Exchequer). Churchill even threatened to resign on 17 November but the next day Cabinet still agreed a treaty with Bolshevik Russia,[81] signed four months later.[82]

So what part did intelligence play, both in Cabinet splits and in Anglo-Russian relations, from initial contacts in February 1920 to the March 1921 agreement? By mid-1920, British policy-makers already prized SIGINT more than HUMINT. Since the war, SIGINT – dispassionate and relatively unambiguous – had been a godsend for politicians, allowing them to dispense with outside opinion if they so chose and assess the raw product themselves.

Laden with potential for deception even at the best of times, HUMINT needed different handling. If to this distinction one adds other factors – the creeping politicisation of intelligence from 1919 on, and the ongoing battle between Sir Basil Thomson and Sir Vernon Kell over subversion[83] – politicians' preference for SIGINT was all but assured. By late 1921, domestic HUMINT on civilian subversion was virtually discredited in Cabinet; the ambitious Thomson and his patrons, who egged him on for their own aims, were equally to blame.

Intercepted correspondence made him rail against the Press, which in his view was not doing enough to counter subversion. In July 1920, Thomson complained that

> working men are against violent revolution, but at the moment they are very sore about a number of minor points such as high prices, shortage of houses, and the impending rise of railway fares in holiday time – grievances which the Press might have done much to alleviate had they cared to explain rather than to exploit.... For the first time ... respectable and well-dressed workers are in evidence at such [extremist] meetings, asking questions and agreeing with the speakers, especially on Russia.[84]

Seeing high prices and housing shortages as minor points reveals a dismissive view of workers' concerns bordering on the comical were the situation not so tragic for those affected. Thomson worried much more about the effect he thought subversion was having on the middle classes, which if radicalised would lead to Britain's collapse.

Over the summer, he argued diplomatic and economic ties with Moscow would only worsen subversion.[85] Yet since Russia had long supplied most of Europe's raw materials and grain,[86] Lloyd George looked to restore trade. First, however, he had 'to get Poland out of the way' and have it 'forget her imperialist ideas':[87] Polish national aspirations could not get in the way of renewed commerce. Norman Davies has said this attitude, 'though not hostile, *was* ambivalent. Whilst sympathetic ... he ... opposed [Warsaw's] ambitions.'[88]

What could have blocked resumption of trade, and nearly did, was persistent agitation[89] by Russian delegates in London, particularly as Moscow's military fortunes against Poland improved. Kamenev and Rothstein had joined the delegation in early July 1920 with orders to stir up domestic opposition to any direct British intervention on Poland's behalf. Within a month, British labour mobilised to prevent just that, forming a Council of Action on 9 August 'to oppose intervention by extra-Parliamentary means'. This was the first instance of the threat of 'industrial action for political ends' in Britain.[90]

A week later, though, the Red Army was unexpectedly defeated within sight of Warsaw and retreated. Tempering this news was the disclosure through SIGINT that Kamenev had concealed from Lloyd George the peace terms Moscow intended to impose on Poland. When GCCS revealed the truth, anti-Bolshevik diehards applied even more pressure on Lloyd George to expel the delegation,[91] urging him to allow publication of deciphered Bolshevik intercepts discussing support for the *Daily Herald*.[92] He relented but agreed only to disclose on 19 August eight wireless (not cable) messages between Copenhagen (not London) and Moscow.[93]

Despite this expedient concession, Lloyd George rose above the frenzy, arguing Britain ought not to 'disclose the sources of our information' that gave 'real insight into Bolshevik intentions and policy'. In any case, this was a period of rising unemployment, 'a far more formidable peril than all the lunacies of Lenin'.[94] Lloyd George was alert to the dangers of joblessness because resulting unrest, Basil Thomson insisted, affected former servicemen. Many were bitter because government had not adequately provided for more than a million disabled veterans and set up a proper pension scheme for them. Aware that thousands of serving and retired Tsarist servicemen had joined the Bolsheviks in 1917, Cabinet worried about how unemployed British veterans might use their training. By late 1920, however, the great majority of ex-servicemen sought not revolution but the peaceful redress of grievances.[95]

Aware of how delicate a touch he needed at such a sensitive point in the trade negotiations, Lloyd George compromised with hardliners. He would allow the delegation to stay but singled out Kamenev on 10 September for his subversive conduct:

> He ... subsidise[d] a newspaper, not merely hostile to the Government. ... This is a newspaper whose object it is to attack the institutions of this country, which every day is trying to sow [class] strife ... to create unrest, and to spread discord.... [I]t is a great mistake ... to think ... an old Government like [ours] ... is so utterly inept that men can do anything they like without its being discovered. Our machinery is fairly efficient.[96]

Due to leave for Moscow the next day anyway, Kamenev was not allowed back into Britain.[97] Nevertheless, for Curzon, Churchill, Long, Thomson and others,[98] these were half-measures.

Foreshadowing methods used in April–May 1923 and October 1924 (see Chapter 5), in mid-September 1920, unknown parties leaked intercepted cables to the right-wing newspapers *Daily Mail* and *Morning Post,* while Curzon publicly quoted cables to support his case.[99] Days later, Churchill insisted Russian delegates would spread propaganda, fund sedition, and collect military and political intelligence; he too demanded their repatriation.[100] In Long's case, not even personal appeals worked. On 24 September, the Cabinet Secretary asked there be 'no divergence between Admiralty instructions and ... Cabinet policy'. Three days later though, Long said trade would only help re-equip the Red Army to attack 'our friends and allies in Europe, and embarrassing our Empire'. Days later, he dismissed prospects of trade resuming, arguing the delegation was 'a danger to the State' and should therefore be sent home.[101] Meanwhile, Thomson called for legislation against the inflow of money for British revolutionaries.[102] Yet despite such pressure (and Russian fears),[103] the Prime Minister refused to expel the delegation.[104] This had as much to do with his political career as with his personal background.

From his election as a Liberal MP in 1890 to leaving office in 1922, Lloyd George[105] – arguably the first British political celebrity[106] of the twentieth century – reinvented politics and government, often supported by an equally radical Winston Churchill[107] looking for social reform. Their partnership was 'a revolution of policy that led to the creation of the welfare state'[108] and representative democracy in Britain. The volatility Lloyd George brought to politics partly explains the *ad hominem* vitriol from conservative quarters: 'It is dreadful ... we have such men in the Cabinet as Winston Churchill and Lloyd George. The one a half-bred American politician, the other a silly sentimental Celt', their views 'scurrilous and Socialist oratory'.[109] Caring little for convention, Lloyd George was innovative in his policies and visceral in his belief on the need for change: 'nine-tenths of mankind have been grinding corn for the remaining tenth, and have been paid with the husks and bidden to thank God that they had the husks'.[110]

Constant reminders of his humble origins and precarious existence throughout his career fuelled indignation and ambition further. He was 'from the first desperately keen'[111] to attain the independence enjoyed by most MPs. This 'radical ... self-made outsider with no University background' remained 'always sensitive of the financial and social barriers between himself and Oxford-trained colleagues'.[112] He was the antithesis of patricians like Curzon, and detested what they represented: inherited wealth and family prestige. For instance, though pleasant to Curzon in private and respectful of his ability, Lloyd George frequently offended him in Cabinet. The Foreign Secretary and many others, in turn, regarded the Prime Minister as a 'political adventurer rather than a patrician figure educated by birth and breeding to lead the nation'.[113] Three events seemingly confirmed this view, giving his enemies grounds for attacking him: transactions of Marconi shares in 1912–13, the sale of British honours from 1916 on and the misuse of a US charitable donation in 1917.

The so-called "Marconi scandal" was misleading because opposition accusations of improper behaviour were selective. There was nothing secret about Lloyd George and his partners' intention to invest, suspicious and improper though it may have seemed.[114] Since Marconi in the US and Britain were separate entities in every sense, there was no genuine wrongdoing. In fact, Lloyd George actually lost money.[115]

The second incident concerned the infamous "Lloyd George fund". Deepening divisions within the Liberal Party over prosecution of the war reached a climax in December 1916 when an impatient War Secretary (Lloyd George) unseated Prime Minister Herbert Asquith.[116] While the former went on to lead a coalition government, the latter retained control over much of the Party's electoral and financial machinery. Thus the "Lloyd George fund" – mainly supporters' donations in exchange for titles – allowed the Prime Minister to endorse candidates and pay for his political activities.[117] The problem was that Lloyd George's 'readiness to adulterate the Peerage with *nouveaux riches* of unsuitable background seemed to indicate a contempt for the ... concept of aristocracy'.[118] Thus, Conservative (and Labour) criticism was expedient at best, since some Coalition Conservative Whips had also sold titles, directly benefiting their Party. Lloyd George seems never to have used the fund personally, only for political work.[119]

The most credible corruption allegation is also the least known, one concerning Solomon Guggenheim's donation of £20,000 (2011: £917,000) in early 1917. Intended as a gift to war charities as Lloyd George saw fit, the money largely disappeared. He failed to appoint trustees to oversee the donation and never properly accounted for it to Guggenheim, who repeatedly sought answers.[120] All this, however, was symptomatic of broader fears. Although some of Lloyd George's actions seemed corrupt and expedient, Conservative hardliners saw them as an opportunity for political reinvention, for the aristocracy to reclaim its rightful place in politics:

> Between 1880 and 1914, the world ... they had been brought up to dominate ... turned against them. And between 1914 and 1918, it was turned completely upside-down.... It was also undermined by the new breed of full-time politicians [like Lloyd George] ... [M]any grandees and gentry

... were prepared ... to resort to ... non-constitutional means, to preach violence and to practise it if needs be, and even to support ... civil war ... to recover their position.... Fearful and anxious, bitter and resentful [the diehards] ... looked to the past with nostalgia and the future with dread.[121]

Many hardliners thus either founded or gravitated towards existing right-wing groups to counter perceived left-wing extremism.[122] They found some kindred spirits within British intelligence.

By working to prevent sabotage and labour unrest, the British intelligence community quickly became a key player in wartime industrial relations. The nature of the work predictably meant the agencies aligned their interests with those of the industrialists; some owners were noted members of radical right-wing groups seeking to roll back socio-political changes. Yet just as unrest increased, the agencies too had a peace dividend to pay.

Table 4. UK Security, Intelligence & Law-Enforcement Expenditure, FY 1913/21 (£)[123]

	1913	1914	1915	1916	1917	1918	1919	1920	1921
Official Secret Service Vote	50,000	110,000	400,000	620,000	750,000	1,150,000	400,000	400,000	300,000
Secret Service Outlay	46,840	107,595	398,697	593,917	740,984	1,207,697	372,337	278,104	195,146
Espionage Bureau (SIS, MI5, DNI)	n/a	n/a	n/a	445,210	594,704	859,197	247,200	n/a	n/a
SIS	n/a	n/a	n/a	400,655	534,404	766,247	205,200	n/a	n/a
MI5	n/a	n/a	n/a	30,850	48,800	79,950	45,000	n/a	22,183
DNI	n/a	n/a	n/a	13,703	11,500	13,000	n/a	n/a	n/a
Home Office Outlay	255,009	248,823	271,379	279,314	286,352	327,672	383,179	448,264	396,197
Police Outlay (England & Wales)	109,241	106,992	158,614	109,241	106,521	1,159,168	5,511,943	6,694,239	6,679,209

Despite the economic predicament Britain was in by 1918,[124] deep cuts to British intelligence occurred just as police funding sharply increased.[125] This paradox reflected a deeper issue. Total war had not only militarised society but also caused socio-economic upheaval, giving rise to the "National Security State". Surveillance bureaucracies grew in size and complexity, accumulating responsibility and power. In 1916–17, emphasis shifted decisively from counter-espionage to political reporting. Information was 'the coin of the new political realm', used to control manpower, combat subversion and shape popular attitudes. Britain too experienced this trend and even in this 'moderately policed society', political police like Special Branch sometimes operated 'beyond ... the law'. After all, 'the germ of political excess' exists in every police force given the ever-present tension between order and legality.[126]

Though prompted also by economic realities, the postwar security and intelligence community underwent rapid changes. Politicians looked to reclaim vast powers given to numerous agencies in wartime, when traditional policing could not cope with new ideological, security and social challenges. One reason for taking powers back was an ultimately futile political attempt to return the country to pre-1914 normality. As decisive as intelligence had been at times during the war and since, many British politicians and officials still detested such "corrupt" and "deceitful" practices so suggestive of "Continental" behaviour.[127]

An interesting pattern emerged after the Armistice: moving eastward from the USA to Russia, increasing social and political dislocation resulted in ever-stronger national security states. This pattern was a reassertion of history and outlook regarding the role of intelligence in each of these societies. The USA, the emerging superpower virtually untouched by war, radically cut its intelligence spending. Britain, still the world's pre-eminent imperial power but financially and physically exhausted by conflict, streamlined and reorganised its intelligence community while maintaining a vigilant posture matching the nation's global responsibilities. France and Germany, devastated by war, actually strengthened their security and intelligence agencies out of mutual suspicion and fear of Bolshevism. Russia – wracked by world war, two revolutions and civil war in six years – was on the brink of dissolution and survived as the cradle of revolution only by becoming what is arguably the ultimate police state so far.[128]

With the Armistice, necessity further strengthened professional, ideological and social affinities already binding British industrialists and intelligence officials. The community could only overcome 'an acute manpower shortage ... by exploiting the resources of those "patriotic" and anti-Socialist groups which [sic] the business community had founded'.[129]

From July 1917 to November 1918, Cabinet called on the British Empire Union and the British Workers' League (BWL) to help counter pacifist and socialist propaganda, and organise counter-demonstrations. Cabinet ordered Special Branch and MI5 to supply right-wing groups with details of leftist meetings so 'spontaneous opposition' could be rallied. In the summer of 1918, Basil Thomson asked BEU and BWL to help him monitor gatherings of pacifists, socialists and conscientious objectors. A year later, he provided agents and intelligence to the Anti-Socialist Union. In early 1920, Thomson attended special sessions of National Propaganda's executive committee (see Chapter 2) to share intelligence on socialist activities. Moreover, as Metropolitan Police Deputy Assistant Commissioner from 1922 to 1938, Lieutenant-Colonel John Carter[130] supported George Makgill's IIB with plain-clothes and uniformed Special Branch officers, and funding. IIB intelligence gathering also benefitted from the friendship between Vernon Kell and the ultra-conservative Makgill. Until his death in October 1926, he repaid Kell by helping him find suitable recruits for MI5.[131]

The nexus was undeniable and wartime intelligence officers,

[e]ven if they had now returned to civilian life, retained close contacts with former colleagues ... [in] the ... agencies and passed on to them information received from ... contacts ... reciprocated by confidences during lunch at London Clubs, or country weekends. It was not just the intelligence community, but more precisely the community of an *élite* – senior officials in Government Departments, men in "the City" ... in politics, men who controlled the Press ... narrow, interconnected (sometimes intermarried), and mutually supportive. Many ... had been to the same schools and Universities, and belonged to the same Clubs.[132]

Contemporary fiction also reflected hardliners' fears. One of the best early postwar examples was John Buchan's *The Three Hostages*.[133] He used the abduction of young aristocrats by Dominick Medina – 'a dangerous cross' between Irish and Latin[134] – to stress what Men of Empire like him feared most: the accelerating decay of civilisation due to wartime mass social movements. Individuality drawing 'life from its roots ... loyalties, memories ... traditions ... family, companionship, Church and locality' was the way forward – not Socialism.[135]

Inspector Macgillivray, in whom Basil Thomson surely saw much of himself, said of the perils of the time:

The moral imbecile ... had been more or less a sport before the War; now he was ... common.... Cruel, humourless, hard, utterly wanting in sense of proportion ... You found [him] among ... young Bolshevik Jews ... the wilder Communist sects, and ... the sullen murderous hobble-dehoys in Ireland.... They are masters of propaganda ... Have you ever considered what a diabolical weapon that can be – using all the channels of modern publicity to poison ... minds? It is the most dangerous thing on earth.[136]

War had tempered Buchan's fictional hero Sir Richard Hannay, the quintessential Man of Empire, giving him a more balanced outlook on the communist threat:

> Their cleverness lay in [using] fanatics ... whose key was a wild hatred of something ... or a ... belief in anarchy.... [T]hese tools ... had no thought of profit, and were ready to sacrifice ... their lives, for a mad ideal. It was a masterpiece of ... devilish ingenuity ... the spectacle of these cranks toiling to create a new Heaven and ... Earth ... thinking themselves ... leaders of mankind, when they were ... at the will of ... scoundrels engaging in the most ancient of pursuits, was an irony to make the Gods laugh.[137]

Arch-villain Medina, who for much of the book is the darling of London high society, summed up his thoughts on postwar upheaval:

> [Politics is a] dingy game as it's played at present, but there are possibilities. There is a mighty Tory revival in sight, and it will want leading. The newly enfranchised classes, especially the women, will bring it about. The Suffragists don't know what a tremendous force of Conservatism they were releasing when they won the vote.... There has never been a true marriage of East and West.... We think of it in material terms.... But it still means, as it has always meant, the control of human souls.[138]

From this context, Lloyd George's reactions to hardline criticism of both Bolshevik subversion and intelligence on Russian activities in Britain make more sense. He was pragmatic and expedient but confident that trade and self-interest, to put it in material terms, would compel Moscow to abandon subversion. This was perhaps unrealistic given his equally improbable expectations of just how much Britain would benefit from renewed trade. Yet the Prime Minister also knew hardliners protested in the name of self-preservation and the status quo, which he had long challenged. Raised in and later an MP for a Welsh rural working-class constituency, he had closer contact with workers than any diehard. He could therefore better understand working-class psychology – and manipulate it. This was, after all, a fight for human souls.

Churchill, Curzon and Long saw trade negotiations with Moscow as the proverbial line in the sand. Resuming trade – and ultimately diplomatic relations – would be disastrous for Britain. The same international trade arteries that had made the country great would now seal its fate, since these arteries would be coursing with the Bolshevik "cancer", allowing it to spread. Britain's physical separation from Europe would matter little against the inevitable influx of people if relations with Moscow were renewed. Diehards viewed Britain and its empire as the body, trade as the delivery vehicle and Bolshevism as the disease. Intelligence agencies – guiding the political, diplomatic and economic isolation of Russia – might help keep the "cancer" in check; resume trade and the "evil" would spread.

Yet the Prime Minister had little time for Thomson's warnings, an approach seemingly vindicated by former CPGB members:

> An organisation whose chief claim to distinction, so far, is that it is composed of drivelling nonentities intoxicated with conceit, who have borrowed the Bolshevik ideas without borrowing the brains necessary to execute them.... Information by the mass, specially preened, pruned, doctored, and cooked by the officials of the old British Socialist Party was sent into Russia with the deliberate object of misleading the Bolsheviks as to the true state of affairs in Britain.... Not until I went to Moscow was I aware that such a tremendously powerful, throne-shaking, Empire-tottering organisation existed in Britain.... Even in Aesop's day the frogs who [sic] burst themselves because they wanted to imitate the cows were recognised. So it is with the British Communists.[139]

At its inception in August 1920, the CPGB had 5125 members but only 2500 by January 1921.[140] Even Walter Long, a supporter of Thomson's reporting on Moscow's crusade 'against Anglo-Saxondom',[141] doubted some of the Directorate of Intelligence product:

> On the one hand, we learn from more than one source of the approaching dissolution of the Soviet Government ... on the other hand, we are told ... their ideas are slowly but surely becoming dominant throughout ... the world. There are undoubted indications that the extremist elements in Moscow are about to give way to a very much more moderate party.... Yet it would be idle to ignore, as it is unwise to exaggerate, the effect of propaganda ... being sedulously advocated throughout the world.[142]

Thomson's reports often promoted the view that 'aliens, Jews, Sinn Féiners, and degenerates'[143] were the cause of unrest in Britain – *The Three Hostages'* argument. This sense of racial superiority underpinned the Victorian public school curriculum and was evident in Thomson's work. The link between unemployment and the spread of subversion was another constant concern, especially when the wealthy ignored pleas to avoid flamboyant displays. By late 1920, when unemployment had nearly reached double digits, public complaints over 'the ostentation and luxury of the idle rich' had soared.[144] Thomson carefully distinguished between the unemployed and those he called "unemployables". The latter posed the real threat for they were the ones communists sought out. The 'true unemployed', Thomson felt, were 'sounder', endured hardship 'in silence' and 'disapprove of such conduct'. Unemployables were different:

> I was offered four days' work ... but ... did not take it. For that ... work I would have received 30/- [but] would have lost my 15/- dole for this week, and my dole for next week, and that is equivalent to what I would have earned by working. Also, I would not have been eligible for any out-door relief. Therefore, I did not take it.[145]

Thomson disliked dishonest unemployables, making him more likely to see them as threatening. This was an underlying theme, both in his reports and threat perceptions more generally. Anything new and different is potentially dangerous and therefore draws attention: new ideas, political actors and social movements. The norm against which Thomson measured such developments was, at least in his case, Anglo-Saxon, Protestant, male, upper middle-class, and educated at elite public schools and universities. The malignancy of the Bolshevik "cancer" meant almost anything outside these narrow parameters was fair game for intelligence agencies. This was especially true once the postwar boom turned to bust and growing numbers of Britons pressed government to slow rising unemployment by resuming trade with Moscow.[146] Ironically, Russian documents show the Bolsheviks knew better: 'the Trade Agreement will not reduce unemployment. We never used this argument because it can be turned against us easily.'[147]

A puzzling feature of Thomson's reporting was he often ridiculed his opponents yet their actions alarmed him. In early 1921, he wrote tongue-in-cheek of British revolutionaries' nicknames. Arthur MacManus, Chairman of the CPGB Executive, was "Little Lenin" and Bert Joy, another Party official, was "Tooting Trotsky". Factional strife within the recently formed CPGB was, in Thomson's view, akin to 'the spectacle of a car with the engine running at full speed and the gear in neutral'. Yet he continued calling for legislation to counter communist-sponsored unrest, lest the 'evil grow'.[148]

This was an unresolved contradiction in Thomson's analysis. Though his domestic and foreign reports included some useful intelligence, they also had much unsubstantiated assertion. Not only did this unnecessarily alarm policymakers but, even worse, it undermined Cabinet confidence in HUMINT agencies and their product for some time. This testified to naivety over the "Red Menace" and the need for an organisation like the JIC, created in 1936. Thomson had long called for the King and the Prime Minister to travel the country,[149] because in his view such symbols of traditional authority could "immunise" Britons against Bolshevism. The CPGB itself seemed to share Thomson's opinion on the innate deference and conservatism of workers:

The movement among ... working classes has no serious connection with Party aims or with ideals – it is based solely on purely economic motives. It is ... impossible to reform the psychology of the British worker in the short time we have at our disposal, and it is no use wasting energy and time ... In England, revolutionary ideas find much less favour amongst the workers than in other countries. The English worker lacks class consciousness. The excitement offered by an active revolutionary fight does not appeal to him. Particularly is this the case in England where life is obstinately carried on in the same old-fashioned style.[150]

Nevertheless, the Bolshevik trade delegation persisted with its subversive work. Equally, SIGINT continued providing insight into not only Russian methods, capabilities and intentions, but also how factional the Kremlin's foreign policy was. Assuming Moscow did not deceive London through SIGINT, it gave London a significant advantage during the trade negotiations and beyond. As the May 1920 trade talks approached, Leonid Krasin in London and Maxim Litvinov in Copenhagen, respectively, had exclusive commercial and political plenipotentiary powers.[151] Deputy Foreign Commissar Litvinov soon attacked Krasin on the proper conduct of discussions, emerging as petty and vindictive.[152] His main concerns during negotiations were that as many people as possible knew of his appointment as chief political negotiator and that Krasin did not take over his powers.[153]

Krasin was not one to shy away, however, soon taking aim at both Litvinov and Foreign Commissar Chicherin who, influenced by his deputy in Copenhagen, made veiled accusations to Krasin. His tone, in turn, was increasingly blunt:

Owing to your aloofness from ... business you are ... not in a position to understand that the importance of the ... Agreement, which is both a useful and a good business, will be radically damaged [by] Litvinoff's diplomatic absurdities and personal grievances ... it is the fatal law of Soviet Russia to begin every new affair with ... elementary mistakes.[154]

Days later, Krasin continued along similar lines:

We [London delegation] ask for concrete directions from you because up to now neither Litvinoff ... nor you yourself, have helped us by any useful and businesslike advice in our complicated and difficult task. Go through your ... telegrams from Litvinoff. They contain nothing but trivialities.... It [is] silly to travel to England merely for the ... conversations to revolve round the slights offered to Litvinoff.... We can understand a rupture ... on the grounds of our unwillingness to recognise the debts ... but no worker will understand a rupture because Litvinoff is not admitted.[155]

One problem for Bolshevik policy-makers at this time was their inability to separate commercial from political issues. Commercial and political negotiators in different countries, however, further slowed and confused Kremlin responses and initiatives. Moreover, Chicherin's indecisiveness only compounded Krasin's confusion: 'I am once more obliged to point out a contradiction in ... your telegrams.... In the name of all saints inform me which of these two instructions, which cancel one another, I am to follow.'[156] With the Krasin–Litvinov feud escalating, the former's criticism of the Deputy Foreign Commissar drew fire. While Krasin travelled to Moscow for consultations in early July 1920, Litvinov let loose a stream of abusive messages undermining his rival:

Krasin [let] himself ... be entangled and terrorised; the visit to London must be considered a *faux pas* as nothing of the sort occurred [here].... [B]e present ... during all ... reports ... by Krasin and ... parry his attacks on the Commissariat ... Do not agree to Nogin and Rosovsky and other nincompoops being included in the Delegation for ... political negotiations. It would be a good reply and a suitable punishment to the British ... for not admitting me.[157]

These and other intercepts offer one explanation why overt subversion largely failed in this period. Key communist officials seem to have worried more about social standing than carrying out Moscow's orders efficiently. No matter how remarkable an ideology may seem, human nature – too often the neglected factor – usually wins out: even Communism does not preclude ego and vanity. Counter-subversive organs naturally helped combat the "cancer". Even so, in Britain (hesitantly) and India (certainly), there was by late 1922 a recognition that overt subversion could be reasonably contained given the ineptitude of many communists.[158]

Still, Litvinov was a professional revolutionary who recognised danger on sight. In July 1920, foreseeing the British raid on ARCOS in May 1927 (see Chapter 7), he cautioned the London delegation: do not 'keep by you the deciphers [*sic*] of radio telegrams which [*sic*] might give grounds for being accused of propaganda'; claims of diplomatic immunity would not stop the British.[159] As professional revolutionaries, the Bolsheviks worried about the physical security of clandestine cells, compartmentalising them. However, when it came to securing communications early on, the Bolsheviks often committed basic errors.

There may be several explanations. Suspicion of sophisticated Tsarist codes and ciphers led the new regime to adopt or retain methods easily compromised by defecting cryptographers. Another possible reason was a poor understanding of changing technology and its possible applications. Though the Bolsheviks appreciated the need for COMSEC they had until recently been on the receiving end of SIGINT. They were a tightly knit minority group whose members communicated either orally or by (coded) written word, delivered by couriers. Hence, few Bolsheviks likely appreciated the vast resources a government determined to intercept and decode enemy communications could assemble.

GCCS intercepts highlighted Bolshevik inexperience (and sometimes dogma). As in any other human endeavour, there was a learning curve and COMSEC behaviours by early 1921 were already better than only six months earlier. Yet as John Ferris has demonstrated, throughout the 1920s, lessons seemingly learnt were seemingly forgotten: in 1920, 1923 and 1927, Moscow persisted in using ciphers known to be exploited[160] by foreign powers. In early 1920, for example, Chicherin often mailed cipher keys to Litvinov in Copenhagen, then compounding the error by notifying his deputy by wireless of the incoming letter. The Foreign Commissar even obliged eavesdroppers by explaining how to retrieve keys: 'they are written between the lines in chemical ink which will show up when subjected to heat'.[161]

Despite initial tradecraft errors, the Russians were always wary of vulnerabilities. Cable traffic between the London delegation and the NKID travelled via the Peterhead line in Scotland. Traffic delays in mid-1920 aroused Moscow's suspicions. Worrying (and plausible) was the possibility these delays sought to isolate Krasin, so Britain could exploit uncertainty and extract binding declarations from him during negotiations. Delays, denounced as 'deliberate [British] scoundrelism' (and which Krasin, incidentally, refused to believe) seem to have been due to telegraph problems in Russia.[162]

In mid-July 1920, Krasin's deputy in London Nikolai Klyshko asked Moscow to replace the MARTA cipher since the West could easily read it. Klyshko

6 Leonid Krasin, the beleaguered Bolshevik representative in London from 1920 to 1923. Jealousy and intrigue within the NKID nearly undid his efforts to secure the critical 1921 trade agreement, which semi-formalised relations with Britain.

appealed for a thousand keys, to which Moscow replied it could not send so many at once. One hundred would soon arrive for the new cipher ZVEZDA (Star) but MARTA remained in use to reach Litvinov in Copenhagen.[163] In August Lev Kamenev, temporarily Head of the London delegation, urged 'great caution'. He advised other legations and NKID to stop using MARTA: it was outdated and possibly compromised. Chicherin's response was both sensible and naive:

> doubts have arisen as to whether our messages are being deciphered.... We consider it absolutely indispensable to encipher all correspondence about secret telegrams, and to make no reference at all to ciphered messages in unenciphered ones. The decipherment of our messages without the keys is very unlikely. Take all possible measures to safeguard the keys of deciphered messages. Specially secret messages must be re-ciphered.

Litvinov's reply was typical: 'I propose to continue using Marta, even if [it is] obsolete.'[164] He and Chicherin understandably upset Kamenev since the Foreign Commissar himself continued using compromised ciphers.[165]

On 19 December 1920, Mikhail Frunze, Red commander of Southern Front forces, finally confirmed Bolshevik suspicions about COMSEC:

> [T]he most secret correspondence of the [NKID] with its representatives in Tashkent and in Europe is known word for word to the English, who have organised a network of stations designed particularly for listening to our radio. This accounts for the deciphering of more than one-hundred of our codes. The keys to those codes which [*sic*] have not submitted to reading are sent from London where a Russian subject [Vetterlein] has been put at the head of cipher affairs having done such work ... in Russia.[166]

New security measures ensued, with double encipherment now required for all secret communications. What Moscow likely did not know was GCCS compromised almost every double-cipher fielded.[167] Perhaps thinking their communications now invulnerable, delegates in London (including the ever-professional Krasin) succumbed to a false sense of security:

> [N]o one here knows officially that the All-Russia[n] Congress of Trade Unions assigned 200,000 [gold roubles] to aid ... British miners. We cannot tell how [they] would regard the actual sending of this money,

but as you did not send it, this ... only gives a further pretext to [anti-Soviet agitation] for interference in England's home affairs.[168]

British intelligence may well have deliberately reinforced the Bolsheviks' faith in their cryptological security. In October 1921 Krasin informed NKID that according to 'very reliable English sources', the most damaging information London collected on Russian affairs came from Moscow: 'from any secretary of any highly placed official it is possible to obtain ... even the most secret information'.[169] Though Britain certainly gathered HUMINT there, reinforcing mistaken Bolshevik assumptions would have been sound counter-intelligence practice.

Knowing Moscow now considered its codes and (double) ciphers safe, Britain could gain much by spreading rumours that leaks came not from communications networks – as the Bolsheviks may have been either led or predisposed to believe – but from disloyal employees. This way, British intelligence could tie up Russian counter-intelligence in fruitless hunts for leaks while leading the scent away from SIGINT successes. Cabinet Secretary Hankey made this very point to Lloyd George in September 1920: foreigners constantly underestimated British cryptological abilities; it would be 'a pity to remove this amiable weakness of theirs'.[170]

Thanks to GCCS, Cabinet had long had proof of Kremlin support for the *Daily Herald* and other organisations in Britain.[171] From late September 1920, the intercepts' distribution list[172] included Lloyd George, since many messages contained instructions for Krasin on the trade negotiations. In mid-December, Board of Trade President Sir Robert Horne joined the list. At the end of that year, GCCS distributed a striking intercept. In it, Krasin reproached Chicherin for taking negotiations with Britain so casually and believing Bolshevik military successes would frighten London into giving in. The text highlights Krasin's anxieties about anything that could block the treaty, for the situation in Russia was increasingly desperate as famine gripped the country.[173] Krasin later told Chicherin the agreement would be the best way of ridding Russia of British influence. Using the treaty as a stepping-stone 'we shall quickly pass to an agreement with Canada, Italy and America' and begin 'to free ourselves from the English political and economic cabal, [and] ourselves be able to threaten England with ... rupture'.[174]

Once trade negotiations started, British intelligence portrayals of the "Red Menace" darkened. One must reiterate how big a foreign policy victory this was for the Bolsheviks, who had seized power not three years earlier and left the Entente in a precarious position by pulling Russia out of the war. Then there was ideology: Bolshevism seemed hostile to all upon which Western nations had based their culture and prosperity. The First World War and the civil war ruined Russia's economy and infrastructure. Outside urban areas, the Reds faced constant challenges to their authority as they, White Guards and other groups sought supremacy (and therefore legitimacy) in the eyes of the population. Even in cities, worker unrest caused considerable alarm. Cold, famished and exhausted, Russia's masses grew restless by 1920.

Diplomatically isolated, torn apart by civil war and economically on its knees, Bolshevik Russia desperately needed commerce with the West to survive and pursue world revolution. Yet just as Britain often misunderstood Russia's internal affairs, so too did Moscow have distorted perceptions of British politics. This was partly because delegates in London perceived Lloyd George as weak, likely to give in to hardliners, end negotiations and sever ties with Moscow.[175] The NKID, in turn, suggested using India as a bargaining chip: 'the East ought to provide the strongest of arguments'. Krasin, however, warned his superiors: 'Do not exaggerate the significance of the Eastern Revolution as the reason for any [British] concessions'. Curzon 'understands that whatever undertakings we might give, there would nevertheless be no complete renunciation of "dirty tricks" in the East'.[176]

What Moscow did not count on, of course, was that even after Frunze's December 1920 warning and the subsequent introduction of double-ciphers, GCCS still solved a substantial amount of diplomatic traffic. As discussed in the next chapter, SIGINT soon played a crucial role in Anglo-Russian relations again, in the tensest crisis between the March 1921 trade agreement and Lenin's death in January 1924. For the moment, however, some observations are due on what intercepts said about Bolshevik foreign policy.

An early theme was one that has frustrated successive Russian rulers in their efforts to reform and govern such vast territory: independent (in) action by local officials. The distances involved, the chaos of civil war and the Bolsheviks' fragile hold on power outside urban centres meant Moscow had trouble getting the periphery either to carry out policy or to consult with the centre about developments. The result was constant admonishment from the centre.[177] Even as the Bolsheviks tailored revolutionary and subversive tactics to the East, there were early signs the struggle would be hard: locals were unreceptive[178] and many Russian officials behaved improperly.[179] Communications between the centre and frontier areas were often disorganised and sometimes non-existent, leaving Moscow unaware of much that happened.[180]

A second prominent feature of the intercepts is how convoluted and inefficient foreign policy formulation could be at times. One reason was the difference in skill among Bolsheviks, obvious when contrasting experienced businessmen-turned-diplomats like Krasin with revolutionaries like Litvinov. Infighting in the NKID and the Politburo only worsened matters. Initial confusion in post-revolutionary Russia, coupled with Allied blockades, no doubt complicated the conduct of diplomacy. Yet the bureaucratic bickering, and egocentrism and amateurism of some officials, is striking.

All this highlights how incomplete knowledge about the GCCS cryptological coup still is. Operational detail on SIGINT triumphs against Russia remains scarce but even less is understood about key people and events in this invisible war. What kind of person was Ernst Vetterlein really? When did he decide to defect and happened next? When and how did Moscow first learn of his successes against its codes and ciphers? A partial answer to this last question may revolve around William Ewer and the Federated Press. Did Moscow experience comparable SIGINT successes against Britain and, if so, how early? British files offer hints but the evidence is not definitive enough to be more specific than what Russian sources suggest.

This chapter highlighted several key developments in the sixteen months from Lloyd George's 1919 speech questioning continued intervention in Russia to the 1921 trade agreement. Politically, he finally began overreaching. Long regarded by the British Establishment as a subversive, insolent and venal demagogue, the Prime Minister gave patricians yet another reason to be furious with his radical methods by negotiating with Moscow. Despite warning of impending doom and misrepresenting the actual subversive threat by politicising some intelligence on it, hardliners could not thwart Lloyd George on the treaty. They and other rivals of his soon made common cause in undermining coalition rule, getting rid of him and seeking power for themselves. Within nineteen months, Lloyd George was gone.

A second trend was a strengthening of ties between British intelligence and right-wing groups, both out of necessity and mutual desire to defend the State as they saw it. While the public face of the enemy was Bolshevism, the broader objectives were in reality checking social change and the rise of the Labour Party. That some of the HUMINT passed on by Basil Thomson to Cabinet on the "Red Menace" was nonsense should be no surprise. Some of this "intelligence" was rumour, collected by private groups funded by industrialists and others with a stake in overstating the impact of subversion on industrial unrest. Information gathered by groups like the BEU and the IIB, and passed on to the agencies, was often warped by personal interest and political prejudice.[181] This skewed the quality and objectivity of HUMINT sent to Cabinet but, more importantly, ministerial perceptions of the relative reliability of HUMINT compared to SIGINT. This just as Moscow gradually switched emphasis from overt to covert subversion.

Which brings up a third issue: that by March 1921 Thomson was fast becoming a liability even for some of his patrons. The (hyperbolical) nature of many of his reports, coupled with his empire-building, made him powerful enemies. Overconfident and underperforming, Thomson also overreached at a time of great stress on the public purse. The combination proved fatal: in October, he had to resign. Chapter 4 examines how disastrous the second half of 1921 was for HUMINT and what that meant for British intelligence in the 1920s. SIGINT would be by year's end the uncontested ministerial favourite. Yet it too was again sacrificed by hardliners at the altar of political expediency, in the hope of causing a breach with Moscow.

CHAPTER 4

The Fall

The Committee, Again ~ The Directorate Undone ~
Lloyd George Departs

[S]ecrecy during war is largely dependent on ... secrecy ...
during peace.   Anonymous[1]

The game of twisting the Lion's tail is very fascinating.
                                       Jacob Kirchenstein[2]

[Lloyd] George thinks he won the election. Well he didn't.
It was the Tories that won the election, and he will soon
begin to find that out.   Walter Long[3]

DISSATISFACTION in government circles over the quality and reliability
of HUMINT peaked in mid-1921. In India, officials felt reports were
only trite compilations of information 'from Foreign Office and War Office
intercepts'. On the effect of Bolshevism on Indian internal affairs, wrote one
politician, there was 'absolutely nothing of interest'.[4] In Britain, Basil Thomson
contradicted himself from one week to the next.[5] This became increasingly
untenable as industrial unrest and unemployment neared their highest levels
between 1917 and 1929,[6] and government looked to cut spending.[7]

In addition to economies demanded of British intelligence, this chapter
focuses on events from March 1921 to November 1922 that led to HUMINT
improvements overseas and domestically. The reforms eliminated some but
not all factors politicising (and therefore distorting) HUMINT on Bolshevism. After all, if ministers expected information to conform to their own
biases, there was little even top intelligence officials could (or would) do. The
challenge was that some ministers and officials shared these preconceptions,
creating a symbiotic relationship. Because reforms only happened when there
was little choice left, the damage done to perceptions of HUMINT was considerable and lasting.

As for SIGINT, events this period highlighted the importance of preserving access to it. GCCS defeated a range of Bolshevik codes and ciphers until December 1920 when Mikhail Frunze warned Moscow about British successes. After Russia introduced new systems in early January 1921, GCCS faced serious difficulties but from 'April 1921 to late 1923 again broke such traffic'. Access faltered once more in January 1924, when the Soviets changed systems, but resumed by spring 1925.[8] What the literature normally neglects is that from Frunze's warning on, GCCS rarely broke Bolshevik diplomatic traffic again in Europe:

> between 1919 and 1932 ... what concerned Britain most about the USSR was its policy in the Middle East, Afghanistan and East Asia, and ... subversion against the British Empire. [M]aterial was plentiful through solutions of Soviet ... systems used in Asia.... Central Europe consistently was the weak spot in its coverage and Asia its strong one, reflecting British interests and access to traffic; [GCCS] was more useful for imperial security than European diplomacy.... It provided first-rate material on second-rate issues, less on significant ones, often nothing on the greatest of them.[9]

For weeks after the 16 March 1921 trade agreement, Russian intercepts did not mention this foreign policy success. In the second half of March, for instance, almost every surviving message concerned the funding of Bolshevik delegations and purchase of British coal. Even later on, the treaty rarely appears. GCCS had limited success against Russian cryptographic systems in Europe but even if Moscow saw the treaty less as an enabler of economic recovery than as a way to soothe London's fears about subversion, the silence was unusual nevertheless.

Historians still believe the most likely reason for the SIGINT blackouts was a British disclosure about its cryptographic successes to White Russians in Crimea, who subsequently exposed the secret to the Bolsheviks after capture.[10] Chapter 6 offers a possible alternative. Moscow may have learnt of GCCS successes well before December 1920 through an Anglo-Russian family, the Lunns. Between 1919 and at least 1926, three of four Lunn sisters at times worked in GCCS and SIS. Of the three, one was dismissed for turning to Communism while a Crown Servant. The fourth sister never did official work but was a longstanding communist who married Andrew Rothstein (the Bolshevik agent in Britain and CPGB founding member).

Regardless of when or how the secret emerged, efforts against Russian systems in Europe did suffer. GCCS head Alastair Denniston indirectly held DNI Hugh Sinclair responsible:

> I wish to call to your attention the remarkable drop in ... output of Russian telegrams by [GCCS]. The immediate reason for this is that the Soviet Government has now furnished its various agents abroad (at London, Berlin, Stockholm, Prague) with a new series of ciphers. In consequence ... experts here are for the present unable to produce anything. Every telegram we receive (amounting to fifty a day) has to be treated on its own merits. The considered opinion of [Vetterlein] is that we can do nothing at present and must wait till the Soviet representatives make some mistake in their ciphering which will give us an *entrée* to their methods. The ultimate cause of this cessation of Russian intelligence was the compromising of the work of [GCCS] in England in August–September 1920, on the question of the 'Daily Herald' and Kameneff.... [T]he results of that coup were in no way commensurate with the complete loss of Russian intelligence.[11]

Sinclair, of course, was one of the hardliners pressing Lloyd George in 1920 to allow the publication of intercepts. Once the consequences of that decision became apparent in early 1921, Sinclair swiftly developed amnesia, condemning the political decision to publish. Reacting to this, Cabinet Secretary Hankey reminded the DNI of his role in the affair.[12]

Sinclair's peculiar condition also affected Curzon. An advocate in Cabinet of publishing SIGINT to justify expelling the trade delegation, the Foreign Secretary must have realised the irony of his July 1921 memorandum in which he declared GCCS 'by far the most important branch of our confidential work'; 'secrecy is essential.'[13] Yet his actions trumped words – so much so that India Secretary Edwin Montagu, in a note to Curzon in August, criticised GCCS for trying to protect sources and methods. Montagu would not likely have written what he did were he not sure Curzon shared at least some of his views. The note highlights how expedient some politicians can be about intelligence when enough political capital is at stake:

> I hear the Cipher authorities are making a great fuss about the use of intercepts.... Well, well, this is quite characteristic. Rather than jeopardise for a single instant their methods ... which has often been done before, they are quite prepared ... there should be no useful results from their laborious work.... They would rather work at their jig-saw

puzzle in obscurity than ... their labours should be any use at all to their employers.[14]

More importantly, Montagu's note highlights the tension between politicians and the agencies over how (much) to protect sources and methods while still allowing them to inform policy-making in a timely fashion. The SIGINT blackout came at a critical point in Anglo-Russian relations (three months before the trade agreement) and Russian internal affairs. With the Bolsheviks' success in October 1917 came the civil war, leading them to impose immediately what is loosely called "war communism".[15] By no means a 'wartime stopgap' starting only in mid-1918 as is often assumed, war communism meant the complete nationalisation of production, radical centralisation of government, imposition of harsh social legislation and grain expropriation. Only this 'total war within the context of civil war' allowed the Reds to raise, equip and field their Army, numbering 5.5 million soldiers by the time it defeated the Whites in November 1920.[16]

Three years of total war devastated Russia. During 1920, rural and urban residents began questioning openly the need for continued sacrifice. War and drought forced authorities to reduce rations and cut other food allowances, worsening famine and spreading disease. Factories in key cities had to close because of scarce fuel and raw materials.[17] Once a Red victory was assured by autumn, the number and intensity of farmer revolts and worker strikes in western Siberia, Tambov Province, the Volga region, Moscow and Petrograd exploded.[18] By early 1921,

> military communism had reached an impasse; violent intervention by the State into all aspects of economic life, particularly ... requisitions from the peasantry, together with ... unemployment and shortages resulting from the ... collapse of the ... economy, had in many places brought ... the population to the verge of open revolt against the [regime].[19]

The tipping point came on 24 February 1921 when desperate Petrograd workers went on strike over better conditions, condemning war communism as a 'bureaucratic, corrupt, violence-ridden parody' of the revolutionary ideal.[20] The Government's brutal response to this 'counter-revolutionary plot' inspired solidarity within the Baltic Fleet (known as the Baltic Sea Naval Forces from March 1918 to January 1935),[21] especially units at Kronstadt fortress on nearby Kotlin Island. A mutiny there between 2 and 18 March by units Leon Trotsky had once called 'the glory and pride of the Revolution' shocked the Government and security organs. Unable to accept (or understand) challenges based on legitimate grievances, the Kremlin also labelled this revolt a counter-revolutionary plot,[22] crushing it in two weeks. The rebellion arose mainly from the authorities' failure to redress longstanding grievances of fleet personnel;[23] worker strikes in Petrograd alone would likely not have been enough to trigger the mutiny.

Kronstadt did influence Lenin at the X Congress of the Russian Communist Party, held in Moscow in March 1921. He favoured a New Economic Policy (NEP) to replace war communism, that 'boiling mixture of revolutionary euphoria, bitter civil war, foreign intervention, economic collapse and growing peasant unrest'.[24] NEP was essentially a new agricultural policy[25] to pacify the peasantry[26] by allowing private and State sectors to coexist in a mixed economy. Peasants could now profit from the sale of surplus grain through cooperatives and markets. Despite some opposition to this partial return to capitalism, Lenin's gamble worked and unrest gradually eased. Perhaps it was fitting the Congress ended the same day British and Bolshevik representatives signed the trade agreement in London.

Relations were now on a semi-official footing. In April 1921, the Politburo approved Leonid Krasin to head the London trade mission, effective 15 May.[27] The Comintern now sought to expand its "illegal" work in Britain spreading subversive literature, though the CPGB soon complained to Moscow about insufficient funding to do so.[28] Party members themselves agreed most of them were neither idealists nor sympathetic to CPGB aims but simply economically self-interested. Convincing those who 'obstinately carried on' living 'in the same old-fashioned style' to turn on national institutions was nearly impossible.[29]

This was one reason why by mid-1921 the CPGB changed tack and began establishing sports clubs across Britain. In so doing, the Party was clearly adapting to government propaganda and trying to answer it by imitating national characteristics. Neglecting this aspect of British life, one CPGB official recognised, was a serious mistake, making 'an organisation that will allow us to influence and reach the workers' essential to 'counter … those run by the Capitalist class in this field'. Players needed not be Party members but the aim was recruiting 'young working-class elements' (mimicking the Young Men's Christian Association). Basil Thomson was not worried about the communists' impact but acknowledged the change showed a growing understanding of the 'British workman's psychology'.[30] The Young Communist League (YCL), the CPGB youth wing, set up Sunday schools for children, and swimming, football and cricket clubs[31] (all features of pre-1914 Socialist and Cooperative groups). These are examples of what some in government viewed as subversive at the time of the trade treaty, for which an end to Bolshevik subversion in Britain and across the Empire was a prerequisite.[32]

A substantial knowledge gap remains concerning British intelligence and subversive operations in Russia at this time. Ten or so works have added much detail,[33] though most focus primarily on Allied intervention (covert or otherwise) between 1917 and 1920. Less is known about the 1920s despite recent official and unofficial SIS histories.[34] What is clear is the opening of the British Commercial Mission in Moscow in July 1921 improved HUMINT collection on Russia.[35] Nine of seventeen people originally named as Mission members had intelligence ties so the primary aim was clearly 'collection of Secret Service information'.[36]

As the primary target for SIS from 1917 to 1929, Russia seems to have been an exception to accepted operational guidelines. Updated and codified in 1919, they dictated the targeting of vital countries from neighbouring ones to ensure security and avoid diplomatic incidents. As early as 1918, SIS began setting up networks in countries bordering Russia; Scandinavia and the Baltic States were especially important. By 1920, SIS had stations and sub-stations in Finland, and by 1921 in Estonia, Latvia and Lithuania.[37] Station identifiers in surviving secret intelligence (CX) reports do show Helsinki (ST; initially Stockholm), Tallinn (BP) and Riga (FR) were at this time the most active stations targeting Russia. Helsinki concentrated on naval intelligence, Tallinn on military and Riga on political, the last one also being the most productive of the Baltic stations.[38]

The high number of intelligence officers originally named to the Moscow Mission therefore seems to have been an exception. This is understandable, given not only how unforgiving an operating environment Bolshevik Russia was for British officers and agents, but also the opportunity the trade agreement presented British agencies. No existing CX in public archives has so far revealed identifiers consistent with a Moscow station in the formal sense (though Petrograd's was "P"). A safe assumption for now might be stations abroad ran agents in Russia but Moscow staff were cut-outs acting 'as contacts, or collectors of information',[39] which was then sent out by diplomatic bag, encrypted transmission or "illegal" couriers. By November 1921, London had already asked Moscow to allow an increase in diplomatic bag weight from eleven to twenty-two pounds. The following month, Foreign Commissar Chicherin rejected the request, fearing larger capacity would be used for 'enemy correspondence'.[40]

Despite SIS's remit as a HUMINT service, its targeting of Russia naturally also included technical operations.[41] These not only served the agency's own intelligence and counter-intelligence work but also supported GCCS efforts. Even though much SIGINT and HUMINT reached government daily, from 1920 to 1923 Foreign Secretary Curzon insisted his department make the best use of all available information, including what is today termed open-source:

> Curzon had a junior member ... collate all news from all sources, gauge each piece in ... light of the whole, and send daily 'problem files' up through his superiors for immediate minutes to the Minister (who demanded speed, thoroughness, and accuracy in the process). Officials found [it] burdensome, and abolished it when he [left] office, mistakenly – it gave [Curzon] a better grasp of information than any other Minister.[42]

This systematic, contextual validation of intelligence was far-sighted and vital, given the sources SIS sometimes recruited to target Russia. Yet no system is perfect and in the early 1920s nowhere did the saying counter-intelligence is a 'wilderness of mirrors'[43] hold truer than in cities like Paris, Berlin or Tallinn. In these and other capitals, White exiles plotted to overthrow the Reds, while Bolshevik intelligence, in turn, tried (and managed) to disrupt these plots. The stakes were high with no quarter given. Sometimes, however,

> SIS was guilty of relying with too great ... credulity on sources ... inherently unreliable, such as competing White Russian opposition groups, Anglo-Russian exiles and returning military men whose service on the Russian borders in the fight against Bolshevism had left them with a somewhat excitable view of the potential for radical change.[44]

Two such lapses occurred in 1921,[45] and though only the second embarrassed London diplomatically, both exposed weaknesses in how SIS assessed its raw product. This led to reforms in 1922 tightening standards and procedures in the Production Branch, responsible for operational work abroad.[46] The more serious incident humiliated Curzon, who sent a diplomatic note to Moscow on 7 September 1921 citing documents later found to be forgeries sold to SIS in Berlin.[47] To say he was upset when the Kremlin pointed this out is an understatement. Led to believe he now had proof of communist subversion in Asia – grounds for cancelling the trade agreement and expelling the delegation from London – Curzon saw this long-sought opportunity slip through his fingers, compounded by Russian ridicule. He 'vented his wrath' on advisers and SIS alike,[48] the humiliation deepening his and other hardliners' faith in intercepts.[49]

Though Sir Mansfield Cumming and SIS had their product's reliability questioned throughout 1921, both still had a future in government. Sir Basil Thomson and the Directorate of Intelligence, however, did not. He had long criticised Lloyd George's Russia policies. Aside from openly advocating the Conservatives' political line, Thomson had let his views on foreigners[50] and the working classes affect his objectivity on the subversive threat. He saw the Labour Party simply as 'the tip of the Bolshevik iceberg' but also 'gave the impression of being incompetent [and] reactionary'.[51] As Head of Special Branch since 1913, Thomson had sought to roll back mass democracy and keep power in "proper" hands. Yet by late 1921, his career was finished, partly due to the outcry over the "forged *Pravda*" incident earlier that year (see Chapter 2). Before being forced to retire, however, Thomson identified what turned out to be the seed of Russia's most successful (known) infiltration of British government.

In September 1920, the Directorate of Intelligence intercepted mail in which British communists urged the clandestine infiltration of 'Government Departments and public offices, the Army, the Post Office, the Telegraph Service, wireless stations, and newspaper offices'. A year later, Thomson examined university Communism, in which students like Arthur Reade[52] at Oxford and Maurice Dobb at Cambridge were involved. In a letter to the YCL Chairman, Reade wrote of creating 'a Communist nucleus among the Varsity men, who will be going out as schoolmasters, scientific workers, literary men and professional and "intellectual" workers'.[53]

Thus, as early as 1920–21, British government had a record of Moscow's likely targets: those from the middle and upper classes attending leading public schools[54] and universities, who would end up in British official, professional or intellectual circles – men like William Ewer, for instance. Four of the Cambridge Five fit this profile in the 1930s. Yet in the 1920s, authorities concentrated on the perceived threat from the working classes. Until the eve of the Second World War, British intelligence recruitment relied almost entirely on personal contacts from exclusive social circles.[55]

This warning was one of Thomson's last acts in office. Given his partisanship, ministerial preference for SIGINT and a worsening economy, Cabinet reconvened the Secret Service Committee on 22 March 1921 to review intelligence spending.[56] If diehards had any illusions about Thomson's fate, they were soon disappointed. On 22 July, five days before the Committee even announced its findings, Colonial Secretary Churchill was already lobbying Lloyd George:

[Prime Minister], I am concerned to hear that it is in contemplation to break up Sir Basil Thomson's department in the near future on grounds of economy, and to split up the work now concentrated in one hand among various departments. In a year, it may be possible to do this, but ... it would be a great mistake to weaken and dislocate the protective organisation at [this] time. I hope in any case this matter will not be decided without consultation among the Ministers who have usually dealt with Secret Service matters, or the Cabinet as a whole.

'This has nothing to do with economy but efficiency'[57] was the Prime Minister's reply.

On 27 July, the Committee presented its findings, which called for cuts to all agencies but singled out Thomson's. The panel accused him of inefficiency, over-spending and exceeding his original mandate to fight civilian subversion by deliberately collecting foreign intelligence[58] and tackling subversion in the military. The suggestion was to wind down his Directorate. Thomson rejected a last-minute attempt by Metropolitan Police Commissioner (and long-time critic) Sir William Horwood in October to bring the unit under his control. Ignoring protests from Cabinet hardliners never consulted on Thomson's fate, Lloyd George ordered him to take a month's leave as of 1 November, his forced retirement being effective 31 December 1921.[59]

Despite the early November uproar diehards caused in Parliament[60] over his sacking, Thomson himself did not seem too distressed:

Dear Quex [Hugh Sinclair], It was awfully good of you to write. I did not resign, but was the victim of the usual intrigue with which [intelligence officers] are familiar. In fact they offered me a bigger pension than I could claim as a condition of my retiring. So I took their dirty money and went. The same day I joined the staff of *The Times* on very favourable terms and I daresay that financially I shall be a gainer.... I am taking a rest for a bit, but ... later I should much like to look you up. I always enjoyed our work together. Yours ever, Basil Thomson.[61]

His 1919 appointment had been the result of 'a policy of desperation to reach some agreement, under pressure from above'.[62] Soon after Thomson's dismissal, the Secret Service Committee met 'to consider the character and scope of ... information required by ... Government, and the best form to give ... the organisation appointed to secure it'.[63] The Committee's mandate was ensuring no similar abuses recurred, determining how best to limit overlapping agency responsibilities and reorganising Home Office intelligence. Lord

Curzon summarised events leading up to the creation of Thomson's Directorate and then did likewise for the Fisher Report, which had suggested an immediate reappraisal of the unit's position by incorporating it into the Metropolitan Police on efficiency and economy grounds. A ministerial conference had discussed all this and tentatively made a decision to divide Thomson's former post between two officials: one to collect intelligence, the other – an Assistant Commissioner – to take executive action. The intelligence officer would be subordinate to the executive. Sir Vernon Kell, provisionally offered the former post, declined it; Sir Wyndham Childs (see below) accepted the executive position.[64]

Home Secretary Shortt commented on recent arrangements. As a collector, Thomson had been independent of the Metropolitan Commissioner but subordinate to him regarding executive duties (surveillance and arrest of revolutionaries). Prompt action was essential and only possible through close liaison between Thomson and the Commissioner, ultimately responsible for executive decisions. Combining both posts was impractical, felt Shortt. Commissioners needed more than what made a collector good, while collectors rarely had the broad skills needed of a good Commissioner. Besides, the new intelligence officer should stay in the shadows. Churchill agreed but had several crucial questions: what the Directorate's scope should be and whether 'there ought to be a general pooling, or focussing in one individual' of information gathered by existing agencies. Should the Director combine domestic and foreign intelligence functions? Should he have domestic executive powers? Churchill argued the Director should only collect information domestically and not even compile information gathered abroad. Thus, three options emerged: the Director could devote himself only to collecting information; he could concentrate on intelligence work but have an independent investigative staff; or Scotland Yard could take over and subordinate the Directorate to the Commissioner.[65]

Churchill supported the first option, rejecting the last. The Director should collect domestic intelligence, consult the Home Secretary regularly and not be under Scotland Yard, but should stay in touch with it through a liaison officer with executive powers. Churchill favoured having all information in one centre but not in the Directorate, which should be separate from other agencies. War Secretary Sir Laming Worthington-Evans went further, suggesting the War Office conduct all intelligence work. Moreover, he argued, the Director's immediate subordinate was the one whose identity should remain secret, allowing him to investigate freely.[66] Ireland Chief Secretary Sir Hamar Greenwood stressed the need for a quick solution of problems identified, suggesting executive and intelligence-gathering powers rest with one individual. Curzon, however, preferred something similar to what Churchill had proposed instead, saying he hoped final arrangements could satisfy both Churchill and Shortt.[67]

Hardliners rallied publicly behind Thomson after his dismissal. Yet two months later Churchill acknowledged Thomson had overstepped his boundaries:

> [T]here was imposed upon Sir Basil ... a sort of vague responsibility for reporting to Cabinet on all Secret Service work, but it was precisely where he stepped outside the geographical limits proper to a Home Secret Service that mistakes were made. ... [SIS] alone have the knowledge, experience, close liaison with the Foreign Office and the War Office, and ... acquaintance with the work of their representatives abroad ... essential for a just appraisement of ... their information and its arrangement ... in true perspective.[68]

Thomson's replacement at Special Branch, Wyndham Childs, took office on 5 December 1921. Known as "Fido" given his 'deep respect for higher authority,'[69] he was an avowed anti-communist like Thomson. Unlike his predecessor and diehard ministers, though, Childs tried to distinguish between Bolshevik subversion and legitimate activism by British labour, something his reports soon reflected. Whereas in late 1921 Thomson commented mainly on unions and demonstrations, by early 1922 Childs already concentrated on the CPGB, related domestic and foreign organisations, and their secret infrastructures.[70]

Since Communism was the most prominent threat to Parliamentary democracy, Childs sought intelligence on CPGB weaknesses. In July 1922, Special Branch obtained a copy of an internal report on the state of the Party. Conclusions were not encouraging:

> The Party has now been in existence for nearly two years.... Yet [it] has made no real progress ... there has been no appreciable increase of membership, and within the period for which we have records there has even been a downward tendency. It has not established the influence that it should have done in the unions and the working class movement.... There have been campaigns, but they have yielded no lasting results. Hundreds of members have drifted in and ... out again because they have found nothing to hold them. ... We believe ... the present weakness ... is due to lack of proper methods in our work and policy. We have been following the lines of the old Socialist Parties: though

in name a Communist Party, we have not yet grasped how to carry on revolutionary Communist organisation and policy.

There were several problems: lack of central organisation; weak local branches; an obsolete Party constitution; no central direction of activities; lack of a Party programme; inconsistent training; a weak press and propaganda machine; and, most importantly, members' poor grasp of their obligations. The most pressing short-term goal was to address these problems.[71]

Childs soon turned to CPGB and Comintern clandestine work. By mid-1922, his reporting again identified methods Soviet intelligence later used in Britain: infiltrating government via universities. J. T. Walton Newbold, the CPGB Central Committee member who in November that year became the first MP elected as a communist, wrote:

> Some of our less well-known comrades could ... be set to work in Government Offices, libraries, to which their University connections would give them ready access. Others ... should be sent to Washington, to Harvard, Columbia, and other great economic research schools of the United States, there to do the work nominally as graduates preparing for further degrees, but, really to do work for the Comintern.[72]

By this time, then, efforts were underway to improve the quality of domestic HUMINT. The same was happening with foreign intelligence. Serious questions in 1921 about some SIS product that year led to an improved assessment process by spring 1922:

> All information ... in intelligence reports had henceforth to be 'submitted to careful consideration, both as regards reliability and value'. The reports were given one of three gradings: A.1. Those whose subject matter suggests their being regarded as of primary importance, and which are actually based on: original documents actually in the possession of SIS or to which a representative of SIS has had access. Statements by agents of exceptional reliability in which the SIS repose especial confidence for peculiar reasons. A.2. Those which ... cannot be classified as A.1, but which are of significance, both as regards subject matter and reliability. B. Those of less importance, but the interest and reliability of which are such as to justify their being issued. Intelligence consumers were also reminded that SIS reports 'should, of course, be considered in conjunction with reports from official sources'.[73]

Ironically, just as SIS assessment capabilities improved, collection capacity declined. Following intelligence spending reviews between December 1921 and February 1922 by the Geddes Committee on National Expenditure, SIS had its FY 1922/3 budget cut by 10%.[74] International pressure was also mounting on Britain to abolish travel visas to and from certain countries, a wartime legacy aimed at monitoring the movement of individuals. The Home Office, the Board of Trade and the Department of Overseas Trade all favoured eliminating visas. Many in intelligence circles resisted, arguing European affairs were still unsettled, visa revenue subsidising overseas operations would vanish and control over 'the movement of undesirables' worldwide would be lost – as would precious cover for SIS officers posing as Passport Control Officers (PCOs). Despite this, the Government abolished visas for Denmark, Holland, Italy, Luxembourg, Norway, Portugal, Spain, Sweden and Switzerland.[75]

To illustrate lost visa revenues alone, by 1923 the main PCO locations were Athens, Berlin, Brussels, Budapest, Copenhagen, Helsinki, Kaunas (in Lithuania), New York, Oslo, Paris, Prague, Riga, Rome, Rotterdam, Sofia, Stockholm, Tallinn, Vienna, Vladivostok and Warsaw. Visa receipts totalled £106,789 (2011: nearly £38 million) while office expenses were only £40,000 (2011: just over £14 million). Running an office in 1923 cost from £1200 for Athens (2011: £425,000) to £8000 for New York (2011: nearly £3 million). In 1922, the London PCO headquarters on Victoria Street consisted of a Director (SIS officer Major Herbert Spencer), an Assistant Director, an establishment officer, several clerks, a typist and a porter. Salaries that year totalled £3005 (2011: £1 million) and in 1923, only £3720 (2011: £1.3 million).[76]

Money was also one reason why by autumn 1922 Lloyd George's political survival was less and less likely. The ruling coalition he had so carefully managed since becoming Prime Minister in December 1916 was collapsing fast: he could no longer justify what Coalition partners saw as an increasingly erratic and autocratic governing style. Post-Armistice, the Conservative Party was reluctant to discard Lloyd George given his 'enormous popular standing' as the 'architect of victory'. Splitting the Coalition at that time would also have been a gamble given growing social and industrial unrest. Postwar suffrage expansion, moreover, changed the electoral calculus. Fear of the Labour Party was a key reason why Conservatives stayed in the Coalition, but not the only one. Some Conservative grandees also believed the enormous postwar challenges temporarily required placing Nation above Party.[77]

By mid-1921, Labour had clearly embarked on a political path, easing fears of revolution.[78] Many Conservatives now started questioning if Lloyd George was indispensable after all, some even preferring defection to Labour to staying in the Coalition.[79] In addition, the December 1921 Anglo-Irish Treaty meant the bloc of eighty-two anti-Conservative Irish MPs was no longer in the House of Commons, making it easier for the Conservatives to form a government. After the 1918 election, these Irish MPs had refused to take their Westminster seats, forming instead the *Dáil Éireann* (which became the lower house of the Irish Parliament).

Conservative impatience increased when Lloyd George announced in June he would end suppression of the Irish Republican movement and negotiate with *Sinn Féin*. Hardliners were furious but, within months, southern Ireland gained effective independence as a British Dominion, allowing the army to withdraw. Colonial Secretary Churchill was instrumental in negotiating the Anglo-Irish Treaty, now expecting Liberals to 'abandon the radical thrust of their social policies' in return. In years before the treaty, Lloyd George accomplished the seemingly impossible task of maintaining coalition unity by moderating his radicalism. Sir Henry Wilson's assassination in London by Irish Republicans on 22 June 1922 only compounded the "betrayal" in Ireland, leading pro-Coalition Conservatives to align gradually with hardliners. This gathered pace in mid-September after Lloyd George ignored Cabinet and European allies, nearly triggering a British attack on Turkey (and a continental war) to help Greece. His recklessness particularly alienated the Conservatives, whose foreign policies traditionally favoured Turkey.[80]

Greece had imposed harsh peace terms on Turkey under the Treaty of Sèvres, signed in 1920 by Entente powers and the Ottoman Empire. Following clashes with Turkish Nationalists led by Kemal Pasha (who had rejected Sèvres), in September 1922 Turkish troops converged on Chanak, a British outpost in the neutral zone. Though danger to Chanak soon passed, the Turks then advanced toward Constantinople, causing divisions in Whitehall and Cabinet over whether to go to war with Turkey (and even Russia).[81] Eventually the "hawks", Lloyd George and Churchill among them, lost out and an armistice was signed in October.[82]

Coalition Conservatives and Liberals alike were by now fed up with Lloyd George, the man 'always on the look-out for ready cash' who had 'demeaned political life'.[83] This was hypocritical coming from the Conservatives, given their own sale of honours and the real reasons they now wanted to ditch Lloyd George (regaining political independence and shielding the Party from his actions). Austen Chamberlain, who replaced Andrew Bonar Law as

Conservative leader upon his temporary retirement in March 1921, was loyal to Lloyd George. Chamberlain believed the Coalition was the only way to stop Labour, something with which most rank-and-file Conservatives now disagreed. By ignoring his Party on these crucial matters, he alienated most of it. Chamberlain called a meeting of Conservative MPs at the Carlton Club in London on 19 October 1922 to crush dissent. However, inspired by Bonar Law and Stanley Baldwin, the rebels voted 187–87 in favour of Party independence. Lloyd George, who had already called a General Election, resigned that afternoon; Bonar Law, re-assuming Conservative leadership, replaced him as Prime Minister four days later. Lloyd George never held office again and the 15 November election saw the Conservatives win 344 Parliamentary seats (versus 142 for Labour, sixty-two for Coalition Liberals and fifty-four for independent Liberals). Labour becoming the official opposition tempered the Conservative landslide.[84]

Lloyd George's political end marked the return to power of a reinvigorated Conservative Party that again saw itself as Britain's natural ruler.[85] This added friction to Anglo-Russian relations. Yet until November 1922, British and Russian documents highlighted three fundamental issues. First, with the insight SIGINT provided into Bolshevik capabilities and intentions, and with the vast majority of British unions and revolutionary groups either penetrated by Special Branch or ineffective (often both), why the "Red Scare" in this period?

Part of the answer, of course, is history. Britain and Russia had long competed for supremacy in Asia. Many who served in India – like Curzon, Viceroy at the turn of the century – had first-hand knowledge of Russian imperialism and now viewed with alarm its strengthening by Bolshevik ideology. For aristocrats like him and Churchill, the new regime embodied humanity's basest instincts. Lenin's unilateral withdrawal from the First World War and subsequent peace with Germany only added to British unease.[86]

The most important part of the explanation, though, is politics. Churchill, Curzon, Long and other hardliners encouraged the ambitious and more pliable Basil Thomson. His politicisation of intelligence served these individuals' aims, which were not only to frustrate politicians favouring relations with Russia but also to stop the loss of status that mass democracy signalled for patricians. To achieve these goals diehards needed someone who would, if not manufacture, then at least magnify a threat that could force Cabinet "doves" to relent. Additionally, some of these men hoped to succeed Lloyd George; Curzon's grief at having lost the premiership to Stanley Baldwin in May 1923 is well documented.[87]

A second theme was tension between HUMINT and SIGINT. Over time, domestic HUMINT lost credibility in Cabinet: ministers came to mistrust Thomson's behaviour (once he became more of a liability than an asset) and he proverbially trod on too many bureaucratic toes while empire-building. There can be no doubt SIGINT won the contest for ministers' affections – after all, for Churchill this was intelligence 'of the kind that never fails'.[88] In the long term, however, this early tension between various kinds of intelligence benefitted Britain. Experiences in wartime and the 1920s taught Churchill the power of intelligence when properly used (particularly SIGINT), preparing him well for his clash with Adolf Hitler. Though Churchill supported SIGINT disclosures in the 1920s to defeat Bolshevik subversion, he grew wiser. His awareness of the sensitivity and value of SIGINT but, more importantly, its unique vulnerability if compromised[89] was just what Britain needed in the Second World War.

The final theme was that some of the very men reforming intelligence from 1919 to 1922 had contributed to problems in the first place. The Directorate of Intelligence was a compromise to combat an ill-understood, ill-defined but nevertheless real threat of communist subversion. Yet the Directorate was just the latest in a growing number of agencies, leading to overlapping duties and numerous disputes dating back to wartime. These turf wars, in turn, created inefficiencies in British intelligence, opening the door to abuses and eventually compelling government to reform its secret machinery. Some of those overseeing this – like Churchill, Curzon and Long – were the same who had in the first place inspired Thomson's more creative powers.

The resulting disconnect between politicians and part of the intelligence community happened as the overt subversive threat (i.e. revolution) eased. This had to do with security and intelligence work, undoubtedly, but much more with Labour's decision to seek social change in Parliament, not on the streets. Yet covert subversion grew but by late 1922, the credibility of Special Branch was suspect and Cabinet had slashed MI5's budget by 72% since the Armistice.[90] As for SIS, examples above highlight its occasional vulnerability to disinformation. This weakness was largely due to the 'frantic nature' of SIS intelligence gathering on subversion (specifically) and Russia (broadly) by a 'motley collection' of officers and agents, in Britain and abroad.[91] GCCS, even if also underfunded,[92] was the most effective agency; unsurprising, given the nature and volume of its product.

When Special Branch reports in early 1923 mentioned Soviet front organisations looking to infiltrate the British Government, Cabinet suspicion of Thomson's excesses undermined the credibility of his successor Childs. Nevertheless, as the next chapter shows, SIGINT and HUMINT again played critical roles in two of the most serious diplomatic crises between Britain and the USSR in interwar years. One incident, the 1924 Zinoviev Letter, had lasting repercussions, both in British politics and international relations.

PART III

Shock Therapy

CHAPTER 5

The Letter

The Curzon Note ~ The Reports ~ The Zinoviev Letter

[A]dvantages of basing the published British case on ...
extracts from the despatches ... outweighed the disadvan-
tages of the possible disclosure of the secret source.

Cabinet conclusion[1]

Unless men of high educational standard and of an age
to learn can be recruited to fill vacancies as they occur,
[GCCS] must gradually become enfeebled and in ... [ten]
to [fifteen] years die of inanition. Anonymous[2]

Socialists have not the slightest idea of fair play or sports-
manship.... We are ... menaced by a foreign propaganda
... anti- and un-English in its character and methods.

Winston Churchill[3]

THOUGH a success for the Conservative Party, the November 1922 General Election was nevertheless a grim omen for hardliners. Labour was now a contender for power, increasing diehard distress over their falling numbers in Westminster at this crucial time. From December 1916 to October 1922, Coalition Cabinets had seven prominent anti-communists; Conservative Cabinets until January 1924 only had three of repute.[4] After November 1922, only Curzon remained yet bilateral ties worsened, with intelligence again playing a central role.

This chapter examines how the Conservatives set out to reclaim perceived lost ground to Moscow, by sending the message relations would no longer be "business as usual" and distancing themselves from Lloyd George's "tainted" premiership. Yet the Conservatives had to bow to economic realities facing Britain. Using SIGINT and then HUMINT, hardliners inside and outside government tried resolving two issues that had since 1917 distressed them even more than Lloyd George: Bolshevik subversion and the political rise of

Labour. Tackling the former was the object of the May 1923 Curzon Note;[5] blocking the latter was the aim of the so-called Zinoviev Letter of October 1924. Together they highlight the dangers of intelligence deception and propaganda becoming public knowledge, creating the need for a political response.

Both crises reflected the fluidity in British politics from Lloyd George's resignation in October 1922 to the collapse of the first Labour government in October 1924. Restoring the traditional party system post-Coalition took two years, three General Elections and three different Prime Ministers from two parties. While these changes did not affect British intelligence structures much, attitudes within the community hardened against the Bolsheviks and Labour.

The new post-Coalition electoral balance benefited the Conservatives. As the 1920s progressed and the Liberals became increasingly marginalised, Labour consolidated its position as 'the Party of urban and industrial Britain'. Still, despite 'much synthetic bitterness', not much had changed since pre-war days: Labour still offered social change and the Conservatives protection.[6] Bolshevik subversion was thus what the Conservatives cited to justify their renewed assertiveness towards Moscow. Once Lloyd George resigned, an emboldened Curzon reclaimed control of British foreign policy.[7]

He quickly signalled what was to come. On 20 October 1922, an international conference started in Switzerland to finalise peace terms with Turkey, which had yet to ratify the Sèvres Treaty (see Chapter 4). Technically, then, Turkey and the Allies were still at war. While chairing proceedings that led to the 24 July 1923 settlement, Curzon proved to be a paradox. Though 'always genial, always courteous, always entertaining' in private, at the conference table he harassed and ridiculed Turkish and Soviet delegates. One participant regarded this as 'ill-judged and productive of little success'. Curzon actually intended to exclude Moscow from the conference and only Franco-Italian pressure beforehand made him relent.[8]

In the first quarter of 1923, Anglo-Soviet tensions rose over the Kremlin's imprisonment of Patriarch Tikhon of Moscow since April 1922 and ongoing suppression of religion; Soviet territorial water boundaries; and detention and execution of British subjects during the civil war. Rhetoric over religion was particularly sharp[9] and heated diplomatic exchanges followed, with Moscow claiming interference in its domestic affairs by London.[10]

Probably anticipating hostile British action, the Politburo of the Central Committee of the Communist Party recalled Nikolai Klyshko to Moscow.[11] London welcomed this since Klyshko had long been a thorn on its side: as

Political Head of Mission (and Krasin's deputy) since May 1920, he funded subversion in Britain. News of the recall set off a contest for Curzon's ear within the Foreign Office. The British representative in Moscow, Robert Hodgson, cautioned London not to isolate the Soviets. Owen O'Malley and his superior Don Gregory, two Northern Department officials, opposed Hodgson, who argued:

> The ... Agreement has not justified itself by positive commercial results.... Nor could a Communist Government ... dissociate itself from propaganda even were it sincerely minded to do so.... [Rupture with Britain] would be in reality regarded as little short of a calamity by the Government.... The [British] Mission has a strong moderating influence and good standing [and has] accumulated knowledge ... it would be a misfortune to lose.... This ... would be ... achieved by immediate curtailment of this Mission to a strict minimum ... for keeping in touch with events and protecting British interests.[12]

O'Malley countered by first reminding all concerned that Curzon had dismissed Gregory's view of 5 April – 'a blow from us would widen the breach between moderates and extremists and create confusion out of which a Government crisis might at last ensue' – as 'purely speculative'.[13] O'Malley then pounced:

> Mr Hodgson [says] a rupture would be regarded as a calamity by the Soviet Government. Is this not exactly what we want? ... He says withdrawal would remove a strong moderating influence.... I do not for a minute believe [he] ever exercised any such influence, or that, if he did, the 'strict minimum' of a mission ... he proposes ... would be able to continue [exercising] this influence. If he means ... it is ... the Trade Agreement rather than the Mission itself which exercises the moderating influence, he is probably right.... We are not dealing with public opinion in Russia but simply with the leaders of the [Communist Party], and [they] will take precious good care to prevent direct contact between us and public opinion.... With them England has nothing in common.... A complete rupture would at least be an interesting experiment ... a gesture clearly intelligible to the rest of the world.[14]

Next day, Gregory – another anti-Bolshevik – pressed the attack:

> Mr O'Malley's moderation will perhaps be more acceptable than my ardent plea for rupture.... When [Hodgson] comes, however, to his

conclusions, I am bound to say again that I differ with him fundamentally.... Our prestige continues to suffer and prestige matters.... Klyshko was openly and contemptuously boasting – so I learned yesterday – that it is ... certain we would take anything lying down, and, if that is the opinion they have of us, their respect, if they ever had any, will not be improved by a continuance of present relations.... By withdrawal we should no doubt be deprived of an observer on the spot. But with all due deference to Mr Hodgson, I do not think that his Mission have [*sic*] been able to supply us with very much more information than we could have obtained, and have obtained, from independent sources or from the neighbouring countries.... The Trade Agreement has not helped our ... industrialists ... [they] are the very people who are now pressing us to withdraw.... It is a great opportunity for us who would like a break anyhow.[15]

Clearly, hardliners sought a trigger to justify breaking with Moscow; a subsequent note by Assistant Under-Secretary Ronald Lindsay is relevant. Lindsay, since 1 January 1921 also the Principal Assistant Secretary and Northern Department Superintendent, wrote on 16 April:

Under repeated insults, and in the presence of repeated barbarities ... honour and feeling call for a rupture. Unfortunately, foreign policy has to take other and more material factors into consideration and when I ask myself what we would get out of a rupture, I fail to find any really satisfactory answer.... Now the Secretary of State ... has called attention to the importance of the Tikhon trial. If it ends in the Patriarch's execution, surely the result will be that unanimous explosion of indignation in England which [*sic*] would facilitate action on our part, and without which would be premature.[16]

Russian documents confirm Lindsay's observation. At a London diplomatic reception in late April, British bankers told Soviet officials Moscow's position on religion was increasing tensions. Britons expected freedom of worship and could accept nothing less; even the recent seizure of the British trawler *James Johnson*, the Soviets heard, paled in comparison. The suggested course of action was for the Kremlin to release the trawler,[17] removing at least one irritant to bilateral ties since Prime Minister Bonar Law was ill and due to go on vacation. This gave Curzon some leeway and on 28 April, Maxim Litvinov received a warning from Assistant Soviet Representative in London, Jan A.

Berzin. A breach would ruin Soviet exports[18] and so by early May Moscow expected the worst from the Conservatives.

A curious aspect of the 2 May 1923 Curzon Note is that the Soviet messages it cited were all intercepted when Bonar Law was in office.[19] This seems a deliberate Conservative break with Lloyd George, since intercepts showed subversive intent and behaviour as early as 1919. Curzon's memorandum is of historical significance: Britain was the first State to protest to another while acknowledging the protest relied on intercepted communications of the recipient nation. The Kremlin's 12 May reply, delivered the following day,[20] denied intercept quotes were genuine but tacitly recognised Britain had compromised Soviet traffic.[21] As for subversion, Moscow restated its longstanding call for a bilateral conference to address this and other issues, and 'regularise ... relations in their full extent'.[22]

Subsequent correspondence between Curzon and Soviet diplomats raised the issue of subversion because Fyodor F. Raskolnikov,[23] Plenipotentiary Representative to Afghanistan, had already conducted 'fresh anti-British activities'[24] since the NKID had received Britain's note on 8 May. If Moscow refrained from such activity, London would give 'an analogous undertaking to refrain from encouraging, either directly or through their representatives or agents' any movement having as 'its object the overthrow of existing institutions in Russia'.[25] This was the clearest admission yet that Great Britain engaged in subversion against the USSR.

In the end, because Moscow saw the 'rupture of trading relations not only as an economic loss, but also as a political disaster', it temporarily agreed to British demands for an end to Eastern subversion.[26] Despite Curzon's use of deciphered Soviet traffic, vulnerable cryptographic systems stayed in place until late 1923 when the Kremlin introduced new ones and temporarily shut out GCCS. The lag in introducing new systems was probably due to the time needed to develop and distribute more secure ciphers. An often-overlooked point is that Cabinet's decision to use SIGINT in Curzon's note was based partly on an understanding the secret source from which diplomatic despatches had been obtained 'was actually known' to the USSR.[27] Even more interesting was Moscow's perspective on the note.

Anxiety leading up to its delivery and, of course, the document itself caused a flurry of exchanges. Soviet officials in London viewed events as serious, offering Moscow two reasons for them: escalating class war and dissatisfaction within British financial circles. Assistant Representative Berzin believed British industrialists regarded the All-Russian Cooperative Society as a monopolistic competitor[28] and so seemed willing to endanger the trade agreement partly because this would end the ARCOS monopoly. Exchanges between NKID and its London delegation highlighted Moscow's greatest fear: that Britain would not simply end trade but start a new blockade or even intervention. In this atmosphere, Berzin wrote, British policy looked 'particularly threatening'.[29]

He also believed Curzon's note sought to draw a sharp response, justifying a break on which London was already set. Berzin urged the Kremlin to answer 'concretely, correctly, not provocatively, but firmly'. At one point, he indirectly criticised Litvinov: for two years, Berzin had been saying abstaining from propaganda would deliver better political results. Now, when replying to Curzon, Moscow should tone down its rhetoric. Meanwhile, the delegation would keep trying to spur Labour into action. For this to succeed, Berzin pleaded, the USSR had to: stop attacking the Party in the Soviet media; keep details of correspondence with British groups secret; and ensure any reply to the note was not 'too sharp'.[30] In May 1923, two objectives for the USSR were to save face internationally, and keep ARCOS and the All-Russian Central Union (*Tsentrsoyuz*) of Consumers' Societies[31] going. Britain could only shut down these organisations by deporting their staff, precisely what Berzin feared London now wanted to do.[32]

Writing to NKID on 11 May from Berlin, Karl B. Radek, the noted revolutionary and Comintern Executive Committee member, argued Britain sought complete Soviet capitulation. The threat of a breach at this time, he felt, was to force Moscow to accept London's terms of a year ago at the Genoa Conference.[33] Fears of renewed intervention persisted because it would prevent the USSR from pursuing 'our Orient policy'. Radek initially pushed for a harsher reply to Curzon. On advice from Soviet military and intelligence officers in Berlin as well as the local *Manchester Guardian* correspondent, Frederick Voigt,[34] he urged the rejection of British demands for a three-mile territorial water limit and removal of Bolshevik agents in the East. Radek also pushed for international arbitration on compensation of British citizens.[35] Within weeks, however, he came round to War Commissar Trotsky's view: do not let London provoke Moscow into a war at this stage, even if appearing to give in to Curzon's ultimatum.[36]

The most publicised Soviet climb-down concerned compensation of two Britons arrested by the *Cheka* for alleged espionage: Charles F. Davison and Mrs Stan Harding (née Sedine Milana, but known also as Stan Harding-Krayl). In September 1919, the *Cheka* accused Davison – described variously as an engineer and businessman – of funding his spying through financial fraud, and executed him on 16 January 1920. In July 1926 Moscow paid his family

£10,000 (2011: £475,000) in compensation.[37] Harding, on the other hand, received £3000 (2011: £134,000) in August 1923 because prominent British politicians took up her case. The *New York World* had earlier commissioned the socialist Harding, who 'greatly desired to see Communist Russia', to cover it from June 1920. Despite official papers and high-level introductions, the *Cheka* arrested her on arrival and took her to Lubyanka prison for interrogation, followed by nine weeks' solitary confinement. After stays in Lubyanka and Butyrka prisons, and threats of execution, Harding finally left Moscow on 26 November 1920.[38]

She later claimed Marguerite Harrison, a US socialite working for American military intelligence under journalistic cover, had informed on her. The *Cheka* arrested Harrison in spring 1920 on espionage charges and said her freedom depended on exposing British and US agents.[39] She pretended to do this but according to Harding stayed loyal to Washington, naming pro-regime sympathisers instead (Harding included). The *Cheka* initially believed the American but as the case against Mrs Harding unravelled, the secret police re-arrested Harrison in October 1920. Much of the subsequent controversy was because despite the evidence, London had been either unwilling or unable to get Washington to honour Harding's compensation claims. The USA (Britain's main postwar creditor) backed Harrison, who spent ten of her eighteen months in Russia in *Cheka* prisons.[40]

Russian documents help fill gaps in British SIGINT coverage of the USSR during the May 1923 crisis. Despite the August–September 1920 revelations in the British Press about GCCS successes, Frunze's warning late that year about poor COMSEC and Curzon's recent use of intercepts in his note, some still seemed to believe in the impenetrability of Soviet cryptographic systems. In a 15 May telegram, Radek suggested codes and ciphers were likely stolen, and that information was probably leaking in Kabul.[41] With Chicherin and his deputy Litvinov in charge of the 13 May response to Curzon, and with the Politburo assigning Krasin plenipotentiary powers to deliver it verbally in London,[42] all the USSR could do now was wait.

Meanwhile, Prime Minister Bonar Law, ill with throat cancer, resigned on 22 May (and passed away in October). Deputy Foreign Commissar Litvinov, unaware of the true reason for the resignation, argued Bonar Law did so only because he did not want blame for any coming breach. However, Litvinov foresaw Stanley Baldwin's appointment as Prime Minister over Curzon. The Foreign Secretary's chances of succession, reasoned Litvinov, would improve only if Moscow conceded on all points in his note (which was unlikely). In the Russian's view, Baldwin's flexibility as a politician and solid reputation in business circles gave him the edge.[43]

Yet Curzon's inflexibility was to some Bolsheviks nothing like that of Sir William Tyrrell (see Chapter 1). As Foreign Office Deputy Permanent Under-Secretary, he headed there what a Soviet official in Berlin called the 'Catholic faction', bent on war with the Soviets.[44] Based largely on exchanges with Voigt of the *Manchester Guardian*, the Department of Diplomatic Information at the Soviet Mission in Berlin felt neither the British Government nor Curzon himself had a detailed plan to deal with Russia. The Department regarded him a slave to his own views on Asian affairs, dissatisfaction within The City about the low profitability of the trade agreement[45] and pressure from oil companies. Royal Dutch Shell had broken industry ranks in March 1922 and negotiated directly with ARCOS to become the sole importer of Russian oil, continuing even after Curzon's note. Moscow believed other oil companies wanted to cancel out Shell's advantage by attacking the legal basis of its contracts, the 1921 trade agreement.[46]

Yet it was not the only thing under attack at this time. Krasin's NKID rivals – mainly Chicherin and Litvinov – questioned his competence almost as soon as he arrived in Britain in May 1920.[47] Petty jealousies and bureaucratic infighting made the situation so poisonous that Krasin had to visit Moscow in early July 1920 for consultations. Despite being the Kremlin's London representative from May 1921 to July 1923 (Britain only granted *de jure* recognition in 1924), in months leading up to Curzon's note rumours persisted in both capitals that Krasin did not have full authority to negotiate on Moscow's behalf. His position within Soviet bureaucracy and as perceived by British counterparts, became delicate. At this point, Russian documents suggest, something baffling occurred.

With Chicherin's backing, Litvinov had repeatedly tried to set Krasin up for failure, out of spite at having neither been picked by the Kremlin nor allowed by Downing Street to negotiate the most important bilateral agreement of the decade for Moscow. Thus, most likely as insurance should a breach happen, Litvinov and Chicherin seem to have forged a decree on Krasin's resignation, backdating it to 2 May 1923. In May and June, both men kept spreading rumours Krasin had no authority to negotiate with Curzon; the Soviet representative in London, as always, fought back with correspondence proving otherwise.[48]

Following Moscow's reply to Curzon and despite the united front Soviet officials showed the world, the NKID was in turmoil over Britain. On 23 May, Krasin wrote Chicherin:

The situation changed yesterday with ... Bonar Law's resignation. Now there are two candidates: Curzon and Baldwin. If Curzon became [Prime Minister], his attitude would be less aggressive because it would not be good to debut in Parliament by breaking off the trade agreement. This is why I tore out my hair today when I received your response note. I told you ... the situation here is changing every day, and asked you not to send the response directly to Curzon, but to me first. If you did this, we could have manoeuvred here to stay in the position of our note from 12 May. I cannot understand how you could send the note to the [Foreign Office] first. Now we cannot use the advantage of Bonar Law's resignation just because of the obstinacy of our [NKID].[49]

Krasin had written Ramsay MacDonald and Lloyd George earlier, who both promised they would denounce in Parliament Curzon's push for a break. However, both speeches, Krasin added sarcastically, had supported the USSR as 'a rope supports a hanged man'.[50] Given the behaviour of Chicherin and Litvinov, others could be forgiven for taking much the same view of them.

Yet Curzon was not as inflexible toward Moscow in private as he seemed in public. One key demand in his 1923 note was the removal of Representative Raskolnikov from Afghanistan to reduce anti-British subversion there. Observers were sceptical of his quiet transfer months later and Moscow's claim it had scheduled the move before Curzon's note anyway. Russian documents show Curzon agreed to Raskolnikov's quiet replacement within a month if the Soviets felt it was beneath their dignity to expel him publicly because of British demands. The Foreign Secretary, however, dealt with declarations of Raskolnikov's innocence by showing Bolshevik delegates in London telegrams the ambassador had sent.[51] Additionally, Curzon's note did force Soviet officialdom to consider the reality and effectiveness of their Eastern presence. Writing to Litvinov in late May, Jan A. Berzin suggested Raskolnikov be transferred immediately and Moscow fundamentally revise its Oriental strategy. Raskolnikov's plans to incite Indian rebellions were 'a childish attempt to lead serious policy without appropriate conditions. ... This kind of mosquito bite won't scare the British elephant'.[52]

Matters came to a head when on 29 May, harassed by NKID officials in Moscow and elsewhere, Krasin hit back. In the contemporary equivalent of a "carbon copy e-mail", he sent a sharp note to Litvinov and Chicherin, copying it to the Politburo and NKID representatives in Berlin, Prague, Riga and Warsaw:

In Litvinov's directive of 18 May, there is a paragraph: 'We telegraphed to Krasin that his mission is just to listen to Curzon's demands without negotiating.' I am strongly protesting against Litvinov's claim. No one ever gave me the instruction only to be listening to Curzon and not to negotiate. It would be an absolutely impossible and impracticable task.... I would never go to London to play a role of recording phonograph that cannot open his mouth.

Krasin concluded by saying:

there has not yet been invented a way of communication between a [foreign] representative and a Minister of Foreign Affairs whereby the representative does not have the right to answer Ministerial questions. The 16 May [Central Committee] cable [instructs] me on how to talk to Curzon. Litvinov himself, in his 22 May cable, suggests ... I draw out negotiations up to the next [Parliamentary session]. I wonder how to do this if 'not negotiating'.[53]

But his protests were of no use. On 4 June, the Politburo acted on Curzon's note. Krasin was to inform Curzon confidentially of Raskolnikov's upcoming transfer, but Krasin was also to receive a Politburo letter criticising him for making unspecified 'intolerable claims' during negotiations.[54] Also that day, Litvinov cabled Krasin that Moscow could not openly recall Raskolnikov (who ironically had been requesting a transfer for nearly a year, it seems, the delay being due to difficulties finding an adequate replacement). Krasin was also to tell Curzon if London did not press the point publicly, Raskolnikov would leave Afghanistan within a week.[55]

Behind all this was simply that Moscow saw any concession as a public relations disaster affecting what one could call the balance of popular perceptions in Asia. As Litvinov put it, 'Any child will understand ... we capitulated on all points. If we ... remove ambassadors, it will make our position ... impossible not only in the East, but in the West, too.'[56] Nevertheless, publicly or otherwise, the USSR did capitulate, at least temporarily. Krasin, in London and unable to defend himself from relentless intrigue in Moscow, was the obvious scapegoat. On 18 June, Chicherin accused him of collaborating with Curzon to undermine the Soviets by helping the Foreign Secretary create 'the fiction of negotiations'. If Moscow had remained firm, asserted Chicherin, this was not thanks to Krasin.[57]

That he had actually persuaded Curzon to resolve the Raskolnikov issue to both sides' satisfaction did not seem to matter.[58] Given the self-serving indignation within NKID over Krasin's "collaboration", and despite his overall success in preventing Moscow's renewed international isolation, the stay of execution was short-lived. Having initially decided on 9 June to postpone Krasin's recall, not two weeks later the Politburo appointed Khristian G. Rakovsky the new Soviet Plenipotentiary Representative,[59] effective 23 July 1923.[60] This set the stage for a Soviet charm offensive in Britain aimed at breaking the tense deadlock in relations.

Meanwhile, the Politburo was already issuing directives to agents and representatives worldwide to ensure their actions compromised neither them nor Moscow.[61] Of course, much of the damage to Soviet interests was self-inflicted. As Krasin put it, 'the continued campaign against me is what is complicating our work here [in Britain].'[62] Paradoxically, while he worried about convincing Cabinet, some Britons were doing what he, the senior representative in London, could not: go to Moscow for guidance. In mid-June 1923, senior CPGB officials went there to discuss which policies to adopt at an upcoming Labour Party conference. The Comintern instructed British communists to organise a campaign with the General Council of the Trades Union Congress to culminate in a day strike to force Britain to change its Soviet policies.[63]

Mid-1923 saw an accelerating but different sort of campaign, due partly perhaps to Curzon's note. Following a transport workers' conference in Berlin earlier in the month, the Executive Committee of the Young Communist International (KIM)[64] issued a 7 June memorandum. A letter to the Red International of Labour Unions (*Profintern*) followed, of which the CPGB's YCL received a copy. These intercepted documents urged that no effort be spared on 'special agitation among the recruits and soldiers who are transport workers', and 'anti-militarist work of the proletarian youth organisations in the Army' receive full support.[65]

The Bolsheviks had long realised popular uprisings across Europe would not easily happen, so covert subversion continued to be refined. Three Special Branch reports in 1923 should have drawn this to Cabinet's attention but they did not seem to, since ministers by then eyed these reports with considerable suspicion. The *Profintern* Mid-European Bureau noted in a message to British delegates how little attention revolutionary work in office employee unions received. Since capitalist states 'carry out their dictatorship through the machinery of government', subverting civil servants was therefore a priority, as was detailed information on the economic situation of certain staff.[66]

In September, the CPGB received an appeal from the International Propaganda Committee of Office and Clerical Workers. The Party was to compile and send information on

> the material situation and legal status of clerical workers and civil serv-
> ants of your country ... [and] also advise us on existing organisations
> of private and Government employees ... giving membership, political
> and industrial tendency, international affiliations, and exact name and
> address.[67]

Only six weeks later, Moscow created the Russo-British Fellowship of Intellectual Workers to appeal to 'all those interested in cooperation and mutual relationships between the two countries', bringing together Russian and British intelligentsia.[68] Despite this, nothing in official or private correspondence examined suggests undue concern by ministers. Alarmism was perhaps no longer as needed as when Lloyd George was in office. Now that a harsher line toward Moscow was Cabinet policy with the Conservatives anyway, by late 1923 the remaining diehards had turned their attention to the rise of the Labour Party.

In one of his last messages of the year to Moscow, Khristian Rakovsky worried about Labour ultimately being unsuccessful.[69] The Party's achievement in the 6 December 1923 election to form a small minority government transformed Britain's political landscape. The Conservatives won 258 seats on 38% of votes (5.5 million), versus Labour's 191 on 31% of votes (4.4 million) and the Liberals' 158 on 30% (4.3 million votes). The poll confirmed that Labour's success in becoming the official opposition the previous year had been no accident.

Yet before 1924 ended, Labour lost power rocked by a scandal that plunged Anglo-Russian relations to lows not seen since the 1918–20 Allied intervention. Moscow reacted cautiously to Ramsay MacDonald's rise from Labour leader to Prime Minister (and Foreign Secretary). On 3 January 1924, Georgi Chicherin urged the Politburo and the NKID to ensure Soviet media moderated its tone towards Labour.[70] This was sensible since it had recently agreed to accept communists as members.[71] The CPGB Political Bureau ordered Party members to seek Labour membership 'without ... ostentation' but this only lasted a week; on 21 December CPGB Chairman Arthur MacManus publicly stated Labour's decision 'now clears the way for the final struggle – the affiliation of the [CPGB], as a whole, to the Labour Party'.[72]

For some Bolsheviks, Labour's acceptance of communists meant nothing. Writing to Litvinov in early January, Rakovsky urged the NKID not to expect much from recent developments. MacDonald, he said, was an opportunist who would try to please The City and the Conservatives.[73] What worried the Soviet representative most was MacDonald's fickleness and vanity, given discussions with Labour MPs on whether to put before both Houses the issue of recognising the USSR. Rakovsky suspected the Lords would not and told Moscow to resolve debt repayment and asset restoration issues quickly, so MacDonald and The City willingly granted recognition.[74] Meanwhile, Rakovsky – the man whose 'great figure gives a delightful impression in England'[75] – pressed MacDonald's inner circle for a result favouring the Kremlin.

On 11 January, Rakovsky updated the Politburo on progress. Of special interest was a conversation with Frank Wise, who had resigned as Board of Trade Acting Assistant Secretary on 1 March 1923 and now advised *Tsentrsoyuz*.[76] Wise had met "X", persuading him recognition should be immediate and unconditional. "X" reportedly had agreed that during the first Parliamentary discussion of the matter, government would announce unconditional recognition but state Moscow would suggest creating an Anglo-Soviet Commission to resolve debt, credit, loan and political issues. In his speech, "X" would not mention having met Rakovsky to avoid suspicion about any arrangement. "X" also suggested Wise and Rakovsky co-write Britain's *de jure* recognition of the USSR. Despite having asked the two men not to mention his name in correspondence, Russian files show "X" was MacDonald. He and "X" were known to have written Rakovsky on 3 January but there is only one letter (MacDonald's).[77]

Little wonder that when firebrands like Comintern Head Grigori Y. Zinoviev spoke on British politics soon after Labour's electoral success, something had changed. Though broadly similar to previous speeches, Zinoviev's on MacDonald were 'quite moderate' and without the 'usual vocabulary'. This was to Chicherin 'quite symptomatic' even if issues like religion remained points of contention between the two governments.[78]

Although Labour's success had been a cataclysmic event for many, some still gave MacDonald the benefit of the doubt. Cabinet Secretary Hankey wrote his daughter Ursula he was busy with the new government, 'who make up in energy what they lack in experience. I like Ramsay MacDonald very much, and get on with him like a house on fire, though I do not promise to like all his measures'.[79] One was recognition of the USSR without serious Parliamentary discussion, a decision for which the Prime Minister gave two reasons. First, discussion would have also required consultation with allied nations, delaying a decision by months. Second, MacDonald wanted to present a result before the All-Russian Congress of Soviets[80] adjourned until further notice on 2 February. By giving recognition beforehand, he secured acceptance 'not merely by M. Chicherin and the [NKID], but also by ... representatives of the Soviets of all Russias, who had in fact sent a very cordial telegram of acceptance'.[81]

MacDonald broke with tradition over recognition – acting both as Prime Minister and Foreign Secretary allowed greater decisiveness – but said he wanted continuity on national security. At the 4 February meeting of the Committee of Imperial Defence (CID), he made clear defence had his attention. There would be 'no break in harmony which [*sic*] had previously existed' and 'old traditions of the Committee' would be maintained. The national interest remained a priority, he said, 'bearing in mind ... existing ... resources'.[82]

Beyond political rhetoric on both sides, resources were undoubtedly at the heart of Anglo-Soviet disputes; simply put, money was the main obstacle to full diplomatic recognition. MacDonald believed that so long as his Soviet policies were sensible and successful enough, neither the Liberals nor the Conservatives would topple Labour from power. Yet he also believed without 'serious loans and credits' Moscow would never recognise its debts and obligations. During a meeting with Rakovsky, MacDonald openly advocated this policy: the USSR should not commit to debt reparations until foreign creditors made sufficient funds available to Moscow. Rakovsky's contacts in Liberal and Labour circles confirmed that what drove Britain's push for normal ties was the need to improve bilateral trade.[83]

Not using this fact in discussions but, more importantly, not solving debt and claim issues quickly would be mistakes, he argued. Moscow also needed to ensure Anglo-Soviet talks on debts or claims stayed just that – bilateral. France, now also discussing reparations with the USSR, should not be allowed to participate. Rakovsky was well aware what was at stake: only in 'England will we be able to combine the solution of our debts with getting credits and loans'.[84] Despite all this, the Kremlin knew the honeymoon period with MacDonald would end; concrete results benefiting both sides were needed soon. By early March 1924, Moscow was already aware of his limitations and weaknesses, at home and abroad. Of special concern was that his decision to push Britain closer to the USSR was 'literally scaring the leaders of English foreign policy'. Jan Berzin wrote from London that his usual scepticism had already replaced the rose-coloured spectacles with which he had viewed Labour's election success.[85] Yet Moscow itself caused many of the problems MacDonald faced.

As part of the bilateral conference starting on 14 April,[86] he met Soviet delegates in London several times. In early May, MacDonald told them his initial decision to ignore anti-British attacks from Soviet officials and media was by now hard to defend. Remaining impassive was starting to affect public perceptions of his government; even close advisers now urged him to make a diplomatic protest, which would mean the end of negotiations. Soviet incitement of the CPGB to say publicly Labour was refusing Moscow requests especially upset MacDonald. The Kremlin, he raged, had better not use the tired old line that Comintern was to blame: 'I know ... the Third International gets all its money from the Soviet Government.'[87]

MacDonald's outburst had the intended effect. Rakovsky cabled the Politburo, Chicherin, Stalin, Krasin in Paris and Nikolai N. Krestinsky in Berlin:

[I]n our counter-offensive, we have crossed the line. All members of the Russian Delegation understand ... the campaign should be stopped if we want positive results from the negotiations. MacDonald is not going to stop the conference; this was just a threat. Still MacDonald himself may be taken away from power ... Zinoviev's idea that our negotiations with Conservatives would be more successful is wrong.... It is getting more ... likely that after MacDonald, Conservatives will come to power.... I repeat my request[:] Moscow should make some official declaration ... to improve the situation.[88]

Despite some normalisation of relations, Moscow's clandestine efforts to undermine British security and prestige had carried on. By mid-1924, Foreign Office correspondence highlighted the renewed intimidation of foreigners and citizens alike. On Soviet espionage: 'It seems ... intolerable ... our Mission should be exposed to this ... treatment while the Bolshevik Delegation here, which includes ... notorious evildoers, is feted and petted.'[89] On the Soviet secret police, now known as OGPU (see Glossary),

[I]nteresting tactic by OGPU ... to isolate Russians ... from the West and ... to isolate Westerners from Russians[:] ... arrest anyone who visited Western missions and especially anyone ... friends with ... diplomatic staff ... or even just acquainted. Result: Western legations stopped inviting Russians over, for fear of putting them at risk.[90]

On Moscow's refusals to share economic data with British officials to assist London in its ongoing negotiations, the view was so long as Soviet authorities 'regard the giving of information respecting the economic conditions inside their territories as the equivalent of high treason, a satisfactory solution would seem unattainable'.[91] And on seeing Russia repeat the mistakes of its tragic past:

> It is unfortunate that … to establish the new regime – the so-called dictatorship of the proletariat – the … Government should find itself compelled to adopt and extend on an unheard-of scale the most revolting expedients of dilation, espionage and administrative tyranny which disfigured the old regime.[92]

A central aspect of these expedients had been intelligence work in Britain, for which 1924 proved decisive. The Federated Press of America network had been active in some form since at least autumn 1919. Because MI5 informant Albert Allen only seemed to know parts of the organisation, the picture until 1924 is incomplete. Yet what he did reveal seemed consistently reliable, according to the Service. The part of the network consisting of Allen, Walter Dale and Rose Edwardes originally operated from an apartment at 51 Ridgmount Gardens, Bloomsbury, London, taken on at Nikolai Klyshko's instructions. In 1923, William Ewer visited Moscow, subsequently running his network under business cover. With help from Carl Haessler in New York, Ewer set to work in room 50, Outer Temple, 222–5 Strand, London, where operations ran smoothly until the May 1927 ARCOS raid (see Chapter 7).

In late 1924, the Federated Press finally caught MI5's attention, leading to developments examined in the final two chapters. One incident the group knew something about was the October 1924 Zinoviev Letter. This forgery, supposedly sent from Moscow to the CPGB Central Committee on 15 September, contained Comintern orders for the Party to prepare for revolution by subverting the military and enlisting Labour to the cause by any means. Appearing in the right-wing *Daily Mail* four days before the 29 October General Election, the letter gave Conservatives their long-sought opportunity to prove Labour did Moscow's bidding. Allen told MI5 the CPGB categorically reassured Ewer it never received the letter. Yet SIS stood its ground, claiming it was authentic and had a copy. Two or three days before the letter was published, Allen insisted, Dale had reported intense activity at SIS offices on Adam Street, leading up to low-key visits by 'three or four' very senior intelligence officials in private cars.[93] Recent research does identify greater involvement by select intelligence officials and diplomats, acting on their own, than formerly believed. The latest scholarship on the Zinoviev Letter concludes it was a forgery, even though the letter resembled in form and content others the Comintern had previously sent the CPGB.[94]

Yet how did Moscow react to the affair? Initially, and as with the 1923 Curzon Note, the worry was the letter was a prelude to renewed British intervention in Russia, or at least a naval blockade; the civil war had left vivid

7 From 1923 to 1927, William Ewer ran Soviet spy rings from the London office of the Federated Press of America, in Outer Temple (door on the left). These networks infiltrated various British and French government departments, including both Foreign Ministries.

memories. Though Soviet leaders were well aware of the impending election – the context for the letter – they still worried. Just as confusing to Moscow was MacDonald's spotlight on Comintern presence in Britain. Why, wrote Chicherin, would the Prime Minister 'run his own Party down'?[95] Another suspicion was "Perfidious Albion" had timed the letter's publication to de-rail French recognition of the USSR.[96] This was plausible in light of recent (and fruitless) Anglo-Soviet talks on loan and debt repayment. Were France to recognise the USSR now, this could trigger near-simultaneous settlements, making it less likely British claims would be addressed first and Moscow would have enough funds to pay them.[97]

Initially, some senior Soviet officials even believed MacDonald might have colluded with the Conservatives. Litvinov wrote to Rakovsky:

> At first we thought [the letter] was an election manoeuvre by MacDonald ... to show his independence from Moscow.... I reject ... MacDonald did not know ... Gregory sent the note. English officials are too disciplined for the sort of action.... If MacDonald knew about the document from the beginning, his responsibility for not preventing the scandal is strong. No matter the election results, we should insist ... the Labour Party carries out an investigation and takes action against ... MacDonald. In spite of our denials, the blow ... [of] the alleged letter ... to the Labour Party will be huge and irreparable.[98]

For a few days, the Politburo hesitated since the British refused to accept a Soviet note denying any involvement.[99] The refusal stemmed partly from the Cabinet appointment of a committee to establish the authenticity of the letter.[100]

Early Moscow suspicions about it fell on one 'Treibish-Lincoln'. Ignacz Timotheus Trebitsch, known in Britain as Ignatius Timothy Trebitsch-Lincoln or I. T. T. Lincoln,[101] was a conman and former Liberal MP. Chicherin believed he had recently been deported from Vienna and was in Riga at the time of the letter; this proved not to be the case. On 1 November, Chicherin told Litvinov 'we have information [the letter] is his creature', adding:

> You may remember that when the war started, there was a scandal in London: a Liberal Deputy, Trebich-Lincoln, who came from America to England and who was close to Asquith, turned out to be a German spy. This was used in a campaign against Asquith. It would be quite juicy if

the same Trebich-Lincoln were the author of the 'Zinoviev letter'. This affair should be investigated.... Comrade Radek could do this well.[102]

Given the unique surname and details listed, either there were two White forgers with the same name and life story operating in Europe or Soviet suspicions were misplaced. Subsequent investigations and evidence failed to tie Trebitsch-Lincoln to the Zinoviev letter.

The 29 October 1924 General Election saw Labour lose power to the Conservatives, now led by Stanley Baldwin. They gained 419 seats on 48% of votes (7.9 million), versus Labour's 151 on 33% (5.5 million) and the Liberals' 40 on 18% (2.9 million). The poll sealed the Liberals' fate for decades as a spent force in politics, largely due to mass voter defections to Labour and the Conservatives, and Labour's resolve to have sole control of the Left. Though Labour lost forty seats in October 1924, the Zinoviev Letter seems not to have affected the Party's popular vote, which actually increased by 1.1 million.[103] These gains were clearly at the Liberals' expense and due to Labour's concentration of support among the working classes.[104]

Khristian Rakovsky, however, cautioned that in Britain generally but mainly under the Conservatives, the 'real power is the City'.[105] Business was delighted with recent results and this letter to Baldwin was representative of many sent to recently elected Conservatives:

> Dear Sir ... on behalf of the Association of British Creditors of Russia [ABCR] ... our hearty congratulations on your great victory.... We feel confident that the restoration of the Government of this country to the Conservative Party under your leadership, will mean that British interests all over the world will receive due protection, and the members of our Association ... whose interests were woefully neglected in the recently signed [Anglo-Soviet] treaties, especially welcome your return.[106]

Despite changes in government and London's hardening stance toward Moscow,[107] the Soviets still wondered if the letter was forged. Chicherin, for one, could not understand why Moscow did not publicise Zinoviev's reported presence in the Caucasus when he had supposedly signed the letter in the capital.[108] Nevertheless, despite their reactions to the affair alternating between outrage and disbelief, in some ways the Bolsheviks responded predictably. If Britain wanted to rage on about foreign meddling in domestic affairs, then two could play that game. Rakovsky, for one, spoke plainly, saying 'your neighbours[109] have ... facts relating to the activities of Hodgson. (?Fel)ix

> **NOTICE**
> SECRET SERVICE.—Labour Group
> carrying out investigation would be
> glad to receive information and details
> from anyone who has ever had any asso-
> ciation with, or been brought into
> touch with, any Secret Service Depart-
> ment or operation.—Write in first in-
> stance Box 573, DAILY HERALD.

8 Advert placed by the Federated Press of America in the *Daily Herald* in 1924 to draw out a man suspected of trying to infiltrate British communist circles. The notice ended up drawing the authorities' attention to William Ewer's work for Soviet intelligence.

[Dzerzhinsky] even promised ... me ... facts that can be communicated even to the British Government.'[110]

At the heart of all this was, of course, the perception of subversion versus its reality. The Kremlin maintained that while Comintern was indeed a Moscow-based propaganda organ, it was independent from government (which London knew was untrue). In private correspondence with the Polit-buro and the NKID, Litvinov was firm: 'anyone who is going to deal with us should be reconciled that Comintern is located here. The price does not exist that the bourgeoisie could pay us for the Comintern.'[111] However, Chicherin urged pragmatism in handling the Conservatives, with 'serious and respon-sible, but not provocative' responses to any British notes.[112]

As part of this conciliatory approach, on 11 December the Politburo agreed to grant 'safety and impunity' to a source who had allegedly given information on the Zinoviev Letter.[113] NKID documents only identify the source as "M", the chief of an unspecified secret department and Comintern member who vanished from Moscow in early October with classified material. Soviet intel-ligence reportedly tried to seize "M" in Berlin but he escaped to London where he contacted hardliners. "M" had allegedly surrendered his secret archive to be published in due course – shades of Mitrokhin seven decades later.[114]

If the British Government were trying to cover up either its ignorance about the letter's origins or the "source's" identity (to play on Soviet paranoia and encourage destructive spy hunts in Moscow), Bolshevik officials were willing to call London's bluff:

In view of the statement made yesterday in the House of Commons by the Minister of [illegible] ... that he could not give any proofs [*sic*] regarding the authenticity of the letter for fear of endangering the safety of the informer, I think a great effect would be produced if Moscow were to state that in the interests of establishing the truth we would guarantee the safe departure of the informers.[115]

Yet support was not universal: the OGPU strongly argued the precedent set would 'encourage foreign spies', with Soviet citizens rushing 'into the British Embassy ... to become ... agents'.[116]

Ironically, as OGPU worried about Soviets becoming British agents, British OGPU sources sought to shake off MI5. On 21 November, the *Daily Herald* had carried this advert:

NOTICE – SECRET SERVICE. – Labour Group carrying out investigation would be glad to receive information and details from anyone who has ever had any association with, or been brought into touch with, any Secret Service Department or operation. – Write in first instance Box 573, DAILY HERALD.

MI5 had instructed one of its staff to answer and attend any meeting, and while nobody met him the first time, Walter Dale – responsible for Federated Press security – constantly watched. William Ewer later met the MI5 man several times, seeking classified information on intelligence agencies. Dale followed the man, eventually uncovering his ties to MI5. Leaving aside for a moment why the Federated Press risked ongoing intelligence work by drawing attention to itself this way, it seems the advert originally aimed to expose an informant (possibly the same man) whose previous efforts to infiltrate CPGB circles had aroused suspicion. The Federated Press promptly terminated all contact.[117]

This chapter highlighted how the misuse and abuse of intelligence, by both government and a group acting independently, set dangerous precedents. That Lord Curzon cited Soviet intercepts verbatim in a diplomatic note to Moscow – the first Foreign Secretary to misuse SIGINT so deliberately – is unusual enough. That unelected officials presumed to know what was best for Britain and attempted to topple a democratically elected government through forgery is something altogether different. The hardliners' twin aims of triggering a rupture with Moscow and ejecting Labour from power seemingly justified almost any means.

On the Soviet side, two broad trends persisted. One was how rivalries in

NKID continued to complicate relations with London. The other development was the ever-clearer duality of the Bolsheviks. They paid lip service to traditional "bourgeois" diplomacy if it brought benefits, but relied on security and intelligence organs to implement policy abroad and tighten the Party's grip at home. Soviet intelligence continued targeting its British counterparts, as well as Whitehall and intellectuals across society. Warnings seem not to have registered with a Conservative Cabinet fixed on a greater political calculus: how to limit, if not reverse, Labour's electoral gains.

If the December 1923 election were a watershed giving Labour its first taste of power, the October 1924 one was arguably even more important: it ended the fluidity of the previous two years in politics, giving the Conservatives five years in office. Even that old renegade Liberal, Winston Churchill, was back in the fold as Chancellor of the Exchequer.[118] The 1924 election and the ensuing peaceful handover of power eased fears of revolution. Yet Labour's choice of the Parliamentary route did not prevent lapses in Ramsay MacDonald's judgement. Suggesting that a Soviet representative co-author Britain's recognition of his country – one overtly and covertly undermining British institutions and interests worldwide – was surely a step too far.

Nevertheless, what fundamentally continued to dictate the course of bilateral relations were economic and financial considerations. These were not as binding for the Conservatives as they had been for postwar Coalition and Labour Cabinets. By 1924, British exports to the USSR had dwindled to under 0.5% of the annual total, so tolerating subversion at home and across the Empire for so little return strengthened the Conservatives' desire for a breach. Europe's sluggish postwar recovery also hit Britain hard. With the Baldwin Cabinet increasingly unable to meet growing demands by both workers and employers, the result was the largest work stoppage in British interwar history: the May 1926 General Strike.

CHAPTER 6

The Strike

Trilby's People ~ The General Strike ~ ARCOS Condemned

> Dobb is anxious to visit Russia ... but ... wants Rothstein to
> help him get there.   MI5 comment on Maurice Dobb letter
> to Andrew Rothstein[1]

> From a British point of view ... the scope of any ... activities
> in which the [Ewer] group may be concerned is of primary
> importance.   MI5 minute on the Federated Press network[2]

> [P]oet ... or politician, the mind of the Russian instinctively
> seeks the twilight that borders on the subconscious. It is
> feline in its discrimination of inner shades, and almost
> unerring in its analysis of individuals.   Anonymous[3]

"**C**"– Hugh Sinclair since June 1923 – felt the 'British Secret Service ... was fundamentally wrong.' Five agencies (GCCS, Indian Political Intelligence, MI5, SIS and Special Branch) operated without 'a central control of policy' and lacked 'coordination and cooperation', resulting in 'overlapping and waste of time'. Though "C" was pursuing the self-serving goal of controlling the entire community, he had valid concerns. For these reasons, Prime Minister Stanley Baldwin reconvened the Secret Service Committee on 10 February 1925 to redress the situation.[4]

Two related issues were at the heart of the Zinoviev affair. First, would a Conservative Cabinet be either willing or able to distinguish between legitimate left-wing opposition and calculated subversion by foreign states? Second, even if government could always make this distinction (which it could not), might hardliners not still attempt to lump both issues together in the name of national security and national interest? Chancellor of the Exchequer Churchill, for instance, had little time for distinctions:

> There is no fundamental difference between the "moderate" Labour men
> and the Communists: the managers and leaders of the Trades Unions

are now nearly all of them Socialists and the "moderate" Socialists are aiming, in effect, at the same things as the Communists: the only difference is their method of procedure. ... The most dangerous position is when a "moderate" party by so-called constitutional methods soothes public opinion while stealthily and with smooth words it proceeds step by step to revolution.[5]

This chapter examines the run-up to and aftermath of the May 1926 General Strike, the closest interwar Britain came to revolution. While British intelligence played a central role, this section concentrates on Soviet involvement in, perceptions of and reactions to the crisis. The chapter also examines Moscow's parallel campaign of covert subversion, specifically the infiltration of British policy and intelligence circles. However, government understanding of the Federated Press network improved in 1925–26. One line of inquiry focused on Andrew Rothstein, the British communist who may have enabled a considerable intelligence success for Moscow in the 1920s. He certainly did not miss the mark in the 1930s by talent-spotting and grooming Melita Norwood,[6] a long-serving British agent for Soviet intelligence.

How could hardliners in a Conservative Cabinet reconcile their distaste for Communism with the need to reduce British unemployment by increasing trade? For if the Government would (or could) not take action, others might. By April 1925, many British businessmen (mainly those with previous Russian investments) were keen to start private talks with Moscow. The Board of Trade President, Sir Philip Cunliffe-Lister, restated the official position: new ideas to promote trade were always welcome but British businesses were not to 'encourage any idea of political concessions' by London.[7]

For many now in office, Russia had long been, was now and would remain for some time the prime threat to British interests. One of Moscow's harshest opponents in Cabinet was Home Secretary Sir William Joynson-Hicks (or "Jix"). Much like Churchill, Curzon, Hall, Long, Sinclair, Thomson and others, Jix had no trouble using and misusing intelligence to expose CPGB and Soviet covert work.[8] As historian Gill Bennett has written,[9] boundaries between the private and public sectors in Britain were rarely clear[10] – something the Zinoviev affair again demonstrated. Even more telling was some grandees' open work in far-right groups (see Chapter 2). Paradoxically, while some private citizens acted publicly when government could or would not improve trade with Moscow, where national security was concerned, some public officials acted privately when government could or would not tackle subversion.

In this sense, 1925 was significant: far-right attacks on communists reached such levels that Special Branch reports to Cabinet covered them for the first time in detail.[11] Of the six Home Secretaries in the period covered in this book, Jix was the boldest advocate of using fascist groups to roll back Communism and ensure continuity during industrial unrest:

There exist the Fascists, the Crusaders and the Organisation for the Supply of Material Services [sic]. One need not say anything about the first two – they are well known, and, I think, to be depended upon. I have seen their leaders several times. The third organisation is being run by Lord Hardinge ... Lord Jellicoe, Colonel [John] Gretton, Sir Francis Lloyd and others. It is forming committees in every London Borough and enrolled, for instance, 1700 men in Hampstead in [two days].[12]

Behind this was the Home Secretary's recognition the intelligence community was struggling with the challenge of communist subversion:

The question of the prosecution of Communist leaders, speakers and writers is becoming a burning one. The old Conservative Party is getting very angry that nothing has been done, but after consultation with the Attorney-General [sic] I have decided against it for the moment. This ... raises the question of the efficiency of the Secret Service. My views are fairly well known as to its inefficiency, but I feel I can do nothing until the ... [Secret Service Committee] appointed by the [Prime Minister] reports. It is essentially urgent that this committee should report without delay in order that a reorganisation of the whole thing, if it so desired, should be carried out before the trouble is likely to arise.[13]

The Foreign Secretary felt the best way to deal with Moscow was to be indifferent. What most irritated the Soviets was to be 'treated in international relations as if they didn't exist' but Austen Chamberlain cautioned Cabinet that Bolshevik activities in Britain should be watched.[14] They were – just not well enough. Writing in July 1925 to Nevile Bland, Secret Service Committee Secretary, Vernon Kell pleaded for more operational funds for FY 1925/6. Otherwise, MI5 could not 'do anything other than touch the fringe of our responsibility'.[15]

In addition to counter-intelligence and counter-espionage, MI5 at this time also dealt with subversion in the armed forces; Special Branch had similar responsibilities in the civilian world. One intriguing aspect of British perceptions of Soviet subversion was just how vague a concept it was, legally and politically, during the twelve years this book covers. Though the Home Office had a working definition of sedition – 'to cause ill-will between the different classes of the King's Subjects'[16] – there was never a universal definition of subversion. As late as February 1927, three months before a breach, Sir Robert Hodgson pointed out in a memorandum from Moscow that Britain had never provided a definition.[17]

Subversion and sedition are not the same. More than just semantics,[18] this was an often-ignored distinction with important judicial and political implications. While sedition generally has a connotation with collective action, the undertone with subversion more often relates to an individual's thoughts or ideas. Subversion is therefore an indispensable precursor to sedition. The earliest recorded reference to State concern with subversion was in 1324 during the turbulent reign of Edward II, who for ten years had been challenged over patronage and choice of confidants (first by the nobility, then his estranged French wife Isabella). Until captured in 1326 by Anglo-French forces loyal to her, Edward and his supporters were constantly on guard against plots originating from across the Channel.[19] The Magna Carta protected merchants' right of movement but not their communications, so English port authorities were instructed to send any intercepted letters to the King 'with the utmost speed'.[20]

State perceptions of subversion became more ideological in Tudor England. In 1534 Parliament ratified the Act of Supremacy signalling the break between Henry VIII and the Papacy, declaring him Supreme Head of the Church and emboldening the English Reformation. Subsequent legislation and edicts described Catholic practices as subversive.[21] Protestant fears peaked during the reign of Elizabeth I. She, and perhaps English Protestantism, survived only because of Sir Francis Walsingham. At the heart of the Court from 1568 to 1590, this devoted Crown Servant laid down the foundations of systematic domestic- and foreign-intelligence gathering. This enabled Elizabeth to overcome the existential threat of Catholic subversion.[22]

In the sixteenth century, the printed word became the vehicle for mass circulation of new (some might say subversive) ideas. By translating the Gospels from Greek, Hebrew and Latin into the vernacular and mass reproducing them, dissenters shifted the balance of power away from clergy toward ordinary people. The effects, later compounded by the French Revolution, are still felt. '*Liberté, égalité, fraternité*' – a simple idea come alive on paper – ultimately toppled a monarchy, the cornerstone of European political power in 1789.[23] This watershed understandably worried British statesmen[24] and criminalising "dangerous" ideas to preserve established political processes gradually became the norm. Seditious publications predictably remained the political activities legal professionals most frequently condemned as subversive.[25]

Bolshevik Russia, and subsequently the USSR, posed complex ideological and security challenges to British governments. Curiously, subversion remained publicly undefined until 26 February 1975 – nearly 650 years after the reign of Edward II. Subversive activities in Britain are generally those threatening 'the safety or well-being of the State, and which are intended to undermine or overthrow Parliamentary democracy by political, industrial or violent means'.[26] Crucially, this definition contains 'no "legality" criterion' so 'neither violence nor unlawfulness' is now a necessary element of subversion.[27] Still, not even the 1975 interpretation changed the centuries-old reality that the concept of subversion does not exist in English constitutional law. Except to justify creating specific criminal offences, British governments have neither given subversion 'precise meaning' nor 'admitted using it ... as a basis for investigating' or suppressing political views.[28] Keeping the definition vague has also maximised the scope of allowable activity within (and sometimes outside) security and intelligence mandates.[29]

The Soviets had not one but two definitions. From a foreign intelligence perspective, subversive activity (*podryvnaya deyatelnost*) was conducted by the intelligence or other agencies 'of the adversary by clandestine means and methods, with the object of causing political, economic, military, scientific and technical or moral damage to another State'. From a counter-intelligence perspective, however, subversive activity (*deyatelnost podryvnaya*) was

[a] form of political warfare conducted by Capitalist States, their intelligence and other special services, bourgeois parties, subversive propaganda centres, anti-Soviet organisations abroad, and hostile elements within the country. Its aim is to subvert or weaken the firm foundations underlying the Soviet Union and other Socialist States, Communist and Workers' Parties, and the national liberation movement by organising and undertaking covert political, ideological, economic, military, intelligence and other subversive operations. The main target of Imperialist States struggling against Socialism is the political, military, economic, moral, scientific and technical potential of the USSR, and the unity of the Socialist States.[30]

These definitions were as open-ended as their briefer British equivalent. All three, however, revealed both what each government feared most and how it envisioned overcoming the other.

By late 1925, Stanley Baldwin struggled to balance defending national interests and institutions, and tackling subversion aimed at worsening an already tense industrial situation. A note by Attorney General Sir Douglas Hogg showed the difficulties inherent in such a balancing act, the convoluted legal language reflecting the complexity of the challenge:

> [T]he definition of sedition generally given to a jury is 'an intention to bring into hatred or contempt, or to excite disaffection against the person of [His Majesty], his Heirs or Successors, or the Government and Constitution of the United Kingdom, as by law established or either House of Parliament, or the administration of justice, or to excite [His Majesty's] Subjects to attempt otherwise than by lawful means, the alteration of any matter in Church or State by law established, or to incite any person to commit any crime in disturbance of the peace, or to raise discontent or disaffection amongst [His Majesty's] Subjects, or to promote ill-will and hostility between different classes of ... Subjects.'[31]

However, a follow-on statement was even more disconcerting:

> *Provided he abstains from these offences* [above] there is nothing to prevent a Communist from stirring up discontent or giving vent to the most revolutionary sentiments; it is to be observed that much of this law is archaic ... it is not easy to decide with precision whether any particular language does or does not amount to sedition and that the necessity of a jury trial involves very considerable delay before a conviction can be obtained ... it is essential to avoid ... undue interference with the freedom of speech.... *I should like to render illegal any strike ... directed against the State and not against the employers,* but so far I have not been able to frame a satisfactory form of words [that] would not unduly limit and interfere with industrial disputes.[32] [my italics]

As 1925 progressed, growing labour unrest played into Jix and other Cabinet diehards' suspicions Moscow was to blame. The so-called "Red Friday", 31 July 1925, had been of special concern: after unions threatened an industry-wide strike, government agreed to subsidise coal miners' wages to stabilise them.[33] The far-right groups Jix and others were involved with had already formed the backbone of the Supply and Transport Organisation (STO), the strikebreaking body working nationwide during the 1926 General Strike.[34]

Rising labour unrest matched reported increases of subversion in the armed forces. Authorities worried about communist efforts between July and September 1925 to enlist and incite unrest. Vernon Kell felt this ulti-mately aimed to undermine government trust in the military should it be called on to subdue civil strife. He thus argued for a decisive blow against the CPGB to reduce its influence in unions and stop subversion in the military.[35] On 13 October Attorney General Hogg stated sufficient evidence existed to arrest and charge leading communists with sedition. Cabinet agreed and the following day Special Branch raided CPGB headquarters at 16 King Street, Covent Garden, London.[36] Twelve communist leaders went on trial in mid-November and found guilty. Five received one-year prison sentences (they had previous criminal records) while the remainder received six-month terms.[37]

At the time, MI5 also monitored the communist and suspected Soviet source Clare Sheridan (see Chapter 2). She was close to William Ewer and George Slocombe of the Federated Press, and reportedly a former lover of Slocombe (who was married to Maria, sister of Fanny Karlinsky, an Anglo-Russian cipher clerk at ARCOS in the 1920s).[38] MI5 suspected Sheridan for her close ties to the Federated Press and receiving correspondence via the Soviet diplomatic bag.[39] Security officials worried about the group's reach even more after intercepting a letter from Ewer to Slocombe dated 20 November 1925, mentioning Sheridan had passed on details of conversations with a Cabinet minister.[40] In late 1922, MI5 had assessed

> This lady, who is well connected and has influential friends and relatives in this country, is most indiscreet, and it is probable ... anything ... told her in confidence will, sooner or later, appear, probably in a distorted version, in the American Press. She is not to be trusted, as her desire to figure in the limelight will outweigh any other consideration.[41]

Sheridan's influential relative was her cousin, Chancellor of the Exchequer Winston Churchill. David Stafford has given an absorbing account of Sheri-dan's involvement with Communism in *Churchill & Secret Service*.[42] The Chancellor was aware of British intelligence efforts in 1920–21 to penetrate Bolshevik activities in Britain and Russia using the unwitting Sheridan.[43] Despite renewed concerns about her in 1925, one could reasonably assume Churchill may still have been deliberately misleading her at this late date.

Yet by late 1925, the Federated Press was itself under growing scrutiny. Authorities had shadowed Walter Dale, leading them to Rose Edwardes, who in turn led MI5 to the group's London office on the Strand. In early February 1925, the Home Office had imposed a mail intercept warrant on the address.

9 George Slocombe, the *Daily Herald* (and William Ewer's) man in France. He handled intelligence from sources inside several French embassies and the Foreign Ministry, and helped launder Soviet funds used to support British organisations like the CPGB.

On the eleventh of that month a package arrived for "Kenneth Milton, Esq." (Ewer), containing reports typed in French on Moroccan, Bulgarian, Serbian and Romanian affairs. Telephone contracts revealed Ewer ran the office with Albert Allen's help. Telephone intercepts outlined Federated Press dealings with ARCOS, ROSTA, the Soviet Embassy (Chesham House, Belgrave Square) and the Vigilance Detective Agency.[44] Contact alone did not imply wrongdoing, obviously. As a leftist news agency, the Federated Press would have been expected to have professional ties to the first three institutions. The detective agency, however, was harder to explain; it watched members of ARCOS, related organisations and certain embassies in London; shadowed some CPGB members; and did likewise to suspected and known British intelligence personnel.[45] Moscow received all this information.

Packets to "Milton" from unknown senders in Paris arrived almost daily, containing at least one of four document types: copies of French ambassadorial dispatches from various capitals; confidential information on French politics and finances; unsigned typewritten letters accompanying English plain-language codes; and occasional messages from either Indian revolutionary Manabendra Nath Roy or his wife to comrades in Britain. An error by Ewer on 8 May 1925, however, exposed his main sub-agent in Paris. That day, the *Daily Herald* carried an article on French Morocco 'from our own correspondent, George Slocombe' that was virtually a reprint of an intercepted note to "Milton" two days earlier. Slocombe was the *Herald's* Foreign Correspondent and Federated Press representative in Paris. The Home Office issued another postal warrant, this time for his private and business[46] addresses.

Coded letters in plain language signed "T" ("Trilby" was Ewer's nickname) were soon intercepted. Correspondence analysis showed Slocombe received about £210 monthly (2011: £9800) from Ewer, spending over a third of that on bribes for copies of classified documents from the French Foreign Ministry and several of its embassies. British authorities deduced from postal intercepts Ewer frequently sent Slocombe Soviet evaluations of intelligence acquired from French government sources; unfortunately, no such assessments survive in MI5 files made public. By October 1925, letters hinted at circumventing the Federated Press in London and sending everything directly to Moscow. This was due to the impending arrival in Paris of a Bolshevik to run Slocombe, who was unhappy with the change. Between December 1925 and March 1927, Outer Temple stopped receiving post for "Milton".[47] British authorities believed Leonid Krasin, by 1925 Soviet Ambassador to France, seemed unaware of Federated Press activity. The idea to send French material straight to Moscow, bypassing London, coincided with the October–November 1925 reassignment to Paris of Khristian Rakovsky to replace Krasin. This suggests that up to his transfer, Rakovsky (or one of his private office staff) oversaw and/or financed the Federated Press in London, and would now do likewise from across the Channel.[48]

In Britain, meanwhile, investigations continued into activities at Outer Temple though with difficulty since Vigilance Agency detectives constantly monitored MI5 watchers. Details obtained in 1928 (corroborated by Walter Dale's diary, seized the following year) confirmed that from 1922 to 1927 Albert Allen was a cut-out between Ewer and his two prize sources. They had revealed locations of British intelligence offices, allowing Vigilance to watch and follow staff.[49] Dale's diary highlighted four areas of responsibility:

- observe 'offices of ... British intelligence ... the staffs ... and ... persons with whom staff ... were in contact';
- observe 'Russians resident in this country ... looked upon with suspicion by [Moscow]';
- investigate 'prominent political or social personages about whom the Soviet Government required information'; and
- ensure 'Ewer and other persons ... were not observed or shadowed by MI5 or the police.'

In the eight years his diary covered, Dale and other Vigilance detectives watched buildings and employees of GCCS, MI5, Special Branch and SIS, among others. They followed official cars and made great efforts to locate homes of intelligence officers and secretarial staff. This was possibly how Ewer's group in 1923 identified a Mrs Moon, an SIS secretary who Rose Edwardes then approached.[50] The recruitment attempt failed but the episode illustrates Soviet tradecraft for handling potential sources with access to information the OGPU and the Kremlin wanted.

In a classic example of "false flag" recruitment, Edwardes posed as an American agent and sounded out Moon, who worked in SIS headquarters. They met at least three times and though Edwardes offered £5 a week (2011: nearly £235) plus bonuses for especially valuable intelligence, she ultimately failed to persuade the nervous secretary. Still, the Government acknowledged Moon made significant disclosures about SIS to Edwardes. And though the secretary reported the contact in June 1923, she hesitated in providing enough detail[51] to allow MI5 to track down Edwardes. Allen added that aside from SIS headquarters at Melbury Road in Kensington, Vigilance detectives watched SIS offices on Adam Street and Broadway Buildings, 54 Broadway, London (which from spring 1926 housed both SIS and GCCS). On Soviet instructions, the Federated Press paid special attention to the London headquarters of the Passport Control Organisation on Victoria Street,[52] the main establishment providing official cover for SIS officers abroad.

Ewer quickly realised British counter-intelligence relied primarily on telephone and postal intercepts. Learning of an MI5 Photostat section in the Post Office copying suspicious correspondence, the Federated Press soon found a way in. Oddly, the group only seems to have realised Vernon Kell headed MI5 – 'the organisation at Cromwell Road' – when 'a longish paragraph in the *News of the World* on 6 April 1924' announced his army retirement. Suspicious of this 'official obituary', the group located Kell's residence (67 Evelyn Gardens, London SW7),[53] kept watch and confirmed his regular trips to Oliver House, 35 Cromwell Road,[54] less than a mile away. Tracking British intelligence agencies in and around London was easy. Not only did Vigilance detectives shadow employees, messengers and official cars effectively but early on, Ewer's most valuable sources also gave him key addresses and names, highlighting further vulnerabilities in British security. As early as January 1920, for example, the sources had already provided information on IPI, years before the agency's name even appeared in print.[55]

The network burrowed elsewhere. A female typist in Naval Intelligence spied for Ewer for several months until the Admiralty dismissed her, reportedly due to personnel cuts. Allen also insisted the group had employed from 1927 on an Indian named Karandikar, who for £10 a week provided information gained from two women at the India and Colonial Offices. MI5 never identified them but according to Allen, Moscow considered their information 'extraordinarily good' since it included details on British troop movements along the Northwest Frontier.[56]

Likewise, the group infiltrated the Foreign Office. When lunching with aides and journalists, Sir Arthur Willert[57] often discussed confidential matters noted by a subordinate. MI5 never identified this "mole" – likely sub-source "F", mentioned in the literature; in London *rezidentura* files, Ewer also listed Don Gregory of the Northern Department and Willert as contacts.[58] To the *Cheka* INO, the biggest weakness in diplomatic coverage by Ewer and his sub-sources was the lack of original documents for verification. Still, reporting was always timely. The 1927 assessment of London operations (see Chapter 2) cited two instances when the *rezidentura* learned of British policy changes on China a month before other stations did (and in one case, a month before any public announcement).[59]

Yet Soviet intelligence may have had earlier and better knowledge of its British counterparts than previously thought. Though published British intelligence records contain no ironclad proof, circumstantial evidence suggests a future reassessment may be sensible. In March 1926, MI5 and SIS concluded a six-year joint investigation into the Lunns, an English family with long-standing ties to Russia. According to a passport application form, Michael Lunn was born on 17 March 1820 in Slaithwaite,[60] West Yorkshire. A spinner by trade, he left for Russia in or about 1845, settling down in Balashikha,[61] fifteen miles east of Moscow. Records exist of another Michael Lunn, likely a son, born in Moscow around 1852. MI5 files put his birth at March 1855 but research suggests it was Edwin Lunn (almost certainly Michael's brother) who was born in Moscow that year. A calico printer by trade, Michael Lunn (Jr) fathered three boys and four girls. The girls are the most relevant here.[62]

Edith was born in Balashikha on 21 March 1887, Lucy in Moscow on

27 December 1891, Helen in Balashikha on 12 August 1895 and Margaret in Moscow on 25 July 1898. A letter of introduction written for Margaret in 1920 (see below) suggested the Lunns lost their possessions and assets during the October Revolution, the inference being therefore the family returned to Britain soon after. Michael Lunn (Sr) only appears in the 1841 Census although Michael Jr appears in those for 1871 and 1901. Oddly, however, neither of them nor any girl shows up in British immigration and travel records.[63]

Little is known about Lucy Lunn. In November 1925, she was listed as having worked as a secretary in the SIS Near East Section since 1919. She lived with her parents in Battersea[64] and in July 1921 travelled on Service business to Constantinople, where she often worked.[65] Not much more is known about the second sister, Helen Lunn. In September 1918, she was due to take up a lectureship at Bordeaux University, France. She subsequently joined GCCS, which appointed her a permanent 'Lady Translator' effective 17 December 1919 (see also Chapter 2). By late March 1921, Helen was also thought to live in Battersea[66] and in August 1925 was still at GCCS,[67] where she had a long career. From 1939 on, as a Foreign Office civilian and part of the second wave of staff billeted at Bletchley Park, she worked at Elmers School[68] and the Diplomatic Section (various locations during the war).[69]

The third sister, Margaret Lunn, briefly worked as an SIS secretary in Helsinki in 1919 before dismissal for suspected espionage, based on communist sympathies and ties to unnamed Bolshevik agents. Neither SIS nor MI5 could account for her subsequent movements, employment or whereabouts. In time, she contacted George Lansbury, *Daily Herald* Editor, about her desire to work for Moscow. In November 1920 he wrote to Deputy Representative in London, Nikolai Klyshko, endorsing her. Yet GCCS somehow took her on as a 'Lady Translator', formally appointed on 1 July 1921. By early 1926, she lived with her parents and was on good terms with her family, occasionally receiving letters from a Russian at ARCOS.[70]

This left Edith (also known as Ethel) Lunn. She worked as a Comintern secretary in 1919; given her work for Moscow, contact with British intelligence (not least through her sisters) and CPGB membership, Edith was predictably suspected of espionage. In 1921, she listed 85 York Mansions as her residence but by 1923 again lived with her parents. By at least March 1921 she already worked at ARCOS and became close to Andrew Rothstein. This professional relationship blossomed into a personal one; in late October 1925, SIS reported the couple had 'been masquerading about the country' as husband and wife ('Mr. and Mrs. Lunn'). That summer, Edith's father had thrown her out of the family home due to her political views and quite likely the courtship, so she moved to 'the Bolshevik colony at Hampstead'.[71] By January 1926, Edith was again on good terms with her family despite her parents' anti-Bolshevism,[72] and finally married Rothstein in Hampstead that September.[73]

As the MI5–SIS investigation ended in 1926, one assessment was:

> correspondence ... doesn't appear to suggest that Edith ... knows anything regarding the present employment of ... Helen ... or ... Lucy ... but I cannot for a moment suggest that I consider that this is evidence ... she doesn't know anything of their work.[74]

While "C" found both 'Lunn girls ... employed under SIS' (Lucy and Helen) to be 'quite sound from a security standpoint',[75] some disconcerting facts are nevertheless inescapable – particularly since Sinclair did not even mention Margaret Lunn.

From 1919 until at least 1925, three of the four sisters at some point worked in SIS and/or GCCS. One of the three (Margaret) was a communist sympathiser who sought work with the Bolsheviks after SIS dismissed her, yet somehow ended up as a translator at the School.[76] The fourth sister (Edith) was openly communist, worked for Comintern and ARCOS, and married Andrew Rothstein. A 'Communist of the purest water',[77] he also oversaw Comintern work in Britain from 1923.[78] Having married Edith in late 1926, this Soviet agent now likely had greater access to three sisters-in-law who either still or had once worked in intelligence.[79] Finally, at least three sisters (Lucy, Margaret and Edith) lived at 67 York Mansions, and all four were in touch from 1919 to at least 1925.

Given the above, it would defy common sense Moscow did not glean any useful information on GCCS and SIS from the Lunns in those six years. In a best-case scenario, this would require simple inference by Edith from any domestic gossip on office locations and daily routines, staff personalities and vulnerabilities, biographical and financial details, family situation and job satisfaction, among others. A worst-case scenario would mean Margaret reporting fully on her SIS and GCCS work, and she and Edith passing on any information gleaned from Lucy and Helen. Either way, Soviet counter-intelligence would have welcomed any such detail to disrupt, recruit or compromise. In 1925, for example, Lucy – an SIS employee – was in debt.[80]

Any such knowledge could also help explain how the Federated Press singled out SIS secretary Mrs Moon for attempted recruitment in 1923, not to mention shadowing intelligence officers, clerical staff, and the offices and vehicles of various agencies over time. Then, of course, there were the Soviet SIGINT

10 Russian-born Edith Lunn worked for the Comintern, later marrying key Bolshevik agent Andrew Rothstein. Three, possibly four, of her siblings worked in GCCS and/or SIS, raising questions over how much (and how early) Moscow may have learned about their work.

successes in the early 1920s, mentioned earlier, facilitated by HUMINT. These (admittedly circumstantial) leads may sound implausible to Western readers. Yet although Operations TREST (Trust, 1921–26) and SINDIKAT (Syndicate, 1922–24)[81] consumed most KRO time and manpower,[82] it is worth remembering the scale of Russian intelligence work historically, and never underestimating the human and financial resources the State devoted to its special services (and still does).

By 1926, the realities of Anglo-Soviet relations were painfully obvious. The British economy remained stagnant and London needed trade – any trade –

to reduce unemployment, which that year neared 10%.[83] Stagnation persisted due to over-reliance on and investment in outdated staple industries like coal, cotton, iron and steel; foreign dumping in international markets at prices lower than British producers set; government's inability to reform and modernise key economic sectors; and the practice started in wartime of linking wages to the cost of living. Furthermore, Churchill's April 1925 decision to return Britain to the gold standard at an overvalued pre-war rate of £1 to $4.86 made export costs 20% higher than they needed to be. Interest rates were also higher than in the rest of the world in order to support this exchange rate and, to top it off, Britain still maintained its traditional policy of free trade on most goods when the rest of the world used high tariffs to keep out imports. Goods were too highly priced from the outset, making them even less competitive exports.[84] In this context, in January 1926 the Conservatives reversed one of their first decisions after ousting Labour from office in late 1924. Backed by the Board of Trade and the Joint Chiefs of Staff, Cabinet approved the sale of 'small coastal defence vessels and submarine mines' by Vickers Ltd to the USSR.[85]

A precarious economy and labour market had contributed to declining trade union membership yet the CPGB's peaked between 1920 and 1929.[86] With growing labour unrest blamed largely on Soviet subversion, British far-right organisations also prospered.[87] These groups first fragmented and then consolidated. By April 1926, a main beneficiary was the Organisation for the Maintenance of Supplies (OMS). Many of its "best" and keenest members had recently joined from similar (but by now extinct) groups.[88] The OMS was one of several entities enabling the Supply and Transport Organisation, and ultimately government, to prevail during the General Strike.

This event had been nearly a year in the making. Factors outlined above forced Cabinet by early 1925 to consider total subsidy cuts to the coal sector, an unsheltered industry. Postwar British coal exports struggled because Polish and German mines had neared pre-war production levels at lower prices;[89] the situation only worsened once Britain returned to the gold standard. Mine owners wanted wages cut so mines remained competitive. As miners vowed to strike, on 31 July 1925 government announced a wage subsidy for nine months and a Royal Commission led by former Palestine High Commissioner Sir Herbert Samuel.[90]

In March 1926 he issued recommendations,[91] including industry consolidation and an immediate wage cut. Owners also wanted to set longer working hours, outraging both the Miners' Union and the TUC. Neither side budged so owners locked miners out on 1 May; a special union conference that day voted for a general strike on 3 May.[92] Though well supported, the strike was 'selective rather than general'. About 1.5 million workers – mainly from the energy, transport and communications sectors – walked out in solidarity with miners.[93]

Anti-Soviet hardliners like Jix were, in Christopher Andrew's words, 'emotionally incapable of seeing the General Strike as anything other than a deep-laid plot'.[94] Churchill's 3 May intervention in Parliament left no doubt:

> It is a conflict which, [*sic*] if fought out to a conclusion, can only end in the overthrow of Parliamentary Government or in its decisive victory. There is no middle course open. Either the Parliamentary institutions of the country ... emerge triumphant ... or ... the existing Constitution will be fatally injured.... [This] will inevitably lead to the erection of some Soviet of Trade Unions on which ... the real effective control of the economic and political life of the country will devolve. Such a transference could only mean the effectual subversion of the State.[95]

Yet to what extent was the USSR involved in the General Strike of 3–12 May 1926?

Preparations began a week before Samuel published his report. Comintern Head Grigori Zinoviev and the Politburo instructed Mikhail P. Tomsky, Chairman of the All-Russian Central Council of Trade Unions (VTsSPS, which played an important role in *Profintern* affairs) to learn what he could about the 'forthcoming conflict of the British miners' and inform their unions they could expect up to a million roubles (2011: around £5 million) in assistance.[96] The TUC knew what being caught with Soviet funds would mean in so polarised a nation, and so returned a cheque sent by VTsSPS and Soviet trade unions, arguing such generosity would be 'wilfully misrepresented and acceptance ... misunderstood'.[97]

British industrial disputes in 1926 were the worst of the interwar period, with more workdays lost that year than in three key others combined (1912, 1921 and 1979). Yet in 1926, the miners' strike accounted for 90% of lost workdays.[98] The Soviets funded this strike, which continued well after the General Strike ended on 12 May. Overall, Moscow sent nearly £1.25 million (2011: nearly £59.5 million), with part of that coming from Soviet miners 'whose wages were smaller than the strike pay received by their British comrades'.[99] One of the earliest decisions to show solidarity with British strikers was not to offload Soviet coal and oil at British ports. Striking Soviet dockers were to do this by refusing to load Britain-bound ships. To add revolutionary drama to the act, these workers would load ships only when or if instructed by the TUC.

What the Politburo did not mention was the USSR could not stop loading of British ships due to an existing agreement. The solution was therefore to rely on allegedly spontaneous acts of solidarity by Soviet dockers. Furthermore, ships on the way to or already docked in Britain were to join strike action.[100]

On 6 May, day four of the General Strike, the Politburo passed several urgent resolutions. One was to publish the announcement VTsSPS would set aside 250,000 roubles (2011: just over £1.25 million) for the TUC. Additionally, if the Strike were a prolonged one, a nationwide campaign would start whereby all workers would devote a quarter of their salary to help British strikers. Soviet ships would neither sail to, nor offload cargo at, British ports. Comintern, meanwhile, was to adopt the same tone as Soviet newspapers: 'calm and explaining' while criticising the British Right. Meanwhile, the CPGB was to do what it could to turn the strike political at the appropriate time.[101]

Moreover, the Politburo decided British trade unions and, if possible, the TUC, were to appeal directly to the British military for solidarity. In Belgium, Czechoslovakia, France, Germany, Italy and Poland, 'committees of action' – essentially assistance committees – were to be set up, with *Profintern* coordinating this campaign to collect money for British strikers. Finally, European communist parties were to campaign against their own governments sending coal to Britain.[102] On 7 May the Politburo accepted Stalin's suggestion to send two million roubles (2011: around £10 million) to British strikers.[103] Next day, a confidential letter to the CPGB Central Committee outlined the need to change strike focus from economics to politics.[104]

As these measures were discussed (and at times adopted), British authorities tried to cope with unrest. They arrested and sentenced rioters, raided Labour and CPGB premises and intercepted TUC telegrams (sent in plain text). Despite this, the Home Office reported 'little effect on the spread of "seditious" literature'.[105] During the General Strike, both sides fought for public sympathy. The Government put its full might behind a media campaign against unions and the CPGB. The Conservatives hired Sydney Walton (see Chapter 2) to run their 'information fund', spending at least £35,000 (2011: over £12 million) on propaganda against the two strikes.[106] Of special concern to Cabinet was the unexpected role of the-then British Broadcasting Company after mainstream printed press stopped.[107] Coverage upset citizens and officials, resulting in many complaints to ministers and MPs regarding BBC impartiality. Cabinet therefore discussed if 'control of the [BBC] should in some form be exercised'.[108]

Addressing rumours of such action, BBC General Manager John Reith wrote to Archbishop of Canterbury Randall Davidson:

The BBC has secured ... the goodwill and affection of the people. It has been trusted to do the right thing at all times.... It is a national institution and ... asset. If it be commandeered or unduly hampered or manipulated now, the immediate purpose of such action is not only unserved [*sic*] but actually prejudiced. This is not a time for dope even if the people could be doped. The hostile will only be made more hostile from resentment. As to suppression, from the panic of ignorance comes far greater danger than from ... knowledge.... If the Government be strong and their cause right they need not adopt such measures.... As for the future, when ... trouble is over, it will be a calamity if public confidence in the BBC has been dissipated through actions, negative or positive, during this emergency. Its pioneer work of 3½ years will have been undermined – an influence of almost unlimited potency ... shaken.[109]

Reith ultimately helped government by giving airtime neither to the Left nor to a 'peace and negotiation appeal by the Archbishop'. Years later, Reith explained his reasoning:

I wondered if it would have been better had the BBC been commandeered. My conclusion was ... it would have been better for me, worse for the BBC and ... the country. Because of Churchill's attitude, supported by ... others in Cabinet, the position was much more difficult than it was in any event bound to be. They were on the look-out for things which would have secured a majority for commandeering.[110]

The Churchill-run *British Gazette*[111] was the Government's counter to the TUC's *British Worker*. The outcome of the contest between the full machinery of government and labour unions was not in doubt; *Gazette* daily circulation dwarfed the *Worker's*.[112] David Lloyd George famously called the *Gazette* a 'first-class indiscretion clothed in the tawdry garb of third-rate journalism'.[113] Yet Churchill defended his role, especially regarding confiscation of newsprint to keep the *Gazette* going and suppression from it of conciliatory messages (most controversially from the Archbishop).[114]

On the first issue, Churchill argued the *Gazette* was the only nationwide publication able to inform Britons in an unbiased way, and should therefore not be deprived of necessary newsprint at such a critical time. Regarding censorship, he implausibly blamed it on the absence of 'expert printers and other classes of experts in the production of a newspaper'. Since so few technicians remained at work, Churchill explained, typesetting was slow. Only crucial articles on daily events could therefore be printed. This already difficult situation was not helped by 'amateurs coming in who have never been in a newspaper office before', to which an opposition MP replied: 'Including the Editor.'[115] The *Gazette* ultimately performed as intended, at a net cost of £10,000 (2011: £475,000) and with a top daily circulation of 2.5 million copies.[116]

Special Constabularies boosted regular police forces. In London, this meant mainly the Metropolitan Police, whose collaboration with MI5 underpinned the Government's intelligence response to the Strike. Preparations had gone on for more than five years. Before the April 1921 Triple Alliance strike (see Chapter 2), the War Office had no dedicated intelligence arrangements to support civil power in a national emergency. Two intelligence officers did work in the War Office, liaising between it and other departments but Special Branch was in charge of gathering all industrial unrest intelligence.[117]

The War Office and National District Commands reinforced their 'defensive, preventive, negative and precautionary' function known as intelligence "B". Military authorities stood up MI(B), a security and secret service section comprising in crisis time the two permanent War Office intelligence officers, seconded MI5 officers, military reserve officers with previous MI5 experience, and clerical staff temporarily seconded from MI5 and elsewhere.[118] The section was particularly concerned with preventing sabotage, blocking 'communists and disloyalists [sic]' from enlisting in the military in times of strife, assessing morale of government forces during an emergency and liaising with Special Branch. Plans called for thirteen MI5 staff to be in MI(B) but in 1926 only twelve deployed.[119] This activity in May 1926 cost MI5 an additional £655 (2011: £227,000)[120] beyond the £14,557 (2011: £5 million)[121] budget for FY 1926/7.

An MI(B) officer went to Special Branch each morning to collect intelligence and authorities formally called up the Special Constabulary early on 3 May. At noon that day, there were 10,687 volunteers but when recruitment ended on 12 May, there were 61,500. The Metropolitan Police budgeted £61,000 (2011: just over £21 million) for contingencies, £13,000 of that for Specials; it actually spent £55,544 (2011: nearly £19.5 million), including £12,728 for Special Constables.[122]

Yet even as the Strike raged on, some in government were already drawing lessons. Conservative grandee Viscount Cecil urged his Party to address underlying issues:

> I am ... convinced [the Government] will be gravely to blame unless as soon as possible ... it takes up a reorganisation of ... industry ... [to diminish] ... suspicion ... between employers and employed.... I am ...

convinced ... unless we can devise some remedy ... [voters will eventually] accept some form of Socialism as the only way.[123]

Already on 8 May, ministers secretly considered a draft Bill addressing the legality of future strikes. Copies circulated in Cabinet but were all collected after. Meeting minutes were held for days, again to preserve secrecy. Among other provisions, the Bill narrowed the scope of what constituted a legal strike, gave government authority to block funds deemed 'in furtherance or support' of any such event, and guaranteed the rights and benefits of workers refusing to walk out during a strike deemed illegal. Northern Ireland was exempt but government only publicly introduced the Bill on 12 May, after Home Secretary Sir John Simon expressed concerns about the timing.[124] The Bill became the Trade Disputes and Trade Unions Act in July 1927.[125]

For the British labour movement, the General Strike brought on the collective realisation nobody benefited from divisive confrontational tactics. Moderation was more productive.[126] Soviet involvement in particular, real or alleged, made many on the Left pause once Britain's chaotic state leading up to, during and after the Strike became clear. Simon now considered prohibiting inflow of foreign funds even for legitimate strikes,[127] let alone illegitimate ones.

In Moscow, meanwhile, the Politburo struggled to understand what had happened – or rather, had not. VTsSPS Head, Tomsky, reported on efforts to prop up British strikers as instructed on 4–5 May. On 8 May, he had met members of the German Communist Party Central Committee in Berlin. They discussed raising food and money to help strikers, with German communists asking for funds to carry out these ultimately fruitless efforts. To Tomsky, the Party did not carry out a 'real mass campaign' of propaganda in the Ruhr Valley, with the Germans in turn arguing they did not have enough people for such work.[128]

By 9 May, Tomsky had moved on to Paris, where he refined a plan for strikers to 'deepen and extend' political and economic demands. In the only meeting of the Comintern Commission on British Affairs on 15 May, Tomsky and his comrades agreed neither the German nor the French Communist Parties had been prepared to carry out active duties.[129] Finally, on 17 May, Tomsky had met Labour MP Albert Purcell, who did not impress the Russian by making excuses why the General Strike had failed. Had there been political demands to the Strike, offered Purcell, it would not have happened. Had it not stopped on a "high note" on 12 May, a complete collapse would have soon followed. Ending the Strike, then, was not a defeat because the goal of restarting negotiations without immediate wage cuts had been achieved.

Furthermore, Purcell argued, miners were undisciplined and had disobeyed the TUC General Council.[130]

Leon Trotsky's assessment was blunter than Tomsky's: the TUC decision to end the Strike on 12 May was a betrayal of British workers. Moreover, Soviet paralysis during the crisis while praising TUC leaders was a fundamental strategy mistake. Trotsky argued the duality in Kremlin policy – the TUC betrayed British workers but still had Soviet support – was highly damaging; 'no one will understand this'.[131] He concluded Moscow failed to capitalise on its best chance so far to destabilise Britain. Soul-searching – or scapegoating, some might say – continued for some time; in July, Zinoviev warned the Communist Party and the Politburo not to confront the CPGB over the May events.[132]

The strategic impact of the General Strike on Anglo-Soviet relations was immense. By early June 1926, ARCOS was a marked entity – almost a year before the raid on its premises triggered a break in bilateral relations.[133] Within a month of the Strike, the Conservatives already spoke openly of a breach. Although the General Strike ended on 12 May 1926, miners continued industrial action well into the autumn with Moscow's financial help (including through ARCOS, which had moved Soviet money to British unions during the Strike, an offer ultimately refused). Cabinet discussed whether to act against ARCOS to block movement of funds.[134] The memorandum underpinning this debate outlined alleged financial support for the Strike from its first day.[135] Subsequent inquiries, however, did not support this assertion and the Government withdrew it.[136] From the Strike on, ARCOS was on borrowed time.

The issue of a diplomatic break with Moscow quickly occupied official circles. A Foreign Office note highlighted the advantages of continued ties:

> A certain amount of trade is already in existence between this country and Russia. Its value to us in our present state of need cannot be dismissed as negligible.... British firms have accepted orders on credits covering a considerable period, and these orders, or the payment for them, will no doubt be lost in the event of a complete breach.[137]

Countering Soviet subversion was already challenging so

> what ... is to be gained by a breach? Our main ... complaint is the propaganda.... It is no doubt facilitated by the presence of a Diplomatic Mission and of trade agencies in this country. But sufficient organisation to maintain it will always be maintained or created anew and money

can always be sent [by another] channel. Our war experience [shows] … nothing short of complete censorship and a financial and economic control scrutinising and allowing or forbidding every business transaction will suffice.[138]

Ultimately, the document argued, British economic sanctions against the USSR would be trivial since it did not follow Western standards and practices. Britain should remember the Soviets did not 'attach the same degree of importance to material considerations as we … do ourselves'.[139]

However, Cabinet was nevertheless unanimous in its view the Government had every right to break ties with Moscow. Still, given Europe's political landscape at the time, British contracts with Soviet firms, the expectation of increased trade, the potential impact of a breach on British unemployment and the difficulties in re-establishing diplomatic relations, most ministers did not endorse an immediate break. The best action for now would be to keep treating 'the attitude of the Soviet with contempt' while 'enlighten[ing] the public as to the menacing character' of Kremlin actions.[140]

Largely, this would only be possible if British intelligence continued monitoring and disrupting Soviet subversion at home and abroad. That challenge, however, had since the war been made tougher first by declining and then stagnating budgets, just as police funding exploded (see also Table 4).

Table 5. Selected UK Security, Intelligence & Law-Enforcement Expenditure: FY 1922/9 (£)[141]

	1922	1923	1924	1925	1926	1927	1928	1929
Official Secret Service Vote	200,000	n/a[a]	n/a	180,000	180,000	n/a	180,000	180,000
Actual Secret Service Outlay	177,030	162,703	162,332	n/a	n/a	164,764	162,453	166,031
Home Office Outlay	332,055	330,880	365,550	418,644 (est.)	421,976 (est.)	422,916	413,225	420,324
Police Outlay (England & Wales)	6,058,479	5,678,313	6,033,595	6,577,672 (est.)	6,914,997 (est.)	6,936,535	7,130,501	7,239,694

[a] The estimated vote in years for which information was not available (n/a) was £180,000.

**Figure: British Intelligence Community and Police
(England & Wales) Expenditure: FY 1913/29 (£)**

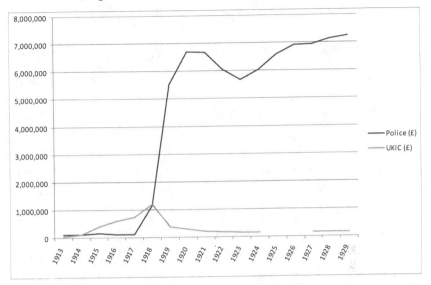

Concern over Bolshevik subversion across the Empire again increased after the General Strike. The Committee of Imperial Defence considered possible measures should subversion in India further damage British standing in Asia. In any case, Winston Churchill argued, recent Soviet actions in the region were simply 'old Czarist policy disguised under the veneer of Communism'. The only way to contain Moscow effectively, he felt, was the 'great counter-poise of alliances and agreements,'[143] with Japan as the prime candidate. William Tyrrell, who succeeded Eyre Crowe after his death in May 1925 as Foreign Office Permanent Under-Secretary, outlined the challenges.

The Soviets wanted the same in the East as their Tsarist predecessors, except communists were 'far more efficient and unscrupulous'. However, reviving the Anglo-Japanese Alliance (1902–23) would be difficult for three reasons. First, London's earlier condemnation of it to please the USA[144] created great antipathy in Tokyo. Second, Japanese industrialisation brought with it a more democratic mindset. The resulting openness toward Moscow, greater than ever before, might therefore counter many possible gains to be had from a renewed alliance. In addition, Japan's changing attitudes also affected its policies on China, no longer the object of Japanese military conquest but rather 'economic penetration'. Tyrrell's final point linked to his second: Japan's new perspective on China could clash with Britain's, leading to further difficulties in restoring the alliance. He felt it was to diplomacy ... we [must] look for the most practical and effective weapon to oppose Bolshevism.... [I]n this choice we can reasonably rely [on] the cordial cooperation of ... [most] Continental Governments ... based ... upon mutual self-interest and sanity – two very powerful factors in the regulation of human relations.[145]

Such commendable views on the merits of sanity while dealing with Moscow would have been unwelcome in some quarters. On 15 July, for instance, a meeting of right-wing groups at the Royal Albert Hall passed a resolution condemning Soviet subversion and pledging to support government. A Foreign Office official, considering the damage such events might cause British diplomacy, noted: '[U]nfortunately these people are working up other anti "Bolsh" demonstrations both in the country and in London.'[146] Robert Hodgson, writing from Moscow, shared his apprehension with Cabinet:

the "Red Bandit" battle-cry may ... serve a useful purpose in political warfare at home.... [Concerning] ... relations with Russia ... the expressions of resentment ... it epitomises are definitely detrimental to our ... interests. First ... it renders us absurd.... We cannot do the Third International a greater service than by ... inveighing against them in the Albert Hall ... encouraging them to believe ... they have got in between the joints of our harness.... [W]hen vehement Conservatives preach ... an Anti-Red Crusade it is assumed ... their vituperations have the sanction and ... sympathy of ... Cabinet; from that to believing ... Cabinet is really weaving ... threads of aggression ... is but a step.[147]

The incisive observations of a young Edward Hallett (E. H.) Carr, working in the British Legation in Riga at this time, complemented Hodgson's description of Kremlin fears. Moscow's distrust centred mainly on the Foreign Office, the armed forces and the PCOs. While 'the Soviet imagination' regarded British diplomats as 'comparatively correct and innocuous', the military warranted considerable concern. The PCOs, however, drew the Soviets' 'darkest suspicions'. A transparent cover for SIS, PCOs were supposedly

engaged in fomenting and financing disaffection in the [USSR] on a scale beside which the comparatively straightforward proceedings of the Third International in ... Britain pale into insignificance.... [A] belief in the nefarious intentions of [the British] has become a psychological necessity to many.... Those fortunate Communists who have faith in a divine mission to convert the world to their doctrine by propaganda or the sword ... need no other justification for the activities of Soviet agents in ... Britain.[148]

What Carr felt the Government needed to understand was

the majority of Soviet officials ... have no particular interest in Communism or belief in missions. A need for self-justification and a capacity for self-delusion are both deeply embedded in human nature; and I think ... many of the servants and supporters of the Soviet Government (at any rate those outside the [USSR]), seeking to justify to themselves the *prima facie* indefensible interference of their Government in the affairs of another power, have ended by acquiring a perfectly genuine belief ... these apparently aggressive measures are essentially defensive in character, and are merely the replica of those initiated and employed by His Majesty's Government against the Soviet Union.[149]

The stage was now set for a break between London and Moscow. Tyrrell again played the proverbial canary in the coal mine when on 4 December 1926 he wrote:

As far as it is possible to forecast Russian tactics ... they will increase their interference in our domestic affairs.... It seems to me therefore that if we continue our ... watchful vigilance we may soon ... catch them in ... *flagrante delicto*, which will enable us to clear them out of this country with almost universal consent.... [I]n order to get the greatest benefit from our breaking off relations with Russia, we should endeavour to force the Labour Party either to associate itself with our policy or frankly to come out into the open on the side of people who are determined upon our destruction.[150]

By the mid-1920s, then, Britain reluctantly acknowledged its financial needs still trumped ideology – the opposite of the USSR. A stagnant British economy, London's perpetual but unfulfilled expectation of strong trade with Moscow and a pressing need to reduce unemployment were the main obstacles to a premature diplomatic break. Britain's return to the gold standard in April 1925 and subsequent labour unrest only hastened the Conservatives' journey to that endpoint.

The 1926 General and miners' strikes were the most significant between 1917 and 1929 in which Moscow was openly involved. Diehards' outrage over this perhaps masked panic that a long-feared revolution had finally come;

censorship of the BBC because of its influence in shaping popular perceptions was an example of how far some would go to stop "subversion". Another
was deepening ties between Conservative politicians, British intelligence and
fascist groups during national crises. Cabinet's reflexive reaction to legislate an
ever-narrowing scope of industrial action was notable but so was the inability
(or refusal) of many European communists to help British strikers in need.

From a British legal standpoint, precisely what constituted Soviet subversion remained unclear. Though government was by 1925–26 at least aware of
Federated Press of America operations, there were potentially serious security
breaches elsewhere, typified by the story of Andrew Rothstein and the Lunn
sisters. Also clear is that from the time Britain suspected Soviet involvement in
the General Strike (perceived) and the miners' strike (real), both ARCOS and
Anglo-Soviet relations were doomed. Different Conservative factions failed to
agree how best to deal with Moscow but eleven months before the supposedly
irrefutable evidence recovered in the May 1927 ARCOS raid, Cabinet hardliners already sought a breach.

CHAPTER 7

The Raids

The ARCOS Tangle ~ Macartney & Mackenzie ~ The Federated Press Undone

[Those] ... engaged in [propaganda] dissemination ... should be discharged forthwith.

Cabinet on communists in military establishments[1]

If [Russia] does get herself into serious trouble, it will be because she has overdone her ... propaganda and ... created a situation ... beyond her control.   Robert Hodgson[2]

I considered [Ewer] by far the most dangerous individual from [a Secret Service] point of view ... the Russians had in this country.   Oswald Harker[3]

B Y early 1927, Anglo-Soviet relations were deteriorating. Russian espionage and open support for industrial unrest in Britain added to the Conservatives' desire for a diplomatic breach, strengthened by growing OGPU harassment of foreign diplomats in the USSR. British officials in Moscow, London and elsewhere had long complained about interference by Soviet security organs. In April 1925, for example, Robert Hodgson informed the Foreign Office that security staff at the Italian Embassy in Moscow had discovered two microphones connected to OGPU headquarters, the Lubyanka.[4] In January 1927, following reliable reports the OGPU had tampered with 'diplomatic bags of a foreign power', Foreign Secretary Austen Chamberlain ordered the British Mission in Moscow to destroy all non-essential ciphers and confidential papers. Should a break occur, this reduced secret material within the premises to a minimum.[5]

He did not believe severing relations would end subversion; that would require blocking money transfers, preventing travellers entering or leaving Britain and censoring communications. Moreover, what he called "trade interests" would exert great pressure to resume ties. Perhaps naively (or simply out of desperation), those interests assumed business would pick up if only bilateral relations settled – wishful thinking driven by memories that Tsarist Russia had been Britain's second largest pre-war export market after Germany.[6] This perpetual self-delusion about potential commercial opportunities in the USSR was a defining feature of Anglo-Soviet relations from 1917 to 1991,[7] and one that again drives post-1991 Anglo-Russian ties. The Foreign Secretary also believed once a rupture happened, the Labour Party – divided since the 1926 strikes – would again argue major contracts and relief for British unemployment were certain if only Moscow were given a chance.[8]

Figures, more than words, showed the reality belying any claims Labour and trade interests could make in favour of continued ties. In 1924–25, Moscow placed orders with British businesses worth £23.5 million; in 1925–26, £20.5 million; in 1926–27, £14 million; and in 1927–28, £6 million. A placed order did not mean one fulfilled and paid for; actual British exports were worth far less than order values. In 1924, for example, actual exports were £4 million and in 1927, £4.5 million.[9]

Early that year, Foreign Office Under-Secretary Don Gregory and key British embassies in Europe assessed the pros and cons of a break. From Paris, the view was 'a man as cautious as Poincaré' would not follow Britain. The National Union Government, observed Chargé d'Affaires Eric Phipps, could only survive without political controversy.[10] From Riga, the view was Baltic nations had originally regarded British recognition of Bolshevism as an error. Having done so, however, London would gain nothing from a breach now. If it occurred, the Baltics expected little political fallout but Latvia and Estonia would face hardship from lost trade (Estonia first stabilised its currency in 1924 and joined what became the Sterling Area[11] in 1926–27). Cutting ties depended on the USA, France, Germany and Italy: they would 'attempt to steal a march' on Britain but only with their support would a breach make sense.[12]

Riga made two other important points. First, a break would be ideal to re-establish British prestige worldwide; resulting commercial and industrial losses paled next to those due to Soviet subversion. Second, London had to consider the safety of Britons in the USSR. These issues could only be resolved to Britain's advantage if it could secure 'the moral support, if not the cooperation, of the other powers', but 'owing to international jealousies', Riga felt, this would be 'next to impossible'.[13]

Sir George Clerk in Constantinople opposed Gregory's perceived fear-mongering in favour of a breach:

[F]rom whom does the well-nigh irresistible agitation for the expulsion of the Bolshevik ... come? Are we to believe that the bulk of popular opinion in [Britain] is really wrought up to such an extent? Can you, even today ... say that Labour ... and the majority of its leaders would be in favour ... ? I doubt it.[14]

On Gregory's question about how soon to resume ties if a breach happened, Constantinople was equally direct. Only time would tell but when the economy made resuming 'broken relations between countries desirable, a face-saving formula is always discoverable'.[15]

Berlin took a broader view, urging London to realise that short of military action against Moscow, this was 'a new kind of war'. Anti-subversive measures could not be piecemeal but as part of a package of 'economic boycott, breach of diplomatic relations, propaganda and counter-propaganda, pressure on neutrals'. Set emotion aside, Berlin argued, and ask how a breach would affect British interests in this new war. By ejecting the Soviets from London, would we 'not blind ourselves more than we should blind them'? Still, Ambassador Sir Ronald Lindsay believed that in doing so, the Government would at least make great progress in 'converting the present peculiar struggle into an armed conflict of the old-fashioned sort'.[16]

Rome was not as forceful. To Ambassador Sir Ronald Graham, the main question was

whether, with a worldwide Empire built ... on prestige, we can afford to submit passively to vicious kicks in the tenderest portions of our anatomy without ... damage to our constitution. My ... feeling is ... the break ... is inevitable ... [what] matters is to choose a moment for that break which is ... best for us and ... worst for them.[17]

Should a break occur, he advised, British interests would be best served by telling Washington and looking for its support, if not similar action.[18]

Warsaw did not see any advantage in a rupture, citing the May 1923 Curzon Note as an example of how to proceed only when 'extracting material concessions'. Threatening a break at this point would bring little advantage since the Soviets ignored the issues of subversion and reparations. The break should be 'an end in itself' and though resuming ties might eventually entail 'a certain loss of dignity and prestige' for Britain, a rupture simply to boost its status worldwide would be 'the satisfaction of an emotion rather than an act of useful diplomacy'.[19]

German and Italian support for Britain at this time was unrealistic because of the 1922 Rapallo and 1926 Berlin Treaties. These were the post-Versailles Treaty foundation for secret German–Soviet collaboration until 1933 on intelligence; weapons research, development and production; and military doctrine. London knew of this, not least because of sensational exposés in December 1926 by Frederick Voigt, the *Manchester Guardian*'s man in Berlin (see Chapter 5). Italy, particularly under Benito Mussolini, had looked from early in the decade to shore up its position in Europe by siding with Germany as a strategic counter-balance to France, going as far as secretly shipping weapons to Berlin in 1923.[20] French and Polish intelligence knew all this so politically, the most important support for London's desired break with Moscow should have come from France, its ally the Second Polish Republic and Czechoslovakia.[21]

Robert Hodgson in Moscow kept urging caution. Severing ties only to show 'resentment at indignities' would be 'trivial' without considering the long-term view. He listed possible benefits from a break: punishing Moscow, ending subversion, setting the stage for renewed bilateral ties on more favourable terms than at present, and forcing the USSR to recognise and settle debts.[22] He then outlined what he saw as the likelihood of success for each.

London could punish Moscow to a certain point and for some time. However, since the Kremlin controlled the media, authorities would soon twist facts to legitimise themselves before Soviet citizens. Any unilateral break would have limited effect because Britain would stand alone in Europe. Desperate to maintain ties with some continental powers, Moscow would likely concede to others more than it had been willing to give London. The USSR was most vulnerable financially but even a break would not cripple their economy.[23]

Regarding subversion, it had never been clearly defined. A break would not only remove any inhibitions the Soviets may have had and increase subversion, Hodgson felt, but would also destroy much of Britain's ability to control it worldwide.[24] As for restoring ties later on when conditions were more beneficial, he thought this equally unlikely:

> The idea of ... world revolution ... in Russia ... has [gradually] been supplanted by the ambition to build up the Socialist State which is to be the beacon to the world.... Again, a clash with ... Britain is likely ... to make the Soviet Government treasure more highly its relationship with countries, notably with Germany, which may entail a serious prejudice to us.... Moscow may come to terms with Washington ... and no doubt to attain that end, the Soviet Government would consent to important sacrifices. We, who had accorded recognition and withdrawn it, would then find ourselves in a position of inferiority in relation to the USA, who [sic] had never accorded recognition at all.[25]

As for debt reparation, Moscow was increasingly unlikely to do so since various Soviet organs of State had continuously bought, sold or dissolved the many affected companies and entities.[26]

Negative effects of a possible break, wrote Hodgson, greatly outweighed possible benefits. He worried about increased subversion, protests by British labour and financial interests over lost trade, loss of mechanisms to address bilateral grievances, turmoil in Central Europe, reversal of what little progress the Soviets had made in normalising their behaviour, and improved relations between the USSR and other powers at Britain's expense.[27] In short, a break

> is a powerful weapon which [*sic*] can be used with crushing effect when circumstances are propitious.... To give force to the blow it must have behind it overwhelming public opinion at home and a consensus ... on the Continent. Neither ... [is] in evidence now.... Counsels of prudence ... suggest ... we hold our hand until that moment occurs.[28]

Even Cabinet did not take counter-subversive measures too far yet, refusing to back a Parliamentary Bill introduced on 18 February 1927 prohibiting 'any person or association from inviting, accepting or using funds from foreign sources for the furtherance or maintenance' of strikes in Britain.[29] Yet aside from the 1926 General Strike, the end of Soviet official presence in London began not there but more than 5000 miles away, in Beijing.

By early 1927, Soviet officials did not see subversion in China harming ties with Britain:

> *In the [Foreign Office] memorandum to yesterday's Cabinet meeting* there was a remark that it is essential to distinguish between our activity in ... independent ... China and activity in ... British Colonies, from which it was concluded ... our policy in China does not give ... grounds for a breach.[30] [my italics]

This intercept suggests the Kremlin still had a source in the Foreign Office (or, less likely, in the Cabinet Office), allowing the trade delegation to cable to Moscow intelligence acquired in London only a day or so before (see also Chapter 2).

Yet by spring, Soviet foreign and military intelligence – INO and IV Directorate, respectively – were reeling from the exposure of several networks worldwide. In March, Poland rolled up a major INO ring, Turkey arrested a Soviet trade delegate on espionage charges and Switzerland seized two Bolshevik agents. In April, Chinese authorities found compromising documents during a raid on a Soviet compound and France dismantled a Paris network run by leading French communist Jean Crémet. In May, Austria arrested some of its diplomats passing on secrets to the Vienna *rezidentura* and Britain raided ARCOS.[31] Unsurprisingly, Soviet fears of a new Western intervention, already high in recent months (the war scare of winter 1926–27), now peaked despite a somewhat reassuring IV Directorate threat assessment.[32] However, given Britain's global interests, events in Beijing were the most worrying.

Early on 6 April, Chinese police – prompted by London and directed by former Manchurian warlord, Nationalist General Zhang Zuolin – raided the Soviet diplomatic compound (but not the embassy building itself, which Beijing deemed inviolable).[33] The Russians set the military attaché's office on fire, which destroyed all but one of the ciphers.[34] Unluckily for Moscow, the police confiscated[35] the archives of the attaché and his "neighbours", leading authorities to three Chinese employees of the British Embassy. One, a Chancellery attendant, operated the Photostat machine; the other two were a telephone operator and a messenger.[36]

Still, the Soviets destroyed much of the Communist Party of China archive, having taken custody of it the previous night. In a separate raid, police seized the Nationalist Party archive, which should have also been delivered to the Soviets the night before. Those files contained reports by Soviet military advisers attached to the Nationalist Army.[37] This reflected the troubled nature of Sino–Soviet ties in the 1920s, when Moscow at times supported both sides.[38]

Given Beijing's actions, Soviet delegates in London became warier but still felt safe:

> I very much doubt the possibility of a raid on our Embassy. I would, however, consider it a very useful … precaution to suspend for a time the forwarding by post of documents of friends, "neighbours", and so forth from London to Moscow and vice-versa.[39]

This showed how senior Soviet officials misunderstood key Conservative ministers, the effect on them of Kremlin support for the 1926 strikes and how they further fuelled anti-communism.

Conversely, senior Foreign Office officials also felt British governments, by not confronting the Bolsheviks decisively since 1917, had also fundamentally misunderstood the challenge. Sir Francis Lindley – a seasoned diplomat posted to Russia from 1915 to 1919 (culminating as Consul-General) and now Minister Plenipotentiary to Norway[40] – argued:

That the Trade Agreement was a first-class blunder, based on a complete misconception both of the Bolshevik mentality and ... potentialities of Russian trade, is common ground.... It has been followed neither by any decrease in open hostility to the ... Empire nor ... any great increase in commerce. But it has fettered our hands ... as the Bolsheviks intended. ... As there is no question of attacking ... with our Armed Forces, how can we best weaken his power of injuring us? ... I was till recently in favour of rubbing along as we were; but ... China ... brought matters to a head. Our patience merely convinces the Soviet ... we are afraid of the breach ... they, in reality, dread far more.... This encourages them, not only in China and the East, but all over Europe. And it confuses our friends.... [T]here is nothing the Bolsheviks fear so much as to be forced back into the underground.... But agitation is a religious mania with them; and, though their reason makes them dread a breach above almost anything, they are ... incapable of refraining from action which makes a breach probable.[41]

From Lloyd George and MacDonald pushing for the 1921 trade agreement and the 1924 *de jure* recognition respectively, to Jix and Churchill's anti-communist campaigns, a duality emerged in British official attitudes. The pendulum swung from contempt to panic due to a combination of personal convictions, political expediency, domestic and foreign policy demands, and the quality and accuracy of information reaching Cabinet on Kremlin intentions and capabilities. By late 1929, for instance, London still seemed unaware of the size of Moscow's intelligence budgets.[42] Yet the 1926 strikes changed everything. Against advice from some of Britain's most experienced diplomats, the day of reckoning came on 12 May 1927 – precisely a year after the General Strike ended.

Any Soviet enterprise wishing to trade in Britain had to use ARCOS. There was evidence it financed Bolshevik subversion in Britain, supported by the Soviet Missions in Berlin and The Hague. British intelligence wanted to learn what it could about ARCOS activities[43] and in October 1926, SIS had the best opportunity. ARCOS employee "X" contacted an SIS officer offering confidential information. Told to go to the police, "X" said he had already done so, been unimpressed and therefore preferred to deal with SIS instead.[44]

"X" met SIS officers for six months, revealing little of interest. That changed on 30 March 1927 when he relayed information from "Y" (a former ARCOS employee) that an army SIGINT document had passed through 49 Moorgate. Given the military dimension, SIS informed MI5, which for several days checked the reliability of the evidence. The opportunity Home Secretary Joynson-Hicks and other hardliners had long sought was finally here. Late on 11 May, he took MI5's information to Prime Minister Baldwin, who approved the raid.[45]

At 4.30p.m. on 12 May, Special Branch and other personnel gathered at Moorgate Street Underground station before entering ARCOS. Authorities had sought a search warrant the day before[46] but intercepted Soviet cables mirror contemporary press accounts of ARCOS Deputy Managing Director M(ark) L. Sorokin[47] only seeing a warrant around 5.30p.m., an hour after the raid started. He and T. V. (Ivan) Boiev (Vice-Chair of the trade delegation, which shared premises with ARCOS) formally complained. However, according to City of London Police Commissioner Sir Hugh Turnbull, the complaint was misleading because Boiev only arrived at 49 Moorgate at 5.45p.m.[48] Until 16 May, the delegation sent messages to Moscow in the clear since, according to London staff, Special Branch had seized all codes and ciphers (untrue).[49]

The raid's planning and execution were chaotic, without clear lines of authority. Nobody knew what to do, either with seized material or with detainees, and few officers understood for what they were actually looking. Seized documentation[50] did not offer as solid evidence of Soviet espionage as Cabinet had hoped. Still, it used the raid as the trigger for suspending the trade agreement, expelling the Soviet delegation and ending diplomatic ties effective 27 May.[51] Throughout the episode, the British Government took care to preserve the identity of "X",[52] the source inside ARCOS. The raid surprised almost everyone (even in the intelligence community). Participating officers were deliberately told they were headed for government dockyards, there was tight operational secrecy and authorities decided to enter Moorgate at the last minute.[53]

Moscow reacted immediately. On 13 May, the Politburo ordered a press campaign against the Conservatives, arguing they were preparing for a breach. Trade Commissar Anastas I. Mikoyan was to organise mass demonstrations and letter-to-the-editor campaigns in the USSR, and review possible economic sanctions. Meanwhile, the All-Russian Central Council of Trade Unions (VTsSPS) was to write the TUC asking British workers to protest against a break. Soviet officials overseas were also to destroy secret documents not deemed vital.[54]

Foreign Secretary Chamberlain's worries were justified and despite government measures, Soviet subversion resumed shortly.[55] Furthermore, the raid and its aftermath became an intelligence disaster. Desperate to prove their case despite the inconclusive nature of seized documents, ministers quoted decrypted Soviet cables in both a White Paper (Cmd 2874) and Parliament. Christopher Andrew has called this 'an orgy of governmental indiscretion about secret intelligence for which there is no parallel in modern parliamentary history'.[56] Unsurprisingly, the USSR introduced theoretically unbreakable one-time-pads (OTPs), shutting GCCS out of high-grade traffic in much of the world for years. For a decade after the disclosures, School staff told every new member about the lost Soviet codes to illustrate politicians' carelessness. The ARCOS raid also underscored problems within the intelligence community again (mainly Special Branch), so the Secret Service Committee re-convened to look for possible solutions.[57]

The fullest assessment of the raid deemed 'the occasion ... insufficient, the timing wrong, and the result not only disappointing but damaging'[58] – a propaganda gift to the Kremlin. State-organised demonstrations, including outside the British Mission in Moscow, swept the USSR. On 23 May, Cabinet voided the trade agreement and cut diplomatic ties. The eventual translation into English of a compromising Russian document seized during the raid came too late to prevent the disclosure of SIGINT in Parliament and therefore a setback for GCCS,[59] eroding trust between the agencies and government. Despite the unease of even prominent Conservatives[60] about a break, the die was cast.

Yet Cabinet deliberations on 23 May 1927 show the Government wanted to have the best of both worlds. Ministers decided to cancel the treaty, expel Bolsheviks guilty of subversion and the delegation, but did not consider it

> desirable ... that the trading activities of ARCOS ... should ... end by [British] action, as it was desirable that trade ... should continue on the same basis ... it is conducted in the [USA] ... and other countries [with] no trade agreement with the Soviet.[61]

In other words, drum out subversives but keep taking their money.[62]

The raid and the subsequent Anglo-Soviet breach cost Britain significantly.[63] An official report concluded 'military espionage and subversive activities throughout the ... Empire and North and South America were directed and carried out from 49 Moorgate'.[64] As in the aftermath of the 1923 Curzon Note, when subversion in South Asia resumed within weeks of a threatened breach,[65] the USSR gradually resumed overt and covert work after the ARCOS raid.

Given British concerns about Paris becoming a new base from which Moscow targeted Britain and its empire, intelligence officials kept their French counterparts informed. Sir Wyndham Childs followed up on the ARCOS raid by meeting the French Special Police Commissioner on 25 May in Calais.[66] Though British authorities found no papers concerning France, Childs felt it right to keep Paris updated but voiced regrets the French had not carried out similar raids simultaneously. This comment, noted the French military attaché in London to his minister, was based purely on a technical approach that failed to consider French political realities. Moreover, added General Ambroise Desprès, similar action in France could only have taken place had London told Paris of the upcoming raid.[67] Still, the *Deuxième* (2e) *Bureau* – French military intelligence, in charge of counter-espionage and counter-intelligence – was delighted at the smooth liaison work. To maintain it, Desprès urged Paris to share with London any intelligence on communist or Soviet activities against Britain.[68]

The British Right celebrated the expulsion of the Bolshevik delegation and the ensuing diplomatic breach. Even before it, local Conservative associations, and right-wing groups and sympathisers had long reported suspected "communist" activity to police.[69] One example illustrates what some at the time perceived as extremism and is interesting, since even Jix got involved. On 7 May 1927, a local newspaper editor wrote to the Chief Constable of Lincoln:

> Sir, I wish to call your attention to the fact that the roadway in front of my house was plastered up with chalk written advertisements on Friday morning ... Inspector Churchill has informed me ... you are powerless to prevent this annoyance to law-abiding citizens. That being so, I beg to warn you that should it happen again, it will probably lead to a breach of peace. That, at least, would be a matter needing your attention.[70]

The adverts supposedly concerned a demonstration by local unemployed during an upcoming visit by the Prince of Wales to Lincoln on 25 May.[71] The Chief Constable replied:

> Sir ... The information given to you ... would appear to be correct. I need hardly remind you ... a breach of the peace is a matter not only for the Police but ... also ... for the Magistrates to deal with. I feel sure ... you personally will refrain from doing or saying anything that might result in a breach of the peace but that you will proceed in a constitutional way and make your protest to the Watch Committee.[72]

Undeterred and dissatisfied, the editor complained directly to the Home Office:

Dear Sir, I beg to call your ... attention to the fact that ... extremists ... are utilizing the undercarriage of the main thoroughfares to chalk insulting advertisements upon them.... [One message] was 'There will be -ell to play in Unity Square'. Unity Square is where the relief-offices are situated. The loyal citizens of Lincoln are getting apprehensive.... The matter has been brought to the attention of both the Town Clerk and the Chief Constable of this city. I have the letters, written reply that nothing can be done.... Surely this cannot be true! Safety first is a good matter – and this is why I [appeal] to you.[73]

The Home Office took up the matter with the Chief Constable, now made to look incompetent and tactless. Further exchanges followed between department officials (including Jix), the editor and the Chief Constable. Not until 20 May was the latter able to convince the Home Office the situation was in hand:

Dear Mr. Dixon ... [This gentleman] has written a most misleading letter to your Department.... [S]ome days ago, I got into touch with the Chairman and Secretary of the local Unemployment Committee and they gave me their assurance ... their Committee had not the slightest intention of doing what is alleged.[74]

The Chief Constable's final note to the Home Office was instructive:

Dear Mr. Dixon ... The Royal Visit to Lincoln passed off without ... anything of an untoward nature. Nothing but demonstrations of enthusiasm and loyalty greeted the Prince.... Knowing the people of Lincoln (both workers and unemployed) as I do, this is just what I anticipated.... If only [some people] would show a little sympathy towards the unemployed, or else leave them alone altogether, instead of trying to ruffle them at every ... turn, some of the bad feeling which exists in this Cathedral City might be lessened, and my duties, if not made easier, would certainly be made more pleasant.[75]

This episode illustrated the traditionalist mindset Moscow had to overcome were revolution to occur in Britain.[76] Two tools at the Soviets' disposal were the leftist media[77] and the CPGB; neither was too effective. As had happened after the Zinoviev letter, Moscow needed a scapegoat in Britain for recent events. Once again, the Kremlin set its sights on the CPGB, particularly on its MP Shapurji Saklatvala.[78] The Comintern demanded an investigation and 'exhaustive report' into his activities, as well as into why, 'when the conditions

... are favourable and ... demand greater activity, there are no signs of special [CPGB] activities'.[79]

David Petrovsky,[80] Chair of the Comintern Anglo-American Secretariat, passed the CPGB reply on to Comintern's Political Secretariat: '[We] have done everything ... to prepare [Saklatvala's] speech [but] he was not allowed to talk in Parliament. We hoped ... he would ... [debate] on trade union law, but he got ill.' Petrovsky ultimately advised: '[C]lose this ... It is not politically expedient to start an open struggle against Saklatvala in present conditions'.[81] While trying to disrupt communist subversion, the Conservatives still needed to trade with Moscow.[82] Yet in another public reminder of ongoing Soviet activities, on 17 November 1927 authorities arrested Wilfred Macartney and his Comintern handler Georg Hansen.[83]

Macartney had a colourful life. Born in 1899 in Cupar, Fife, to an American mother and a Scots-Irish American father, Macartney had a peripatetic childhood and grew up in places like Panama and Russia.[84] Inheriting a considerable estate on his father's death in 1916, Macartney served in the Naval Reserve, working in the Levant and Aegean for both Naval Intelligence and SIS under Captain (later Sir) Compton Mackenzie.[85] The £70,000 (2011: nearly £4 million) inheritance, however, did not last long. By 1925, almost penniless, he claimed he had an epiphany about Communism but seemed to see it 'as a business opportunity rather than a spiritual home'.[86] Passing himself off at different times as an aristocrat, a naval officer and an army officer, among others, Macartney was in SIS's view 'completely unscrupulous, can never tell the truth ... is very clever but not quite so clever as he thinks'.[87]

In October 1926, following a nine-month prison term for a botched burglary, a bankrupt Macartney contacted the *Sunday Worker* and the *Daily Herald*, offering them information on his secret wartime work. Of greater interest to British intelligence, though, were Macartney's attempts to get closer to Soviets in Britain. In late March 1927, George Monkland, an insurance broker who knew Macartney, contacted former DNI Sir Reginald Hall claiming to have information of interest.[88] At a lunch with a senior SIS officer on the 29th Monkland gave them a thirteen-item questionnaire on the RAF. SIS quickly understood a foreign power (likely the USSR) was involved; given the foreign element and SIS's own views on MI5 abilities, the Service was reluctant to call on Vernon Kell.[89]

Monkland himself was like Macartney: expensive tastes but unable to pay for them. SIS carefully investigated Monkland in case he was a Soviet plant or just looking for easy money. He eventually passed scrutiny, at least in the eyes of his SIS case-officer, Major Desmond Morton, Head of Production and member of Section V (counter-intelligence and counter-Soviet work). Monkland told him Macartney had confessed to being a Comintern agent and that Moscow sought details on 'insurance of [munitions] cargoes ... to ... States bordering the [USSR]'. As a Lloyds insurance broker, Monkland was ideally placed to supply such details.[90]

Though he had previously sold information, the questionnaire was a more dangerous proposition; Morton believed 'Monkland was both frightened ... and ... honestly unwilling ... to betray his country.'[91] Macartney intrigued Morton not so much for his importance as an agent (not great) but for his ability to shed light on Soviet covert work run out of ARCOS. In April 1927, Morton gave Monkland information on the RAF to test him and find out how Macartney communicated with Soviet contacts. When Morton and Monkland met for the third time on 30 May, the recent ARCOS raid had added importance and urgency to the Macartney case.[92]

The British closely monitored Macartney's illicit travels[93] across Europe (particularly France, Germany and Holland). In early May, French intelligence confirmed he was a Soviet agent but questions remained, namely who handled Macartney and from where. When Monkland received a letter from a "Mr Johnson" arranging a meeting for the evening of 16 November 1927 in London, the trap was set. At this meeting, a man later identified as Georg Hansen – a IV Directorate "illegal" acting as a cut-out, likely sent by Jacob Kirchenstein from Hamburg – discussed tradecraft, including personal security and safe houses. Immediately after, Monkland told Morton of a second meeting scheduled for the following day between Macartney and Hansen. In case the latter planned to escape afterward, authorities arrested both men on 17 November. Hansen's lodgings contained no incriminating evidence but Macartney's did. On 18 January 1928, the pair received ten-year prison terms,[94] though an intervention by Vernon Kell, on clemency and financial grounds, resulted in Hansen's release and deportation in 1935.[95]

While London had a positive start to the year in the intelligence war with Moscow, 1928 left British agencies in turmoil. The Federated Press ring, which had far greater reach than Macartney and Hansen, was wound down. According to MI5 source and former Federated Press manager Albert Allen, the group had no financial problems until the ARCOS raid. When Britain expelled the Soviet delegation, it only gave William Ewer enough funds for a month's work. Afterward, his network limped on for a few months more by borrowing money.[96]

Eva Reckitt,[97] who may have helped Ewer out in 1927, had often received funds from abroad intended for him. US dollars were sometimes used, with

Moscow forwarding the required amounts to agents in the USA, who in turn passed everything on to Carl Haessler at the Federated Press office in New York. He then redirected the money either to Reckitt in London or to George Slocombe in Paris.[98] Before the ARCOS raid, funding in dollars for the CPGB, the National Minority Movement (NMM)[99] and the Federated Press arrived at Chesham House (the Soviet Embassy) via diplomatic bag. Ewer received the share meant for his group, while Andrew Rothstein collected sums quarterly for the CPGB and the NMM, each respectively receiving £4110 and £3290 annually (2011: £195,000 and £156,000). Rothstein then handed funds over to CPGB Secretary Albert Inkpin and Nathaniel Watkins of the NMM.[100]

Ewer's top lieutenant, Walter Holmes,[101] sometimes also arranged conversion of dollars into sterling. After the ARCOS raid, Inkpin started travelling to Berlin to collect funds even though CPGB and NMM annual stipends had by then dropped to £3290 and £2470 respectively (2011: £161,000 and £121,000). Inkpin normally took dollars to Paris where he met at least one of three female couriers (usually Rose Cohen),[102] as arranged by Slocombe. The women brought the notes back to London, where Holmes then arranged for exchange into sterling. Several people (e.g. Robin Page Arnot, Secretary of the Fabian/Labour Research Department between 1914 and 1926)[103] sometimes laundered small denominations through exchange bureaux and travel agencies. Inkpin and Watkins then collected clean funds for their organisations. After delivering money to Paris, Inkpin normally returned to Berlin, re-entering Britain via Harwich, Essex – an ideal entry point since according to Ewer's prize sources, Special Branch officers there were known to be lax. MI5 never noticed Inkpin's movements.[104]

Authorities also wanted to learn about communication arrangements. Albert Allen explained that on Wednesdays and Fridays, Chesham House received collected intelligence. Rose Edwardes carried the material, always watched by Vigilance Agency detectives on her journeys to and from the embassy. After the ARCOS raid, information went to Paris instead by secret ink in a book, with Edwardes and Dale acting as couriers. Ewer communicated with Slocombe and others abroad using ordinary post, cover addresses and coded language.[105]

Who at Chesham House handled this intelligence was always concealed from Federated Press members but Allen once heard the name 'Vasiloff or Vasiltseff'. MI5 had records of one Nikolai Vasiltsev, who the NKID sent to London in May 1924 as Assistant Head of the Consular Section. He stayed for two years until Timofei Kuznetsov replaced him. MI5 records listed Kuznetsov, who requested permission in 1925 to travel from Berlin to Britain to buy textiles. He arrived on 30 March 1926 but left in April, reapplying for entry in November. Ivan Mingulin, appointed in June 1924 as a clerk to the trade mission, eventually replaced Kuznetsov. Mingulin arrived in 1925, now listed as a correspondent with the embassy Press Section.[106] Once or twice, Allen said, the Federated Press suspected Moscow of inspecting their work. On one occasion, a man did come over to monitor operations, causing Ewer to protest to Chesham House.[107]

Interviewed in 1950 as part of final inquiries into Federated Press operations decades earlier, Ewer was clear. He and Walter Holmes visited the Soviet Embassy and trade delegation, where several Bolsheviks facilitated his group's operations – namely Nikolai Klyshko, one Maisky, one Radomsky and one of the Miller brothers (Peter A. or Anton A.), then Second Secretary[108] at the legation. Ewer described Holmes, his chief assistant, as 'a complete Communist fanatic' who betrayed any information to Moscow. As for the November 1924 *Daily Herald* notice, Ewer said the aim had been to draw 'the fire of the ... authorities'.[109] On who in his organisation knew the collected intelligence was for Moscow, he replied 'all'. Finally, Ewer urged 'a keen eye' be kept on Andrew Rothstein, another 'fanatical Communist'.[110]

In June 1928, seven months after Allen left the Federated Press and now in financial difficulties, MI5 'induced [him] to talk'. He initially demanded £1500 (2011: nearly £74,000) for the full story of his time with Ewer but the Service negotiated the figure down.[111] To the astonishment of MI5 officers, Allen subsequently revealed two Special Branch officers had long worked for Ewer.[112] This was significant because contrary to perception and until a September 1931 reorganisation of the intelligence community,[113] Special Branch – not MI5 – was the lead agency tackling communist subversion in Britain.

Holding out for as much money as possible, Allen did not name the men immediately so a full-scale investigation began to see if anyone previously based out of the Federated Press office on the Strand still worked for Moscow. Authorities shadowed Rose Edwardes on her regular travels to Holborn, London, where she allegedly ran the Featherstone Typewriting Bureau. This new cover for Ewer's group was set up in or just after October 1927, when Soviet intelligence officials in Paris told Ewer his existing organisation was to be closed down. He, Holmes and Dale – the latter now using his work as an enquiry officer for Shoreditch Borough Council as cover – regularly met Edwardes in Holborn; afterwards, either Ewer or Holmes visited Eva Reckitt. Surveillance soon paid off, uncovering Dale's meetings with the Special Branch

11 Photocopied page of Walter Dale's diary. On the lower right (week ending 25 December 1926), note surveillance of Captain H. A. O'Connor of 'Sec[urity] Intel[ligence]' at '35 Crom[well] Rd' – MI5's address. Note that Dale also knew O'Connor's home address.

"moles" – Dutch-born Inspector Hubert van Ginhoven and Sergeant Charles Jane.[114]

For around a decade, these prized sources provided Bolshevik intelligence with lists of suspects, subjects of mail intercept warrants, addresses of British intelligence offices and personnel, and detail on Special Branch operations – all for £20 a week.[115] MI5 informed the Home Office of this serious security breach and on 11 April 1929, authorities arrested van Ginhoven, Jane and Dale, whose work for Moscow was undeniable. In an election year, the Government chose not to prosecute, reportedly to avoid an outcry similar to that following publication of the 1924 Zinoviev Letter (not to mention disclosures about British intelligence – including awkward questions about how well MI5 could really do its job on such limited funds). Scotland Yard dismissed van Ginhoven and Jane on 2 May 1929.

Dale's diary showed he was the Federated Press's private detective from at least January 1922 to May 1927. With Allen's departure in November 1927 following a dispute with his employers[116] (whether Ewer or the Soviets is unclear), Dale also assumed the role of cut-out between Ewer and the two Special Branch officers until their April 1929 arrest.[117] The moles supplied up-to-date lists of people whose mail was to be intercepted; on whom 'special instructions had been issued to Aliens Officers at ports' like Harwich; and about whom 'any of the Intelligence Services had communicated with Scotland [Yard]'. Both officers also forewarned Ewer of imminent raids against communist individuals or organisations.[118]

According to Allen, former National Union of Police and Prison Officers General-Secretary (and Labour MP) Jack Hayes initially recommended van Ginhoven to Ewer in 1918 as someone who could obtain inside information at Scotland Yard. Allen first met the Dutchman at Vigilance Detective Agency, from where they worked closely until November 1927. As for Jane, Allen first noticed him when van Ginhoven reportedly accompanied a Dutch dignitary on a visit to northern England. Someone else had to maintain contact with the Federated Press; van Ginhoven suggested Jane, who filled in when needed. Allen categorised the vital intelligence received from both officers:

- accessing '[Special Branch] Registry and see what developments these cards indicated';
- providing 'any information regarding lists of suspects sent to the ports';
- supplying 'information on ... individuals whose correspondence might be on check'; and
- securing 'any ... information ... [on Scotland Yard] activities ... [of interest to] ... the Russians or the CPGB'.[119]

They obtained this by either infiltrating the registry at night or gathering intelligence during their daily duties – particularly the Dutchman, who often translated sensitive papers. He also seems to have acquired information by seducing or doing favours for female registry clerks.[120]

The October 1925 raid on CPGB headquarters illustrates advance warnings given to the Federated Press. Jane, involved in the action, telephoned Rose Edwardes about it but spoke guardedly, fearing eavesdroppers. She misinterpreted Jane and failed to warn others, making the raid a success in the eyes of British authorities.[121] Yet the London *rezidentura* felt Ewer (and the USSR) came out ahead since his two moles 'removed the most compromising documents' from police archives afterward. Soviet intelligence thus felt a June 1926 government report on the raid 'made a very feeble impression and did not contain any really secret material'.[122] Without knowing which documents were taken, one cannot say who was right.

The 1927 ARCOS raid was a rare occasion about which Ewer had no prior warning.[123] Yet his moles eventually identified intelligence officers involved in the operation and those who later visited ARCOS. One was Guy Liddell, the leading Special Branch counter-subversion expert who was 'cross not to be told about the raid'[124] by superiors until the last moment. The INO also tasked the Federated Press with sending former NUPPO General-Secretary James Marston to Uxbridge, west London, to look up "X", the former British ARCOS employee who 'had worked the [P]hotostat' and was the suspected source of information that triggered the raid.[125]

On 3 May 1929 the *Daily Mail* publicised the Federated Press case:

> Two officers of the Political Branch ... were yesterday dismissed.... They were Inspector Ginhoven, who has for many years been entrusted with important Secret Service missions, and Sergeant Jane, whose special work brought him into close touch with the Reds.... Ginhoven ... is a Dutchman by birth. Early in life, he became naturalised, and has served in the Police for more than twenty years. About a year ago, he was promoted Inspector. He was easily Scotland Yard's best linguist, and is stated to have an expert knowledge of [at least] eight tongues.... Jane also had an excellent reputation. His knowledge of the Communist movement was vast and intelligent.[126]

In 1950, Ewer confirmed all of the above and went further, saying his network revolved around the two officers. The Federated Press obtained most of its intelligence in Britain from them because van Ginhoven and Jane, said Ewer, were communists above all else.[127]

Within days of their dismissal, the Featherstone Typewriting Bureau closed down. Ewer (who MI5 previously thought had used Polish diplomatic channels for correspondence regarding his clandestine work) reportedly left for Poland, returning in September. Weeks later he fell out with the CPGB, which disapproved of an article of his in *Labour Monthly*. In December 1929, Ewer resigned the Party.[128] Despite knowing Indian communists used the "Kenneth Milton" (Ewer) channel from Paris to London, and though he had been a Party founding member, MI5 thought it unlikely the CPGB knew much about Ewer's espionage.[129]

The Service warily covered Ewer's subsequent declarations of anti-communism. Though seeming to have parted with the CPGB, remarked one MI5 officer, there was perhaps 'more to [the] resignation ... than meets the eye'. Such public disavowals, after all, were what the Cambridge Five would soon use to burnish their anti-communist credentials and deflect official suspicions. Following the 1929 dismantling of the Federated Press's known remnants, Ewer's journalistic career went from strength to strength and he remained a celebrated professional. His top lieutenant, Walter Holmes, had left the *Daily Herald* in 1928 to edit the *Sunday Worker*. With the 1930 launch of the *Daily Worker*, Holmes became its roving correspondent, with postings to the USSR and Manchuria. George Slocombe stayed in Paris until 1940, returning to Britain not having drawn much official interest since the "Milton" episode in 1925. Rose Edwardes, Walter Dale and Allen seem to have severed ties with Soviet intelligence. Edwardes moved to Sheffield while Allen held various jobs in the Bournemouth area as a café owner, boxing match promoter, and 'a masseur and sunray specialist'.[130]

As for the two Special Branch moles, Allen told MI5 Hubert van Ginhoven visited him on 12 May 1929, confiding he had a young Special Branch officer 'ready to take on [Federated Press] duties',[131] but authorities had no more leads than that. Allen reported van Ginhoven (and the others) seemed unaware of how much authorities already knew at this stage, the Dutchman saying they intended to keep working for Moscow. Van Ginhoven stayed in touch with Ewer via Jack Hayes MP,[132] which surprised both Allen and MI5. The Dutchman also stayed in occasional touch with Charles Jane, who after dismissal resumed his previous trade as a tailor's presser. The two ex-officers sometimes went out together but, as van Ginhoven reportedly told Ewer in 1949 at the British Legation in Copenhagen, Jane was by then 'very much down and out, and on the verge of going off his head'.[133] None was ever prosecuted despite a wealth of evidence from years of surveillance, outright confessions and seized documentation.

How, then, do these revelations change existing perceptions of Bolshevik interwar efforts to subvert British government? Soviet military intelligence arguably remained Moscow's best source of foreign intelligence until the 1936–38 Stalinist purges. Not only was the IV Directorate more focused in what it targeted but also it skilfully used the Comintern as a front, getting communists and "fellow travellers" worldwide to work *for* the USSR, and not exclusively against Capitalism and Fascism. Many IV Directorate and Comintern OMS officers and head agents – quite a few of them Central and Eastern European – were accomplished professionals and linguists in their own right. Comfortable among European polite society,[134] these individuals differed early on from their *Cheka* peers, many of whom were worse educated and better suited for internal repression in provincial Russia than sparkling conversation in fashionable Paris. That said, the *Cheka* undeniably had exceptional officers, as Operations TREST and SINDIKAT proved. Yet from the *Cheka's* inception, operations abroad remained above all domestic in their ultimate goal: suppressing White and affiliated counter-revolutionaries. Or so it was thought.

The Federated Press of America case revealed a group of agents, sources and sub-sources who for a decade infiltrated British security, intelligence and policy circles. Although the network penetrated several government departments up to 1929, the argument could be made that except for Special Branch, these infiltrations seem to have been fairly low-level and certainly unlike the Cambridge Five, for instance. Though strictly accurate, such a view would miss the critical lesson the two cases in this chapter illustrate: being of intelligence value to a hostile power rarely hinges on high rank; access alone is the true discriminator.[135] To how many more people like Macartney, for example, did unidentified, corruptible Passport Office clerks give false British travel papers?

Between 1918–19 and 1929, what eventually became the Federated Press ring infiltrated Special Branch; the Foreign, India, Colonial and Post Offices; the French Foreign Ministry and some of its embassies; and the Admiralty. Naval affairs at that time were of course especially sensitive for Britain. Commander Harold Grenfell,[136] Naval Attaché in St Petersburg/Petrograd from 1912 to 1917 and a convert to Communism, shocked British intelligence officials in the 1920s by corresponding and exchanging draft articles with Ewer for possible publication in the *Daily Herald*. These intercepted letters particularly alarmed "C" – himself a career naval officer – because they detailed work done by naval attachés and Passport Control Officers in countries bordering the USSR.[137] Furthermore, Ewer's group obtained information harmful to British national security on IPI, MI5, SIS and GCCS, along with arrangements between the

Home and Post Offices and cable companies to intercept postal and telephone communications; and possibly on Woolwich Arsenal.[138] Moreover, since Vigilance Agency detectives in London watched select foreign embassies, Soviet intelligence may also have penetrated them through the Federated Press (though no evidence of that has emerged).

In many European countries, and surely in Britain, the *Cheka* recruited among Russian émigrés who often needed money, remained patriotic to their Motherland, and wanted to return to the Russia portrayed by Bolshevik propaganda (and some British intellectuals) as a Socialist paradise.[139] Ewer's group was a repetition of a scheme originally invented in Germany in 1919, where the Communist Party created from its secret members, supporters and sympathisers several underground networks working on intelligence, counter-intelligence and military affairs. All groups worked for the Party and actively collaborated with all branches of Bolshevik intelligence. These networks also provided an excellent pool of future recruits for the Soviets. After Germany it was France (Jean Crémet's organisation, dismantled in April 1927), followed by Britain (Ewer's). Noticeably, all these groups operated largely by themselves at first and were not yet as strictly controlled by Moscow as they would be from the early 1930s onward.[140]

Another feature was that at least nine members of the Federated Press ring were disaffected policemen. One former officer, Vigilance Detective Agency and NUPPO Head Jack Hayes, was even re-elected Labour MP in the May 1929 General Election.[141] Thus, at least one Soviet source worked in Parliament. Ironically, militancy in supposedly conservative police forces was what enabled Moscow to infiltrate Special Branch. By compromising the lead agency tasked with fighting them, the Bolsheviks applied lessons perfected during long years as clandestine revolutionaries, constantly but unsuccessfully fighting off *Okhrana* infiltration.[142]

Also curious is that the Federated Press targeted GCCS, the newest and most secretive British intelligence agency, within one to two years of its creation in late 1919. Conversely, Ewer's group did not learn of Vernon Kell's role as MI5 Director until mid-1924. Perhaps this reflected a temporary Bolshevik priority, since the leading Tsarist codebreaker Ernst Vetterlein had begun working for London in June 1918. Moscow would have wanted to find out just how much the British now knew. By enabling GCCS to defeat Bolshevik codes and ciphers, among others, Vetterlein gave Britain a vital strategic edge in international affairs throughout the 1920s.

Events in this book therefore suggest incidents previously seen as isolated Soviet successes (e.g. cipher clerk Ernest Oldham's August 1929 decision to

12 Metropolitan Police sergeant Jack Hayes headed the Vigilance Detective Agency, which ensured the security of Federated Press operations. This future Labour MP (and Party Whip) reportedly talent-spotted for William Ewer as early as 1918.

sell Foreign Office secrets)[143] should be viewed in the context of a longer-term campaign to expose and exploit Whitehall vulnerabilities. In the late 1920s, Ewer began corresponding with a noted Orientalist and a young economist. Entirely unremarkable in itself, were it not that the two were Harold St John Philby and Maurice Dobb. One was the anti-Establishment father of Harold "Kim" Philby; the other the Cambridge don who introduced young Philby to Communism while he studied at Trinity College in the early 1930s. St John Philby sent Ewer copies of confidential government documents on Arab affairs[144] and the sons, moreover, picked up where their fathers left off. A biography of Victor Rothschild reveals that a colleague who went to Trinity with him in 1935 soon joined the CPGB, recruited by yet another College man: Denis Ewer, William's son.[145]

Yet gaps remain in the Federated Press story. Due to incomplete records in case files made public, some inconsistencies remain that deserve further research. For instance, questions surround the 1927–28 winding down of operations. Did MI5 staff (or anyone else's, for that matter) pose as Soviets to reactivate remnants of the network and identify unknown agents still at large? Allen never revealed names immediately, hoping for more money. Even the Special Branch moles, van Ginhoven and Jane, were unmasked without his direct help; he only confirmed their names to MI5 the day after their arrest.[146]

One question asked in and of Cabinet in months leading up to the May 1927 Anglo-Soviet breach was "And then what?" The Conservatives might well sever ties but either Labour or the Liberals would eventually return to power. Were Cabinet hardliners willing to settle for the short-term satisfaction of giving Moscow a metaphorical black eye, only to see this ultimately ineffective fit of pique reversed one or two, or five years later? While popular with parts of British society, a break with Moscow was by no means universally supported.

This chapter highlighted two important issues. First, Cabinet's determination to retaliate for Moscow's subversion and involvement in the 1926 strikes led ministers to ignore not only a sizeable portion of the electorate but also advice from some of Britain's most experienced diplomats. Though only one Head of Mission out of seven mentioned here supported outright war if needed, three others urged Cabinet to break ties only in concert with other Powers. The remaining three Heads of Mission essentially argued London's desire for a break went against British popular sentiment and since the negatives outweighed the positives, a rupture should not occur simply for its own sake or out of anger.

Yet Cabinet did break with Moscow, proving critics right. The challenge for British intelligence actually increased, given Parliamentary disclosures and the move to continental Europe of the Soviet apparatus targeting Britain. That all major intelligence disclosures (1920, 1923 and 1927) were either prompted by or occurred under the Conservatives is paradoxical, given their horror of subversion. Hardliners' disregard for intelligence sources and methods, however, should be viewed in light of the postwar political climate. Conservatives tended to view information on Russia through the lens of high Party politics and in relation to Labour's menacing rise. This made the British intelligence community expendable if needed. Subversion did not decline noticeably between 27 May 1927 and the resumption of ties on 3 October 1929. Renewing relations with Moscow was an easy choice for Ramsay MacDonald, who in June 1929 had become Prime Minister leading a second minority Labour government, thanks mainly to a stagnating economy and rising unemployment.[147]

A second issue was consolidation of a near-decade-long SIS practice of operating domestically, as shown by its involvement in the ARCOS and Macartney affairs. This, of course, was another symptom of intelligence community dysfunction blurring inter-agency boundaries, and duplicating effort and expenditure. SIS's need to run networks and collect its own intelligence on the "Red Menace" domestically stemmed from longstanding concerns about MI5 competence and Special Branch trustworthiness. On the last issue, at least, SIS concerns proved justified. As far back as 1918–19, when the over-ambitious Basil Thomson roamed Whitehall, Special Branch was already a broken institution. The Federated Press case only confirmed publicly what many in intelligence circles had long argued privately: they could not trust the police with sensitive information. While such assertions conveyed some condescension – recall the typical socio-economic backgrounds of intelligence officers versus police officers – in William Ewer's own words, his Special Branch moles were communists 'first and foremost'. On existing evidence, therefore, the Federated Press of America ring was the most extensive – and arguably most effective – Soviet network operating in Britain in the 1920s.[148]

Ewer's group damaged British counter-intelligence and counter-subversive efforts throughout that decade, and probably well into the 1930s too. An MI5 officer reviewing the case in late 1949 wrote:

> It became abundantly clear that for … ten years, any information regarding subversive organisations and individuals supplied to Scotland Yard by SIS or MI5, which had become the subject of [Special Branch] enquiry, would have to be regarded as having been betrayed to Ewer's group. Through his sources in [Special Branch], Ewer was enabled to

give warning to suspects and subversive organisations of suspicions entertained or of projected police action, to nullify the effects of security measures, to cripple enquiry, and thus positively to enhance the successful operations of the Communist conspiracy in the United Kingdom and its promotion from abroad.[149]

Conclusion

> The new is no more than a reinvention of the old which [sic] has been forgotten. ... The new flows out of the old and you [must] know the old to understand the new.
>
> Vasily N. Mitrokhin[1]

THE end of the USSR on 26 December 1991 closed a seventy-four-year period unlike any before in history. Competing visions for the future of humanity led to a global struggle that several times nearly ended in a nuclear holocaust. To generations of Westerners used to the relative predictability of the original 'long twilight struggle',[2] the 'new world order'[3] after the Cold War was unfamiliar and therefore unsettling. The only certainty in international affairs was now uncertainty, and decades-old concepts like "ideology", "subversion" and "radicalisation" virtually overnight became relics of a dangerous time gone by.

Having paid a steep price tackling totalitarianism since 1917, the West complacently neglected those valuable lessons after 1991. In 1992, for instance, MI5 stopped monitoring political subversion.[4] That same year, US political scientist Francis Fukuyama articulated a view others in American government shared, declaring 'the end of history' from an ideological standpoint. Historians the world over must have cringed at such euphoric triumphalism, understandable though it was.

Within ten years – during which Western powers largely focused on domestic affairs while some nations violently disintegrated, genocide unfolded and Islamicist extremism spread – even Fukuyama, to his credit, revised his opinions.[5] On 11 September 2001, "ideology", "subversion" and "radicalisation" roared back into mainstream discourse – and after a decade of concentrating on economic growth, the West was predictably short on ideas. Only after years of combat in Afghanistan, Iraq and elsewhere as part of 'the long war'[6] on terror did political leaders again acknowledge that in international affairs, ideology does matter after all.[7]

Examining Bolshevik subversion and British responses to it from 1917 to 1929 reveals striking parallels with the present. A deep recession forced London to trade even with regimes as openly hostile as Moscow, dividing politicians and voters alike on how to balance the creation of much-needed jobs with safeguarding national security. Meanwhile, Bolshevik security organs increasingly isolated Russian citizens by proscribing interaction with foreigners and tightening censorship. Yet there are also crucial differences, which make Britain in the early twenty-first century less capable of handling the Russian State threat than in the early twentieth.

Why? At that time, and despite competition from rival states, Britain was still a manufacturing powerhouse of repute,[8] giving its politicians and senior officials great influence in world affairs. Nowadays, despite globalisation and the information revolution – or perhaps, because of them – most British politicians and senior officials paradoxically seem more insular and self-interested than their counterparts did a century ago. Few have spent significant time living, working or managing – let alone fighting – overseas, and fewer still have done military service. The role of the Commonwealth after the end of empire has also declined sharply, as has the public-service ethos in the broader society from which most politicians and officials now come. These days, the average politician or civil servant is worse equipped to cope with or understand the modern Russian State threat, and therefore less able to protect Britain. In politics, the term 'statesman' has lost virtually all meaning.

One key finding of this research was the extent of Moscow's decade-long access to sensitive information on British security/intelligence operations and personnel, and policy decisions, mainly through what became the Federated Press of America ring. Just as unexpected was how during twelve years of diplomatic exchanges about subversion, London never defined it. Given how well funded subversion was, another striking fact was how underfunded yet relatively effective British agencies still were in this period, despite being the sacrificial lamb at times for politicians and senior officials willing to compromise years of painstaking work and significant expense.

Economics, shrouded in the convenient trappings of ideology by both sides, drove Anglo-Russian relations in the period this book examines. Yet the steep rise in British police funding from 1918 on (coinciding with sharp reductions in intelligence spending and staff) undermined Cabinet arguments about lack of resources. The extent to which the intelligence community relied on and was tied into the British Right to combat Bolshevism was one visible outcome of this between 1917 and 1929. An example of shortages adding to community dysfunction was the degree to which SIS felt it had to deviate from its charter and operate domestically, due to concerns over MI5 competence and Special Branch reliability.

On the Soviet side, a salient point was just how disjointed the early formulation of foreign policy could be. Yet despite incoherence in some areas,

Moscow had foresight in others. At least as early as September 1920, Cabinet was told of Kremlin intentions to penetrate British institutions via universities. GCCS (the newest and most secretive British agency) was one of Moscow's earliest targets for penetration – as was law enforcement. This book demonstrates how the 1918–19 strikes left London Metropolitan and other police officers exposed professionally, economically and socially, and how susceptible that made some of them to Soviet recruitment.

Successful penetration elsewhere allowed Bolshevik delegates in London to send intelligence to Moscow gleaned only a day or so earlier from Foreign Office documents. Yet despite this access, the Kremlin seems not to have realised how soon after the General Strike (and how long before the ARCOS raid) the Conservatives were already set on a diplomatic breach. Preceded by ministerial disclosures on SIGINT successes, the May 1927 break underscored the reality of the relationship between (British) politicians and intelligence. When enough political capital is at stake, the agencies are expendable.[9]

Evidence leads to three conclusions regarding how Britain tackled communist subversion from 1917 to 1929. First, it is human nature – and therefore that of bureaucracies – to identify lessons when absolutely needed but seldom to learn them, especially if a crisis has passed. Diehards in Cabinet and intelligence circles compromised the vital strategic edge provided by GCCS not once, not twice, but seven times between 1919 and 1927.[10] More unsettling still was politicians then disparaging the School for protecting the very sources and methods enabling Britain to cope with Moscow. As for HUMINT, perhaps the best examples of government inability (or unwillingness) to learn lessons identified were the unheeded September 1920, November 1921 and August 1922 Directorate of Intelligence and Special Branch warnings about what Russian intelligence went on to do to such effect in the 1930s: recruit undergraduates from prominent British families.

Yet Bolshevik leaders were equally good at ignoring common sense. A good illustration was the puzzling insistence throughout 1920 by Georgi Chicherin, his deputy Maxim Litvinov and others in NKID, despite warnings, to keep using codes and ciphers known to have been compromised by Western codebreakers. This was even more confusing when Moscow began sensitive trade talks with London on 31 May 1920. Allowing enemies to read communications when the Kremlin had staked its domestic and international legitimacy on the outcome of these negotiations made little sense, unless there were other motives.

A second conclusion is successive Cabinets faced a new Bolshevik threat from 1917 but from a security and intelligence perspective, at least, they still looked to fight the last enemy. The unwillingness of many politicians and officials to face postwar socio-economic realities is documented. Challenges like universal suffrage and mass democracy made many long for pre-war days, a time of greater clarity and stability. Instinctive aversion to this brave new (postwar) world meant most were psychologically unprepared to appreciate fully how multifaceted Bolshevik subversion could be. Post-Armistice events in Britain illustrated these difficulties.

Nobody would deny the peace dividend demanded from British intelligence was not only needed but also good for democracy. Such radical cuts so soon after 11 November 1918, however, signalled the will of nostalgic politicians to reclaim vast powers given to an expanding national security apparatus out of wartime necessity. The unprecedented devolution of power had been essential to take on perceived existential threats (first German espionage and subversion, then Pacifism and Socialism) with which traditional policing could not cope. Yet many Victorian and Edwardian men comprising the British body politic detested such distasteful yet necessary practices, which in their eyes were very much in the Continental tradition.

Their approach was to ignore some new postwar realities, reduce below a bare minimum the number of specialists who could tackle communist subversion in all its forms, and look back to a more comforting (and therefore plausible) past for answers. These men again chose traditional policing to fight what seemed the pre-eminent postwar danger: overt revolution as in Romanov Russia. Logically, such threat perceptions meant the Government's main concern was containing potentially violent outbreaks and restoring public order.

The trouble, however, was that by virtue of their origins, development and success as a clandestine revolutionary group, the Bolsheviks put greater stock in covert subversion. Infiltrating enemy institutions was for Lenin's followers something upon which their very survival depended, a lesson seared into their collective psyche throughout a relentless fourteen-year campaign against the Tsarist *Okhrana*. Perhaps the greatest failure of the British political classes from 1917 to 1929 was not realising that, just as the First World War was a total war requiring the mobilisation of every national institution, combating communist subversion effectively would require an equally comprehensive approach from national security structures. This would involve carefully legislated vigilance at home, aggressive operations abroad, targeted economic sanctions as needed and a propaganda effort matching Moscow's. To do all this, though, a great deal of money was needed; by 1918, there was little of it to go around.

From the Armistice, MI5, SIS and even GCCS subsisted on tiny budgets, ensuring a degree of coverage but little more. Vernon Kell's plaintive letters over an additional few hundred pounds here and there, and Alastair Denniston's struggles with the Treasury bear witness to this. Conversely, police funding grew enormously from 1918. Perhaps because one of MI5's roles was liaison with Chief Constables nationwide,[11] this may have given the impression of sufficient scrutiny of all Bolshevik activities. On the overt side, this may even have been possible; on the covert side, however, postwar budgets and staff did not allow proper coverage of more than a few priority targets. The Federated Press network, which operated undetected for five years before finally catching MI5's attention in 1924, illustrated the problem. Ironically, the ring penetrated the intelligence community via the police, the institution sidelined in 1914 for its perceived inability to cope with new wartime threats like espionage and foreign subversion.

So how did the four agencies fare overall in informing British policy toward Moscow from 1917 to 1929? Unquestionably, GCCS was from its creation in November 1919 the most valuable and valued of the four. The insight decrypts gave into Russian capabilities and intentions largely explains the two-year bureaucratic tussle between the Admiralty and the Foreign Office for School control. SIS would have to rank a close second despite some unflattering episodes in the twelve years here examined. Customers genuinely seemed to like and respect SIS Chiefs in this period, Mansfield Cumming and Hugh Sinclair, in contrast to their counterparts in MI5 and Special Branch. This helped SIS not only to survive but in fact to thrive (despite a faltering performance at times), as evidenced by the September 1923 subordination of GCCS to the Service.

Conversely, MI5's ability to influence politicians suffered because of Vernon Kell's reputation as bookish and timid, even though he was as much an anti-communist as many others in Whitehall and Westminster. Only when discussing imagined or actual subversion of the military did Kell really get undivided attention. All agencies faced postwar budget cuts but, given its broad remit to tackle (military) subversion and foreign espionage at home and across the Empire, MI5 certainly suffered most. These tasks are resource-intensive in money and people terms; from November 1918, MI5 had less and less of both.

Paradoxically, the agency whose intelligence warned politicians of Moscow's many-sided approach to subversion – Special Branch – was also the most discredited. Even as communist intentions became clearer, Basil Thomson and Wyndham Childs found it difficult to get Cabinet's attention. Thomson's excesses from 1917 to 1921 meant the agency was largely suspect throughout the 1920s, a view confirmed by the 1928–29 rolling-up of the Federated Press network. Though Cabinets since 1917 had feared revolution most, the greater threat was in fact covert subversion of British institutions.

Yet what exactly constituted subversion? This was arguably the prickliest question affecting bilateral relations. From 1917 to 1929, the British Government neither formally nor fully defined all it regarded as illegal behaviour. Given the Bolsheviks' revolutionary ethos, any definition, no matter how comprehensive, would have been in vain anyway. Moreover, since London's perception of subversion covered a wide range of State and State-sponsored activities, fully defining boundaries of acceptable behaviour would have been almost impossible. Yet why Britain never even attempted this properly begs some questions. Could it have concluded this was not viable? Was the concept of subversion allowed to remain legally and diplomatically vague to give British government increased room for manoeuvre in countering the USSR? No evidence to suggest this has yet emerged, but some measures diehards advocated[12] would have been harder to justify (let alone conduct) had there been a legal definition of subversion.

This term ultimately came to mean anything undermining British prestige and perceived national interests. After all, as the Foreign Office's Don Gregory argued in April 1923, prestige mattered – especially in the context of the old Great Game, of which Bolshevik imperialism was but the most recent manifestation. The last conclusion is that the meaning of subversion changed with time. By late 1917, given the First World War and the overthrow of the Romanovs, British hardliners regarded Bolshevik "internationalism" as something out of the Book of Revelation. By late 1922, however, diehards viewed Moscow's activities more as an admittedly serious irritant, but one to be exploited in preventing what would for these men be truly apocalyptic: Labour's rise to power. Shifting official perceptions of subversion – and how intelligence was (mis)used along the way – can be broadly traced over five distinct phases.

The first essentially started with the Bolshevik uprising on 25 October 1917 and ended with David Lloyd George's speech on 8 November 1919, the second anniversary of the Revolution. In that speech, he first signalled a shift away from British intervention in Russia toward a mutually beneficial trading relationship. This period was initially characterised by shock, then confusion and finally anger. Lenin had toppled one of the world's most powerful dynasties, withdrawn Russia from the war and sued for peace with Imperial Germany, allowing it to bring even more firepower to bear on the Western

Front. The remaining Allies felt betrayed but also expected Bolshevism to collapse quickly. When it did not, support grew for the Whites, culminating in multinational military intervention. The Lloyd George speech was therefore a watershed. With Britain's precarious postwar finances and gradual realisation the Bolsheviks were here to stay, policy shifted from overt and covert intervention in Russia to covert alone.

The second phase started with Lloyd George's 1919 speech and ended with the signing of the Anglo-Russian trade agreement on 16 March 1921. Realising the Prime Minister would ignore their misgivings in hopes of improving bilateral ties, hardliners – several of them prominent intelligence men – played up the "Red Card" even more. While many of them still feared overt revolution in light of recent industrial unrest, military mutinies and police strikes, for most of them, even the nation's grim postwar economy and desperate need for new trade were not compelling enough. During this phase, hardliners not only encouraged the politicisation of HUMINT on Bolshevik activities but also compromised sensitive SIGINT sources and methods publicly, in attempts to undermine closer bilateral ties and thus Bolshevik legitimacy.

The third stage began with the signing of the trade agreement and ended with the 6 December 1923 General Election. Lloyd George's 19 October 1922 resignation was another watershed. The ensuing general election not only restored the Conservatives to Downing Street for the first time since 1905 but also confirmed Labour as the official opposition. This seemed to confirm longstanding diehard fears that Labour's political rise and the spread of Bolshevism across Britain would one day converge. Yet though ideologically closer to Moscow, Labour was far from being in lockstep with the Bolsheviks, who actually mistrusted the Party but had no problem exploiting it to bring communist rule to Britain.

Nevertheless, by October 1922 the Conservatives still vilified Labour and at once reasserted their own, more antagonistic policies toward Moscow. Debt recognition, reparations, religious freedom and subversion were all grist to the Conservative mill. The last issue increasingly became a useful political tool with which to hit back at the Bolsheviks for not delivering what London most wanted at a time of stalled economic recovery: sizeable trade increases to improve national finances and reduce unemployment. Their stubborn failure to materialise made Conservatives readier to threaten a break. That was what happened in May 1923 when Cabinet again compromised SIGINT publicly in an attempt to coerce the USSR to fulfil the terms of the trade agreement.

The fourth phase lasted from the December 1923 General Election to the one on 29 October 1924. Having failed to prevent the doomsday scenario of a

Labour government, the Conservatives used incidents like the Zinoviev Letter to portray their opponents as Moscow stooges. This was not quite the case, despite Labour's initial naivety toward the USSR. Ramsay MacDonald's anger at continued subversion and Soviet media attacks on his government actually threatened to derail bilateral negotiations in early 1924. Though diehards in Conservative and intelligence circles mistrusted Labour, MacDonald seemed as committed as his predecessors at least to monitoring Soviet activities in Britain.

The fifth and final stage lasted from the October 1924 election to the resumption of ties in October 1929. Given the upheaval the Zinoviev affair caused in British politics, and with the Conservatives again in power, what little goodwill they may have had left toward Moscow evaporated with the 1926 strikes. Outrage at Soviet interference (including financial support for miners) meant that by May 1926, a diplomatic break was a matter of time. The clearest indication subversion had increasingly become a Conservative political tool from October 1922 emerged even before the May 1927 rupture. With a diplomatic breach and the expulsion of Soviet delegates only days away, Cabinet nevertheless decided to retain Britain's insignificant trading relationship with Moscow even while subversion continued. To make matters worse, Parliamentary disclosures about British SIGINT successes led the USSR to introduce theoretically unbreakable OTPs, shutting GCCS out of most Soviet traffic for years.

The implicit message in Cabinet's 1927 decision to keep taking Stalin's rouble was much the same sent from February 1920, when exploratory trade contacts began between the two governments. The message repeatedly confirmed the Bolsheviks' one enduring stereotype about their enemies: that at the expense of nearly all else – including many principles supposedly underpinning its democratic traditions – the West's primary motive was expectation of profit. For two hundred and fifty years, but especially since 1917, Russia has cleverly exploited this weakness with promises of quick and substantial profits, and preferential access to vast natural resources. Under Putin and Medvedev (and now Putin again), Russia today does simply what it did under Lenin and Stalin. Then, as now, it looked to seduce the West by buying its compliance. Now, as then, the West fails to recognise this and learn lessons at its own peril.

Notes

Introduction

1 This book does not cover Ireland; see Christopher Andrew, *Her Majesty's Secret Service: The Making of the British Intelligence Community* (New York, 1986), chapters (ch.) 7–8; Paul McMahon, *British Spies and Irish Rebels: British Intelligence and Ireland, 1916–1945*, History of British Intelligence (Woodbridge, 2008).

2 Michael Smith, 'The Government Code and Cipher School and the First Cold War', *Action This Day: Bletchley Park from the Breaking of the Enigma Code to the Birth of the Modern Computer*, ed. Michael Smith and Ralph Erskine (London, 2001), 15–40. See also Keith Neilson, *Britain, Soviet Russia and the Collapse of the Versailles Order, 1919–1939* (Cambridge, 2006).

3 Michael Occleshaw, *Dances in Deep Shadows: Britain's Clandestine War in Russia 1917–20* (London, 2006).

4 The term *siloviki* comes from *silovye struktury* (force structures), 'a reference to the armed services, law-enforcement bodies, and intelligence agencies that wield the coercive power of the State'. United 'more by outlook and interests', the *siloviki* are a hierarchical, 'informal network of ... officials and businessmen ... who share similar political views, pursue a common policy agenda, and seek joint control over economic assets'. Ian Bremmer and Samuel Charap, 'The Siloviki in Putin's Russia: Who They Are and What They Want', *The Washington Quarterly* 30:1 (2007), 83–92: page (p.) 86. See Andrei Soldatov and Irina Borogan, *The New Nobility: The Restoration of Russia's Security State and the Enduring Legacy of the KGB* (New York, 2010), Part I.

5 See Glossary and Robert Pringle, 'The Heritage and Future of the Russian Intelligence Community', *International Journal of Intelligence and Counter-intelligence (IJIC)* 11:2 (1998), 175–84.

6 Sergei Kovalev, 'Why Putin Wins', *The New York Review of Books* 54:18 (2007), 64–6; Julie Elkner, 'Spiritual Security in Putin's Russia', 2005, www.historyandpolicy.org; Julie Fedor, *Russia and the Cult of State Security: The Chekist Tradition, from Lenin to Putin*, Studies in Intelligence (London, 2011).

7 Nicholas Riasanovsky, *A History of Russia* (Oxford, 2000), p. 63.

8 Under Tsardom, the term came to mean 'practices needed to organise a study circle, a meeting, a trade union or a revolutionary party' without alerting the police. Yet a parallel term 'developed in the newly-created Soviet intelligence services'. Years of underground struggle 'equipped them with a "tradecraft" which worked ... well for their new role ... overseas'. Being a 'hunted revolutionary in your own land was a good preparation for acting as a spy in someone else's'. David McKnight, *Espionage and the Roots of the Cold War: The Conspiratorial Heritage*, Studies in Intelligence (London, 2002), pp. 2–3.

9 Fredric Zuckerman, *The Tsarist Secret Police Abroad: Policing Europe in a Modernising World* (Basingstoke, 2003), ch. 4; Christopher Andrew and Oleg Gordievsky, *KGB: The Inside Story of its Foreign Operations from Lenin to Gorbachev* (London, 1990), pp. 4–18.

10 Pringle, 'The Heritage', p. 177.

11 Yet in the context of *konspiratsya*, 'to regard the words "legal" and "illegal" as equivalent to "lawful" and "unlawful" would be to misunderstand both Bolshevist semantics and ... practice'. More correctly, 'substitute "overt" for "legal" and "clandestine" or "conspiratorial" for "illegal"'. Günther Nollau, *International Communism and World Revolution: History and Methods* (London, 1961), p. 157.

12 Julie Anderson, 'The Humint Offensive from Putin's *Chekist* State', *IJIC* 20:2 (2007), 258–316.

13 The USSR was created on 30 December 1922.

14 'State of the Nation Address', 25 April 2005, www.fas.org.

15 Francis Fukuyama, *The End of History and the Last Man* (London, 1992), expanding on his essay 'The End of History?', *The National Interest* (Summer 1989), 1–17: p. 1: '[W]e may be witnessing ... not just the end of the Cold War ... but the end of history as such'; that is, 'the end point of mankind's ideological evolution and the universalization of Western

liberal democracy as the final form of human government'.

16 In 1990 the North Atlantic Treaty Organisation (NATO) military budget was £283 billion (2011 value: £748 billion; see 'Currency', Glossary); in 1997 it was £256 billion (2011: £465 billion). From 1991 to 1996, US Congress cut intelligence budgets by 19% and ordered a 17.5% reduction in personnel by 1999. Between 1991 and 1998, US intelligence lost 20,600 staff. In 1991 the British intelligence community numbered 'significantly in excess of 15,000' with an annual budget of £1 billion (2011: £2.5 billion). By 1998–99, the Single Intelligence Vote (SIV) for the Secret Intelligence Service (SIS), the Government Communications Headquarters (GCHQ) and the Security Service (MI5) had declined to £694 million (2011: £1.3 billion). In 2003, the British community was thought to comprise 10,000 staff although Sir Gerald Warner, Intelligence and Security Coordinator at the Cabinet Office from 1991 to 1996, estimated total annual costs to be up to 2.5 times higher. *NATO Handbook 2001*, ch. 9, Tables 3 and 4; Roger George and Robert Kline, *Intelligence and the National Security Strategist: Enduring Issues and Challenges* (Lanham, MD, 2006), p. 185; Michael Herman, *Intelligence Power in Peace and War* (Cambridge, 1996), p. 38; Dan Arbel and Ran Edelist, *Western Intelligence and the Collapse of the Soviet Union, 1980–90* (London, 2003), p. 133; Parliamentary Papers, *Intelligence and Security Committee* [ISC] *Annual Report, 1997–98*, Cmd 4073 (1998), p. 9; Stephen Dorril, *MI6: Fifty Years of Special Operations* (London, 2001), pp. 799–800.

17 Of individuals holding high government or business posts in 2008, nearly 80% had served in either the KGB or its main successors. Francesca Mereu, 'Putin Made Good on Promise to FSB', *The Moscow Times*, 8 February 2008, www.cdi.org; Julie Anderson, 'The *Chekist* Takeover of the Russian State', *IJIC* 19:2 (2006), 237–88; Edward Lucas, *The New Cold War: How the Kremlin Threatens both Russia and the West* (London, 2008), ch. 1. By 2010, it was under 25%. Idem, *Deception: Spies, Lies and How Russia Dupes the West* (London, 2013), p. 72.

18 Fredric Jameson, *Postmodernism, or, the Cultural Logic of Late Capitalism* (London, 1991), p. ix.

19 Peter Hennessy and Gail Brownfeld, 'Britain's Cold War Security Purge: The Origins of Positive Vetting', *The Historical Journal* (*THJ*) 25:4 (1982), 965–74; Peter Hennessy, *The Secret State: Whitehall and the Cold War* (London, 2003), pp. 90–9.

20 See Amy Knight, *How the Cold War Began: Igor Gouzenko and the Hunt for Soviet Spies* (Toronto, 2005); 'Istoriia Voennoy Razvedki' [History of Military Intelligence], www.agentura.ru; Lurie and Kochik, *GRU*, pp. 7–97.

21 This was State policy: 'As soon as *Chekists* first put *rezidentura* [intelligence stations] in Soviet diplomatic and trade missions abroad', each chief (*rezident*) 'was ordered by Party Instructions of 1920 to give highest priority to inserting agents into the enemy's intelligence and [counter-intelligence] organs by recruiting people working there'. Tennent H. Bagley, *Spy Wars: Moles, Mysteries and Deadly Games* (New Haven, CT, 2007), p. 134. The first *Cheka* Foreign Section (INO) *rezident* Moscow appointed to London was Józef Krasny (alias Rotstadt, former head of the Communist International [Comintern] bureau in Vienna) but Britain rejected him. Private correspondence. We now know penetration of British secret machinery pre-dated even the 1920 directive (see Chapter 2).

22 Margaret Thatcher, *The Downing Street Years* (London, 1993), p. 377.

23 Keith Jeffery and Peter Hennessy, *States of Emergency: British Governments and Strike-breaking since 1919* (London, 1983).

24 'The modern British intelligence community effectively came into being during the [First World War] and the years immediately following it'. Keith Jeffery and Alan Sharp, 'Lord Curzon and Secret Intelligence', *Intelligence and International Relations, 1900–45*, ed. Christopher Andrew and Jeremy Noakes (Exeter, 1987), 103–26: p. 103. The term "United Kingdom [UK] intelligence community", however, did not become common until after 1945.

25 Hennessy, *The Secret* (2003), pp. 79–83.

26 Stuart Ball, 'Davidson, John Colin Campbell, first Viscount Davidson', *Oxford Dictionary of National Biography* (*ODNB*), ed. Colin Matthew and Brian Harrison (Oxford, 2004).

27 Andrew and Gordievsky, *KGB*; Christopher Andrew and Vasili Mitrokhin, *The Mitrokhin Archive: The KGB in Europe and the West* (London, 1999); McKnight, *Espionage*. These efforts included the Comintern's International Liaison Service (OMS). Until the 1943 dissolution of the Comintern, the INO and especially the military's *Razvedupr*/IV Directorate regularly used it as cover for intelligence work. See also Raymond Garthoff, 'Foreign Intel-

ligence and the Historiography of the Cold War', *Journal of Cold War Studies* 6:2 (2004), 21–56. One exception to the Cambridge Five trend was Raymond Leonard, *Secret Soldiers of the Revolution: Soviet Military Intelligence, 1918–33*, Contributions in Military Studies (Westport, CT, 1999).

28 *KGB: The Inside Story* and *The Mitrokhin Archive* total 1558 pages, nine of them on the targeting of Britain between 1917 and 1934. McKnight devoted one page out of two hundred to the topic and Leonard seventeen of 204.

29 Andrew, *Her Majesty*; Gordon Brook-Shepherd, *Iron Maze: The Western Secret Services and the Bolsheviks* (London, 1999); Alan Judd, *The Quest for C: Mansfield Cumming and the Founding of the Secret Service* (London, 2000); Michael Smith, *The Spying Game: The Secret History of British Espionage* (London, 2003); David Stafford, *Churchill & Secret Service* (London, 2000); Richard Thurlow, *The Secret State: British Internal Security in the Twentieth Century* (Oxford, 1994). Not even early official histories looked at interwar Bolshevik efforts to penetrate British government. F. H. Hinsley *et al.*, *British Intelligence in the Second World War* (London, 1979–90), particularly volume (vol.) 4: F. H. Hinsley and C. A. G. Simkins, *Security and Counter-Intelligence* (1990). See also Richard Thurlow, 'The Historiography and Source Materials in the Study of Internal Security in Modern Britain (1885–1956)', *History Compass* 6:1 (2008), 147–71, for the same omission. British historians have recently begun redressing the imbalance, thanks to new record releases: Christopher Andrew, *The Defence of the Realm: The Authorized History of MI5* (London, 2010); Gill Bennett, *Churchill's Man of Mystery: Desmond Morton and the World of Intelligence* (London, 2006); Keith Jeffery, *MI6: The History of the Secret Intelligence Service* (London, 2010); Michael Smith, *Six: A History of Britain's Secret Intelligence Service – Part 1: Murder and Mayhem 1909–1939* (London, 2010).

30 David Burke, *The Spy Who Came in from the Co-Op*, History of British Intelligence (Woodbridge, 2008). This is the biography of Melita Norwood (née Sirnis), who from 1934 to 1972 passed atomic and other secrets to Moscow. See also idem, *The Lawn Road Flats: Spies, Writers and Artists*, History of British Intelligence (Woodbridge, 2014), and Boris Volodarsky, *Stalin's Agent: The Life and Death of Alexander Orlov* (Oxford, 2014), ch. 7.

31 Amy Knight, 'Russian Archives: Opportunities and Obstacles', *IJIC* 12:3 (1999), 325–37: p. 333.

32 The concept of *dezinformatsiya*, integral to Russian intelligence doctrine, has been described as 'aiming at pollution of the opinion-making process in the West' and as 'the "heart and soul" of the KGB, its "subversive half"'. By 1923, the *Cheka* already had a disinformation department. Max Holland, 'The Propagation of Power of Communist Security Services *Dezinformatsiya*', *IJIC* 19:1 (2005), 1–31: pp. 3–4, 22 note (n.) 9.

33 Some works have nevertheless added significantly to knowledge about Russian intelligence. Lurie and Kochik, *GRU*; Aleksandr Kolpakidi and Dmitriy Prokhorov, *Imperiia GRU: Ocherki Istorii Rossiyskoy Voennoy Razvedki* [The GRU Empire: Essays on the History of Russian Military Intelligence] (Moskva, 2000); T. A. Soboleva, *Tainopis v Istorii Rossii: Istoriia Kriptograficheskoi Sluzhby Rossii 'XVIII' – nachala 'XX' v.* [Cryptography in Russian History: The History of the Russian Cryptographic Service from the XVIII to the Beginning of the XX Century] (Moskva, 1994) and idem, *Istoriia Shifrovalnogo Dela v Rossii* [The History of Encryption in Russia] (Moskva, 2002).

34 Kolpakidi and Prokhorov, *Imperiia*, chs 2–3. An interwar *Razvedupr* innovation was the systematic use of trade as cover. Brian Champion, 'Spies (Look) Like Us: The Early Use of Business and Civilian Covers in Covert Operations', *IJIC* 21:3 (2008), 530–64: pp. 552, 554–5; Leonard, *Secret*, pp. 58–9.

35 Prime ministerial biographies scarcely mention intelligence in Anglo-Soviet relations at this time. Peter Clarke, *A Question of Leadership: Gladstone to Thatcher* (London, 1991); John Grigg, *Lloyd George: War Leader, 1916–18* (London, 2002); Ian Packer, *Lloyd George* (London, 1998); R. J. Q. Adams, *Bonar Law* (London, 1999); Robert Blake, *The Unknown Prime Minister: The Life and Times of Andrew Bonar Law, 1858–1923* (London, 1955); H. A. Taylor, *The Strange Case of Andrew Bonar Law* (London, 1932); Roy Jenkins, *Baldwin* (London, 1987); Philip Williamson, *Stanley Baldwin: Conservative Leadership and National Values* (Cambridge, 1999); David Marquand, *Ramsay MacDonald* (London, 1997); Duncan Watts, *Ramsay MacDonald: A Labour Tragedy?* (London, 1998).

36 Lloyd George's views on Russia mirrored President Woodrow Wilson's own:

> Russian Bolshevism was a condition to be cured ... the spiritual appeals of the Bolshevik ideology were far from negligible; the reactionary consequences of a military crusade against Bolshevism

could not be ignored; and a military truce combined with economic aid [or trade, in Britain's case] was most likely to redirect the revolutionary currents into reformist channels in Russia.

Arno Mayer, *Politics and Diplomacy of Peacemaking: Containment and Counterrevolution at Versailles, 1918–19* (London, 1968), pp. 27–8. On 6 August 1920, Henry Wilson wondered in his diary if Lloyd George 'is deliberately shepherding England into chaos and destruction', later concluding that 'LG^s attitude is incomprehensible unless he is terrified of the Bolsheviks or unless he himself is Bolshevik'. Richard Ullman, *Anglo-Soviet Relations, 1917–21, vol. 3: The Anglo-Soviet Accord* (Princeton, NJ, 1972), p. 276.

37 29 December 1920, *fond* (f.) 04, *opis'* (op.) 4, *papka* (p.) 19, *delo* (d.) 261, *listy* (ll.) 9–17, Foreign Policy Archive of the Russian Federation (AVP RF), Moscow. "Toryism" was not monolithic: two main wings of Conservatism and anti-Bolshevism clashed in the period covered here. One was strident and brash, personified by Winston Churchill. The other was preacher-like, embodied by Stanley Baldwin. His approach was to use flattery to woo workers whose minds were the ultimate guarantors of whether or not Communism spread. Baldwin aimed to fight Socialism not by being anti-socialist but by offering workers something positive and enticing as a viable alternative.

38 'A Monthly Review of Revolutionary Movements in British Dominions and Foreign Countries – Report 25' (foreign), November 1920, p. 44, Cabinet Paper (GT/CP) 2352, The National Archives (TNA), London, CAB 24/117. Basil Thomson, *The Scene Changes* (London, 1939), p. 376. Thomson saw Bolshevism as 'a sort of infectious disease, spreading rapidly, but insidiously, until like a cancer it eats away the fabric of society'. He used four terms to describe Bolshevism and Communism in his reports: 'cancer', 'infection', 'disease' and 'evil'.

39 Keith Jeffery, 'The British Army and Internal Security, 1919–39', *THJ* 24:2 (1981), 377–97, examines the military's role in preserving domestic order.

40 Yulia Sinyagina-Woodruff, 'Russia, Sovereign Default, Reputation and Access to Capital Markets', *Europe-Asia Studies* 55:4 (2003), 521–51: p. 522.

41 On politicians' historical reluctance to spy, see Ann Rogers, *Secrecy and Power in the British State: A History of the Official Secrets Act* (London, 1997), p. 22; Bernard

Porter, *The Origins of the Vigilant State: The London Metropolitan Police Special Branch before the First World War* (Woodbridge, 1991), pp. 182–3; David Vincent, *The Culture of Secrecy: Britain, 1832–1998* (Oxford, 1998), pp. 1–25; Smith, *The Spying*, pp. 12–14; John Fisher, *Gentleman Spies: Intelligence Agents in the British Empire and Beyond* (Stroud, 2002), pp. 10–12.

CHAPTER 1
The Committee

1 Major Ernest Walter Brudenell Gill, Royal Signals, 'Policy on Organisation for Detection of Illicit Wireless Transmissions in Time of War 1939–45, November 1940', vol. 2, serial 37A, TNA KV 4/62. See also Brian Austin, 'EWB Gill–Taking Wireless to War', *The Journal of the Royal Signals Institution* 29:2 (2010), 48–56.

2 Graham Goodlad, 'Ditching the Goat: The Fall of Lloyd George', *Modern History Review* 10:4 (1999), 5–8: p. 6.

3 Robert Littell, *The Company: A Novel of the CIA* (London, 2003), p. 823.

4 Dobb introduced Harold "Kim" Philby to Communism. Andrew and Gordievsky, *KGB*, p. 151. See also Eric Hobsbawm, 'Dobb, Maurice Herbert', *ODNB*.

5 'The Russian Revolution', 1920, p. 2, DD [lectures] 4, Maurice Dobb (DOBB) manuscripts (MSS), Trinity College Library, Cambridge. This end-of-days view of Bolshevism was the basis of a book by Sir Samuel Hoare, 1st Viscount Templewood. He wrote of his interest in Russia, his experiences there in 1916–17 as a member (and eventual Head) of the Military Intelligence Liaison Mission in Petrograd (as St Petersburg was renamed in 1914), and his impressions of the Bolsheviks. *The Fourth Seal: The End of a Russian Chapter* (London, 1930). See also Templewood MSS, Part II (Russia, 1915–24), Cambridge University Library. On the Bolshevik "Red Terror", see Arno Mayer, *The Furies: Violence and Terror in the French and Russian Revolutions* (Princeton, NJ, 2000), ch. 8.

6 A. J. P. Taylor, *English History, 1914–45*, The Oxford History of England, ed. Sir George Clark (Oxford, 2001), p. 94.

7 The best work is Gerald Reynolds and Anthony Judge, *The Night the Police Went on Strike* (London, 1968), but see also Arthur Sellwood, *Police Strike, 1919* (London, 1978) and Joseph King, *The Development of Modern Police History in the United Kingdom and the*

United States, Criminology Studies (Lewiston, NY, 2004).

8 See Andrew, *Her Majesty*, ch. 7; Victor Madeira, '"No Wishful Thinking Allowed": Secret Service Committee and Intelligence Reform in Great Britain, 1919–23', *Intelligence and National Security* (*INS*) 18:1 (2003), 1–20; Jeffery, *MI6*, chs 5–7; Smith, *Six*, ch. 16.

9 See Nicholas Hiley, 'Counter-Espionage and Security in Great Britain during the First World War', *English Historical Review* 101:400 (1986), 635–70; Bernard Porter, *Plots and Paranoia: A History of Political Espionage in Britain, 1780–1988* (London, 1989); idem, *The Origins*. The designation "MI5" first appeared in January 1916. Hiley, 'Counter', p. 664. On MI5's origins, see Andrew, *Her Majesty*, ch. 2; idem, *The Defence*, pp. 113–38; Andrew Cook, *M: MI5's First Spymaster* (Stroud, 2004), chs 9–10; John Curry, *The Security Service, 1908–45: The Official History* (Kew, 1999), pp. 63–9; Hinsley and Simkins, *Security*, pp. 4–17; Smith, *The Spying*, ch. 5.

10 The designation "SIS" first appeared in February 1920 and became official in 1921. Despite the division of labour between the Home and Foreign Sections of the Secret Service Bureau set up in 1909, MI1$_{(c)}$ operated domestically. Jeffery, *MI6*, p. 162, ch. 7; Bennett, *Churchill*, chs 3–6; Judd, *The Quest*, chs 3–5.

11 Thurlow, *The Secret*, p. 49; Hinsley and Simkins, *Security*, p. 9; Hiley, 'Counter', p. 667.

12 Cabinet cut MI5 funding from £79,950 (2011: £22 million) in financial year (FY) 1918/19 to £45,000 the next (2011: nearly £11.5 million). In FY 1921/2, MI5 received £22,183 (2011: £7.5 million). 'Funds Devoted to [MI5] by the Foreign Office, vol. 1', serial 28, TNA KV 4/198; 'Foreign Secret Service Accounts, 1916–20', TNA FO 1093/61. Most cuts came from eliminating port controls, staffing of military missions overseas and wartime central registry slots, which accounted for about six hundred staff out of 844. Private correspondence.

13 The Bolsheviks created the Comintern in March 1919 with the 'far from modest' goal of fomenting world revolution. Tim Rees and Andrew Thorpe, 'Introduction', in *International Communism and the Communist International, 1919–43*, ed. Tim Rees and Andrew Thorpe (Manchester, 1998), 1–11: p. 1. On Comintern intelligence work, see McKnight, *Espionage*, chs 1–4; Andrew and Gordievsky, *KGB*, chs 3, 6; Peter Huber, 'Structure of the Moscow Apparatus of the Comintern and Decision-Making', in *International*, ed. Rees

and Thorpe, pp. 41–64; Leonard, *Secret*, pp. 17–18.

14 Curry, *The Security*, pp. 3–5, 47–8; Gill Bennett, *'A Most Extraordinary and Mysterious Business': The Zinoviev Letter of 1924* (London, 1999), p. 44; Andrew, *Her Majesty*, p. 264.

15 Peter Hopkirk, *Setting the East Ablaze: On Secret Service in Bolshevik Asia* (Oxford, 1986), p. 15. Two million gold roubles in late 1917 equalled around £200,000 (2011: £70.5 million), given the wartime exchange rate of ten Russian roubles (RR) to £1. J. D. Smele, 'White Gold: The Imperial Russian Gold Reserve in the Anti-Bolshevik East, 1918–? (An Un-concluded Chapter in the History of the Russian Civil War)', *Europe-Asia Studies* 46:8 (1994), 1317–47: p. 1339 n. 3. See Vladimir Lenin, *The National-Liberation Movement in the East* (Moscow, 1962), p. 218 (Afghanistan) and p. 248 (India) on the "Eastern question"; and T. H. Rigby, *Lenin's Government: Sovnarkom, 1917–22* (Cambridge, 1979), ch. 1, on SNK's origins.

16 To Winston Churchill, Lenin was the 'Grand Repudiator': '*God, King, Country*, morals, treaties, debts … laws and customs of centuries … contracts … the whole-structure … of human society'. Walter Laqueur, *The Fate of the Revolution: Interpretations of Soviet History* (London, 1970), pp. 60–1.

17 '"The Greatest Power on Earth": Great Britain in the 1920s', *The International History Review* 13:4 (1991), 726–50: p. 740.

18 Richard Millman, *British Foreign Policy and the Coming of the Franco-Prussian War* (Oxford, 1965), p. 3.

19 Philip Williamson, 'The Doctrinal Politics of Stanley Baldwin', in *Public and Private Doctrine: Essays in British History Presented to Maurice Cowling*, ed. Michael Bentley (Cambridge, 1993), 181–208: p. 185. On changing feminine roles in society, see Martin Pugh, *The March of the Women: A Revisionist Analysis of the Campaign for Women's Suffrage, 1866–1914* (Oxford, 2000), chs 8–10. By 1914, for the first time in history due to a need to free up men to fight, women occupied positions previously off-limits to them. In 1918, 920,000 women worked in armament factories. King, *The Development*, pp. 104–5.

20 Williamson, 'The Doctrinal', p. 185.

21 Stanley Baldwin speech, 1 July 1929, ibid. See also Peter Clarke, *Hope and Glory: Britain, 1900–90* (London, 1997), pp. 90–3, 97–8; Neil McCrillis, *The British Conservative Party in the Age of Universal Suffrage: Popular Conservatism, 1918–29* (Columbus, OH, 1998),

ch. 1; and David Cannadine, *Class in Britain* (New Haven, CT, 1998), ch. 4.

22 Stanley Baldwin speech, 29 June 1923. Williamson, 'The Doctrinal', p. 185. On Labour's postwar rise, see Andrew Thorpe, *A History of the British Labour Party* (Basingstoke, 2008), ch. 2, and Keith Laybourn, *A Century of Labour: A History of the Labour Party, 1900–2000* (Stroud, 2000), ch. 3.

23 In 1918, unemployment was 0.8%; by 1921, it was 12.2% (2.2 million) of insured British workers (15.9 million). W. R. Garside, *British Unemployment, 1919–39: A Study in Public Policy* (Cambridge, 1990), pp. 4–5, Tables 1, 2.

24 Williamson, 'The Doctrinal', p. 185.

25 Jon Lawrence, 'Forging a Peaceable Kingdom: War, Violence and Fear of Brutalisation in Post-First World War Britain', *The Journal of Modern History* 75:3 (2003), 557–98: p. 559.

26 See 'Thomson', Appendix.

27 'During the nineteenth century ... public school education took on moral and class connotations that made alternative forms of secondary education not just different but less worthy.' Gail Savage, 'Social Class and Social Policy: The Civil Service and Secondary Education in England during the Interwar Period', *Journal of Contemporary History* 18:2 (1983), 261–80: p. 263.

28 On MI5's reported wartime successes against German espionage, see Nicholas Hiley, 'Entering the Lists: MI5's Great Spy Round-Up of August 1914', *INS* 21:1 (2006), 46–76. See also idem, 'Internal Security in Wartime: The Rise and Fall of PMS2 [Parliamentary Military Secretary Department, no. 2 Section], 1915–17', *INS* 1:3 (1986), 395–415; idem and Julian Putkowski, 'A Postscript on PMS2', *INS* 3:2 (1988), 326–31.

29 Carson was briefly (and ineffectively) First Lord of the Admiralty from December 1916 to July 1917, when he became a Minister without Portfolio in the War Cabinet. D. George Boyce, 'Carson, Edward Henry, Baron Carson', *ODNB*. See also John Hostettler, *Sir Edward Carson: A Dream Too Far* (Chichester, 1997), pp. 250–62.

30 Thomson's first regular monthly report to Cabinet (24 November 1917) was entitled 'Pacifism' due to rising domestic unrest fuelled by war weariness and growing military demands for manpower. On 20 February 1918 the title became 'Pacifist Revolutionary Propaganda'; Russia's decision the previous December to negotiate peace with Berlin meant Thomson readily combined the German and Bolshevik threats. On 10 April,

report titles changed to 'Pacifism and Revolutionary Organisations in the UK'. By then, government regarded Bolshevik subversion as a potential domestic threat. Thus in May Thomson started reporting twice a month, the title becoming 'Fortnightly Report on Pacifism and Revolutionary Organisations in the UK' on 12 August. By 21 October it was 'Fortnightly Report on Pacifism and Revolutionary Organisations in the UK, and Morale [Abroad]', reflecting an end in sight to the war. By late 1918, Thomson was manoeuvring to head the entire intelligence community, straying into foreign work. Although he failed in his aim, Cabinet appointed him Home Office Director of Intelligence from 1 May 1919. On 30 April, he settled on 'Report on Revolutionary Organisations in the UK'. These key historical documents survive in GT 2809, TNA CAB 24/34; GT 3674, TNA CAB 24/42; GT 4199, TNA CAB 24/47; GT 4463, TNA CAB 24/50; GT 5407, TNA CAB 24/61; GT 6079, TNA CAB 24/67; GT 7196, TNA CAB 24/78.

31 See 'Childs', Appendix.

32 Thurlow, *The Secret*, pp. 64, 140. On Childs and Communism, see his *Episodes and Reflections* (London, 1930), chs 20–7.

33 Rogers, *Secrecy*, pp. 6, 9, 26; Arthur Waldron, *The Great Wall of China: From History to Myth* (Cambridge, 1990), pp. 182–3, quoted in Rogers, *Secrecy*, p. 28.

34 John Grigg's multi-volume biography is the best on the subject. *Lloyd George: The Young Lloyd George*; *Lloyd George: The People's Champion, 1902–11*; *Lloyd George: From Peace to War, 1912–16*; *Lloyd George: War Leader, 1916–18* (London, 2002).

35 Lawrence, 'Forging', p. 559.

36 Ibid., pp. 559–60. Mutinies by British soldiers at the Calais and Folkestone demobilisation camps were early indications of potential postwar unrest. Taylor, *English*, p. 138.

37 Lawrence, 'Forging', p. 560.

38 The top public schools (Charterhouse, Eton, Harrow, Merchant Taylors', Rugby, Shrewsbury, St Paul's, Westminster and Winchester) were known as the Clarendon schools, supplemented by other leading institutions like Loretto, Marlborough, Oundle and Radley. A Clarendon school was one belonging to the Headmasters' Conference whose students paid for board and tuition. R. K. Kelsall, *Higher Civil Servants in Britain: From 1870 to the Present Day* (London, 1955), pp. 147–8. On psychological and physical conditioning of pupils, see John Wakeford, *The Cloistered Elite: A Sociological Analysis of*

the *English Public Boarding School* (London, 1969), ch. 1.

39 The Archbishop was a strict disciplinarian. E. I. Carlyle, 'Thomson, William', *ODNB*.

40 Thurlow, *The Secret*, p. 45; Thomson, *The Scene*, pp. 8–9, 13; Andrew, *Her Majesty*, pp. 60, 177, 232–3. See also Noel Rutherford, 'Thomson, Sir Basil Home', *ODNB*. As Assistant Commissioner for CID from 1913, he also oversaw its Special Branch. The Directorate of Intelligence was essentially a renamed Special Branch. 'Changes at Scotland Yard', 24 April 1919, p. 12, *The Times* digital archive.

41 Daughter of James Skene, British Consul at Aleppo, and his wife Rhalon Rizo-Rangabé, 'a Greek beauty of aristocratic descent'. Carlyle, 'Thomson', *ODNB*. Thomson wrote of his mother: 'I never saw her impatient or ungentle. No thoughtlessness of ours could ruffle her serenity.' Thomson, *The Scene*, p. 8. See also E. C. Rickards, *Zoe Thomson of Bishopthorpe and Her Friends* (London, 1916).

42 Harold Kirk-Smith, *William Thomson, Archbishop of York – His Life and Times, 1819–90* (London, 1958), pp. 160, 165.

43 Ibid., p. 166.

44 Thomson, *The Scene*, pp. 14, 16–17.

45 Rutherford, 'Thomson', *ODNB*; Thomson, *The Scene*, p. 17.

46 Ibid.

47 Wakeford, *The Cloistered*, p. 22.

48 By the early twentieth century, India alone bought more British steel than the rest of Eurasia or the Americas combined. India also consumed 42% of British textile exports – crucial, since Britain's textile industry accounted for around 25% of exports, employing 10% of all manufacturing workers. Another reason why Britain depended on India so much was its export earnings financed over 40% of Britain's total deficit. Don Dignan, *The Indian Revolutionary Problem in British Diplomacy, 1914–19* (New Delhi, 1983), pp. 5, 13–14.

49 J. A. Mangan, *The Games Ethic and Imperialism: Aspects of the Diffusion of an Ideal* (Harmondsworth, 1986), pp. 18–21. For a broader perspective, see idem, '*Manufactured' Masculinity: Making Imperial Manliness, Morality and Militarism* (London, 2012), especially chs 4, 7, 16 and 20.

50 Mangan, *The Games*, pp. 62–3, 23. Headmasters of leading public schools gathered annually to discuss their curricula and how best to advance the imperial cause. See idem, '"The Grit of Our Forefathers": Invented Traditions, Propaganda and Impe-

rialism', *Imperialism and Popular Culture*, ed. John MacKenzie, Studies in Imperialism (Manchester, 1986), pp. 113–39; idem, *Manufactured*, ch. 15.

51 Dr Hely Almond, Loretto Headmaster from 1862 to 1903. Mangan, *The Games*, pp. 24–8.

52 14 May 1895 speech by the Reverend Dr James Welldon, Harrow Headmaster from 1885 to 1898. Mangan, *The Games*, pp. 33–42. Leo Amery, a Welldon pupil and future Colonial Secretary, often acknowledged his influence. Winston Churchill was also a Welldon pupil. Paul Addison, 'Churchill, Sir Winston Leonard Spencer', *ODNB* (see Appendix). Sir Eric Holt-Wilson, founding Deputy Director of MI5 and a Harrovian during Welldon's time, wrote: 'all my life and ... strength were given to the finest cause on this Earth – the ennoblement of all mankind by the example of the British Race'. Welldon's influence is unmistakable and in a sparse diary, Holt-Wilson nevertheless felt it important to note his headmaster's dates of birth and death. Diary, 28 February, A5 sheet of light blue paper, Eric Holt-Wilson MSS, Cambridge University Library; diary, p. 9, Holt-Wilson MSS.

53 Mangan, 'The Grit', pp. 120–1.

54 In 1932, socialist intellectual Bertrand Russell commented:

> Those ... taught from an early age to fear the displeasure of their group as the worst of misfortunes will die on the battlefield ... rather than suffer the contempt of fools. The English public schools have carried out this system to perfection and have largely sterilised intelligence by making it cringe before the herd. This is what is called making a man manly.

Wakeford, *The Cloistered*, p. 22. See also Mangan, *Manufactured*, ch. 12.

55 Mangan, *The Games*, p. 56. Colonial administrator Lord Lugard wrote in 1922: 'We hold these countries because it is the genius of our race to colonise, to trade and to govern.' Robert Young, *Colonial Desire: Hybridity in Theory, Culture and Race* (London, 1995), p. 29.

56 Mangan, *The Games*, p. 58.

57 Sir Mansfield Cumming, the first Chief ("C") of SIS, called pre-1914 espionage 'capital sport'. Christopher Andrew, 'Cumming, Sir Mansfield George Smith', *ODNB*. Captain Arthur Conolly, a veteran of Central Asian campaigns, coined the term "Great Game". This was a mix of 'exploration, espionage and intrigue', carried out by the Russian and British Empires in Afghanistan and Central Asia from the early nineteenth century to the

early twentieth. Richard Popplewell, *Intelligence and Imperial Defence: British Intelligence and the Defence of the Indian Empire, 1904–24*, Studies in Intelligence (London, 1995), pp. 19–21. John Fisher offers good accounts of British operations in *Gentleman*; chs 4, 6 focus on the Anglo-Russian rivalry.

58 Thomson, *The Scene*, pp. 12–13.

59 Ibid.

60 Ibid., pp. 13–14, 16. On the impact of public schools on British intelligence recruitment, see Porter, *Plots*, pp. 175–96, 233–4.

61 In *Queer People* (London, 1922), pp. 299–301, Thomson commented on the post-1917 situation:

> for the first time ... the revolutionary agitator need not be a fanatic, for his profession had now become lucrative, and a loud voice and a glib tongue became worth anything from £6 to £10 a week ... [O]ne result ... was to augment the little band of intellectual revolutionaries who have always bloomed among us modest and unseen ... [E]ven ... at Oxford and Cambridge, and in one or two public schools, there are ... "parlour Bolsheviks" ... [N]ot a few [revolutionaries] are ex-officers in the Navy and Army.

62 'Report 20' (foreign), June 1920, pp. 53–5, CP 1587, TNA CAB 24/108. As Karl Marx argued in *The Communist Manifesto*, workers had no country.

63 In his 1851 work *Social Static*, Herbert Spencer argued human society resembled the natural world, particularly regarding natural selection. He justified growing socio-economic inequality in a rapidly modernising Britain as a natural process neither politics nor the State should disrupt. As Ivan Hannaford has suggested, if 'evolution and natural selection were the principles of natural existence and therefore applicable to social life', then 'it must be true ... the poor ... were in their natural condition [due to] some deficiency in their physical and intellectual capacity'. These words mirror Thomson's. *Race: The History of an Idea in the West* (Washington, DC, 1996), pp. 277–8.

64 In descending rank: Secretaries, Deputy Secretaries, Under-Secretaries, Principal Assistant Secretaries and Assistant Secretaries. Kelsall, *Higher*, pp. 147–8, 123, Table 13, p. 127, Table 15, p. 138, Table 22.

65 Ibid., pp. 150–1, Table 24, pp. 157–8, Table 26. Insufficient data were available for 1929.

66 Ibid., pp. xiv–xv. Note the education of key anti-communist hardliners, according to the *ODNB*. Winston Churchill (Harrow, Sandhurst Military Academy); George Curzon (Eton, Oxford); Reginald Hall (HMS *Britannia*); Samuel Hoare (Harrow, Oxford); Walter Long (Harrow, Oxford); Reginald McKenna (King's College School, Cambridge); Hugh Sinclair (HMS *Britannia*); Edward Shortt (Durham School, Durham University); F. E. Smith (Sandringham, Liverpool University, Oxford); and Henry Wilson (Marlborough).

67 'Report 5' (foreign), 28 May 1919, p. 14, GT 7368, TNA CAB 24/80.

68 'Report 24' (UK), 21 October 1918, p. 5, GT 6079, TNA CAB 24/67. For Thomson and his peers, to question the status quo was to be disloyal. General Richard Haking, Head of the British Military Mission to Russia and the Baltics in 1919, believed

> every man who finds life going hard with him [asks] himself the question why the conditions should not be changed. This is the first germ of Bolshevism, and, in every country, it finds suitable soil in which to flourish and spread itself with alarming speed. It affects the individual in the first instance, and thrives mainly on self-interest. The individual who suffers from it knows no patriotism, love of country, or regard for other people, though he pretends that he possesses all these qualities.

'The Defeat of Bolshevism', 31 March 1919, p. 1, GT 7086, TNA CAB 24/77.

69 On CPGB interwar history, see Francis Beckett, *Enemy Within: The Rise and Fall of the British Communist Party* (London, 1995), chs 1–2; James Eaden and David Renton, *The Communist Party of Great Britain since 1920* (Basingstoke, 2002), ch. 1.

70 Thomson, *Queer*, p. 301.

71 'Communists', 'Report 97' (UK), 17 March 1921, CP 2740, TNA CAB 24/121.

72 'Pacifism', 22 January 1918, pp. 1–2, GT 3424, TNA CAB 24/40.

73 Ibid.

74 Thurlow, *The Secret*, p. 60.

75 Much information coming out of Russia in those three years struck a chord in Britain. The right-wing *The Morning Post* blamed 'Russian Jews of German extraction' for the troubles. In mid-1920, the newspaper printed frenzied articles claiming to expose the roots of the Revolution and global instability: the so-called Protocols of the Elders of Zion. Stories in *The Times* from 1917 to 1920 included some on the nationalisation of women and on a series of monuments

to Judas Iscariot supposedly erected by the Bolsheviks. For a while, even *The Times* believed in the Protocols. Despite having a seasoned correspondent in Petrograd, *The Times* reported nothing untoward on 6 and 7 November 1917; not until 9 November did it report on the Bolsheviks' 'organised outbreak'. Communism was a 'synonym for destruction, anarchism, a conspiracy to throw the whole world into chaos', while communists 'were moral imbeciles, fanatics, sadists, negating all traditional values ... willing to sacrifice everything, including their lives, for the realization of a mad ideal'. Laqueur, *The Fate*, pp. 8–9, 157, 10–11. See also Keith Wilson, *A Study in the History and Politics of* The Morning Post, *1905–26*, Studies in British History (Lewiston, NY, 1990), pp. 138, 175. On *The Times'* remarkable man in Russia, see Arkady Borman, 'Harold Williams: A British Journalist and Linguist in Russia', *Russian Review* 28:3 (1969): 327–37; Ariadna Tyrkova-Williams, *Cheerful Giver: The Life of Harold Williams* (London, 1935).

76 Bennett, *Churchill*, p. 46. Captain Francis Cromie, the British Naval Attaché in Petrograd, wrote despairingly to Director of Naval Intelligence (DNI) Rear-Admiral Reginald "Blinker" Hall:

> [T]he extraordinary amount of duplication of work [is] due to the overlapping of Departments; I refer to ... General Poole and Boyce.... [T]his is principally due to a lack of combination and contact between these Departments, resulting very largely from a professional as well as personal jealousy.... With us I find there is no Head to direct different Departments as a homogenous organisation, much less direct their policy. Each wanders along, more or less indifferent to the policy and ignorant of the work of its neighbour.

Roy Bainton, *Honoured by Strangers: The Life of Captain Francis Cromie, 1882–1918* (Shrewsbury, 2002), p. 210. By August 1918, London already intercepted Bolshevik cable and wireless traffic. The Admiralty wanted to end cipher communication to and from Russia, fearing German interception could compromise British systems. 'Wireless Communications with Russia', 3 August 1918, p. 245, file 134846, TNA FO 371/3330.

77 The primary HUMINT agencies were SIS and the War Office Directorate of Military Intelligence (DMI), while GCCS provided most foreign SIGINT.

78 Under Leonid B. Krasin, later Head of the Bolshevik Trade Delegation in London, the Trade Commissariat jealously guarded its role in foreign trade. Anthony Heywood, *Engineer of Revolutionary Russia: Iurii V. Lomonosov (1876–1952) and the Railways*, Science, Technology and Culture, 1700–1945 (Farnham, 2011), p. 213.

79 Occleshaw, *Dances*, and A. J. Plotke, *Imperial Spies Invade Russia: The British Intelligence Interventions, 1918*, Contributions in Military Studies (Westport, CT, 1993).

80 See Jonathan Rose, *The Intellectual Life of the British Working Classes* (New Haven, CT, 2001), ch. 9. In his diary entry for 8 January 1918, Colonel Edward House (President Woodrow Wilson's closest adviser) wrote: 'I have partially succeeded in frightening not only the President but [also] the English ... regarding ... "the Russian peril". Personally, he wrote, 'there is not as much danger as I make'. Mayer, *Politics*, p. 342. In July, Sir Robert Nathan, the India Office representative, met House. Popplewell, *Intelligence*, pp. 322–3; Jeffery, *MI6*, p. 112. The House–Nathan link was a key channel through which politicised assessments on the "Red Menace" reached London.

81 'Pacifist Revolutionary Propaganda', 20 February 1918, p. 1, GT 3674, TNA CAB 24/42.

82 'Pacifism and Revolutionary Organisations in the UK', 10 April 1918, p. 2, GT 4199, TNA CAB 24/47.

83 Cabinet Secretary Sir Maurice Hankey wrote in his diary (Churchill Archives Centre, The Papers of Sir Maurice Hankey, HNKY 1/5, 30 August 1918, p. 12):

> the opportunity ... should be taken to sweep away the anomaly of our present police force with its semi-independent Metropolitan Commission, City Police, Borough Police, County Police, Watch Committees, etc., and to replace it by a unified State police under proper discipline. I would put London temporarily under military control pending ... passage of a police law ... allow the old police to return temporarily ... redress their ... legitimate pay grievances; I doubt if the Govt will have the courage to do this.

Little wonder a superior once described Hankey as 'Napoleonic in his ideas and Cromwellian in his thoroughness'. Diary, HNKY 1/3, 19 July 1918, p. 270. See also John Naylor, 'Hankey, Maurice Pascal Alers, first Baron Hankey', *ODNB*; Stephen Roskill, *Hankey: Man of Secrets, vol. 1: 1877–1918* (London, 1970), pp. 595–8. Educated at Rugby public school, Hankey believed in the Victorian quality of "manliness" with all it implied for national and racial fitness, as symbolised by military strength and readiness. See Michael L. Roi, 'German Holidays: Sir Maurice Hankey Meets the "Ultimate Enemy." Nazi Indoctrination and Physical Training and the DRC's Threat Assessment', in *Incidents and International Relations: People, Power and Personalities*, ed. Gregory C. Kennedy and Keith Neilson (Westport, CT, 2002), 113–34.

84 Grigg, *Lloyd George: War*, p. 588.

85 Lydia Morris, *Dangerous Classes: The Underclass and Social Citizenship* (London, 1994), p. 15.

86 King, *The Development*, pp. 94–106.

87 Sellwood, *Police*, p. 7.

88 Ibid., pp. 17–18. On grievances, see King, *The Development*, pp. 112–15; Reynolds and Judge, *The Night*, ch. 3. Other than low pay, the most critical issue was long hours: twelve-hour days and extra shifts were common, to make up for conscription-related staff shortages. Sellwood, *Police*, p. 25.

89 Sir William Nott-Bower, City of London Police Commissioner from 1902 to 1925. *Fifty-Two Years a Policeman* (London, 1926), p. 283 and ch. 20.

90 Ron Bean, 'Police Unrest, Unionisation, and the 1919 Strike in Liverpool', *Journal of Contemporary History* 15:4 (1980), 633–53: p. 638.

91 V. L. Allen, 'The National Union of Police and Prison Officers', *The Economic History Review* 11:1 (1958–59), 133–43: p. 134.

92 Grigg, *Lloyd George: War*, p. 582; Reynolds and Judge, *The Night*, pp. 17–19. Created in 1860, the Council was an early effort to bring together London trade unions.

93 On Cave's time at the Home Office, see Charles Mallet, *Lord Cave: A Memoir* (London, 1931), ch. 7; Thomas Legg and Marie-Louise Legg, 'Cave, George, Viscount Cave', *ODNB*.

94 Grigg, *Lloyd George: War*, p. 582.

95 For Macready's views on the 1918 police strike, see his *Annals of an Active Life: vol. 1* (London, 1924), ch. 12; Keith Jeffery, 'Macready, Sir (Cecil Frederick) Nevil, first Baronet', *ODNB*.

96 Sellwood, *Police*, p. 20.

97 Grigg, *Lloyd George: War*, pp. 582–4; Reynolds and Judge, *The Night*, chs 4–5. Grigg states only the Special Constabulary and Thomson's CID did not strike (p. 583), though Reynolds and Judge say they did (p. 52). An internal history supports the latter: twenty-five Special Branch men 'refused to leave the briefing room' on the 30th. 'Special Branch

Introduction and Summary of Responsibilities', www.met.police.uk, p. 24. City of London Police, chiefly responsible for the financial centre known as The City or Square Mile, should not be confused with its larger counterpart, the Metropolitan Police, responsible for the rest of Greater London.

98 Grigg, *Lloyd George: War*, pp. 584–6.

99 Ibid., p. 588.

100 Ibid., p. 584. The May 1917 French Army mutiny at Verdun and 'a vivid perception of the part played by the Soldiers' and Sailors' Committees in the disintegration of Tsarist Russia' were key considerations for a government faced with the notion of a police union. Sellwood, *Police*, p. 25. By early 1919, however, soldiers were no longer idolised. Many Britons now treated them with indifference, even hostility, and fears grew demobilised soldiers might one day take scarce jobs in times of unemployment. 'Report 33' (UK), 10 February 1919, p. 7, GT 6816, TNA CAB 24/75. See also Jane Morgan, *Conflict and Order: The Police and Labour Disputes in England and Wales, 1900–39* (Oxford, 1987), pp. 66–72.

101 'Bolshevist Propaganda', 22 February 1918, p. 1, GT 3704, TNA CAB 24/43. Cave felt Russian agitators held little sway over British workers but could 'cause serious trouble among Russian and Jewish soldiers and munition workers and in the mixed population of the East End'. Cave left out one reason for Litvinov's success: the 1917 Military Service (Allied States Conventions) Act, empowering the British Government to conscript Russian nationals in Britain. David Englander and James Osborne, 'Jack, Tommy, and Henry Dubb: The Armed Forces and the Working Class', *THJ* 21:3 (1978), 593–621: p. 606 n. 43.

102 On the release of intelligence files, see Oliver Hoare, ed., *British Intelligence in the Twentieth Century – A Missing Dimension? INS* 17:1 (2002), Special Issue, particularly Gill Bennett, 'Declassification and Release Policies of the UK's Intelligence Agencies'. See also Thurlow, 'The Historiography'.

103 Bennett, 'Declassification', pp. 26–8. Exceptions were files released on the Special Operations Executive and access given to Bennett for work on the 1924 Zinoviev Letter. Cook spoke in Parliament on 2 November 1998.

104 The best account is Andrew, *Her Majesty*. See also his preface to Curry's 1946 MI5 history. Other useful works include Andrew, *The Defence*; Bennett, *Churchill*; Robin Denniston, *Thirty Secret Years: Alastair Denniston's Work in Signals Intelligence,*

1914–44 (Clifton-upon-Teme, 2007); Hinsley and Simkins, *Security*; Jeffery, *MI6*; Judd, *The Quest*; Porter, *Plots* and *The Origins*; Popplewell, *Intelligence*; Smith, *The Spying and Six*; and Thurlow, *The Secret*.

105 See 'Morton', Appendix.

106 Andrew, *Her Majesty*, p. 533 n. 34. The Committee convened for specific purposes, at different times, by order of different Prime Ministers, with different membership. Gill Bennett, 'The Secret Service Committee, 1919–31', *The Records of the Permanent Under-Secretary's Department Liaison between the [Foreign Office] and British Secret Intelligence, 1873–1939* (London, 2005).

107 Created in July 1936, the JIC provides 'Ministers and senior officials with co-ordinated inter-departmental intelligence assessments' on issues 'of immediate and long-term importance to national interests ... in the fields of security, defence and foreign affairs'. Percy Cradock, *Know Your Enemy: How the Joint Intelligence Committee Saw the World* (London, 2002), p. 7; 'Joint Intelligence Committee', www.intelligence.gov.uk.

108 'Memorandum by Sir Charles Hardinge on the Tampering with Papers at Petersburg Embassy (Conversation with [Russian Ambassador] Count Benckendorff)', 26 March 1906, TNA HD 3/132.

109 'War Cabinet: Revision of Secret Service', 28 January 1919, TNA WO 32/21380. Curzon chaired the Committee. Also attending were Edward Shortt (Home Secretary), Ian Macpherson (Ireland Chief Secretary), Lord Lytton (deputising for Walter Long), Lord Peel (deputising for Winston Churchill), Lord Hardinge (Foreign Office Permanent Under-Secretary) and S. Harris (Home Office; Committee Secretary). 'Secret Service Committee: First Meeting', 3 February 1919, p. 1, TNA KV 4/151.

110 See Alvin Jackson, 'Long, Walter Hume, first Viscount Long', *ODNB*; Charles Petrie, *Walter Long & His Times* (London, 1936).

111 David Gilmour, *Curzon* (London, 1994) is an excellent biography but G. H. Bennett and Marion Gibson, *The Later Life of Lord Curzon of Kedleston – Aristocrat, Writer, Politician, Statesman: An Experiment in Political Biography* (Lewiston, NY, 2000) also dispels much of the mythology around Curzon.

112 Edward Carlyle, 'Shortt, Edward', *ODNB*.

113 See Martin Gilbert, *World in Torment: Winston Churchill, 1917–22* and *Prophet of Truth: Winston Churchill, 1922–39* (London, 1990).

114 Greenwood held the post from January to April 1919. Martin F. Seedorf, 'Greenwood, Hamar, first Viscount Greenwood', *ODNB*.

115 Curry, *The Security*, p. 4.

116 See Jeffery, *MI6*, pp. 55, 58–61; Bennett, *Churchill*, p. 40.

117 'War Cabinet: Revision', pp. 1–2, TNA WO 32/21380.

118 Ibid., p. 2. By the first committee meeting, MI5 was already down to 450 officers and clerks. 'Secret Service Committee: First Meeting', 3 February 1919, p. 1, TNA KV 4/151.

119 Private correspondence; Raymond Challinor, *The Origins of British Bolshevism* (London, 1977), ch. 6; David Burke, 'Theodore Rothstein and Russian Émigrés in the British Labour Movement, 1884–1920' (unpublished Ph.D. thesis, University of Greenwich, 1997), ch. 5.

120 'War Cabinet: Revision', p. 3, TNA WO 32/21380. On military intelligence, see Occleshaw, *Dances*, chs 1–2; Peter Freeman, 'MI1$_{(b)}$ and the Origins of British Diplomatic Cryptanalysis', *INS* 22:2 (2007), 206–28.

121 'War Cabinet: Revision', pp. 6–7, TNA WO 32/21380. Agency financing occupied the Committee. 'Security Service Organisation, 1918–39: Reports of the Secret Service Committee, 1919–23', TNA KV 4/151; 'Secret Service Committee', TNA CAB 127/356. See also 'Secret Service Blue Notes, 1913–37', TNA T 165/445; Eunan O'Halpin, 'Financing British Intelligence: The Evidence Up to 1945', in *British and American Approaches to Intelligence*, ed. Ken Robertson (Basingstoke, 1987), 187–217; 'Thomson to Walter Long (and reply)', 15 and 16 October 1918, pp. 2–4, old reference 947/672, Walter Long MSS, Wiltshire and Swindon Archives (WSA), Chippenham. On PMS2, see Hiley, above.

122 'Secret Service Committee: First Meeting', 3 February 1919, p. 3, TNA KV 4/151.

123 Ibid.

124 'Secret Service Committee: Second Meeting', 7 February 1919, TNA KV 4/151. Curzon chaired the Committee. Also attending were Ian Macpherson (Ireland Chief Secretary), Lord Peel (deputising for Winston Churchill), S. Harris (Home Office; Committee Secretary), Sir Edward Troup (Home Office Permanent Under-Secretary), Basil Thomson (Special Branch), Vernon Kell (MI5) and Mansfield Cumming (SIS).

125 Ibid., p. 3.

126 Ibid.

127 'Secret Service Committee: Third Meeting', 4 April 1919, p. 1, TNA KV 4/151. Curzon chaired the Committee. Also

attending were Edward Shortt (Home Secretary), Warren Fisher (Permanent Under-Secretary, Treasury), Basil Thomson (Special Branch), Stephen Gaselee (Foreign Office) and S. Harris (Home Office; Committee Secretary). On the Directorate's functions, see Andrew, *Her Majesty*, ch. 7; Curry, *The Security*, p. 92.

128 In November 1917 the Imperialist and novelist John Buchan, Head of the Department of Information tasked with wartime propaganda, urged ministers to move his intelligence bureau to the Foreign Office to improve 'flow of information to his experts and their effectiveness'. In February 1918, seconded staff formed PID. Alan Sharp, 'Some Relevant Historians – The Political Intelligence Department of the Foreign Office', *Australian Journal of Politics & History* 34:3 (1988), 359–68: pp. 359–61; H. C. G. Matthew, 'Buchan, John, first Baron Tweedsmuir', *ODNB*. In October 1920, the Foreign Office disbanded PID due to budget cuts. Zara Steiner and Michael Dockrill, 'The Foreign Office Reforms, 1919–21', *THJ* 17:1 (1974), 131–56: p. 135. See also Erik Goldstein, 'The Foreign Office and Political Intelligence, 1918–20', *Review of International Studies* 14 (1988), 275–88.

129 See 'Tyrrell', Appendix.

130 'Secret Service Committee: Third Meeting', 4 April 1919, p. 1, TNA KV 4/151.

131 For decades, MI5 was believed to have rounded up all German spy rings in Britain within days of the war starting; reality seems to have been different. According to Nicholas Hiley, most "agents" were either not in the country at the time of their supposed arrest or were already in prison for other offences. Hiley, 'Entering'. See also Andrew, who disagrees in *The Defence* (pp. 53–109), and Hiley's subsequent reassertion of his original thesis. 'Re-entering the Lists: MI5's Authorized History and the August 1914 Arrests', *INS* 25:4 (2010), 415–52.

132 Keith Jeffery, 'Wilson, Sir Henry Hughes, Baronet', *ODNB*; idem, *Field Marshal Sir Henry Wilson: A Political Soldier* (Oxford, 2006).

133 Andrew, *Her Majesty*, pp. 191–2, 229–30. Hall favoured one man being in charge of 'contre-espionage and secret service'. 'Notes on Reorganisation and Future Status of MI5', 14 November 1918, serial 1a, TNA KV 4/182.

134 One difference between the periods from 1917 to 1929 and 2001 to the present is that the British Government now admits recent counter-intelligence funding has been inadequate, given the vast sums allocated

to counter-terrorism (around 87% of MI5's 2010–11 operational budget, for instance) and growing hostile foreign activity. MI5 funding has risen since 2001 but most of that has gone to counter-terrorism. In 2004, the Security Service allocated 9% of its budget to counter-intelligence and counter-espionage but only 6% in 2006 and 4% in 2009, though annual budget increases have made this decline in counter-intelligence funding relative. Parliamentary Papers: *ISC Annual Report, 2004–05*, Cmd 6510, p. 14; *ISC Annual Report, 2010–11*, Cmd 8114, p. 27; *ISC Annual Report, 2011–12*, Cmd 8403, pp. 21, 28. The lesson has been identified – but has it been learnt? If not, others will in future be writing about how Russian intelligence again infiltrated British Government while its attention was elsewhere.

135 'It is a tribute to Sir Vernon Kell's personality that the organisation was kept in being under such conditions ... when there was ... danger of its being abolished.' Curry, *The Security*, p. 99. The Army Council also resisted Thomson's plan, refusing to let civilians run postwar counter-espionage. Private correspondence.

136 Andrew, *Her Majesty*, pp. 231–3. Thomson inflated the communist threat to head the community but by 1919–20 his reports did offer proof of subversion. In the end, Kell outlasted his rival by two decades. In late 1931, following a community reorganisation, Kell rejoiced at having finally taken over 'Scotland Yard intelligence'. Andrew, *Her Majesty*, p. 362. See also Bennett, *Churchill*, pp. 127–34. Contrary to conventional wisdom, postwar cuts were not driven largely by what John Ferris calls the anachronistic term "ten-year rule", whereby the Treasury ostensibly vetoed additional defence and security funding from August 1919, based on the assumption London would not fight another major war for a decade. He argues the rule did not have a significant impact until 1925. 'Treasury Control, the Ten-Year Rule, and British Service Policies, 1919–24', *THJ* 30:4 (1987), 859–83: p. 861.

137 Andrew, *Her Majesty*, pp. 231–3, 271–2.

138 Thomson, *Queer*, pp. 12–14, 16, 306.

CHAPTER 2

The Mutinies

1 William Gallacher, *Revolt on the Clyde: An Autobiography* (London, 1936), p. 179.

2 'Long to Lloyd George', 9 May 1919, pp. 1–2, old reference 947/746, Long MSS.

3 Evan Mawdsley, *The Russian Civil War* (Edinburgh, 2000), p. 217.

4 See 'Hayes', Appendix.

5 Title devised by Sir Victor Forbes, of the Foreign Office Communications Department. 'Historical Notes on [GCCS]', p. 1, TNA HW 3/33. The School was initially at Watergate House, Adelphi, London WC1, with a starting annual budget of between £13,268 and £21,217 (2011: £3.65 million and £5.8 million), depending on requirements. 'Code & Cipher School, 1919–22', 24 October 1919, p. 14, and document "A" C.E. 16337/19, TNA FO 1093/104.

6 See Patrick Beesly, *Room 40: British Naval Intelligence, 1914–18* (London, 1982); David Ramsay, *'Blinker' Hall: Spymaster – The Man who Brought America into World War I* (Stroud, 2009); and Nicholas Hiley, 'The Strategic Origins of Room 40', *INS* 2:2 (1987), 245–73.

7 See Martin Pugh, *The Pankhursts* (London, 2002), ch. 14; 'Sylvia Pankhurst', TNA KV 2/1570.

8 'Report 27' (UK), 2 December 1918, p. 4, GT 6425, TNA CAB 24/71.

9 Ibid., p. 1.

10 Englander and Osborne, 'Jack', pp. 600–1 (e.g. daily pay in a British division in France was a sixth that of colonial and Dominion troops).

11 J. M. Winter, *The Great War and the British People* (Basingstoke, 1987), p. 38.

12 Ibid., p. 39.

13 'Troops & Trade Unions, 1919', *History Today* 37 (March 1987), 8–13: pp. 8–9. This concept of total war heralded 'an administrative revolution in Britain and central Government assumed wide powers of supervision and control over many, if not most, areas of national life'. This set the precedent for government to suspect strikes in both war and peace, officials now regarding industrial unrest merely as 'the precursor of political revolution'. After the 1917 Bolshevik uprising, what Cabinet feared most was the 'subtle, and to some more insidious, challenge posed to the State by an extra-Governmental power-centre – the trade unions'. At stake was therefore

the State's legitimacy to rule. Jeffery and Hennessy, *States*, pp. 3–6.

14 Englander and Osborne, 'Jack', p. 602.

15 John Sweetman, 'Crucial Months for Survival: The Royal Air Force, 1918–19', *Journal of Contemporary History* 19:3 (1984), 529–47: p. 533; Stephen Graubard, 'Military Demobilisation in Great Britain Following the First World War', *The Journal of Modern History* 19:4 (1947), 297–311: p. 309; Englander and Osborne, 'Jack', n. 77, put Navy strength at 407,316; War Office, *Statistics of the Military Effort of the British Empire during the Great War, 1914–20* (London, 1922), p. 29, Table ia. By February 1920, the RAF had let 24,600 officers and 249,000 airmen go. Graubard, 'Military', p. 309; Andrew Rothstein, *The Soldiers' Strikes of 1919* (London, 1980), p. 98.

16 Fraud arose as men sought discharge by any means. Graubard, 'Military', pp. 297–302.

17 Englander, 'Troops', p. 9. The main government concern in adopting original demobilisation plans had been avoiding mass unemployment. Graubard, 'Military', p. 298. War Secretary Churchill had the revised plan published on 29 January 1919 (p. 304). As Sir Edward Carson, then Minister without Portfolio and Chairman of the Economic Offensive Committee, stated in early 1918: 'Our primary aim is to place ourselves in a position of security during the period of reconstruction.' 'War Cabinet: Economic Offensive Committee, G-190 (January 1918)', 21 January 1918, p. 8, file 70, John Colin Davidson (DAV/) MSS, Parliamentary Archives, London.

18 Calculations put the desirable minimum at between 150,000 and 500,000 men, depending on the amount of heavy weaponry committed. Rothstein, *The Soldiers*, pp. 99, 97. British strength in Russia never reached 15,000; of those deployed, 327 died (including 194 in action). W. P. Coates and Zelda K. Coates, *Armed Intervention in Russia, 1918–1922* (London, 1935), p. 174; Gilbert, *World*, p. 383. See also Clifford Kinvig, *Churchill's Crusade: The British Invasion of Russia 1918–20* (London, 2006), particularly chs 5–6, 9, 17.

19 Occleshaw, *Dances*, and Rothstein, *The Soldiers*, chs 1–2, offer contrasting views on invasion plans.

20 On the decision to extend conscription, see Graubard, 'Military', pp. 305–8. Despite denying Russia influenced British demobilisation policies, Cabinet agreed 'not to extend demobilisation to the British forces in Russia' on 31 December 1918. Rothstein, *The Soldiers*, p. 25.

21 The 1918 election was the first involving females, thanks to the 1918 Representation of the People (or Fourth Reform) Act. Moreover, abolishing household franchise extended the vote to all men over twenty-one which, combined with female suffrage, trebled electorate size. All parties now looked to reduce 'the legal maxima for expenses' mainly because wartime inflation had reduced the wealth of the middle and upper classes, from where most MPs came. Re-districting smaller constituencies and consolidating them made even relatively high spending nearly ineffective, except in a few cases. With the expansion and rationalisation of voter registries, the need for permanent 'extensive and expensive' Party machineries between elections disappeared. By 1920, Labour could finally afford competing, and portray itself as a natural party and contender for power, making critical inroads into rural and some urban areas traditionally either Liberal or Conservative strongholds. Michael Dawson, 'Money and the Real Impact of the Fourth Reform Act', *THJ* 35:2 (1992), 369–81, mainly pp. 375–81.

22 'Russia Must Wait' (*Daily Mail*, 22 November); 'Are We to Be Committed to a War with Russia?' (*Daily Express*, 3 January 1919); 'Withdraw from Russia' (*Daily Express*, 4 January). Rothstein, *The Soldiers*, pp. 31–5.

23 Ibid., pp. 68–75.

24 Archangel (22 February 1919). Ibid., pp. 76–81.

25 Personnel involved was mainly from the Army (51,000), followed by the Air Force (2500) and the Navy (800). The largest protests were in Folkestone (3 January; 10,000 men) and Shoreham (6 January; 8000 men). Ibid., pp. 37–85. By mid-February, attempts were also underway to create a union for Navy ratings. Englander and Osborne, 'Jack', pp. 617–18. First Lord of the Admiralty Long wrote Lloyd George: 'An outbreak in the [Navy] would indeed be a disaster and a blot on the escutcheon of England.' 8 May 1919, p. 2, old reference 947/746, Long MSS. To avoid unrest Cabinet chose conciliation with Navy ratings. Later that month, however, Long had different views on the Metropolitan Police: '[T]he men in the Navy are watching ... the ... police very closely.... I hope that the Government will deal drastically with ... insubordination in police ranks.... This kind of thing is very infectious.' 'Long to Lloyd George', 28 May 1919, pp. 1–2, old reference 947/746, Long MSS.

26 Other grievances were 'insufficient food, badly cooked ... indescribable sanitary conditions ... exploitation by the officers, who required the men to do private jobs', demands for 'shorter working hours ... no church parades on Sunday ... weekend passes when not on duty ... [and] all training to stop'. Rothstein, *The Soldiers*, pp. 42, 45–6.

27 Graubard, 'Military', p. 308. On labour's attitude towards servicemen, see Englander and Osborne, 'Jack'.

28 Grigg, *Lloyd George: War*, p. 614.

29 Englander and Osborne, 'Jack', p. 602.

30 See 'Rothstein', Appendix.

31 Rothstein, *The Soldiers*, pp. 94–5. These fears likely explain why military authorities charged so few mutineers after the Armistice. From 4 August 1914 to 31 March 1920, there were 1807 mutiny charges for all ranks, with only fifty-one filed between 1 October 1918 and 30 September 1919. War Office, *Statistics*, pp. 651–2, 658, 667, 669.

32 16 February 1919, pp. 1–3, LG/F/8/3, piece 18, David Lloyd George MSS, Parliamentary Archives, London.

33 17 February 1919, pp. 1–2, LG/F/8/3, piece 19, Lloyd George MSS.

34 At an early July Cabinet meeting to discuss intervention in Russia, Churchill's calls for more men and resources prompted Curzon to pass a note to H. A. L. Fisher, President of the Board of Education: 'What a dangerous man he is!' Churchill Archives Centre, The Papers of Sir James and Agnes Headlam-Morley 3, H. A. L. Fisher diaries, 9 July 1919, ACC 800.

35 22 September 1919, pp. 1–6, LG/F/9/1, piece 20, Lloyd George MSS. Lloyd George later admitted to Fisher, 'Winston is probably a greater source of weakness than of strength to the Government.' Headlam-Morley MSS 3, H. A. L. Fisher diaries, 23 September 1919, ACC 800. Yet Churchill would not budge. As late as March 1920, when the Bolsheviks were well on their way to defeating the Whites, he wrote: 'My dear Prime Minister ... since the Armistice my policies ... have been "Peace with the German people, war on the Bolshevik tyranny." ... you have followed something very near the reverse.' 24 March 1920, p. 1, LG/F/9/2, piece 20, Lloyd George MSS.

36 'Report 35' (UK), 10 March 1919, pp. 2–3, GT 6976, TNA CAB 24/76; Andrew, *Her Majesty*, p. 239. In a self-serving but prescient memorandum, Thomson advocated he should become the Royal Family's intelligence chief for as he put it, every 'institution of any importance has depended during the war for its existence on an intelligence organisation'. Not only was the monarchy 'deficient in its system of intelligence but it runs the risk of depending upon unreliable and tainted chan-

nels for what little information it receives'. While Prime Ministers so far had been loyal to the Crown, there was good reason to fear 'that the next few years will bring ... disloyal Prime Ministers. For example, [Labour Party leader] Ramsay MacDonald might quite conceivably be Prime Minister in five years'. Thomson to Hoare, 'Note on Intelligence & Importance of the Monarchy', 1919, Part I (Political and Other Correspondence), pp. 1–7, file 2, document 37, Templewood MSS.

37 'Report 30' (UK), 20 November 1919, p. 2, CP 168, TNA CAB 24/93; 'Report 31' (UK), 27 November 1919, p. 1, CP 217, TNA CAB 24/93; 'Report 35' (UK), 23 December 1919, p. 2, CP 343, TNA CAB 24/95.

38 'Report 34' (UK), 18 December 1919, p. 1, CP 319, TNA CAB 24/95.

39 'Report 33' (UK), 10 February 1919, p. 8, GT 6816, TNA CAB 24/75.

40 'War Cabinet: Unemployment and the State of Trade', 14 March 1919, p. 1, TNA CAB 27/58.

41 'Long to Lloyd George', 3 June 1919, pp. 1–6, old reference 947/746, Long MSS.

42 Constables James Marston (Chair), Jack Zollner, George Simmonds, Joe Paul, Alf Patterson and Alf Pack; Sergeant W. Sell; John Crisp (Secretary); and Warden Renshaw. Reynolds and Judge, *The Night*, p. 89.

43 Ibid., p. 73. Like many senior officials (including Basil Thomson), Henry had been a colonial administrator. Though experienced, such officials were often handicapped by a mindset developed dealing with different challenges in different cultures. What may 'have been good for India in Victoria's Golden Jubilee year was not necessarily so for London, four decades later'. Selwood, *Police*, pp. 21–2.

44 Although an Army man, Macready was well suited for his new post, with extensive experience as a military policeman and staff officer. Jeffery, 'Macready', *ODNB*.

45 In 1884, during his first posting as a young lieutenant in Egypt, Macready shocked superiors by having medical officers monitor the health of European prostitutes spreading disease to British soldiers. He acted just as declining sexual and physical health standards of British forces in Egypt were becoming a sensitive political issue in London. Reynolds and Judge, *The Night*, p. 75.

46 Morgan, *Conflict*, p. 17. For events at Tonypandy, see ibid., pp. 44–9; Barbara Weinberger, 'Police Perceptions of Labour in the Interwar Period: The Case of the Unemployed and of the Miners on Strike', in *Labour, Law, and Crime: An Historical Perspective*, ed.

Francis Snyder and Douglas Hay (London, 1987), 150–79: pp. 163–4; and Clive Emsley, *The English Police: A Political and Social History* (London, 1996), pp. 117–20.

47 Morgan, *Conflict*, pp. 44–5. The Glamorganshire Chief Constable, Captain Lionel Lindsay, ferociously anti-socialist (shocking even Macready) and close to the owners, 'was the source of the original reports which led to the calling-in of the troops'. Weinberger, 'Police', p. 164.

48 Reynolds and Judge, *The Night*, pp. 76–7.

49 Macready rejected constant 'invitations to himself and his officers ... from the local coal owners'. Emsley, *The English*, p. 117. Moreover, he insisted the military be a last resort and even then as backup to police; it alone should deal directly with the public. Morgan, *Conflict*, p. 47. Macready also made himself and his staff officers available to strikers for daily meetings on grievances. Childs, *Episodes*, p. 82.

50 The intelligence committee included Captain Wyndham Childs and Major William Horwood. Using intelligence to monitor industrial unrest was a new 'pattern for military and police action, both in coping with civil disorder and in maintaining a viable relationship with the local population'. Morgan, *Conflict*, pp. 46–7. Childs and Horwood subsequently became Assistant Commissioner (Special Branch) and Metropolitan Commissioner, respectively. As unrest subsided, Macready told Home Secretary Churchill 'without the excellent intelligence system ... inaugurated, it would have been impossible to have kept one's finger on the pulse of the two "belligerents"'. 1 January 1911, CHAR 12/6/50–1, Winston Churchill MSS, Churchill College, Cambridge.

51 Reynolds and Judge, *The Night*, p. 77. Every Commissioner in the interwar period was a military officer. Clive Emsley, 'Police Forces and Public Order in England and France during the Interwar Years', in *Policing Western Europe: Politics, Professionalism, and Public Order, 1850–1940*, ed. Clive Emsley and Barbara Weinberger, Contributions in Criminology and Penology (New York, 1991), 159–86: p. 162.

52 Macready initiated the practice of visiting stations and eliminated a 'system of fines by reduction in pay spreading over several months and even years' that had 'often taken the heart out of a man who found himself and his family suffering for long periods because of one mistake'. Reynolds and Judge, *The Night*, p. 81. Macready increased the

number of Chief Constables from three to four, sending them away from headquarters for the first time to head each of the four new districts into which he had divided London. Chief Constables were responsible for everything in their districts and were instructed to keep Macready informed. He also moved the promotion system away from seniority to merit. Police section houses, 'austere and cheerless', were re-decorated; canteens also improved, while the refreshment allowance – 'static for decades' – was doubled. Selwood, *Police*, pp. 23, 28.

53 Reynolds and Judge, *The Night*, p. 79.

54 Selwood, *Police*, ch. 2.

55 Reynolds and Judge, *The Night*, p. 83. Lifting the ban led to a sharp rise in NUPPO membership, from a few hundred men in London only to nearly 40,000 nationwide (p. 89).

56 Ibid., pp. 83–4.

57 Ibid., pp. 90–1.

58 Ibid., pp. 95–9.

59 On 27 February, Marston spoke at the National Industrial Conference and was elected to the Joint Committee of Unions and Management. Ibid., pp. 102, 111.

60 Parliamentary Papers, *Report of the Committee Appointed to Enquire into the Claims of the Men Dismissed from the Police and Prison Services on Account of the Strike of 1919*, Cmd 2297 (1924), p. 12. The Committee first suggested improvements in May 1919. Emsley, *The English*, p. 134; *Report*, Cmd 2297 (1924), p. 12.

61 Reynolds and Judge, *The Night*, pp. 104–7.

62 Ibid., pp. 108–9.

63 Ibid., pp. 115–16.

64 Nevil Macready, *Annals of an Active Life: vol. 2* (London, 1924), p. 364.

65 Reynolds and Judge, *The Night*, pp. 121–2.

66 Ibid., p. 130. Even before publication, the Government had already incorporated most Desborough findings (including union activity) into the Bill that became the 1919 Police Act in August. This crippled NUPPO's chances of a second successful strike. See Allen, 'The National', pp. 140–2 on the Act.

67 Reynolds and Judge, *The Night*, p. 130.

68 Ibid., pp. 133–5. During the strike Basil Thomson wrote:

There is prevailing belief ... the ... strike was engineered by ... revolutionaries ... as a prelude to a general attempt to upset ... order. I believe this [is] only partly true. The real cause ... was the certitude in the

minds of the leaders that if the ... Bill became law, the ... Union [paying] their salaries, would cease to exist ... Policemen are notoriously slow in their apprehension ... of political [trends].

'Report 15' (UK), 7 August 1919, p. 1, GT 7933, TNA CAB 24/86.

69 Allen, 'The National', pp. 142–3.

70 Reynolds and Judge, *The Night*, p. 151. Hayes later wrote: 'Thus was their birthright sold for a mess of pottage.' *Some Observations on the Police Strikes, 1918 & 1919* (London, 1921), p. 24.

71 Set up in London on 11 June 1920. Edmund Osmańczyk and Anthony Mango, ed., *Encyclopedia of United Nations & International Agreements* (London, 2003), p. 124. By 31 August, there was already a Home Office mail intercept warrant on ARCOS House, Lincoln's Inn Fields. 'ARCOS', serial 9, TNA KV 2/818.

72 See 'Ewer', Appendix.

73 BBC, *BBC London Calling, vol. 3–4* (London, 1963), p. 213; Andrew Defty, *Britain, America and Anti-Communist Propaganda 1945–53: The Information Research Department* (Abingdon, 2004), p. 87, chs 1–2.

74 Christopher Andrew, 'F. H. Hinsley and the Cambridge Moles: Two Patterns of Intelligence Recruitment', in *Diplomacy and Intelligence during the Second World War: Essays in Honour of F. H. Hinsley*, ed. Richard Langhorne (Cambridge, 1985), 22–40: p. 30; Andrew and Gordievsky, *KGB*, pp. 155–80; Andrew and Mitrokhin, *The Mitrokhin*, pp. 55–88. See also Madeira, 'No'.

75 See 'America', Appendix.

76 'William Ewer', TNA KV 2/1016; John Callaghan and Kevin Morgan, 'The Open Conspiracy of the Communist Party and the Case of William Ewer, Communist and Anti-Communist', *THJ* 49:2 (2006), 549–64: p. 560. This article responded to the one that first revealed the extent of Ewer's espionage. Victor Madeira, 'Moscow's Interwar Infiltration of British Intelligence, 1919–29', *THJ* 46:4 (2003), 915–33.

77 Nigel West and Oleg Tsarev, *The Crown Jewels: The British Secrets Exposed by the KGB Archives* (London, 1999), p. 9. Their account draws on Soviet intelligence records containing MI5 files supplied by Anthony Blunt.

78 Callaghan and Morgan, 'The Open', p. 553.

79 Ewer wrote Anglo-Russian tensions had ideological and historical roots due to 'old rivalries as Asiatic powers'. John Beavan, 'Ewer, William Norman', *ODNB*; 'Ewer', Part II

(Ewer), September 1949, p. 1 and serial 1101, p. 6, TNA KV 2/1016. After his CPGB expulsion, he gradually became a vocal anti-communist until his death in 1977.

80 'Ewer', Part II (Slocombe), p. 2, TNA KV 2/1016. The communist Clare Sheridan, Winston Churchill's cousin, was thought to be Slocombe's mistress. 'Renseignements a/s de Clare Sheridan [Information on Clare Sheridan]', 10 April 1923, pp. 9–10, 14, carton 1034, dossier 4614, *Fonds Moscou*, Army Historical Service, Vincennes, France. Sheridan, born Clare Frewin in London in 1885, was Churchill's relative on her maternal side. Her mother, like Churchill's, was from the noted Jerome family of New York. 'Clare Sheridan', TNA KV 2/1033. See also 'George Slocombe', TNA KV 2/485, and his autobiography *The Tumult and the Shouting: The Memoirs of George Slocombe* (London, 1936), pp. 184, 255 (on Sheridan) and p. 37 (on Ewer).

81 'Ewer', September 1949, p. 1, serial 1101, TNA KV 2/1016. See 'Walter Dale', TNA KV 2/997–/999.

82 'Dale', precautionary index, TNA KV 2/998; 'Arthur Lakey', 20 August 1928, serial 72A, TNA KV 2/989. IPI was the London liaison office of the Indian Government's security section, the Delhi Intelligence Bureau.

83 'Lakey', 20 August 1928, p. 8, serials 72A and 62A, TNA KV 2/989; 'Ewer', September 1949, p. 1, serial 1101, TNA KV 2/1016. See 'Lakey', TNA KV 2/989–/990.

84 See '(V)Cheka', Glossary; private correspondence; Andrew and Mitrokhin, *The Mitrokhin*, p. ix; Vasiliy Mitrokhin, ed., *KGB Lexicon: The Soviet Intelligence Officer's Handbook* (London, 2002), p. xiv.

85 See 'Wilkinson', Appendix.

86 A useful definition combines the work of two leading thinkers on the subject: 'the study of the organisation and behaviour of the intelligence [activities] of foreign states and entities, and [the strategic] application of the resulting knowledge [in identifying, assessing, neutralising, and exploiting hostile activities and capabilities]'. John Ehrman, 'What Are We Talking About When We Talk About Counterintelligence?', *Studies in Intelligence* 53:2 (2009), 5–20: p. 6; Michelle K. Van Cleave, *Counterintelligence and National Strategy* (Washington, DC, 2007), p. 5.

87 'Lakey', p. 3, serial 71A, TNA KV 2/989.

88 West and Tsarev, *The Crown*, p. 12.

89 See 'Klyshko', Appendix.

90 'Ewer', September 1949, pp. 6–7, serial 1101, TNA KV 2/1016; 'Lakey', 27 June 1928,

p. 3, serial 2A, TNA KV 2/989. By 1972, MI5 was no longer sure about the nature of Klyshko's intelligence work:

It is virtually impossible at this … time to determine with any accuracy what Klyshko's role was in … the Russian intelligence service and the Comintern; certainly contemporary assessments, suggesting that he was the OGPU "Resident" or the UK representative of the Third International, are misleading. Klyshko was not a trained intelligence officer; what he had to offer the Soviet regime in the post-Revolution period were his contacts and an experience of conspiratorial work in the UK before the revolution…. Although we have detailed evidence of their own activities from both Allen and [Jacob] Kirchenstein [see Appendix] … the part played by Klyshko remains somewhat obscure. It would be misleading to suggest … he controlled these operations; he was probably the channel through which … communications and reporting to Moscow passed, but his main role would seem to have been … providing support and above all as paymaster.

'Nicolas Klyshko', 4 January 1972, section V, p. 17, TNA KV 2/1415. See also 'Klyshko', TNA KV 2/1410–/1416.

91 Knight disagreed: '[T]his I am not prepared to accept. It is … impossible to run a [counter-espionage] organisation of this kind without performing acts which [*sic*] are to all intents and purposes espionage. Also, it seems … equally impossible to run an organisation like the [Federated Press] without obtaining information which [*sic*] is not purely "counter".' 'Ewer', 30 January 1950, p. 2, serial 1105a, TNA KV 2/1017.

92 Ibid.

93 West and Tsarev, *The Crown*, p. 11; Callaghan and Morgan, 'The Open', p. 553; 'Meeting with British Delegation', 16 June 1923, f. 495, op. 100, d. 97, l. 3, RGASPI.

94 'Ewer', 30 January 1950, p. 2, serial 1105a, TNA KV 2/1017.

95 Challinor, *The Origins*, p. 172; Callaghan and Morgan, 'The Open', p. 561; Brian Pearce, '1921 and All That', *Labour Review* 5:3 (1960), 84–91; *Parliamentary Debates*, House of Commons, 18 May 1931, vol. 252, columns 1654–5, and 3 March 1921, vol. 138, columns 2043–4; Brian Pearce, 'Top Cop Who Came Unstuck', *The Newsletter*, 1 November 1958.

96 While still at Special Branch in 1918–19, Allen entered Sir Nevil Macready's office several times and went through secret papers,

passing information to NUPPO. 'Lakey', 4 July 1928, serial 72A, TNA KV 2/989.

97 French security records mention a Max Grinfeld, a suspected INO Counter-intelligence Section (KRO) officer. 'Compte-Rendu Spécial no. 56/CPLE a/s de Grinfeld, Délégué de l'OGPU à CONS/PLE, [Special Report 56 on Grinfeld, OGPU Delegate in Constantinople]', 5 April 1927, carton 229, dossier 1548, p. 202, *Fonds Moscou* finding aid. The *Cheka* formally established KRO in May 1922 to tackle 'espionage, White Guard counter-revolution, conspiracies, gangsterism, smuggling, and illegal border crossings'. Mitrokhin, ed., *KGB*, p. 239. According to the French records, Nathan was a Comintern courier in Europe (including Britain). Carton 229, dossier 1548, p. 64; carton 1324, dossier 2812, p. 7, *Fonds Moscou*. French authorities may have mixed up the biographies.

98 'Ewer', September 1949, p. 1, serial 1101, TNA KV 2/1016; 'Lakey', serials 66a, 69A, 84a and 84b, TNA KV 2/989; 'Ewer', September 1949, pp. 6–7, serial 809a, TNA KV 2/1016.

99 French security records mention a Bittner (alias "Ignaz Perl"), born in Austria but claiming Czechoslovak nationality. Carton 1349, dossier 2540, pp. 15, 47, 53, *Fonds Moscou*.

100 Among them was Joe Paul, an ex-NUPPO executive and Vigilance Agency chief detective before Walter Dale. Paul's daughter, Rose Edwardes, was a Federated Press courier. Ex-NUPPO General-Secretary James Marston worked for ARCOS but sometimes helped Ewer. 'Ewer', September 1949, pp. 6–7, serial 809a, TNA KV 2/1016.

101 Idem, September 1949, p. 1, serial 1101; 'Lakey', serials 84 (illegible), 84a, 84b and 69A, TNA KV 2/989; 'Ewer', September 1949, pp. 6–7, serial 809a, TNA KV 2/1016. Hayes's brother Charles briefly worked for the Federated Press, conducting inquiries about weapons purchases 'by one of the Balkan or Baltic' states from the Birmingham Small Arms Company. Allen stated in 1928 he did not believe John Hayes 'had very much knowledge' of what the Federated Press did and 'was not cognisant of any' details. 'Lakey', p. 2, serial 84; p. 11, serial 66a, TNA KV 2/989. However, John Ottaway, head of MI5's three-man Observation Section and Allen's main debriefer, disagreed: evidence indicated Hayes was 'perfectly cognisant of Ewer's activities towards the end of 1920 and 1921 ... That he helped it ... at its inception, with full knowledge of what it was doing, there is ... no doubt.' 'Lakey', 29 April 1929, p. 2, serial 105a, TNA KV 2/990; Andrew, *The Defence*, p. 128.

102 'Report 29' (UK), 13 November 1919, p. 5, CP 125, TNA CAB 24/93.

103 'Report 44' (UK), 4 March 1920, p. 7, CP 791, TNA CAB 24/99.

104 Brigadier John H. Tiltman, 'Experiences 1920–1939', 1–13: p. 1, www.nsa.gov. Vetterlein's assistants early on were 'two very competent girls, refugees from Russia, with a perfect knowledge of the language, who subsequently became permanent members of the staff'. A. G. Denniston, 'The Government Code and Cypher School between the Wars', *INS* 1:1 (1986), 48–70: p. 54. Nigel West mentions a 'Miss Anderson' and a 'Miss Hayller' [*sic*]. *The SIGINT Secrets: The Signals Intelligence War, 1900 to Today: Including the Persecution of Gordon Welchman* (London, 1990), pp. 101, 117. These were E. Anderson (Junior Assistant; temporary status as of 20 November 1920) and F. C. Hayllar (Junior Assistant/Translator; resigned on 31 January 1920), who both joined GCCS after wartime service in MI1$_{(b)}$. However, GCCS records indicate these women did not fit the profile above. They knew French, German and Italian – 'The services of these ladies are invaluable ... in the working out of all kinds of codes' – but not Russian, unlike Helen Lunn and her sister Margaret. Russian-born Britons whose family fled the Bolshevik Revolution, GCCS appointed them translators on 17 December 1919 and 1 July 1921 respectively (see Chapter 6). Royal Naval Volunteer Reserve (RNVR) Lieutenant Gabriel Woods, who replaced Hayllar in February 1920, had worked on various ciphers (including Bolshevik) from 1917 to 1919. Admiralty minute of appointments, 10 January 1920, and handwritten GCCS salaried staff list (undated) and typed staff list, 29 October 1919, TNA FO 1093/104. 'Nominal Roll of MI1$_{(b)}$', 2 August 1919; 'Summary of Documents relating to Staff of GCCS', 7 July 1922, p. 2; 'Work Done by Staff of ID 25 during the War', 15 May 1919; 'Record of Cryptographic Work' (undated); 'Services of Lieutenant G. S. Woods, RNVR, in the Intelligence Division', 12 May 1919, TNA HW 3/35.

105 The scale and complexity of the Second World War forced the automation of cryptography, with mathematicians replacing linguists and philologists as leaders in the field. Friedrich L. Bauer, *Decrypted Secrets: Methods and Maxims of Cryptography* (Berlin, 2007), pp. 2–3.

106 Private correspondence. Originally Prussian, the family anglicised its surname once in Britain (the German 'V' has an 'F' sound in English). Private correspondence.

107 The reconstruction of British keys, he

wrote to Foreign Minister Count Lamsdorf in 1904, was 'very difficult' and 'time-consuming'; Sabanin spent over three years on one key alone before solving it. Irina Rybachenok, 'Takiye Raznyye Klyuchi: Shifrovalnaya Ekspeditsiya MID' [Such Different Keys: Cryptographic Expedition of the Ministry of Foreign Affairs], *Rodina* 9 (2003), 54–6: p. 55. See also 'Savinsky', Appendix.

108 Rybachenok, 'Takiye', p. 55.

109 A. V. Babash and E. K. Baranova, 'Kriptograficheskiye Metody Obespecheniya Informatsionnoi Bezopasnosti do Pervoi Mirovoi Voiny' [Cryptographic Methods to Ensure Information Security before the First World War], *Tekhnologii Tekhnosfernoi Bezopasnosti* [Technosphere Security Technologies] 6:34 (2010), 1–11: p. 4, http://ipb.mos.ru/ttb; Robert K. Massie, *Nicholas & Alexandra* (London, 1967), pp. 160–1; Michael Smith, *Station X: The Code Breakers of Bletchley Park* (London, 2007), pp. 12–13. See also 'Savinsky', Appendix.

110 Soboleva, *Istoriia*, pp. 281, 344, 349; Thomas R. Hammant, 'Russian and Soviet Cryptology I: Some Communications Intelligence in Tsarist Russia', *Cryptologia* 24:3 (2000), 235–49: p. 238; 'Baltic Operations, Sea', Spencer C. Tucker, ed., *The Encyclopedia of World War I: A Political, Social, and Military History* (Santa Barbara, CA, 2005), p. 179; www.saintanna.ru; Andrew, *The Defence*, pp. 143–4; Smith, *Station*, pp. 12–13. See also Ralph Erskine and Michael Smith, *The Bletchley Park Codebreakers* (London, 2011), pp. 15–22.

111 'Pavel Vetterlein', memoirs (6 sections), Imperial War Museum (IWM) London, section 2.

112 Smith, *Station*, p. 13; Denniston, *Thirty*, p. 7.

113 John F. Clabby, *Brigadier John Tiltman: A Giant among Cryptanalysts* (Fort Meade, MD, 2007), p. 6, www.nsa.gov; Tiltman, 'Experiences', p. 1.

114 'Paul Fetterlein (Sr)', police report, TNA HO 144/17121. Pavel Karlovich slipped across while the Bolshevik border guard was on a tea break. Private correspondence. His son did not mention Finland, saying only the family went from Moscow to Riga, from where they sailed to Britain on a vessel belonging to the 'British Baltic something or other fleet'. 'Vetterlein', IWM, section 2.

115 Ibid.

116 'N. A. Helsingfors', telegram 55, 9 March 1918, TNA ADM 223/743; Occleshaw, *Dances*, pp. 93–4.

117 'Ernest Fetterlein', naturalisation memorial and questionnaire, TNA HO 144/2848. He was naturalised in October 1923. TNA HO 334/97/10573; Denniston, *Thirty*, p. 71; private interview and correspondence. Records show one Tilbury-bound vessel around those dates: the Norwegian-built *Saphir*, which on 16 May 1918 arrived in Gravesend, Kent, where it then likely waited for the right tide before crossing the Thames over to Tilbury. 'Gravesend: Arrivals', 18 May 1918, *Lloyd's List – Overseas Shipping Intelligence* (January–June 1918), and 'Saphir', *Lloyd's Register*, 1918. Caird Archive & Library, National Maritime Museum, Greenwich.

118 P. William Filby, 'Bletchley Park and Berkeley Street', *INS* 3:2 (1988), 272–84: p. 280.

119 Norman Davies, *White Eagle, Red Star: The Polish-Soviet War, 1919–20* (London, 1972), p. 81; Brian Boyd, *Vladimir Nabokov: The Russian Years* (Princeton, NJ, 1993), p. 227; W. K. von Korostowetz, *Lenin im Hause der Väter* [Lenin in the House of the Fathers] (Berlin, 1928), pp. 4–6; 'GCCS Naval Section Translations of German Press Articles on British, German and Russian Sigint Organisations', TNA HW 3/12; Thomas R. Hammant, 'Russian and Soviet Cryptology II: The Magdeburg Incident, the Russian View', *Cryptologia* 24:4 (2000), 333–8; Smith, *Station*, p. 13; 'Work Done by Staff of ID 25 during the War', 15 May 1919, TNA HW 3/35.

120 John Rushworth Jellicoe, *The Crisis of the Naval War* (London, 1920), Appendix, p. 298.

121 Admiralty letter, 17 December 1919, TNA FO 1093/104; Denniston, *Thirty*, p. 95; Denniston, 'The Government', p. 50; 'Fetterlein', naturalisation memorial, TNA HO 144/2848. Curzon had long wanted the Foreign Office, not the Admiralty, to oversee GCCS since most of its work targeted diplomatic messages. By 1921, GCCS was already under Foreign Office operational control though a formal transfer did not occur until FY 1922/3. John Ferris, 'Whitehall's Black Chamber: British Cryptology and the GCCS, 1919–29', *INS* 2:1 (1987), 54–91: p. 57. Gill Bennett puts the operational transfer at August 1921. *Churchill*, p. 338 n. 24.

122 'Code and Cipher Personnel', 2 August 1919, p. 2, TNA HW 3/35. The GCCS head later said Vetterlein was one of 'our original [three] key men'. Denniston, 'The Government', p. 54.

123 Tiltman, 'Experiences', pp. 1, 3–4; Clabby, *Brigadier*, pp. 6–7. Appointed BP Chief Cryptographer in 1942, Tiltman said Ernst Vetterlein was 'still in my opinion far the best general-purpose cryptanalyst' by 1929.

'Experiences', p. 9. See also 'Vetterlein, Pavel P', Appendix.

124 Established on 1 October 1938, the Commercial Section worked largely for the Ministry of Economic Warfare, decrypting commercial traffic that might become the only intelligence source on enemy capabilities and intentions if war caused GCCS problems reading diplomatic and military traffic. Jacket cover X 11226, 16 November 1938, TNA FO 366/1024; Denniston, 'The Government', p. 62; Jacket cover X 3495/2300/504, 'Staffing of Code & Cypher School. Commercial S', 4 April 1939, TNA FO 366/2378.

125 The Air Section dealt with non-ENIGMA enemy codes and ciphers. 'BP 1939–1945: Roll of Honour Explanatory Notes', p. 2, www.bletchleypark.org.uk.

126 Zdzisław Jan Kapera, *The Enigma Bulletin* 2 (1997), pp. 66, 68; Denniston, 'The Government', p. 56; Michael J. Cowan, 'The Breaking of Floradora: The German Diplomatic Cipher', *The Cryptogram* 77:6 (2011), pp. 4–5; Bauer, *Decrypted*, p. 172; P. William Filby, 'Floradora and a Unique Break into One-Time Pad Ciphers', *INS* 10:3 (1995), 408–22. At one point during the war BP employed thirty-seven staff (including thirteen cryptanalysts and linguists, led by Vetterlein) to attack FLORADORA. Denniston, *Thirty*, p. 156.

127 Jacket cover X 1715, 21 February 1938, TNA FO 366/1024; West, *The SIGINT*, p. 117; 'Vetterlein', IWM, section 4; 'Nigel de Grey's History of Bletchley Park', p. 80, TNA HW 3/95; Martin Sugarman, 'Jewish Personnel at Bletchley Park in World War 2', www.jewishvirtuallibrary.org; 'Fetterlein, Ernst Constantine', 'BP Roll of Honour' and 'BP Roll of Honour Notes', pp. 1–2, 4–5, www.bletchleypark.org.uk; private correspondence; 'England & Wales Probate Calendar (Index of Wills and Administrations), 1856–1966', www.ancestry.co.uk.

128 Until Germany launched Operation BARBAROSSA against the USSR on 22 June 1941, BP was reading 'relatively minor' Russian military traffic. That day, Prime Minister Winston Churchill ordered BP to stop breaking Soviet signals (but said nothing about interception). British 'analytical work on Russian cryptosystems' but not necessarily 'interception or certain work farmed out to the [Polish Wireless Research Unit at Stanmore]' was 'more or less discontinued by September 1941'. In 1943, however, Project ISCOT began. 'Seventy Years Ago this Month at Bletchley Park: June 1941 – Barbarossa: Intelligence Relations with Russia', www.bletchleypark.org.uk; Craig Graham McKay,

'British SIGINT and the Bear, 1919–1941', *Kungl Krigsvetenskaps-Akademiens Handlingar och Tidskrift [KKrVAHT*, The Royal Swedish Academy of War Sciences Proceedings and Journal, online edition] 2 (1997), 1–15: pp. 9, 11. See Richard J. Aldrich, *GCHQ: The Uncensored Story of Britain's Most Secret Intelligence Agency* (London, 2010), pp. 37–8; Nigel West, *Historical Dictionary of Signals Intelligence*, ed. Jon Woronoff (Lanham, MD, 2012), p. 128; and 'Vetterlein, Pavel P', Appendix on ISCOT.

129 Ferris, 'Whitehall', pp. 57, 61; McKay, 'British', p. 2; Robin Denniston, 'Diplomatic Eavesdropping, 1922–44: A New Source Discovered', *INS* 10:3 (1995), 423–48: p. 429. On the School's creation, see Freeman, 'MI1$_{(b)}$'; and Denniston, *Thirty*, ch. 6.

130 Paul Addison, *Churchill on the Home Front, 1900–55* (London, 1992), p. 211.

131 Andrew, *Her Majesty*, p. 259. British government first discussed a postwar service on 10 December 1918. Freeman, 'MI1$_{(b)}$', p. 218.

132 James Bamford, *Body of Secrets: How America's NSA [National Security Agency] and Britain's GCHQ Eavesdrop on the World* (London, 2001), p. 397. On GCCS interwar performance, see John Ferris, 'The Road to Bletchley Park: The British Experience with Signals Intelligence, 1892–1945', *INS* 17:1 (2002), 53–84.

133 Abyssinia, Afghanistan, Argentina, Austria, Belgium, Bokhara (in present-day Uzbekistan), Brazil, Chile, Denmark, Egypt, France, Georgia, Germany, Greece, Hungary, Italy, Japan, Kingdom of Hejaz, Netherlands, Norway, Persia, Poland, Portugal, Romania, Soviet Union, Spain, Sweden, Syria (Hashemite), Turkey (Constantinople and Angora), Ukraine, USA, Uruguay and Yugoslavia. TNA HW 12 finding aid.

134 Denniston, 'Diplomatic', p. 429.

135 James Bamford, *The Puzzle Palace: Inside the National Security Agency, America's Most Secret Intelligence Organization* (New York, 1983), p. 30.

136 Part of the HW 12 series at TNA. See also Victor Madeira, '"Because I Don't Trust Him, We are Friends": Signals Intelligence and the Reluctant Anglo-Soviet Embrace, 1917–24', *INS* 19:1 (2004), 29–51.

137 GCCS had difficulty decrypting Russian traffic from January 1921 but from 'April 1921 to late 1923' again broke it. Only an estimated 0.75% of intercepts produced from 1919 to 1929 survive. Ferris, 'Whitehall', pp. 74, 72.

138 Popplewell, *Intelligence*, pp. 19–21.

139 British elites believed administrators and

rulers of sufficient talent to run the Empire could only come from a small pool of the right people. Traditionally, however, "Englishness" had actually been anti-imperial and instead parliamentary, constitutional and liberal. India and those in its favour, in fact, were often suspect. The underlying struggle at the heart of British politics was whether to hold on to India for prestige or to let go, much more the English tradition. Complicating matters was a Civil Service mindset of exaggerated realism and powerful pragmatism, according to which no problem was beyond solution. Private correspondence.

140 The Bolshevik danger 'to Persia and ... India seems to me to be ... largely the fault of the Home Govt in their anti-Mohammedan policy. ... We could have made pan-Islamism friendly to Great Britain. We are making it hostile.' [India Secretary Edwin] Montagu to [Foreign Secretary Lord] Curzon, 5 January 1920, AS 1/12/122, Edwin Montagu (MONTAGU) MSS, Trinity College Library, Cambridge.

141 Laqueur, *The Fate*, p. 10.

142 'All unofficial news from and in Russia must be received with much reserve and matters seen to be believed.' 'Russian Situation', 9 May 1918, file 82354, TNA FO 371/3330.

143 Christopher Andrew, 'The British Secret Service and Anglo-Soviet Relations in the 1920s – Part I: From the Trade Negotiations to the Zinoviev Letter', *THJ* 20:3 (1977), 673–706: pp. 688–91; idem, *Her Majesty*, pp. 278–82.

144 Denniston, 'Diplomatic', p. 73; Andrew, *Her Majesty*, p. 261; idem, 'British Intelligence and the Breach with Russia in 1927', *THJ* 25:4 (1982), 957–64: p. 957. Vetterlein and others had made British communications just as vulnerable. While posted in Petrograd in 1916 to the British Intelligence Mission to the Russian General Staff, Lieutenant-Colonel Sir Samuel Hoare, MP, warned London Russia could easily decrypt British communications. 'One of the codes ... was so compromised ... the [Russian] Admiralty General Staff called attention to the fact.' As for Foreign Office codes, 'they are seldom changed and ... according to common talk they can be easily deciphered.' Hoare urged the British Admiralty, War Office and Foreign Office to copy Russia's elaborate security since 'we take far too small precautions. I ... think ... [the Russians] themselves are in possession of most of our codes.' 'The Russian Use of Codes', 1 December 1916, Part II (Russia, 1915–24), pp. 1–3, file 1, document 14, Templewood MSS. A 1918 British security assessment found Admiralty codes and ciphers provided 'sufficient

security' but Foreign Office ones did not. Corrective measures ensued. 'Notes on Cryptography', Appendix C, MS 2788/2/4, Malcolm Hay MSS, Special Collections Centre, University of Aberdeen.

145 TNA HW 12/1 (19–26 October 1919) to TNA HW 12/9 (6 May–2 June 1920).

146 For instance:

We learn ... of a political note of the Foreign Relations Department addressed ... to the Government of Bokhara. This note was presented not only without the sanction of the Central Government, but also without the knowledge of the Foreign [Commissariat]. We remind you once more ... the Foreign Relations Department has not the right to take ... steps of a political nature without the knowledge of the Central Government.... A repetition ... will make it necessary to recall all persons responsible.

(Sender to receiver) Karakhan, Moscow–Eliava, Tashkent; (GCCS internal distribution date and serial number) 5 January 1920–000693; (original intercept date) 3 January 1920, p. 1, TNA HW 12/3.

147 Karakhan, Moscow–Eliava, Tashkent; 31 December 1919–000653; 27 December 1919, p. 1, TNA HW 12/3; Karakhan, Moscow–Eliava, Tashkent; 29 January 1920–001041; 25 January 1920, p. 1, TNA HW 12/4.

148 On his dealings with Britain, see Timothy O'Connor, *Diplomacy and Revolution: Georgi Chicherin and Soviet Foreign Affairs, 1918–30* (Ames, IA, 1988), ch. 3.

149 Chicherin, Moscow–Eliava, Tashkent; 27 January 1920–001002; 24 January 1920, p. 1, TNA HW 12/4; Karakhan, Moscow–Eliava, Tashkent; 4 January 1920–000694; 3 January 1920, p. 1, TNA HW 12/3.

150 Ferris, 'Whitehall', pp. 54, 81 n. 6. In September 1920 GCCS noted the possibility of deception:

This telegram is purposely ciphered on a "Marta" key. Since July 15th the Russian Delegation in London have considered Marta keys as compromised and on August 19th Kameneff [temporary Head of Delegation] himself requested that the use of Marta ... should cease ... Presumably ... Kameneff's intention was to make sure that this message could be deciphered by the British Government.

Kamenev, London–Chicherin, Moscow; 15 September 1920–004155; 11 September 1920, pp. 1–2, TNA HW 12/14.

151 Karakhan, Moscow–Eliava, Tashkent; 30

January 1920–001057; 27 January 1920, p. 1, TNA HW 12/4.

152 Soboleva, *Tainopis*, p. 321.

153 'Report 18' (foreign), April 1920, p. 4, CP 1130, TNA CAB 24/104.

154 Leonard, *Secret*; idem, 'Studying the Kremlin's Secret Soldiers: A Historiographical Essay on the GRU, 1918–45', *The Journal of Military History* 56 (1992), 403–21: pp. 406–17; Dennis Kux, 'Soviet Active Measures and Disinformation: Overview and Assessment', *Parameters, Journal of the US Army War College* 15:4 (1985), 19–28.

155 Chicherin, Moscow–Litvinov, Copenhagen; 12 March 1920–001607; 20 February 1920, p. 1, TNA HW 12/6.

156 G. H. Bennett, 'Lloyd George, Curzon, and the Control of British Foreign Policy, 1919–22', *Australian Journal of Politics & History* 45:4 (1999), 467–82: p. 479.

157 Soboleva, *Tainopis*, pp. 333–5; idem, *Istoriia*, pp. 399–400. On Russian HUMINT enabling SIGINT successes, see Andrew and Mitrokhin, *The Mitrokhin*, pp. 46–8, 67–70; D. Cameron Watt, 'Francis Herbert King: A Soviet Source in the Foreign Office', *INS* 3:4 (1988), 62–82; Richard Thurlow, 'Soviet Spies and British Counter-Intelligence in the 1930s: Espionage in the Woolwich Arsenal and the Foreign Office Communications Department', *INS* 19:4 (2004), 610–31; Christopher Andrew and Oleg Gordievsky, 'Ciphers and Counter-Intelligence', in 'More "Instructions from the Centre": Top Secret Files on KGB Global Operations, 1975–85', *INS* 7:1 (1992), Special Issue, 99–121: pp. 99–100; Christopher Andrew and Keith Neilson, 'Tsarist Codebreakers and British Codes', *INS* 1:1 (1986), 6–12; Hammant, 'Russian ... I: Some', pp. 236–7; David Kahn, 'Soviet Comint in the Cold War', *Cryptologia* 22:2 (1998), 1–24: p. 11; David Schimmelpenninck van der Oye, 'Tsarist Codebreaking: Some Background and Some Examples', *Cryptologia* 22:4 (1998), 342–53: pp. 345–7, 350. France was renowned for solving Tsarist cables by buying or stealing codebooks. 'Notes', Hay MSS.

158 Chicherin, Moscow–Litvinov, Copenhagen; 6 April 1920–001976; 30 March 1920, p. 1, TNA HW 12/7; Litvinov, Copenhagen–Chicherin, Moscow; 6 April 1920–001977; 2 April 1920, p. 1, TNA HW 12/7. For an (ideologically rosy) overview of Frunze's early life and military career, see Makhmut Gareev, *M. Frunze – Military Theorist* (Washington, DC, 1988), pp. 7–78. See also Ivo Juurvee, 'Estonian Interwar Radio-Intelligence', *Baltic Defence Review* 10:2 (2003), 123–37.

159 Kamenev was a founding member of the ruling Politburo in 1919. Between 11 July and 11 September 1920, he temporarily headed the London Mission (see Chapter 3).

160 Kamenev, London–Chicherin, Moscow; 21 August 1920–003854; 19 August 1920, p. 1, TNA HW 12/13.

161 Soboleva, *Istoriia*, pp. 397–9.

162 8 November 1920, TNA HW 3/39.

163 'Conference on GCCS: Miscellaneous', 10 January 1921, p. 10, TNA HW 3/39.

164 For instance, Krivosh-Nemanjic, Vetterlein's former Foreign Ministry colleague. Soboleva, *Istoriia*, p. 417.

165 Moscow accepted an offer of service from a wireless telegraphy expert named Rozitsky in late 1920. Krasin, London–Chicherin, Moscow; 11 October 1920–004393; 30 September 1920, p. 1, TNA HW 12/15; Krasin, London–Chicherin, Moscow; 12 October 1920–004409; 8 October 1920, p. 1, TNA HW 12/15. Faced with a somewhat similar offer earlier that year, the British declined. A Bolshevik expert named Jukovski claimed he had solved German ciphers during the war and was now writing an account of his work, for which he needed 'a quantity of German ciphers sent from and received here [Persia] before the war'. The Russian Chargé d'Affaires in Tehran asked the British Minister there, Sir Percy Cox, saying if London helped, it could have Jukovski's product. The Foreign Office declined. 'Telegram from Sir Percy Cox' (12 January 1920) and 'Telegram from Foreign Office' (20 January 1920); © British Library Board L/P&S/11/167, P 600/1920: P 600/20; Asia, Pacific & Africa Collections; British Library, London. In 1926, a Soviet cipher clerk in Kabul recalled to Moscow fled to the British Embassy but officials there, to GCCS dismay, forced him to leave. Tiltman, 'Experiences', p. 8.

166 See 'Wise', Appendix. Like Lloyd George, Wise felt a trade agreement was a key first step in getting Moscow to 'behave properly in other areas if ... given the hope of full recognition, either *de facto* or *de jure*'. Andrew J. Williams, *Trading with the Bolsheviks: The Politics of East–West Trade, 1920–39* (Manchester, 1992), p. 60.

167 'Economic Aspects of British Policy concerning Russia', 6 January 1920, pp. 2–4, TNA CAB 21/200.

168 Rail staff (one-third of the resurrected "Triple Alliance" of February 1919 that included miners and transport workers) walked out in September over proposed wage

cuts at a time of high inflation. Taylor, *English*, pp. 140–1.

169 Stephen White, *Britain and the Bolshevik Revolution: A Study in the Politics of Diplomacy, 1920–4* (London, 1979), p. 3; 'Report 36' (UK), 9 January 1920, pp. 1–2, CP 429, TNA CAB 24/96: 'the most serious factor at the moment is unemployment, which is driving many of the more moderate ex-Service men into the revolutionary camp ... most urgent need ...: solution for unemployment and housing problems'.

170 'Civic Unrest in Great Britain: Steps to Safeguard Against', 17 January 1920, pp. 1–2, file 12, TNA CAB 1/29. The Supply and Transport Organisation (STO), the Government's strike-breaking machinery, was already under development, playing a critical role in keeping Britain functioning during the May 1926 General Strike (see Chapter 6). See also Jeffery and Hennessy, *States*, ch. 2, on the STO.

171 'Report 36' (UK), 9 January 1920, p. 4, CP 429, TNA CAB 24/96. As an academic wrote to James Headlam-Morley, PID Assistant Director: 'The Englishman is so honest and sound at heart that with a little patience and tact, one can always get him to look at things soberly and sanely.' 'Winthrop Bell to Headlam-Morley', Churchill Archives Centre, The Papers of Sir James and Agnes Headlam-Morley, HDLM, 2 January 1920, box 1, folder 1.

172 Thurlow, *The Secret*, p. 129.

173 'Special Report 14', 2 February 1920, pp. 1–3, 12, CP 544, TNA CAB 24/97; 'Report 38' (UK), 22 January 1920, pp. 2, 6, CP 491, TNA CAB 24/96:

Communism will be best served by using the Parliamentary machine.... Bolshevik propaganda ... ably written, will inevitably [increase] when trade is opened ... and there is no way of stemming the flow without legislation.... The decision to reopen trade ... has been ... welcomed by most sections of labour.... The extremists hope for easier communication and for financial assistance on a much larger scale than has ... been possible, and it is difficult to see how this can be prevented, since the law provides no penalty for preaching revolution or ... financing revolutionary propaganda.

174 John Hope, 'Surveillance or Collusion? Maxwell Knight, MI5, and the British Fascisti', *INS* 9:4 (1994), 651–75: p. 665.

175 'Propaganda Sub-Committee', 9 March 1920, p. 2, TNA CAB 27/84. On such groups, see Thomas Linehan, *British Fascism, 1918–39:*

Parties, Ideology, and Culture (Manchester, 2000), ch. 2; Mike Hughes, *Spies at Work: The Rise and Fall of the Economic League* (Bradford, 1995), chs 1–3; David Miller and William Dinan, *A Century of Spin: How Public Relations Became the Cutting Edge of Corporate Power* (London, 2008), ch. 3.

176 See 'Makgill', Appendix.

177 Founded in April 1915 by members of the British Empire Producers' Organisation, of which Makgill was General-Secretary, the BEU rallied popular support for efforts to eradicate German influence across the Empire. German "espionage" soon became a concern so to fight it Makgill set up a network of agencies collecting intelligence on suspect individuals and organisations. Special Branch and MI5 were by mid-1916 receiving information, though it was often unreliable. Hope, 'Surveillance', pp. 657–8. MI5's Maxwell Knight belonged not only to BEU but also to a sister group, the British Fascisti, where he was Deputy Chief of Staff and Director of Intelligence. Linehan, *British*, p. 44. The postwar BEU had a Fascist outlook on the danger posed by Bolshevik and Jewish conspiracies to Britain and empire. John Ferris and Uri Bar-Joseph, 'Getting Marlowe to Hold His Tongue: The Conservative Party, the Intelligence Services, and the Zinoviev Letter', *INS* 8:4 (1993), 100–37: p. 106.

178 Eunan O'Halpin, 'Hall, Sir (William) Reginald', *ODNB*; 'Propaganda Sub-Committee', 9 March 1920, p. 2, TNA CAB 27/84. See also Miller and Dinan, *A Century*, pp. 40–6. Formally known as The Central Committee for National Propaganda, it was reorganised and renamed The Central Council of Economic Leagues in 1924, retaining its coordinating role under new Chairman Sir Auckland Geddes. Two years later, the name was shortened to The Economic League, which survived into the 1990s. Hope, 'Surveillance', pp. 659–61; Hughes, *Spies*, ch. 1; Miller and Dinan, *A Century*, pp. 42–3.

179 Hope, 'Surveillance', pp. 659–61. Hall held the founding conference in his suite at the Savoy.

180 'Propaganda Sub-Committee', 9 March 1920, pp. 7–8, TNA CAB 27/84. Sources put Hall's budget between 1919 and 1921 at £250,000 (2011: nearly £77 million). Miller and Dinan, *A Century*, p. 41.

181 Jacquie L'Etang, 'Public Relations and Democracy: Historical Reflections and Implications for Practice', in *Handbook of Corporate Communications and Public Relations: Pure and Applied*, ed. Sandra M. Oliver (London,

2004), 342–55: p. 350; Miller and Dinan, *A Century*, pp. 17, 41.

182 'Propaganda Sub-Committee', 9 March 1920, pp. 9–10, TNA CAB 27/84. Industrial Information clearly meant to counteract public relations work by the Left:

> the Labour publicity ... office ... is ... organised for any conditions that may arise. It is well staffed; it has famous writers at its disposal; its telephone and general communications organisation is complete; it welcomes press representatives at any hour and goes to endless trouble to supply articles and material. The Press are making more and more use of this establishment. (p. 4)

183 Ibid., p. 3. Neither William James, *The Eyes of the Navy: A Biographical Study of Admiral Sir Reginald Hall* (London, 1955) nor Ramsay, *'Blinker'* mentions his role in National Propaganda. The identities of its leaders and advisory council were to remain secret. Hope, 'Surveillance', p. 660.

184 Ibid., p. 655.

185 Ibid., p. 658.

186 Bennett, *Churchill*, pp. 71–9; idem, *A Most*, p. 38. Aside from gathering intelligence, IIB also conducted covert operations. In Liverpool, an IIB agency provided vetting (i.e. blacklisting) services to local employers by identifying leading socialists and communists in the area. The Bureau acquired information on planned industrial action or demonstrations by infiltration and theft, if needed. Other practices included sabotage, break-ins, theft of correspondence and membership lists, and forgery of documents. Hope, 'Surveillance', pp. 658–9.

187 Thomson had recognised the value of telegraphy as an intelligence source years earlier:

> Thomson asked me to go into the question of the intercepts, and of the proposed new clause of the Official Secrets Bill, before a conference which [*sic*] he was going to ask the Home Secretary to summon.... Thomson wished to incorporate into the Bill two clauses: (1) instructing that either the public or the cable company were to arrange to supply a copy of each telegram; (2) that only people on a register be allowed to ... use ... private codes.

'SIGINT Exploitation of Diplomatic Telegrams', 4 May 1918, TNA HW 3/37.

188 Thomson was on to something. In the same report, a railway union leader was quoted saying he wanted a 'revolution, but ... no bloodshed here'. 'Report 43' (UK), 26 February 1920, pp. 4–8, CP 748, TNA CAB 24/99.

189 'Report 49' (UK), 8 April 1920, p. 5, CP 1039, TNA CAB 24/103.

190 The intelligence cycle broke down at two points: tasking and assessment. Diehards egged Thomson on to find "evidence" of Bolshevik subversion. He in turn, seeking advancement and keen to please his political masters, obliged by often exaggerating the extent of such activity. Reginald Hall also 'succumbed to the professional temptation of manipulating good intelligence' to influence Cabinet decisions and actions. O'Halpin, 'Hall', *ODNB*.

191 'Report 53' (UK), 6 May 1920, p. 6, CP 1239, TNA CAB 24/105.

CHAPTER 3

The Agreement

1 'Financial Dependence [on USA]', October 1916, TNA CAB 42/23, quoted in John Cooper Jr, 'Command of Gold Reversed: American Loans to Britain, 1915–17', *The Pacific Historical Review* 45:2 (1976), 209–30: p. 220.

2 Robert James, ed., *Winston Churchill – His Complete Speeches: vol. 3, 1914–22* (New York, 1974), pp. 3025–6.

3 'Solution of Codes', 29 October 1917, TNA ADM 137/4652.

4 'Intelligence Methods in Peacetime: Russian System', 1909, pp. 3, 11; TNA KV 1/4.

5 Basil Thomson complained of this in 1919: 'Owing to the lack of internal communication, it is very difficult to obtain news from the [Russian] interior.' 'Report 30' (UK), 13 January 1919, p. 2, GT 6654, TNA CAB 24/73.

6 For instance: Churchill (India, South Africa); Curzon (Asia); Hankey (Mediterranean); Long (Ireland); Shortt (Ireland); Thomson (Tonga); and Wilson (Burma, South Africa).

7 White, *Britain*, p. 3.

8 By 1918–19, MI5 had hired Japanese-speaking Cambridge graduates to tackle Tokyo's aggressive intelligence gathering. At an Intelligence and Police (IP) Club dinner on 26 November 1920, Cabinet Secretary Hankey learned Japan posed the gravest espionage threat. Vernon Kell founded the IP Club in 1919 to bring together past and current male MI5 members, and guests like Lloyd George and Churchill. Diary, HNKY 1/5, 16 and 26 November 1920, p. 170; diary, 26 November 1920, Holt-Wilson MSS; The Papers of Major

General Sir Vernon Kell KBE, p. 173, PP/ MCR/120, IWM; 'Interim Report on [MI5] by Lord Hankey', p. 5, TNA CAB 63/193; Ferris and Bar-Joseph, 'Getting', pp. 111–16.

9 'I had long coveted' heading CID. Thomson, *The Scene*, p. 226. He cleverly manipulated the Press with selective leaks. "Black propaganda" was one of his duties between 1913 and 1921, and he worked closely on this with Ralph Blumenfeld, editor of the *Daily Express*. Ferris and Bar-Joseph, 'Getting', p. 116. Thomson had personal ties to the Tsarist regime. His cousin, Helen Rangabé, married 'Vice-Admiral Petroff', the 'Chief of the Naval Staff at Petrograd' who fled abroad in October 1917. Thomson, *The Scene*, p. 360. Petrov likely headed the Main Naval Staff rather than the Naval General Staff: its acting chief between June and September 1917 was Count Alexei P. Kapnist, arrested on 15 November. 'Bolsheviki Outlaw Military Opponents', 2 December 1917, *The New York Times* digital archive. See WarChron, 'Russian Navy Commander Name File', http://warchron.com; Evgenii Podsoblyaev, 'The Russian Naval General Staff and the Evolution of Naval Policy, 1905–14', *The Journal of Military History* 66:1 (2002), 37–69: pp. 42–3.

10 H. A. L. Fisher, 'Strikes in the Civil Service', 4 May 1920, pp. 1–3, CP 1267, TNA CAB 24/105.

11 The Lord Mayor's Banquet at which the Prime Minister signalled a policy shift, away from intervention and toward a mutually beneficial relationship based on trade. Curtis Keeble, *Britain, the Soviet Union and Russia* (Basingstoke, 2000), p. 67. Richard Toye has written that where Lloyd George 'differed from Churchill was not on the desirability of a White victory but over the amount of effort that should be expended by the British to bring it about'. *Lloyd George and Churchill: Rivals for Greatness* (London, 2007), p. 201.

12 He relied on Maurice Hankey, Philip Kerr (Private Secretary) and Frank Wise (Food Ministry). Keeble, *Britain*, p. 69. Churchill and Curzon loathed Kerr who, as Lloyd George's right-hand man, foiled Churchill's plans for large-scale intervention in Russia and undermined Curzon by acting as a 'second Foreign Office'. Curzon regarded Kerr 'a most unsafe and insidious intermediary, being full both of ability and guile. He was the chosen agent of most of his master's intrigues.' John Turner, ed., *The Larger Idea: Lord Lothian and the Problem of National Sovereignty* (London, 1988), p. 55, quoted in Alex May, 'Kerr, Philip Henry, eleventh Marquess of Lothian', *ODNB*.

13 We 'are simply converting them through

a gentlemanly process of instruction' for 'to love one's neighbour' is 'not only good sound Christianity: it is good business'. White, *Britain*, pp. 26, 24.

14 T. S. Willan, 'Trade between England and Russia in the Second Half of the Sixteenth Century', *The English Historical Review* 63:248 (1948), 307–21: p. 308. While foreigners invest for profit in Russia, it seeks foreign capital for state-building: 'The geo-economic resources of Russia sustain these principles today as much as they did two centuries ago.' Herbert Kaplan, 'Commerce, Consumption, and Culture: Hope & Co. and Baring Brothers & Co. and Russia', *Proceedings of the American Philosophical Society* 142:2 (1998), 258–62: pp. 260, 258–9.

15 Repudiation decision made on 21 January 1918; decree issued 8 February. Moscow also nationalised banks and trading companies often owned by foreign investors, who 'dismissed these decrees as illegal' and 'reached several secret agreements' with the Whites during the civil war. Investors traded 'support for promises to honour pre-revolutionary debt obligations in case of victory'. John Landon-Lane and Kim Oosterlinck, 'Hope Springs Eternal … French Bondholders and the Soviet Repudiation (1915–19)', Working Paper WP-CEB 05/013, Solvay Business School, Brussels, 2005, p. 20; Sinyagina-Woodruff, 'Russia', p. 532. Repudiation extended to all Russian domestic creditors. Peter Gatrell, 'Poor Russia, Poor Show: Mobilising a Backward Economy for War, 1914–17', in *The Economics of World War I*, ed. Stephen Broadberry and Mark Harrison (Cambridge, 2005), 235–75: p. 249.

16 From 1914 to 1929, some hardliners held directorships in public companies: Reginald Hall, Samuel Hoare, William Joynson-Hicks (known as "Jix"), Walter Long, Edward Shortt and F. E. Smith. Directorships were primarily in banks, insurance, utilities and energy companies – some of the most affected by Bolshevik renunciation of debt. In most cases, the number of directorships per individual rose once war started. Thomas Skinner, ed., *The Directory of Directors for [1914, etc.] – A List of Directors of Joint Stock Companies of the UK* (London, 1914–29). Curzon married two wealthy Americans. David Cannadine, *The Decline and Fall of the British Aristocracy* (New Haven, CT, 1990), p. 397; Richard Davis, '"We are All Americans Now!" Anglo-American Marriages in the Later Nineteenth Century', *Proceedings of the American Philosophical Society* 135:2 (1991), pp. 140–99. For additional income, Churchill wrote and

lobbied. Neither man appeared in *The Directory* during this period.

17 Niall Ferguson, *The World's Banker: The History of the House of Rothschild* (London, 1998), p. 901. On the political motives for French floating of Russian bonds, see Landon-Lane and Oosterlinck, 'Hope', pp. 2–12; and Kim Oosterlinck and Ariane Szafarz, 'One Asset, Two Prices: The Case of the Tsarist Repudiated Bonds', Working Paper WP-CEB 04/022, Solvay Business School, Brussels, 2004, pp. 3–4.

18 Figures based on an exchange rate of RR 9.45 to £1. Ferguson, *The World*, p. 1038, Appendix 2, Table C. In 1887, Russian debt was RR 4.42 billion (£395 million); by 1913, it was RR 8.86 billion (£937 million). Adjusting for rouble depreciation versus the pound, the rise was only two-thirds. Losing the 1904–05 Russo-Japanese War added to.debt growth. Besides seeking foreign funds to develop industry, Russia also sought them for military modernisation: that spending grew by 18.5% between 1894 and 1913. Ibid., p. 944, Table 29c; p. 942, Table 29a.

19 Two Russian measures led to such growth. One was the gradual transition to the gold standard (1895–97) that 'strengthened the confidence of foreign investors in Russian Governmental and industrial securities'. The other was an aggressive effort to court foreign investment. John Sontag, 'Tsarist Debts and Tsarist Foreign Policy', *Slavic Review* 27:4 (1968), 529–41: pp. 530–1.

20 Having only arrived in Russia in the 1770s, by the early 1850s 'Barings were [in effect now] the official agents of the Russian Government'. Philip Ziegler, *The Sixth Great Power: Barings, 1762–1929* (London, 1988), pp. 171, 311–50; Kaplan, 'Commerce', p. 259.

21 Ferguson, *The World*, pp. 909, 934, 926.

22 Russian national debt in 1913 was around 47% of net national product. Ibid., pp. 945–6.

23 Oosterlinck and Szafarz, 'One', pp. 3–6.

24 Original figure: French francs (FF) 3.3 million. Sinyagina-Woodruff, 'Russia', p. 532. Figures based on an exchange rate of FF 25.22 to £1. Ferguson, *The World*, p. 1038, Appendix 2, Table C.

25 Sinyagina-Woodruff, 'Russia', p. 522.

26 Ferguson, *The World*, p. 929.

27 In 1870, 47% of Russian exports went to Britain, which supplied 31% of Russian imports. In 1890, it was 29.5% of exports and 22.5% of imports; in 1910, 22% (£33.5 million) of exports and 14% (£16 million) of imports; and in 1913, 19% (£28 million) of exports and 14% (£18 million) of imports. Jules Gay, 'Anglo-Russian Economic Relations', *The Economic Journal* 27:106 (1917), 213–37: p. 215, Table I.

28 In 1870, 21% of Russian exports went to Germany, which supplied 39.5% of Russian imports. In 1910, it was 27% (£41.5 million) of exports and 42% (£48 million) of imports; in 1913, 32% (£48 million) of exports and 53% (£68 million) of imports. Ibid.

29 Argentina, Australia, Canada, New Zealand and South Africa: 25%; India: 13%; and the USA: 5%.

30 I. Drummond, 'Britain and the World Economy, 1900–45', in *The Economic History of Britain since 1700, vol. 2: 1860 to the 1970s*, ed. Roderick Floud and Donald McCloskey (Cambridge, 1981), 286–307: pp. 290–3. From 1909 to 1913, Britain imported 79% of its wheat and flour, and 56% of cereals and pulses. Stephen Broadberry and Peter Howlett, 'The United Kingdom during World War I: Business as Usual?', in *The Economics of World War I*, ed. Stephen Broadberry and Mark Harrison (Cambridge, 2005), 206–34: p. 211.

31 The Royal Commission on the Supply of Food and Raw Materials in Time of War felt Britain could survive any future war given sufficient ships and money. Alan Milward, *The Economic Effects of the Two World Wars on Britain* (London, 1984), p. 51.

32 Ibid.; Nicholas A. Lambert, *Planning Armageddon: British Economic Warfare and the First World War* (Cambridge, 2012), especially chs 1–2. Britain had £4 billion of foreign investments before the war, compared to a £2.3 billion GDP. Barry Eichengreen, 'The British Economy between the Wars', in *The Cambridge Economic History of Modern Britain, vol. 2: Economic Maturity, 1860–1939*, ed. Roderick Floud and Paul Johnson (Cambridge, 2004), 314–43: p. 318. Others put foreign investment in 1914 at between £3.1 and £4.5 billion, and GDP at £2.5 billion. P. J. Cain and A. G. Hopkins, *British Imperialism, 1688–2000* (Harlow, 2002), pp. 160–5.

33 Milward, *The Economic*, p. 52. In 1914, exports were £526 million; in 1915, £484 million; in 1916, £604 million; in 1917, £597 million; in 1918, £532 million. Broadberry and Howlett, 'The United', p. 221, Table 7.11.

34 The British trade deficit in 1914 was £170 million. By 1915 it was £368 million; by 1916, £345 million; by 1917, £467 million; and by 1918, £784 million (not taking inflation into account). Ibid.

35 Milward, *The Economic*, pp. 55, 52. Wartime exchange rate variations and

currency depreciation worsened Britain's plight since most nations (Britain too) had suspended the gold standard. Derek Aldcroft, *From Versailles to Wall Street, 1919–29*, The Pelican History of World Economy, ed. Wolfram Fischer (Harmondsworth, 1987), p. 32. Pre-1914 parity was $4.86 to £1. By 1916, it was $4.76; by early 1920, after the March 1919 peg was dropped, parity hit a post-1914 low of $3.20. N. H. Dimsdale, 'British Monetary Policy and the Exchange Rate, 1920–38', *Oxford Economic Paper* 33 (1981) supplement, 306–49: p. 307; Cooper Jr, 'Command', p. 211. British foreign investment income in 1913 was £200 million; in 1920, it was £120 million. C. K. Hobson, 'The Measurement of the Balance of Trade', *Economica* 2 (1921), 132–46: p. 146. This would all be worse factoring in inflation.

36 "Invisibles" were defined as 'receipts of the British mercantile marine in the foreign trade, less expenses in foreign ports, but plus expenses of foreign vessels in British ports'; 'services rendered by persons in the [UK] in connection with the financing and insurance of trade'; 'income from overseas investments'; and 'miscellaneous items'. Ibid., p. 133.

37 Milward, *The Economic*, p. 52. British shipping receipts in 1911 were £97 million; in 1913, £107.5 million. Stephen Broadberry, *Market Services and the Productivity Race, 1850–2000: British Performance in International Perspective*, Cambridge Studies in Economic History (Cambridge, 2006), p. 155, Table 8.9. By May 1915, estimated receipts were £100 million. C. K. Hobson, 'The War in Relation to British Foreign Investments', *The Economic Journal* 25:98 (1915), 244–55: p. 254. In 1920, receipts were £340 million. Hobson, 'The Measurement', p. 146. Others put the 1920 value at £345 million. Henry Macrosty, 'Statistics of British Shipping', *Journal of the Royal Statistical Society* 89:3 (1926), 452–543: p. 506.

38 Broadberry and Howlett, 'The United', p. 221, Table 7.11; p. 216, Table 7.7.

39 Or 18.5% if some non-tax revenue were omitted. Aldcroft, *From*, p. 31 n. 43.

40 A rapidly expanding money supply, sharply rising public debt, and declining precious metal reserves of banks in relation to their notes and deposits were the main causes of inflation. Ibid., pp. 31–2. Commodity prices and transition from a consumer to a war economy (without controlling prices and wages) also added to inflation.

41 Ibid., p. 56.

42 Albert Lauterbach, 'Economic Demobilisation in Great Britain after the First World War', *Political Science Quarterly* 57:3 (1942), 376–93: p. 392.

43 Milward, *The Economic*, p. 34. Debt rose even after war's end, peaking at around £8.1 billion in December 1919. Lauterbach, 'Economic', p. 392. By 1921, it was still £7.8 billion. Earl Hamilton, 'Origin and Growth of the National Debt in Western Europe', *The American Economic Review* 37:2 (1947), 118–30: p. 130.

44 Broadberry and Howlett, 'The United', p. 221; Aldcroft, *From*, pp. 79, 93.

45 Broadberry and Howlett, 'The United', p. 221. Throughout the war,

> normal accounting and payments settlements were suspended between Britain and France, Britain providing liberal loans to cover the cost of exports to France to sustain the war effort there. France followed the same principle with Russia and, eventually, the United States did the same for Britain … each country allowing massive debts to accumulate with one of its partners on the assumption that in the postwar world the international position of the debtor would soon be strong enough to regulate the situation.

Milward, *The Economic*, p. 56.

46 Once Russia could not rely on internal financing alone, the Bolsheviks changed their mind. Moscow informed creditors it would 'consider recognising pre-revolutionary debts in exchange for new money'. On 27 August 1918, Russia reached one such agreement with Germany, agreeing to pay £127 million in instalments by floating a new bond in Germany on 1 January 1919. When Germany surrendered, Russia denounced the terms (Sinyagina-Woodruff, 'Russia', pp. 532–3), renewing its resolve not to repay creditors until conditions were right.

47 Milward, *The Economic*, pp. 56–7; Robert Self, *Britain, America and the War Debt Controversy: The Economic Diplomacy of an Unspecial Relationship, 1917–1941* (Abingdon, 2006), particularly chs 1–4.

48 Pre-war debt was £26.5 million and wartime debt £568 million.

49 N. von Tunzelmann, 'Britain, 1900–45: A Survey', in *The Economic History of Britain since 1700, vol. 2: 1860 to the 1970s*, ed. Roderick Floud and Donald McCloskey (Cambridge, 1981), 239–64: pp. 239–40. Keith Middlemas, however, has argued "normalcy" was artificial from 1918 to the mid-1960s and due to manufactured popular consent. With a quasi-corporate State arising to prosecute total war, and the elevation at the same time

of employer associations and trade unions to
the status of indispensable governing partners,
the challenge for government was finding
the balance between accommodating and
confronting threats to industrial harmony.
*Politics in Industrial Society: The Experience of
the British System since 1911* (London, 1979).

50 Eichengreen, 'The British', p. 318.

51 Ibid., p. 319.

52 Ibid., p. 321.

53 Ibid., pp. 326–8. Excess capacity affected
the British economy for much of the interwar
period. Coal demand declined sharply as new
seams opened on the continent. European
iron/steel output was 50% higher by the mid-
1920s than before the war. Global shipbuilding
nearly doubled in wartime, producing enough
ships to meet ten years' demand without new
building. Aldcroft, *From*, pp. 47–8.

54 Dimsdale, 'British', p. 306; Aldcroft,
From, pp. 64–5; Susan Howson, 'Slump and
Unemployment', in *The Economic History of
Britain since 1700, vol. 2: 1860 to the 1970s*,
ed. Roderick Floud and Donald McCloskey
(Cambridge, 1981), 265–85: p. 265.

55 Howson, 'Slump', p. 265; Aldcroft, *From*,
p. 68; Eichengreen, 'The British', pp. 329–30.
One obstacle to wage adjustment was Britain's
unemployment insurance scheme. In the 1920s
'the ratio of average weekly benefits to average
weekly wages' neared 50%, removing the
incentive for many unemployed to find work.
In the same period, the normal workweek
was cut by 13% without a corresponding wage
adjustment.

56 Aldcroft, *From*, p. 111.

57 Howson, 'Slump', p. 265. Average annual
unemployment in 1921 was around 2.2 million,
17% of insured unemployed as a proportion of
insured employees (or 12% of total workers).
Garside, *British*, p. 5, Table 2.

58 Aldcroft, *From*, pp. 73, 96. See also Zara
Steiner, *The Lights that Failed: European
International History, 1919–33* (Oxford, 2005),
ch. 4.

59 Aldcroft, *From*, pp. 13, 111.

60 Ibid., p. 13; Gatrell, 'Poor', pp. 259–60 and
Table 8.20. From August 1914 to the end of
the Russian Civil War in November 1920, an
estimated nine to twelve million Russians
died. Mawdsley, *The Russian*, p. 287.

61 Gatrell, 'Poor', p. 239. Brest-Litovsk's
terms forced the Bolsheviks to accept 'a vast
amputation of territory ... unprecedented in
Great-Power relations'. Russia ceded Poland,
Lithuania and Western Latvia; essentially
recognised Ukraine as independent; and

pulled troops out of Estonia, Finland and the
Southern Caucasus. Mawdsley, *The Russian*, p.
33. Feliks E. Dzerzhinsky (Head of the *Cheka*)
sided with War Commissar Trotsky in January
1918 in opposing Lenin's decision to accept
these terms. Soviet authors keen to mytholo-
gise Dzerzhinsky subsequently airbrushed this
embarrassing alliance. Svetlana Lokhova, 'The
Evolution of the *Cheka*, 1917–26' (unpublished
M.Phil. thesis, University of Cambridge, 2002),
pp. 8–9.

62 Aldcroft, *From*, p. 34.

63 Gatrell, 'Poor', p. 256, Table 8.16.

64 Aldcroft, *From*, p. 121.

65 Mawdsley, *The Russian*, p. 287.

66 Between the November 1918 Armistice
and Lloyd George's speech, Britain spent
£100 million (2011: £27.5 billion) to topple the
Bolsheviks. Keeble, *Britain*, p. 69. Curzon put
the cost at £94 million (2011: £25.8 billion).
Bennett, *Churchill*, p. 46. Such spending was
unsustainable given Britain's postwar national
debt.

67 Preliminary trade discussions occurred in
February 1920. Richard Debo, 'Lloyd George
and the Copenhagen Conference of 1919–20:
The Initiation of Anglo-Soviet Negotiations',
THJ 24:2 (1981), 429–41.

68 'The Soviets have nothing to offer but
gold and precious stones, acquired by naked
robbery.' Even of gold 'they possess so little
that were we to acquire it all it would make
no material difference to the British economy'.
Winston Churchill memorandum, 16
November 1920, quoted in M. V. Glenny, 'The
Anglo-Soviet Trade Agreement, March 1921',
Journal of Contemporary History 5:2 (1970),
63–82: p. 75.

69 See Ullman, *Anglo-Soviet, vol. 3*; Glenny,
'The Anglo-Soviet'; Keeble, *Britain*, pp. 67–83.

70 Glenny, 'The Anglo-Soviet', pp. 66, 70.
'[C]essation of military action, propaganda
and other hostile action'; 'exchange of all
prisoners and detainees'; mutual recognition
'in principle' of all outstanding debts; and
'exchange of official missions, subject to the
right of each Government to prohibit entry
to any proposed mission member deemed
persona non grata to the host country'.

71 France sent six hundred military officers to
Poland. Andrew, *Her Majesty*, p. 265. Britain
turned down Polish requests for arms and
munitions in October 1919. Official policy was
that France should be the main Polish sponsor
since Britain was already heavily committed,
financially and materially, to White forces in
Russia. Lloyd George also opposed supplying
Poland with weapons for offensive use; were

Poland attacked, however, that would be different. Norman Davies, 'Lloyd George and Poland, 1919–20', *Journal of Contemporary History* 6:3 (1971), 132–54: pp. 136, 141.

72 Glenny, 'The Anglo-Soviet', p. 71; Keeble, *Britain*, pp. 72–3, 75–9; Mawdsley, *The Russian*, pp. 250–61; Brook-Shepherd, *Iron*, pp. 223–4.

73 Glenny, 'The Anglo-Soviet', pp. 71–2.

74 Ibid., p. 72 n. 31. Lloyd George told Kamenev 'he would not be welcome back after his impending trip'. Stafford, *Churchill*, p. 118.

75 Glenny, 'The Anglo-Soviet', p. 66.

76 He 'shared Churchill's hatred of Bolshevism [but] not his readiness to fight it'. Davies, 'Lloyd', p. 137.

77 Persia was both a key target for and a facilitator of subversion. On 8 September 1920, the NKID cabled the London delegation: 'For Krasin ... from Lezhava. The Persians are offering up to 50,000 kilos of opium ... Telegraph urgently what quantities you will be able to sell and what is the market price'. Chicherin, Moscow–Krasin, London; 13 September 1920–004115; 8 September 1920, p. 1, TNA HW 12/14. See Ahmad Seyf, 'Commercialisation of Agriculture: Production and Trade of Opium in Persia, 1850–1906', *International Journal of Middle East Studies* 16:2 (1984), 233–50: pp. 241, 246; S. Shahnavaz, 'Afyuún', *Encyclopædia Iranica*, www.iranica. com. British intelligence knew a sizeable portion of the London *rezident*'s operational budget came from narcotics sales. 'Organisation & Activities of the Russian Intelligence Services (General: 1930–45)', 23 May [illegible], serial 36a, TNA KV 3/141.

78 Glenny, 'The Anglo-Soviet', pp. 73–4. Actual repatriation did not start until 5 November.

79 See 'Long', Appendix.

80 See 'Chamberlain', Appendix.

81 Glenny, 'The Anglo-Soviet', pp. 75–6. Curzon, Churchill, Long, Lord Milner (Colonial Secretary), Chamberlain and Wilson opposed continued negotiations. Diary, HNKY 1/5, 16 and 18 November 1920, p. 166.

82 For a legal assessment of the treaty, including diplomatic immunity, see Kenneth Starr, 'The Framework of Anglo-Soviet Commercial Relations: The British View', *Law and Contemporary Problems* 37:3 (1972), 448–64.

83 Eric Holt-Wilson wrote of Thomson's attempts to absorb MI5 into the Directorate of Intelligence:

It has taken many years to train the ... staff of MI5 to its present high standard: we cannot afford to waste this ... in recreating what must ... be a repetition of its present organisation.... [F]our of the officers serving under ... Thomson are ex-officers of MI5 ... not considered to be up to the high standard necessary for retention on the permanent staff ... in peace. This ... alone would make it most difficult to transfer without grave injustice any members of the permanent staff ... to the Directorate ... in any subordinate capacity.... This was a scheme by which B. [asil] T. [homson] sought to capture MI5 (in collusion with [SIS]). Had no prospects: – chiefly from failure to grasp several fundamental principles and difficulties.

'Security Intelligence Policy & Organisation: Notes by Holt-Wilson (1920 Onwards)', piece 19 ('Future Organisation of MI5, December 1920'), p. 4; piece 25 ('Secret Service Reorganisation: Draft Letter Proposing Amalgamation with SIS, March 1923), marginalia in pencil on the back of A3 chart. TNA KV 4/416–/417.

84 'Report 66' (UK), 29 July 1920, pp. 1, 6, CP 1706, TNA CAB 24/110. Others shared Thomson's views of the media. Major-General Sir Wilfrid Malleson, Head of the British Military Mission in Turkestan (1918–20), had written to the Chief of the General Staff in India three months earlier:

[According to *The Times*] Bolsheviks have the advantage of secure strategical [*sic*] railways [into] Afghanistan ... Afghans and Indians hate the British. We may be forced into ... hostilities with Bolsheviks for which we are badly prepared. Article closes with pessimistic remarks concerning incompetence of present military authorities in India ... Would it not be possible to represent to *The Times* the great disservice of such articles[?] ... They are reproduced in thousands ... and on the Bolsheviks have the most encouraging effect.

'Bolsh. Accusations of GB Scare-Mongering: from Malleson, Meshed', 9 April 1920, © British Library Board L/P&S/11/171, P 3070/1920.

85 'Report 22' (foreign), August 1920, p. 14, CP 1942, TNA CAB 24/112.

86 M. E. Falkus, 'Russia and the International Wheat Trade, 1861–1914', *Economica* (New Series) 33:132 (1966): 416–29, p. 423, Table 3.

87 'Notes of a Conversation held at ... Lucerne', 22 August 1920, p. 14, TNA CAB 21/179. Earlier that year, Board of Education President H. A. L. Fisher had urged Lloyd George not to help Poland: 'It would be sheer

cruelty and the grossest impudence to spur this unstable, starving, bankrupt little State into a military adventure against Russia.' Headlam-Morley MSS 3, H. A. L. Fisher diaries, 29 January 1920, ACC 800.

88 Davies, 'Lloyd', p. 133. It 'was highly important to get trade with Russia restarted as soon as possible…. Cabinet had been informed that morning [that] British trade was inclined to sag and it was essential to open up new … business'. Cabinet conclusion 33(20), Appendix V1a, 3 June 1920, TNA CAB 23/21.

89 Activities included financial support and political guidance for the "Hands Off Russia" committee, the socialist newspaper *Daily Herald* edited by George Lansbury, assorted leftist publications and the CPGB, when it was created in August. Andrew, *Her Majesty*, pp. 262–4; L. J. Macfarlane, 'Hands Off Russia: British Labour and the Russo-Polish War, 1920', *Past and Present* 38 (1967), 126–52.

90 Davies, 'Lloyd', p. 147; Andrew, *Her Majesty*, p. 265.

91 Ibid., p. 266.

92 Churchill, Curzon and DNI Sinclair led the charge; see ibid., pp. 266–70, for details.

93 Stafford, *Churchill*, p. 118.

94 'Proposal to Expel Messrs. Kameneff and Krasin. By Lloyd George, Lucerne', 2 September 1920, pp. 1, 4, TNA CAB 21/173. Unemployment at this time was 4% and would soon hit 17%. Garside, *British*, p. 4, Table 1.

95 Stephen Ward, 'Intelligence Surveillance of British Ex-Servicemen, 1918–20', *THJ* 16:1 (1973), 179–88: pp. 179, 180–1, 187. Ironically, radical right-wing groups aligned with the Government used servicemen for 'sometimes savagely violent' attacks on leftists. The BEU formed paramilitary units (comprising regular and reserve military personnel, and merchant seamen) active from 1917 to 1922. Hope, 'Surveillance', pp. 667–8.

96 'Secretary's Notes of Conference with Trade Delegation', 10 September 1920, pp. 2–3, TNA CAB 21/173.

97 Days before, Kamenev wrote: 'In our relations with England a dead period is inevitable…. [A]ll the intelligence work which it was possible to do has been done.' Kamenev, London–Chicherin, Moscow; 1 September 1920–003981; 30 August 1920, p. 1, TNA HW 12/14. Foreign Office Russia experts Reginald Leeper and Edward Carr urged Lloyd George not to expel Theodore Rothstein, whose long-standing work with them had helped set up unofficial diplomatic contacts with Moscow in January 1918. However, an ill-timed trip by Rothstein in August 1920 seems to have

given hardliners an opening. The Russians believed Thomson had used Lloyd George's absence from Britain in early September not to readmit Rothstein. Burke, 'Theodore', pp. 13, 17–18; Goldstein, 'The Foreign', p. 280; Chicherin, Moscow–Kamenev, London; 4 September 1920–004000; 1 September 1920, p. 1, TNA HW 12/14.

98 [Sir Hugh] 'Trenchard thinks … like … Thomson, that LG is a traitor.' Henry Wilson diary, 24 August 1920, quoted in Ullman, *Anglo-Soviet, vol. 3*, p. 280. Trenchard was Chief of the Air Staff and Churchill's friend.

99 Andrew, *Her Majesty*, pp. 269–70; 'Krasin and Klyshko: Memorandum by Curzon', 16 September 1920, p. 3, TNA CAB 21/173. He quoted a cable:

> [R]ecognition of … [private English claims] is only accorded in principle … application of this principle is left … to … future … peace negotiations. Nevertheless, we must exploit this colossal concession as [much] as possible for … agitation. In principle it is an enormous step. We must not sell it too cheaply.

Chicherin, Moscow–Krasin, London; 1 July 1920–003177; 26 June 1920, p. 1, TNA HW 12/11.

100 'Krasin and Klyshko: Memorandum by Churchill', 21 September 1920, p. 1, TNA CAB 21/173.

101 'Hankey to Long', 24 September 1920, p. 1, TNA CAB 21/173; 'Trade with Soviet Russia: Admiralty Memorandum', 27 September 1920, p. 1, TNA CAB 21/173; 'Russian Trade Delegation: Admiralty Memorandum', 30 September 1920, p. 1, TNA CAB 21/173. Long lacked no conviction: 'I would follow the Devil himself in doing what we can to destroy the enemy.' Long to Lady Londonderry, 9 November 1915, quoted in Richard Murphy, 'Walter Long, the Unionist Ministers, and the Formation of Lloyd George's Government in December 1916', *THJ* 29:3 (1986), 735–45: p. 736.

102 'Report 73' (UK), 23 September 1920, p. 6, CP 1885, TNA CAB 24/111.

103 Curzon's and Churchill's 'resignations … to which rumours allude, may, with George's lack of character, compel [him] to yield.' Krasin, London–Chicherin, Moscow; 3 June 1920–002771; 8 June 1920, p. 1, TNA HW 12/10.

104 Key issues for the Prime Minister were whether subversion by Russian delegates was enough of a threat and if their expulsion would definitely end such subversion. 'To both questions he replied in the negative.' Andrew, *Her Majesty*, p. 267. The Bolsheviks them-

selves were unsure how far to push: '[A]sk for a precise definition of "propaganda", lest an arbitrary interpretation of that word' enable the British 'to declare that the Treaty has automatically lapsed, whenever they [choose] to do so for political or other reasons.' Litvinov, Christiania [Oslo]–Soviet Delegation, London; 30 September 1920–004291; 24 September 1920, p. 1, TNA HW 12/15.

105 See 'Lloyd George', Appendix.

106 Kenneth Morgan, *David Lloyd George, 1863–1945* (Cardiff, 1981), p. 35.

107 Churchill defected from the Conservatives to the Liberals in 1904. After Lloyd George tabled his "People's Budget" in April 1909 to ease poverty through higher direct taxation of the wealthy and their estates, relations between the two men soured and were never the same. Ibid., pp. 29–33.

108 Ibid., p. 29. Some of Lloyd George's most radical actions were old age pension plans (1908); House of Lords reform and national health insurance (1911); suffrage reform (1918); and a settlement of the Irish question (1921).

109 Diary of General Spencer Ewart, Director of Military Operations and Intelligence: February, November–December 1909, quoted in Stafford, *Churchill*, pp. 34–5.

110 Lucy Masterman, *Charles Masterman: A Biography* (London, 1939), p. 150.

111 John Grigg, 'Lloyd George: Crusader or Crook?', *Modern History Review* 1:1 (1989), 20–3: p. 23.

112 Morgan, *David*, pp. 25, 35.

113 Bennett, 'Lloyd', p. 477. Lloyd George 'always bullies' ministers with 'little popular following'. Diary, HNKY 1/5, 16 November 1920, p. 165.

114 Bentley Gilbert, 'David Lloyd George and the Great Marconi Scandal', *Historical Research: The Bulletin of the Institute of Historical Research* 62:149 (1989), 295–317: p. 297. Some patricians also engaged in dubious practices. In 1923, Churchill took £5000 (2011: around £233,000) from Royal Dutch Shell and Burmah Oil to lobby Prime Minister Stanley Baldwin for their intended merger with the Anglo-Persian Oil Company. Churchill was not in office but it was 'very improper for him not to have revealed to Baldwin ... he was acting as a paid lobbyist ... rather than as a disinterested advocate'. Toye, *Lloyd*, p. 254. See also Geoffrey Searle, *Corruption in British Politics, 1895–1930* (Oxford, 1987), ch. 8; Gareth Jones, 'The British Government and the Oil Companies, 1912–24: The Search for an Oil Policy', *THJ* 20:3 (1977), 647–72.

115 Toye, *Lloyd*, p. 94; Morgan, *David*, p. 37; Searle, *Corruption*, ch. 15; Cannadine, *The Decline*, ch. 7.

116 See Toye, *Lloyd*, pp. 167–85, and Murphy, 'Walter'.

117 Morgan, *David*, p. 79.

118 Goodlad, 'Ditching', p. 7.

119 Grigg, 'Lloyd', p. 23. The CPGB also had a dim view of Labour in power: 'The office-seeking elements of the Labour Party will be as conservative as their ... predecessors.' Saddled 'with the Monarchy, the Court, and the Aristocracy ... Labour ... will follow the lead of all bourgeois parties, selling honours as well as honour'. 'Report 66' (UK), 5 August 1920, p. 8, CP 1743, TNA CAB 24/110.

120 Grigg, 'Lloyd', p. 23.

121 Cannadine, *The Decline*, pp. 2, 13, 37, 86, 183, 298, 517–19, 546–7. See also idem, *Class*, pp. 126–60; Ross McKibbin, *Classes and Cultures – England, 1918–51* (Oxford, 1998), pp. 35–7.

122 See Linehan, *British*, ch. 2; Hope, 'Surveillance'; Bennett, *Churchill*, chs 3–6; Thurlow, *The Secret*, pp. 173–9; idem, *Fascism in Modern Britain* (London, 2000), ch. 4; Ferris and Bar-Joseph, 'Getting', pp. 111–16.

123 Security and intelligence spending from 1913 to 1922 varied but the post-1917 rise in police funding was startling. Politicians and civil servants with outdated mindsets struggled to adapt to a brave new (postwar) world defined by mass democracy and economic turmoil. To rely primarily on law enforcement to tackle perceived Bolshevik subversion of social order was to misunderstand the nature of this new threat. Law enforcement mostly coped with overt subversion but drastic postwar cuts to the agencies' budgets affected government's ability to monitor and counter covert efforts (e.g. espionage) already underway by 1919. Data from: 'Secret Service Blue Notes, 1913–37', Civil Services Class II., 34–1921–2, TNA T 165/445; 'Funds Devoted to [MI5] by the Foreign Office, vol. 1', 'Cost of Maintenance of Defence Security Service (Estimate for 1921–22)', serial 28, TNA KV 4/198; Parliamentary Papers, 'Estimates for the Civil Services, 1922: Paper 32', Microfiche 129.146, TNA; Parliamentary Papers, 'Estimates for the Year ending 31 March 1926: Paper 27', Microfiche 134.183, TNA; 'Foreign Secret Service Accounts, 1916–20', TNA FO 1093/61.

124 See Andrew McDonald, 'The Geddes Committee and the Formulation of Public Expenditure Policy, 1921–22', *THJ* 32:3 (1989), 643–74.

125 Deflation further raised high budgets throughout the 1920s.

126 Peter Holquist, '"Information is the Alpha and Omega of our Work": Bolshevik Surveillance in its Pan-European Context', *The Journal of Modern History* 69 (1997), 415–50: pp. 440–3, 435; Michael Geyer, 'The Militarisation of Europe, 1914–45', in *The Militarisation of the Western World*, ed. John Gillis (New Brunswick, NJ, 1989), 65–102; Tom Bowden, 'Guarding the State: The Police Response to Crisis Politics in Europe', *British Journal of Law and Society* 5:1 (1978), 69–88: pp. 72–3.

127 Rogers, *Secrecy*, chs 2–3; Thurlow, *The Secret*, ch. 2; Vincent, *The Culture*, pp. 140–1.

128 Private correspondence. See Christopher Andrew, *For the President's Eyes Only: Secret Intelligence and the American Presidency from Washington to Bush* (London, 1996), ch. 2; Andrew Barros, 'Le 2ᵉ Bureau dans les Années Vingt: L'Impact de la Guerre Totale sur les Renseignements' [The 2ᵉ Bureau in the 1920s: The Impact of Total War on Intelligence], in *Naissance et Evolution du Renseignement dans l'Espace Européen (1870–1940): Entre Démocratie et Totalitarisme: Quatorze Etudes de Cas*, ed. Fréderic Guelton and Abdil Bicer (Paris, 2006), 189–210; Martin Alexander, 'Did the *Deuxième Bureau* Work? The Role of Intelligence in French Defence Policy and Strategy, 1919–39', *INS* 6:2 (1991), 293–333; Olivier Lahaie, 'Le Renseignement Militaire Français dans l'Allemagne d'Après-Guerre (mai 1919–mars 1920): A la Recherche d'Une Nouvelle Sécurité' [French Military Intelligence in Postwar Germany: In Search of a New Security], *Revue Historique des Armées* 256 (2009), 32–42; Leonard, *Secret*, ch. 6; Arthur Smith, 'The German General Staff and Russia, 1919–26', *Soviet Studies* 8:2 (1956), 125–33; John Erickson, *The Soviet High Command: A Military-Political History, 1918–1941* (London, 2001), chs 6, 9; Lennart Samuelson, *Plans for Stalin's War Machine: Tukhachevskii and Military-Economic Planning, 1925–1941*, Studies in Russian and East European History and Society (Basingstoke, 2000), pp. 31–4.

129 Hope, 'Surveillance', p. 662; Hughes, *Spies*; Miller and Dinan, *A Century*, ch. 3.

130 See 'Carter', Appendix.

131 Hope, 'Surveillance', pp. 661, 663–5; Bennett, *Churchill*, p. 71. Agency heads often attended meetings of the Makgill-run Monday Club (unrelated to its Conservative Party namesake set up in 1961). Idem, *A most*, p. 38.

132 Ibid., p. 28; idem, *Churchill*, p. 79.

133 Buchan was 'sometimes called a Tory radical' and an imperialist, 'but one of a distinctly liberal' bent. Karl Miller, introduction, John Buchan, *The Three Hostages* (Oxford, 1995), p. xx.

134 Ibid., p. x.

135 Jon Parry, 'From the Thirty-Nine Articles to the Thirty-Nine Steps: Reflections on the Thought of John Buchan', in *Public and Private Doctrine: Essays in British History Presented to Maurice Cowling*, ed. Michael Bentley (Cambridge, 1993), 209–35: pp. 217, 213, 211.

136 Buchan, *The Three*, pp. 23–4, 49. Buchan himself was a wartime intelligence officer working on propaganda. Colin Matthew, 'Buchan, John, first Baron Tweedsmuir', *ODNB*.

137 Buchan, *The Three*, p. 49.

138 Ibid., pp. 54, 119.

139 Former CPGB member quoted in 'Report 75' (UK), 7 October 1920, p. 4, CP 1937, TNA CAB 24/112.

140 Andrew Thorpe, 'The Membership of the Communist Party of Great Britain, 1920–45', *THJ* 43:3 (2000), 777–800: p. 781, Table I.

141 'Report 24' (foreign), October 1920, p. 51, CP 2192, TNA CAB 24/115.

142 'Bolshevik Propaganda: Memorandum by Long', 12 November 1920, p. 1, TNA CAB 21/200.

143 See 'Report 80' (UK), 11 November 1920, p. 1, CP 2089, TNA CAB 24/114.

144 'Report 84' (UK), 9 December 1920, p. 1, CP 2273, TNA CAB 24/116.

145 'Unemployment' section, 'Report 85' (UK), 16 December 1920, CP 2316, TNA CAB 24/117; 'Report 125' (UK), 29 September 1921, p. 1, CP 3350, TNA CAB 24/128.

146 'Report 85' (UK), 23 December 1920, pp. 3–4, CP 2351, TNA CAB 24/117.

147 'Krasin to Chicherin', 29 December 1920, f. 04, op. 4, p. 19, d. 261, l. 10, AVP RF.

148 'Report 93' (UK), 17 February 1921, p. 8, CP 2603, TNA CAB 24/120; 'Report 94' (UK), 21 February 1921, p. 11, CP 2631, TNA CAB 24/120.

149 'Friday last, the King visited the Grand National ... 35,000 people watching'. His interest 'in a game ... nearer the heart of the people of the North' than any political question 'has done immense good'. 'Report 48' (UK), 30 March 1920, p. 5, CP 1009, TNA CAB 24/103. The Prince of Wales 'inspected the Jewish Lads' Brigade and attended a concert organised by the police in aid of the unemployed'. He had 'a great reception' and

'the visit ... will have more than a transient effect'. 'Report 98' (UK), 23 March 1921, p. 2, CP 2765, TNA CAB 24/121.

150 'Report 106' (UK), 19 May 1921, pp. 3–4, CP 2952, TNA CAB 24/123.

151 Chicherin, Moscow–Litvinov, Copenhagen; 6 April 1920–001978; 1 April 1920, p. 1, TNA HW 12/7. See also Richard Debo, 'Litvinov and Kamenev – Ambassadors Extraordinary: The Problem of Soviet Representation Abroad', *Slavic Review* 34:3 (1975), 463–82.

152 'Krasin [feels] Europe is doing us a favour by condescending to talk to riff-raff like [us] and we must ... agree to all her demands ... If ... you ... give him a ... free hand I (?will be obliged) to return immediately'. Litvinov, Copenhagen–Chicherin, Moscow; 26 May 1920–002606; 19 May 1920, p. 1, TNA HW 12/9.

153 Litvinov, Copenhagen–Krasin, London; 5 June 1920–002740; 2 June 1920, pp. 1–2, TNA HW 12/10; Litvinov, Copenhagen–Chicherin, Moscow; 29 June 1920–003138; 24 June 1920, p. 1, TNA HW 12/11.

154 Krasin, London–Chicherin, Moscow; 19 June 1920–002972; 16 June 1920, p. 1, TNA HW 12/10.

155 Krasin, London–Chicherin, Moscow; 26 June 1920–003099; 23 June 1920, pp. 1–2, TNA HW 12/11.

156 Krasin, London–Chicherin, Moscow; 24 November 1920–004821; 22 November 1920, p. 1, TNA HW 12/17; Krasin, London–Chicherin, Moscow; 18 December 1920–005020; 11 December 1920, p. 1, TNA HW 12/17.

157 Litvinov, Copenhagen–Chicherin, Moscow; 7 July 1920–003253; 3 July 1920, pp. 1, 3, TNA HW 12/11; Litvinov, Copenhagen–Chicherin, Moscow; 8 July 1920–003264; 5 July 1920, p. 1, TNA HW 12/11: 'Urgent. Krasin's return ... was only ... to influence Lenin and ... obtain ... widening ... powers ... [B]e on your guard.'

158 This awareness paradoxically reinforced complacency that blinded Cabinet to infiltration of the British Government.

159 Litvinov, Copenhagen–Soviet Delegation, London; 24 July 1920–003510; 22 July 1920, p. 1, TNA HW 12/12.

160 Ferris, 'Whitehall', p. 74. He has determined British successes against Soviet traffic continued even after Moscow introduced theoretically unbreakable one-time-pads (OTPs) following the ARCOS raid. 'The Road', p. 67.

161 Chicherin, Moscow–Litvinov, Copenhagen; 19 April 1920–002225; 18 January 1920, p. 1, TNA HW 12/8.

162 Chicherin, Moscow–Krasin, London; 16 June 1920–002905; 10 June 1920, p. 1, TNA HW 12/10; Chicherin, Moscow–Krasin, London; 23 June 1920–003033; 19 June 1920, p. 1, TNA HW 12/11; Chicherin, Moscow–Krasin, London; 24 June 1920–003051; 20 June 1920, p. 1, TNA HW 12/11; Krasin, London–Chicherin, Moscow; 29 June 1920–003140; 25 June 1920, p. 1, TNA HW 12/11.

163 Klyshko, London–Chicherin, Moscow; 20 July 1920–003422; 9 July 1920, p. 1, TNA HW 12/12; Chicherin, Moscow–Klyshko, London; 22 July 1920–003469; 18 July 1920, p. 1, TNA HW 12/12.

164 Kamenev, London–Litvinov, Copenhagen; 7 August 1920–003685; 5 August 1920, p. 1, TNA HW 12/13; Kamenev, London–Litvinov, Copenhagen; 10 August 1920–003704; 7 August 1920, p. 1, TNA HW 12/13; Chicherin, Moscow–Kamenev, London; 9 August 1920–003699; 6 August 1920, p. 1, TNA HW 12/13; Litvinov, Copenhagen–Kamenev, London; 17 August 1920–003795; 13 August 1920, p. 1, TNA HW 12/13.

165 Kamenev, London–Chicherin, Moscow; 21 August 1920–003855; 19 August 1920, p. 1, TNA HW 12/13: 'ciphering of telegrams in "Rosa" and "Marta" keys should cease at once. You have already been informed of this at least twice'. The wireless messages on Bolshevik subsidies for the *Daily Herald* the British Government released to newspapers in August 1920 were in the compromised MARTA cipher.

166 'Frunze to Lenin, Trotsky, Chicherin, Military High Command and Central Committee', 19 December 1920, piece T628, Trotsky Archives, quoted in Ullman, *Anglo-Soviet, vol. 3*, p. 308.

167 Chicherin, Moscow–Klyshko, London; 27 January 1921–005341; 23 January 1921, pp. 1–2, TNA HW 12/18:

> telegrams ciphered on ... keys of other Departments and destined for ... representatives of those Departments abroad, despatched from Moscow to the address of our representatives, will be despatched by us only on the condition that the contents of such telegrams and the system of keys on which they are ciphered are known to us [NKID]. On the despatch of such cipher telegrams addressed to us and signed by our representatives abroad but destined for other Departments, the contents and cipher system on which they

are ciphered should be presented to our representatives who decide on the question of despatch[;] ... particularly secret information that might compromise us should be despatched only by courier and not by radio or telegraph.... It is essential that secret information should be sent only with the help of double-ciphering. DEPARTMENT [GCCS] NOTE. This Department has solved almost every 'double-cipher' system up to date, of which the above telegram is the latest – and presumably, in the opinion of Moscow, the safest – example.

168 Krasin, London–Chicherin, Moscow; 2 July 1921–007203; 27 June 1921, p. 1, TNA HW 12/24.

169 Krasin, London–Chicherin, Moscow; 21 March 1922–009793, 8 October 1921, p. 1, TNA HW 12/32; Phil Tomaselli, 'C's Moscow Station: The Anglo-Russian Trade Mission as Cover for SIS in the Early 1920s', *INS* 17:3 (2002), 173–80; Ivo Juurvee, 'Välisministeeriumi Informatsiooniosakond: Kas Maailmasõdadevhelise Eesti Välisluureteenistus?' [Did Interwar Estonia Possess an Exterior Intelligence Service?], *Akadeemia* 2007 (10), 2083–2119.

170 Andrew, 'The British Secret Service', p. 682.

171 Chicherin, Moscow–Litvinov, Copenhagen; 24 March 1920–001811; 29 February 1920, p. 1, TNA HW 12/7: 'reply as soon as possible how much you consider we ought to give the *Herald*'; Kamenev, London–Chicherin, Moscow; 24 August 1920–003878; 20 August 1920, p. 1, TNA HW 12/13: 'We have sold some of the stones ... we ... brought with us. £40,000 [2011: £1.3 million] of the money realised was paid over to the newspaper'; Krasin, London–Chicherin, Moscow; 24 August 1920–003883; 21 August 1920, p. 1, TNA HW 12/13: 'The embargo on our gold is one of the chief means of fighting us'; Krasin, London–Chicherin, Moscow; 28 October 1920–004580; 26 October 1920, p. 1, TNA HW 12/16: 'do not refer in your telegrams to us openly to the *Daily Herald* ... unless you desire the sudden departure of the whole Delegation, strictly ... forbid this'.

172 SIGINT distribution within Cabinet was tightly regulated, and usually only went to the Prime Minister, the Foreign and War Secretaries, the First Sea Lord and the Chiefs of Staff. Ullman, *Anglo-Soviet, vol. 3*, p. 115.

173 Krasin, London–Chicherin, Moscow; 29 December 1920–005084; 23 December 1920, pp. 1–3, TNA HW 12/17:

I ... deliver once more a warning against treating too lightly the question of a rupture ... with the British.... The [Foreign Commissar] frequently gives expression to the thought ... there is no harm in a rupture of negotiations, since England will in any case soon renew them.... Without ... the English ... we shall not develop trade with a single country.... Do not exaggerate the significance of military victories, for all European Governments still hope ... we shall ... perish of exhaustion and ... helplessness.... We are ... at the most dangerous stage and our policy should be most cautious and restrained without any husteria [*sic*].

174 Krasin, London–Chicherin, Moscow; 4 January 1921–005132; 30 December 1920, p. 1, TNA HW 12/18.

175 Krasin: 'Lloyd George is wobbling under pressure from the Curzonites and the Court politicians. He is afraid to take any definite steps'. Krasin, London–Chicherin, Moscow; 2 June 1920–002700; 29 May 1920, p. 1, TNA HW 12/10. This was a mistake. Lloyd George 'knew that in order for him to get what he wanted or needed, for political survival', he had to discover 'what the other party to a bargaining situation wanted or needed for his survival'. Ullman, *Anglo-Soviet, vol. 3*, p. 464.

176 Chicherin, Moscow–Krasin, London; 22 June 1920–003011; 15 June 1920, p. 1, TNA HW 12/11; Krasin, London–Chicherin, Moscow; 26 June 1920–003096; 23 June 1920, p. 1, TNA HW 12/11. Chicherin persisted: 'Even a simple break with us would harm the (British) ... to a considerable extent'. Chicherin, Moscow–Krasin, London; 26 June 1920–003114; 24 June 1920, p. 2, TNA HW 12/11. For economic and political reasons, Russia could not do this. Reconstruction could only happen by restoring economic ties with the West.

177 See TNA HW 12/1–/3.

178 Events between 1917 and 1920 showed that 'the inherent contradiction between the political and social theories of Communism, and the tenets of religion in general, and of Islam in particular' would prevent 'any widespread acceptance of Bolshevik doctrines by Eastern races'. 'Special Report 17: Notes on Central Asia', June 1920, p. 5, CP 1585, TNA CAB 24/108. The NKID agreed: 'The Muslim world may become either ... ally or ... enemy'. 'Chicherin to Berzin', 4 March 1921, f. 04, op. 4, p. 19, d. 271, l. 1, AVP RF.

179 Eliava, Tashkent–Chicherin, Moscow; 19

January 1920–000873, 7 January 1920, p. 1, TNA HW 12/3:

> The [Collegium] of the Turkestan Executive Committee is extremely unsatisfactory: complete absence of technical knowledge, inactivity, oppression of the inhabitants, drunkenness, abuses, bribery, arrests without reason, protection of the criminal element. A complete reorganisation ... is being contemplated.

Eliava, Tashkent–Chicherin, Moscow; 22 January 1920–000926; undated, pp. 1–2, TNA HW 12/4: 'When attempting to apply the decrees of the ... People's Commissaries ... the Commission meets with the most hostile attitude on the part of the local Soviet officials, most of whom belong to the ... Party.'

180 'Up to now we have received practically no information from you'. The 'Foreign Relations Department has not despatched a single courier, in spite of our instructions. ... Our questions are systematically left unanswered'. Karakhan, Moscow–Eliava, Tashkent; 30 January 1920–001057; 27 January 1920, p. 1, TNA HW 12/4.

181 Guy Liddell of Special Branch wrote in 1926 the BEU was 'a sound organisation but the information it supplies ... is not invariably reliable'. TNA FO 371/11775/33, quoted in Hope, 'Surveillance', pp. 658, 673 n. 28.

CHAPTER 4
The Fall

1 'Fleet Ciphering and Coding Organisations', CW 4128/22, 25 March 1922, case 1422, TNA ADM 116/2101.

2 'Jacob Kirchenstein', undated, p. 20, after serial 98a, TNA KV 2/1391.

3 5 March 1919, A. J. P. Taylor, ed., *Lloyd George: A Diary* (New York, 1971), p. 169.

4 'Reports on Bolshevism & India, P 1229: Edwin Montagu to Sir William Duke', 21 March 1921, file 1229/1920, Part 2, © British Library Board L/P&S/10/887, Asia, Pacific & Africa Collections, British Library. Montagu meant Delhi Intelligence Bureau reports, the intelligence section of the Government of India Home Office. Andrew, *Her Majesty*, p. 277. Duke was the India Office Permanent Under-Secretary.

5 'Report 96' (UK), 10 March 1921, p. 1, CP 2698, TNA CAB 24/120: 'Unemployment is not decreasing and [tempers are] becoming bitter. The Communists are taking full advantage of this.'; 'Communists', 'Report 97' (UK), 17 March 1921, CP 2740, TNA CAB 24/121:

> No one could ... [foresee] that, at a time [of] widespread ... hardship from unemployment and when ... agitators [are funded] from abroad, there should [be] so little growth of revolutionary feeling. It is ... testimony to the good sense and moderation of the English [worker].

6 General Strike aside, industrial strife peaked in 1921: average monthly loss of working days was 7,156,000 and aggregate duration of disputes was 85,872,000 days. In 1918, average monthly loss of working days was 490,000 and the aggregate duration of disputes was 5,875,000 days. 'Industrial Unrest Committee: The CPGB', 25 April 1924, Appendices I (p. 3) and II (p. 1), TNA CAB 27/239. Unemployment hit 23.5% during the May 1921 coal strike, with overall unemployment that year hitting 12%. Howson, 'Slump', p. 265; Garside, *British*, p. 5, Table 2.

7 Sir Eric Geddes chaired the Committee on National Expenditure, set up in August 1921. In early 1922, he called for around £87 million in cuts from budget estimates of about £528 million. McDonald, 'The Geddes', p. 643.

8 Ferris, 'Whitehall', p. 74.

9 Idem, 'The Road', pp. 67–9. Moscow usually changed Asian ciphers last. Idem, 'Whitehall', p. 74.

10 Freeman, 'MI1(b)', n. 94. See also Thomas R. Hammant, 'Russian and Soviet Cryptology III: Soviet COMINT and the Civil War, 1918–1921', *Cryptologia* 25:1 (2001): 50–60.

11 'Correspondence concerning Damage Caused by Release of Deciphered Bolshevik Telegrams to the Press: Denniston to Sinclair', 18 March 1921, p. 1, TNA HW 12/338.

12 'Idem: Sinclair to Crowe' and 'Hankey to Sinclair', 22 March 1921, TNA HW 12/338.

13 Keith Jeffery, ed., 'The Government Code and Cypher School: A Memorandum by Lord Curzon', *INS* 1:3 (1986), 454–8: pp. 454–5.

14 'Montagu to Curzon', 26 August 1921, AS 3/3/156, Montagu MSS.

15 Mawdsley, *The Russian*, pp. 73–4. The term "war communism" dates from 1921 when Lenin first used it retroactively in his notes. See also Bertrand Patenaude, 'Peasants into Russians: The Utopian Essence of War Communism', *Russian Review* 54:4 (1995), 552–70.

16 Mawdsley, *The Russian*, pp. 73, 245; Jacob Kipp, 'Lenin and Clausewitz: The Militarisation of Marxism', *Military Affairs* 49:4 (1985), 184–91: p. 189.

17 Lokhova, 'The Evolution', p. 24.

18 Mawdsley, *The Russian*, pp. 245–6.

19 Robert Daniels, 'The Kronstadt Revolt of 1921: A Study in the Dynamics of Revolution', *American Slavic and East European Review* 10:4 (1951), 241–54: p. 241. Not coincidentally, rebellions erupted as the Red Army began demobilising in late 1920.

20 Ibid., p. 249.

21 A. V. Basov, ed., *Boevoi put Sovetskogo Voenno-Morskogo Flota* [Combat History of the Soviet Navy] (Moskva, 1988), Appendix 2.

22 Evan Mawdsley, 'The Baltic Fleet and the Kronstadt Mutiny', *Soviet Studies* 24:4 (1973), 506–21: p. 506; Lokhova, 'The Evolution', pp. 25–6. Lokhova shows Kronstadt was an early example of intelligence politicisation. *Chekists* on the ground found no evidence of either White or foreign involvement in the mutiny but *Cheka* leaders sought evidence to the contrary to please the Kremlin (pp. 25–41).

23 See Mawdsley, 'The Baltic', on conditions before the revolt. He identifies four problem areas: ship and supply quality, personnel, discipline and morale. See Daniels, 'The Kronstadt', on government reactions. Given previous mutinies there during the 1905 and (February) 1917 Revolutions, Kronstadt clearly had a revolutionary pedigree.

24 Alan Ball, 'Lenin and the Question of Private Trade in Soviet Russia', *Slavic Review* 43:3 (1984), 399–412: p. 399.

25 V. N. Bandera, 'The New Economic Policy (NEP) as an Economic System', *The Journal of Political Economy* 71:3 (1963), 265–79: p. 268.

26 Simon Johnson and Peter Temin, 'The Macroeconomics of NEP', *The Economic History Review* (New Series) 46:4 (1993), 750–67: p. 752. Lenin first spoke of the need for a new policy at the VIII Party Congress in December 1919. Robert Himmer, 'The Transition from War Communism to the New Economic Policy: An Analysis of Stalin's Views', *Russian Review* 53:4 (1994), 515–29: p. 518.

27 20 April 1921, f. 17, op. 3, d. 153, l. 3, RGASPI, Moscow; Keeble, *Britain*, p. 364. For Krasin's views, see Lubov Krasin, *Leonid Krasin: His Life and Work* (London, 1929), ch. 13.

28 16 May and 12 September 1921, f. 495, op. 100, d. 23, ll. 7–28, RGASPI.

29 'Report 106' (UK), 19 May 1921, pp. 3–4, CP 2952, TNA CAB 24/123. See also Stuart Macintyre, 'British Labour, Marxism, and the Working Class Apathy in the Nineteen Twenties', *THJ* 20:2 (1977), 479–96.

30 'Report 112' (UK), 30 June 1921, pp. 9–10, CP 3100, TNA CAB 24/125.

31 'Report 137' (UK), 5 January 1922, p. 11, CP 3600, TNA CAB 24/131. These were like old Socialist cycling clubs, some of them still active today minus the politics (e.g. National Clarion and Willesden Cycling Clubs).

32 Other measures can be more effective than agitation: 'If we help the Emir to build factories and bridges these cannot be considered as actions forbidden by the Agreement.... [C]onstruction in Afghanistan ... is ... completely peaceful.' 'Chicherin to Berzin', 11 July 1921, f. 04, op. 4, p. 19, d. 271, l. 18, AVP RF.

33 Bainton, *Honoured*; Bennett, *Churchill*; Brook-Shepherd, *Iron*; Andrew Cook, *Ace of Spies: The True Story of Sidney Reilly* (Stroud, 2003); Harry Ferguson, *Operation Kronstadt* (London, 2008); Judd, *The Quest*; Occleshaw, *Dances*; Plotke, *Imperial*. See also Andrew, *Her Majesty*, pp. 203–14; Keith Neilson, '"Joy Rides"? British Intelligence and Propaganda in Russia, 1914–17', *THJ* 24:4 (1981), 885–906.

34 Jeffery, *MI6*; Smith, *Six*.

35 Tomaselli, 'C', p. 173. London also appointed Robert Hodgson as Official Agent. Keeble, *Britain*, p. 363.

36 Tomaselli, 'C', pp. 174–6. Of the nine men, four were SIS (Alfred Ferdinand Hill, Lionel G. M. Gall, Oswald Rayner and Gerald Fitzwilliams), two Military Intelligence (Charles J. Dunlop and Lawrence Collas), one India Office (W. F. O'Connor), one Information Ministry in Russia in 1918 (Edward Charnock) and one Foreign Office (Percy Gent). Gall, Hill and O'Connor ended up not going to Moscow.

37 Bennett, *Churchill*, p. 42; Jeffery, *MI6*, pp. 172–93.

38 Phil Tomaselli, *Tracing Your Secret Service Ancestors* (Barnsley, 2009), p. 194; Jeffery, *MI6*, p. 184.

39 Tomaselli, 'C', p. 177; idem, *Tracing*, p. 195. Stations usually comprised at least one intelligence officer, a small office staff, and cut-outs between the officer(s) and local agents. 'Secret Service Committee: Minutes, Third Meeting', 2 June 1921, p. 2, TNA CAB 127/356.

40 12 November 1921–008504, p. 1, TNA HW 12/28; 23 December 1921–009070, p. 1, TNA HW 12/29. The weight cap for Bolshevik diplomatic bags was seven pounds per week. *Parliamentary Debates*, House of Lords, 16 December 1924, vol. 60, columns 129–30.

41 'Fishing Rights in the Arctic Ocean and the White Sea', Major Malcolm Woollcombe (SIS Section Va) to Reginald Leeper (Foreign Office Northern Department), 4 November 1921, p. 73, TNA FO 371/6912 (N12258): 'I am attaching a translation of a telegram trans-

mitted by Krasin through Reval [Tallinn], to Chicherin. ... It was tapped from the direct private line between Moscow and the Hotel Petrograd at Reval.' See 'Woollcombe', Appendix. Given SIS difficulties spotting forgeries from Estonian agents in 1921 (see below), the translation raises questions about reliability, depending on who did the tapping: Estonian agents, SIS/GCCS or others. If the British did it themselves, it would be a question of assessing potential Russian deception instead. Private correspondence.

42 Ferris, 'The Road', p. 55. One wonders if the start date reflected Curzon's unhappiness with HUMINT.

43 James Angleton, Head of Counter-Intelligence Staff (1954–74) at the US Central Intelligence Agency, popularised the term. He is thought to have drawn it from T. S. Eliot's poem *Gerontion* (1920): 'In a wilderness of mirrors. / What will the spider do, / Suspend its operations, will the weevil Delay?' See also David C. Martin, *Wilderness of Mirrors* (New York, 1980), p. 10; Michael Holzman, *James Jesus Angleton, The CIA, & the Craft of Counterintelligence* (Amherst, MA, 2008), pp. 302, 320.

44 Bennett, *Churchill*, p. 43; see also pp. 33–60 and Jeffery, *MI6*, ch. 6. On White intrigues, see Andrew, *Her Majesty*, pp. 273–97; Andrew and Gordievsky, *KGB*, chs 2–3; Andrew and Mitrokhin, *The Mitrokhin*, ch. 2; Brook-Shepherd, *Iron*, chs 3–14.

45 The first case began in February 1921. Colonel Ronald Meiklejohn, SIS station chief in Tallinn, claimed an agent of his, BP 11, had infiltrated the office of Deputy Foreign Commissar Maxim Litvinov. Until early July, BP 11 gave SIS more than two hundred 'summaries and paraphrases' of traffic between Moscow, Litvinov in Tallinn and Krasin in London. However, once GCCS again started solving Russian traffic (mainly Middle Eastern) in April 1921, SIS realised BP 11's product was forged. Jeffery, *MI6*, pp. 184, 187; Andrew, *Her Majesty*, pp. 277–9.

46 Jeffery, *MI6*, pp. 188, 164.

47 In July 1921, SIS claimed to have a source in the office of the Bolshevik representative in Berlin, Viktor L. Kopp. By September, Curzon believed he had enough proof of renewed subversion in Asia, a clear violation of the trade agreement. The material actually came from SIS source Z51, Vladimir G. Orlov, the shadowy but gifted White forger with high-level contacts across Europe. Soon, however, SIS suspected that at least some of his product came from another known forger, Bernhard

von Uexkull. He ran *Ost Information*, a political bureau linked to German intelligence. *Ost Information* documents, many of them forgeries, were the basis of much of Curzon's note. Andrew, *Her Majesty*, pp. 280–1; Bennett, *Churchill*, pp. 53–4, 336 n. 61.

48 Andrew, *Her Majesty*, p. 281.

49 'I attach more importance to them as a means of forming a true judgement of public policy ... than to any other source of knowledge at the disposal of the State.' David Kahn, ed., 'Churchill Pleads for the Intercepts', *Cryptologia* 6:1 (1982), 47–9: p. 49. To Sir Eyre Crowe, Foreign Office Permanent Under-Secretary, SIGINT was 'exceedingly instructive' and 'a much more valuable source of information' than secret service reports. 'Secret Service Committee: ... Reappointed', 4 March 1922, p. 5, TNA CAB 127/356. In 1940, by-then Lord Hankey described intercepts as 'the most reliable of all our secret sources of information' since 1914. 'Correspondence and Background Notes into Investigation and Brief History of [MI5] by Lord Hankey', 1940, p. 4, TNA CAB 63/192.

50 Matthew Hendley, 'Anti-Alienism and the Primrose League: The Externalisation of the Post-War Crisis in Great Britain, 1918–32', *Albion: A Quarterly Journal concerned with British Studies* 33:2 (2001), 243–69.

51 Eunan O'Halpin, 'Sir Warren Fisher and the Coalition, 1919–22', *THJ* 24:4 (1981): 907–27, p. 923.

52 See 'Reade', Appendix.

53 'Report 74' (UK), 30 September 1920, p. 6, CP 1908, TNA CAB 24/112; 'Report 132' (UK), 24 November 1921, pp. 8–11, CP 3509, TNA CAB 24/131. This work was open since 'there was no history of underground work in Britain.' McKnight, *Espionage*, p. 132. While the II Comintern Congress (July–August 1920) pointed to the need for clandestine structures, the III Congress (June–July 1921) highlighted the necessity 'to combine illegal work with legal' (p. 50). See ibid., chs 1–2, on the origins of Soviet conspiratorial tradition and Comintern clandestine methods.

54 See allegations by Brian Sewell, *Outsider II – Almost Always: Never Quite* (London, 2012), about Andrew Gow, Assistant Master at Eton (1914–25) and Fellow of Trinity College, Cambridge (1911–14, 1925–79).

55 Larry Hannant, 'Interwar Security Screening in Britain, the United States, and Canada', *INS* 6:4 (1991), 711–35: pp. 713–17; Porter, *Plots*, pp. 185–7; Hope, 'Surveillance'; Tammy Proctor, 'Family Ties in the Making of Modern Intelligence', *Journal of Social*

History 39:2 (2005), 451–66; 'Interim Report on [MI5] by Lord Hankey', 11 March 1940, p. 5, TNA CAB 63/193; 'Report on the Administrative Services of [MI5]', Appendix 1, TNA KV 4/19: 'Before the war, recruitment ... was by private introduction and selection, the willingness of a candidate to accept the post and salary offered being the sole criterion'; 'Director General's Report on [MI5]', February 1941, p. 6, TNA KV 4/88: 'selection was made too much on personal qualifications and too little on business ones'; Ferris, 'Whitehall', pp. 61–3: GCCS 'selected its clerical staff from an old girls' network of people known to its members or those of Room 40' while cryptologists came 'from a charmed circle of the wartime cryptanalytical units, the Services, and Oxford and Cambridge – not the "provincial universities"'; 'Regulations for the Recruitment of Candidates for Posts in the C&CS', 28 November 1924, p. 357, file 324, TNA FO 366/815: however, any attempt by 'a candidate to enlist support for his application, through [MPs] or other influential persons, will disqualify him for appointment'. As for SIS, until the Cambridge Five case broke in May 1951, recruitment was via the "old boys' network". Positive vetting became compulsory in late 1951 though already under review by 1947–48. Hennessy and Brownfeld, 'Britain'; Peter Hennessy, *The Secret State: Preparing for the Worst, 1945–2010* (London, 2010), ch. 3.

56 Sir Warren Fisher, Sir Eyre Crowe and Sir Maurice Hankey (the Treasury and Foreign Office Permanent Under-Secretaries, and the Cabinet Secretary) met five times in May and June. Bennett, *Churchill*, pp. 57–8; Andrew, *Her Majesty*, pp. 282–5; O'Halpin, 'Sir', pp. 922–6.

57 Churchill Archives Centre, The Papers of Sir Winston Churchill, CHAR 22/6, 22 July 1921, p. 79.

58 Contrary to what Christopher Andrew has written, SIS and Thomson's Directorate worked closely in one area. Four Special Branch officers were by 1921 seconded to SIS, collecting anti-subversive intelligence across Europe. Thomson then received their foreign intelligence from "C". 'Secret Service Committee: Third Meeting', 2 June 1921, p. 2, TNA CAB 127/356. See Andrew, *Her Majesty*, p. 284.

59 Ibid., p. 283; 'Sir Basil Thomson: Reminiscences for *The Times*', 1 November 1921, p. 10, *The Times* digital archive; 'Thomson to Walter Long', 27 October 1921, old reference 947/855, Long MSS. In October, Horwood attacked Thomson's excesses, including using Special Branch as a political weapon:

[It] has achieved ... a reputation for espionage on Labour which [*sic*] causes resentment among ... the working classes. ... English public opinion ... is most suspicious and resentful of anything approaching the Continental system of domestic espionage.

Andrew, *Her Majesty*, p. 282.

60 Ibid., pp. 283–4; O'Halpin, 'Sir', p. 925; 'Parliament: Sir B. Thomson's Retirement', 4 November 1921, p. 14, *The Times* digital archive.

61 'Thomson to Sinclair', 1 November 1921, MSS 81/091 (scrap book, blue paper), vol. 1 of 2, Hugh Sinclair MSS, Caird Archive & Library, National Maritime Museum, Greenwich.

62 Private correspondence. Horwood stated 'in no instance' had the Directorate's intelligence led to successful prosecution of political crime. Andrew, *Her Majesty*, p. 282.

63 'Reports of Secret Service Committee, 1919–23: First Meeting', 15 November 1921, TNA KV 4/151. Curzon chaired the Committee. Also attending were Churchill (Colonial Secretary), Sir Laming Worthington-Evans (War Secretary), Edward Shortt (Home Secretary), Sir Hamar Greenwood (Ireland Chief Secretary), Sir Eyre Crowe (Foreign Office Permanent Under-Secretary), Sir Archibald Sinclair (Private Secretary to Winston Churchill) and Nevile Bland (Foreign Office; Committee Secretary).

64 Ibid., pp. 2–3.

65 Ibid., pp. 3–6.

66 Ibid., pp. 6–7.

67 Ibid., pp. 7–8.

68 'Reports of Secret Service Committee, 1919–23: Churchill Note', 24 December 1921, p. 2, TNA KV 4/151.

69 Andrew, *Her Majesty*, p. 284.

70 See 'Report 125' (UK), 29 September 1921, CP 3350, TNA CAB 24/128; 'Report 151' (UK), 12 April 1922, CP 3939, TNA CAB 24/136.

71 'Report 163' (UK), 13 July 1922, Appendix 1, pp. 2–3, 5–6, CP 4102, TNA CAB 24/138. From August 1920 to October 1929, CPGB membership fluctuated from a low of 2000 in January 1921 to a high of 12,000 in October 1926. In June 1922, the month before Special Branch obtained this internal report, membership was 5116. By October, it had dropped to 3293. Thorpe, 'The Membership', p. 781, Table 1.

72 'Communists & Research Work', 'Report 166' (UK), 3 August 1922, pp. 1–3, CP 4144, TNA CAB 24/138.

73 'Memorandum on the Classification of Reports', attached to 10 May 1922 report, LG/F/26/1/30, Lloyd George MSS, quoted in Andrew, *Her Majesty*, pp. 281–2. See Jeffery, *MI6*, pp. 187–8, for a fuller description.

74 Bennett, *Churchill*, p. 65. All military and intelligence budgets were cut. McDonald, 'The Geddes'.

75 'Reports of Secret Service Committee, 1919–23: Sir Robert Horne Memorandum', 10 July 1922, pp. 1–3, TNA KV 4/151. See also Bennett, *Churchill*, pp. 36, 58–9, 65–71 on SIS finances; McDonald, 'The Geddes'.

76 '[PCOs] in Foreign Countries, 1923–24', 4 December 1923, pp. 65, 68, file 22, TNA FO 366/808; 'Lakey', p. 3, serial 63A, TNA KV 2/989; Bennett, *Churchill*, p. 68; Parliamentary Papers, 'Estimates for the Civil Services, 1922: [PCO] HQ Staff Salaries: Paper 32', Microfiche 129.148, TNA.

77 This was hard for ordinary members who knew Conservatives gave 70% of Coalition support in the Commons but had only twelve of twenty-one Cabinet posts. Goodlad, 'Ditching', p. 5; David Close, 'Conservatives and the Coalition after the First World War', *The Journal of Modern History* 45:2 (1973), 240–60: p. 241; Patrick Renshaw, 'Anti-Labour Politics in Britain, 1918–27', *Journal of Contemporary History* 12:4 (1977), 693–705: pp. 693–4.

78 Macintyre, 'British'; Rose, *The Intellectual*, ch. 9.

79 Goodlad, 'Ditching', p. 6; Richard Lyman, 'Ramsay MacDonald and the Leadership of the Labour Party, 1918–22', *The Journal of British Studies* 2:1 (1962), 132–60; Martin Pugh, '"Class Traitors": Conservative Recruits to Labour, 1900–30', *The English Historical Review* 113:450 (1998), 38–64: p. 39.

80 Goodlad, 'Ditching', pp. 6–7; Addison, *Churchill*, pp. 221–2; John Fair, 'The Anglo-Irish Treaty of 1921: Unionist Aspects of the Peace', *The Journal of British Studies* 12:1 (1972), 132–49; Thurlow, *The Secret*, p. 128; Jeffery, *Field*, p. vii; Peter Jensen, 'The Greco-Turkish War, 1920–2', *International Journal of Middle East Studies* 10:4 (1979), 553–65: p. 564.

81 Cabinet had little operational but good strategic intelligence available, confusing policy-making. John R. Ferris, '"Far Too Dangerous a Gamble"? British Intelligence and Policy during the Chanak Crisis, September–October 1922', in *Power and Stability: British Foreign Policy, 1865–1965*, ed. Erik Goldstein and B. J. C. McKercher (London, 2003), 139–84.

82 Addison, *Churchill*, p. 225; A. E. Montgomery, 'The Making of the Treaty of Sèvres of 10 August 1920', *THJ* 15:4 (1972), 775–87. With the end of the Ottoman Empire, Turkey found itself with two governments: the Sultan in Constantinople and the Nationalists in Ankara. The former refused to ratify Sèvres; the latter rejected it outright. Joseph Grew, 'The Peace Conference of Lausanne, 1922–3', *Proceedings of the American Philosophical Society* 98:1 (1954), 1–10: p. 2; Edgar Turlington, 'The Settlement of Lausanne', *The American Journal of International Law* 18:4 (1924), 696–706; Jeffery and Sharp, 'Lord Curzon and Secret', pp. 109–10, 117; Keith Jeffery and Alan Sharp, 'Lord Curzon and the Use of Secret Intelligence at the Lausanne Conference: 1922–3', *The Turkish Yearbook of International Relations* XXIII (1993), 79–89: pp. 79, 84.

83 Addison, *Churchill*, p. 225; Clarke, *A Question*, p. 91.

84 Goodlad, 'Ditching', pp. 7–8; Toye, *Lloyd*, p. 236; Clarke, *Hope*, pp. 109–10; Addison, *Churchill*, pp. 225–6; Jessica Yonwin, 'UK Election Statistics, 1918–2001', Research Paper 04/61, House of Commons Library, London, 2004, p. 10, Table 1a.

85 The Conservatives were in power for fifty out of the next seventy years. Clarke, *Hope*, p. 119.

86 Not that White Russians were trusted either: 'My dear Winston … I do not trust [White Russian leader Boris] Savinkoff … and my information is quite contrary to yours, which you may have derived from him.' 'Correspondence with the Palaces, 1919–23: Curzon to Churchill', 30 December 1921, p. 89, TNA FO 800/157. See Chapter 7 on Russo-German defence and security cooperation in the 1920s.

87 Philip Williamson and Edward Baldwin, ed., *Baldwin Papers: Conservative Statesman, 1908–47* (Cambridge, 2004), pp. 82–5; Clarke, *Hope*, pp. 122–3; Gilmour, *Curzon*, ch. 37; Bennett and Gibson, *The Later*, p. 139.

88 Stafford, *Churchill*, p. 95.

89 See Emily Wilson, 'The War in the Dark: The Security Service and the *Abwehr* [German military intelligence], 1940–44' (unpublished Ph.D. thesis, University of Cambridge, 2003) on the British Double-Cross System.

90 'Secretary of State for War [on] Organisation and Functions of MI5', 19 March 1920, p. 2, TNA KV 4/159.

91 Private correspondence; Bennett, *A Most*, pp. 28–32; idem, *Churchill*, pp. 92–134.

92 From 1919 to 1929, annual GCCS funding ranged from £15,000 to £25,000. Freeman, 'MI1$_{(b)}$', pp. 218–20.

CHAPTER 5
The Letter

1 2 May 1923, p. 216, conclusion 23(23), TNA FO 371/9365 (N3360).

2 'Suggested Draft of [Foreign Office] Letter to Treasury', 14 August 1924, TNA HW 3/49.

3 Robert James, ed., *Winston Churchill – His Complete Speeches: vol. 4, 1922–8* (New York, 1974), p. 3496.

4 Hardliners in Lloyd George Cabinets: Chamberlain, Churchill, Curzon, Long, Milner, Shortt and Smith. Hardliners in Bonar Law and Baldwin Cabinets: Curzon, Hoare and Jix. David Butler and Gareth Butler, *Twentieth Century British Political Facts, 1900–2000* (Basingstoke, 2000), pp. 6–12; Clarke, *Hope*, pp. 120–1; Taylor, *English*, pp. 195–6. Some lost seats in the election, but others retired and others still briefly withdrew from politics to protest the post-Coalition direction Party leaders chose.

5 In Parliamentary Papers, 'Correspondence between His Majesty's Government and the Soviet Government respecting the Relations between the Two Governments', Cmd 1869 (1923). The note raised the issues of religious freedom, maritime boundaries and reparations for ill-treated Britons, as well as persistent Soviet subversion in India, Afghanistan and Persia (citing intercepted cables to prove Moscow's activities).

6 Clarke, *Hope*, pp. 118–20; Taylor, *English*, p. 195.

7 Keeble, *Britain*, pp. 93–4.

8 Grew, 'The Peace', p. 4; Keeble, *Britain*, p. 93. See also Jeffery and Sharp, 'Lord Curzon and Secret'; idem, 'Lord Curzon and the Use'; William Norton Medlicott *et al.*, ed., *Documents on British Foreign Policy (DBFP), 1919–39*, First Series, vol. XVIII (London, 1972).

9 Early British political discourse on Communism was insular. Those most worried by it were those who saw themselves as Christians above all else, the prime example being Stanley Baldwin.

10 Keeble, *Britain*, p. 95; 'His Grace, Bishop Tikhon (Belavin) of Moscow', www.oca.org; Constantine Krypton, 'Secret Religious Organisations in the USSR', *Russian Review* 14:2 (1955), 121–7: pp. 122–4.

11 5 April 1923, f. 17, op. 3, d. 346, l. 1, RGASPI.

12 'Notes & Memoranda on Russia', 13 April 1923, Moscow, © British Library Board EUR F112/236, Curzon MSS, British Library; 'Proposed Rupture with Soviet Government', 14 April 1923, pp. 121, 123–4, TNA FO 371/9365 (N3334).

13 'Proposed Rupture', 14 April 1923, p. 126, TNA FO 371/9365 (N3334).

14 Ibid., pp. 127–8.

15 'Proposed Rupture', 15 April 1923, pp. 129–32, TNA FO 371/9365 (N3334). Gregory was right: reputation did matter. A fortnight later Turkish officials informed London that the Soviets, immediately after delivering offensive notes to Hodgson, telegraphed the content to the Turks to lower Muslim respect worldwide for the British. 'Relations between His Majesty's Government and Russia', 30 April 1923, p. 189, TNA FO 371/9365 (N3804).

16 'Proposed Rupture', 16 April 1923, p. 132, TNA FO 371/9365 (N3334). Tikhon was imprisoned in April 1922, tried in April 1923 but finally released in the summer. Krypton, 'Secret', p. 124.

17 On 31 March 1923, a Soviet cruiser seized the Hull-based trawler *James Johnson* ten miles off Murmansk, on charges of illegal fishing. Moscow had since 1917 claimed territorial waters out to twelve miles but London only recognised three. The trawler captain was to be jailed for a month and pay a £10 fine; crew and vessel were released after five weeks' captivity. *Parliamentary Debates*, Commons, 25 April 1923, vol. 163, columns 424–6, and 7 May 1923, vol. 163, columns 1891–3; 'Best Cure for Bolshevism – 1923', www.britishpathe.com.

18 27–28 April 1923, f. 04, op. 4, p. 24, d. 332, ll. 1–3, AVP RF. Not to be confused with Jan K. Berzin, the Latvian officer and Head of *Razvedupr*/IV Directorate from March 1924 to April 1935, and June to August 1937. Lurie and Kochik, *GRU*, p. 106.

19 The dates of quoted intercepts were November 1922, 8 November 1922, February 1923, 17 February 1923, 21 February 1923, 16 March 1923 and 17 March 1923. Cmd 1869 (1923), pp. 7–8.

20 Parliamentary Papers, 'Reply of Soviet Government to His Majesty's Government respecting the Relations between the Two Governments', Cmd 1874 (1923), pp. 3–4.

21 '[E]xtracts and quotations ... by [London] are combination of invention, with deciphered parts of telegrams tendenciously [*sic*] manipulated and arbitrarily extended.' Cmd 1874 (1923), p. 4; Andrew, *Her Majesty*, p. 293.

22 Cmd 1874 (1923), p. 8.

23 See 'Raskolnikov', Appendix.

24 Parliamentary Papers, 'Further Correspondence between His Majesty's Government and the Soviet Government respecting the Relations between the Two Governments', Cmd 1890 (1923), p. 7.

25 Ibid., p. 8.

26 Ibid., pp. 12–13. Using GCCS intercepts, Northern Department Head Don Gregory confirmed a temporary observance of this undertaking. Andrew, *Her Majesty*, pp. 295–6.

27 3 May 1923, conclusion 23(23), minute 2, TNA CAB 23/45.

28 5 May 1923, f. 04, op. 4, p. 24, d. 332, l. 5, AVP RF. British industrialists and mistreatment of British subjects were pressuring Curzon to withdraw from the treaty. See Gregory, above, and the Harding case below.

29 Ibid., ll. 6–7.

30 Ibid., l. 7.

31 *Tsentrsoyuz* primarily oversaw internal USSR trade.

32 11 May 1923, f. 04, op. 4, p. 24, d. 332, l. 15, AVP RF.

33 The conference started on 10 April 1922, with participants seeking Soviet assurances on an end to subversion, as well as commercial and financial guarantees on debt recognition and seized private property. Keeble, *Britain*, pp. 89–90. See also Medlicott *et al.*, ed., *DBFP*, vol. XIX (London, 1974), chs 2–3.

34 See 'Voigt', Appendix.

35 11 May 1923, f. 04, op. 4, p. 24, d. 338, l. 4, AVP RF. See 'Berens', Appendix.

36 'The Curzon Ultimatum: Report to the Sixth All-Russia Congress of Metal Workers', 16 June 1923, Brian Pearce, translator, *The Military Writings and Speeches of Leon Trotsky, vol. 5: 1921–1923: How the Revolution Armed* (London, 1979); Xenia Joucoff Eudin and Harold H. Fisher, *Soviet Russia and the West, 1920–1927: A Documentary Survey* (Stanford, CA, 1959), pp. 188–9.

37 Private correspondence; Hans Kollwitz, ed., Richard and Clara Winston, translators, *The Diary and Letters of Kaethe Kollwitz* (Evanston, IL, 1988), p. 6, 45–6; Parliamentary Papers, 'Correspondence between His Majesty's Government and the Soviet Government respecting the Murder of Mr. C. F. Davison in January 1920', Cmd 1846 (1923); Paul Dukes, *Red Dusk and the Morrow: Adventures and Investigations in Red Russia* (London, 1923), p. vii; *Parliamentary Debates*, Commons, 14 July 1926, vol. 198, columns 388–9; Parliamentary Papers, 'Correspondence with the Russian Soviet Government

respecting the Imprisonment of Mrs. Stan Harding in Russia', Cmd 1602 (1922), p. 4; Pearce, 'The Curzon'.

38 Cmd 1602 (1922), pp. 3–6; Stan Harding, *The Underworld of State* (London, 1925), pp. 223–4, 29, 39–41, 188, 245. Curzon, Labour's Philip Snowden and the Liberal John Simon, for example, supported Harding.

39 Harrison reportedly knew at least one: Captain Francis McCullagh, the vocal anti-Bolshevik allegedly also using journalistic cover. One source suggests Bolshevik agents in America (including in military intelligence) had actually blown Harrison's cover by describing her identification of a communist agent and giving the *Cheka* some of her reports. Murray Seeger, *Discovering Russia: 200 Years of American Journalism* (Bloomington, IN, 2005), p. 229, 232.

40 Harding, *The Underworld*, pp. 59, 11–12. On Harrison's intelligence work, see Seeger, *Discovering*, ch. 14; Catherine M. Griggs, 'Beyond Boundaries: The Adventurous Life of Marguerite Harrison' (unpublished Ph.D. thesis, George Washington University, 1996), chs 4–7; and works by Harrison herself. In 1938, Mrs Harding successfully sued Harrison's publisher for libel over claims about her 1920 imprisonment. Harrison denied she had exposed the Briton, saying 'the Russians knew Harding was also an intelligence agent'. Seeger, *Discovering*, p. 244.

41 15 May 1923, f. 04, op. 4, p. 24, d. 338, l. 26, AVP RF.

42 21 May 1923, f. 17, op. 3, d. 355, ll. 1, 6–7, protocol 7, no. 1, RGASPI.

43 22 May 1923, f. 359, op. 1, d. 5, ll. 78–9, RGASPI. See 'Baldwin', Appendix.

44 'Memorandum by Lapinsky', 22 May 1923, f. 04, op. 4, p. 24, d. 338, l. 42, AVP RF. On his suspicions of the USSR, see 'Tyrrell', Appendix, and Keith Neilson and T. G. Otte, *The Permanent Under-Secretary for Foreign Affairs, 1854–1946*, British Politics and Society (Abingdon, 2009), ch. 10, particularly pp. 193–9.

45 'Memorandum by Lapinsky', 22 May 1923, f. 04, op. 4, p. 24, d. 338, l. 42. From 1913 to 1929, British exports to Russia as a percentage of annual British exports decreased from around 3.5% (£18 million) to around 0.5% (£3.7 million). In 1917, the figure was 9.3% (£49 million); in 1920 it was 0.9% (£12 million); in 1924 it was 0.5% (£4 million); and in 1927 it was 0.6% (£4.5 million). Parliamentary Papers, 'Annual Statement of Trade of the [UK] with Foreign Countries and British Possessions. 1920 Compared with the Years 1913 and 1919',

Cmd 1506 (1920), vol. IV, p. 139, Table 2, and Cmd 1503 (1920), vol. I, p. 1, Table 2; Parliamentary Papers, 'Statistical Tables relating to British Foreign Trade and Industry (1924–30). Part I – General Tables', Cmd 3737 (1930), p. 10, Table 1 and pp. 34–41, Table 8; Parliamentary Papers, 'Annual Statement of Trade of the [UK] with Foreign Countries and British Possessions. 1917 Compared with the Four Preceding Years', Cmd 9136 (1918), vol. II, p. 20, Table 4, and Cmd 9127 (1918), vol. I, p. 20, Table 5.

46 'Memorandum by Lapinsky', 22 May 1923, f. 04, op. 4, p. 24, d. 338, ll. 42–6, AVP RF. See Jones, 'The British'; Hans Heymann Jr, 'Oil in Soviet-Western Relations in the Interwar Years', *American Slavic and East European Review* 7:4 (1948), 303–16.

47 See Litvinov, Copenhagen–Chicherin, Moscow; 26 May 1920–002606; 19 May 1920, p. 1, TNA HW 12/9; Litvinov, Copenhagen–Krasin, London; 5 June 1920–002740; 2 June 1920, pp. 1–2, TNA HW 12/10; Litvinov, Copenhagen–Chicherin, Moscow; 29 June 1920–003138; 24 June 1920, p. 1, TNA HW 12/11; Krasin, London–Chicherin, Moscow; 9 June 1920–002784; 7 June 1920, pp. 1–2, TNA HW 12/10.

48 (Illegible) 1923, f. 04, op. 4, p. 24, d. 338, ll. 113–17, AVP RF.

49 23 May 1923 (copied to Litvinov and Stalin), f. 04, op. 4, p. 24, d. 332, l. 25, AVP RF.

50 'Krasin to Chicherin', ibid., l. 22.

51 'Berzin to Litvinov', 29 May 1923, f. 04, op. 4, p. 24, d. 332, ll. 37–8, AVP RF.

52 Ibid., l. 40.

53 'Krasin to NKID', ibid., ll. 42–3.

54 4 June 1923, f. 17, op. 3, d. 358, ll. 1–2, protocol 10, no. 1, RGASPI.

55 'Litvinov to Krasin', 4 June 1923, f. 359, op. 1, d. 5, ll. 80–1, RGASPI. Officially, Raskolnikov's posting ended in June 1924 but one source states he left Afghanistan in November 1923. His replacement, Leonid N. Stark, only presented his credentials in July 1924. 'Polnomochnyye Predstavitelstva, Missii, Posolstva: Afganistan' [Plenipotentiary Representatives, Missions, Embassies: Afghanistan], *Spravochnik po Istorii Kommunisticheskoy Partii i Sovetskogo Soyuza, 1898–1991* [Reference Book on the History of the Communist Party and the Soviet Union, 1898–1991], www.knowbysight.info; Fazal-ur-Rahim Khan Marwat, *The Evolution and Growth of Communism in Afghanistan, 1917–79: An Appraisal* (Karachi, 1997), p. 79.

56 'Litvinov to Berzin', 4 June 1923, f. 04, op. 4, p. 24, d. 333, l. 12, AVP RF.

57 'Chicherin to Berzin', 18 June 1923, f. 04, op. 4, p. 24, d. 333, l. 29, AVP RF.

58 'Krasin to Chicherin', 8 June 1923, f. 04, op. 4, p. 24, d. 332, l. 77, AVP RF.

59 9 June 1923, f. 17, op. 3, d. 359, l. 1, protocol 11, no. 1, RGASPI; 21 June 1923, f. 17, op. 3, d. 361, l. 1, protocol 13, no. 1, RGASPI.

60 Keeble, *Britain*, p. 364. The Kremlin then sent Krasin to repair relations with France.

61 14 June 1923, f. 17, op. 3, d. 360, l. 1, protocol 12, no. 1, RGASPI.

62 'Krasin to Chicherin', 22 June 1923, f. 04, op. 4, p. 24, d. 332, l. 87, AVP RF.

63 'Meeting with British Delegation', 16 June 1923, f. 495, op. 100, d. 97, l. 3, RGASPI.

64 Created in 1919 and disbanded in 1943 like the Comintern, KIM was its international youth affiliate.

65 'Report 211' (UK), 21 June 1923, pp. 4–7, CP 285(23), TNA CAB 24/160.

66 'Report 200' (UK), 5 April 1923, pp. 6–7, CP 183(23), TNA CAB 24/159, from domestic postal intercepts.

67 'Report 222' (UK), 13 September 1923, CP 400(23), TNA CAB 24/161.

68 'Report 233' (UK), 29 November 1923, CP 473(23), TNA CAB 24/162. See 'Münzenberg', Appendix.

69 'Rakovsky to Litvinov', 29 December 1923, f. 028, op. 1, p. 101, d. 59438, l. 249, AVP RF.

70 3 January 1924, f. 04, op. 4, p. 27, d. 391, l. 1, AVP RF. Moscow suspected Labour for ideological and more practical reasons: reformist Socialists were rivals for worker support. Hennessy, *The Secret* (2003), p. 24.

71 'Report 237' (UK), 3 January 1924, p. 1, CP 5(24), TNA CAB 24/164.

72 Ibid.

73 'Rakovsky to Litvinov', 9 January 1924, f. 325, op. 2, d. 38, l. 59, RGASPI. 'Ramsay MacDonald was even more proletarian [than Lloyd George]: he was poor and illegitimate; he took to high society (to his great political cost) with all the ardour of the outsider.' Cannadine, *The Decline*, pp. 227–8.

74 'Rakovsky to Litvinov', 11 January 1924, f. 325, op. 2, d. 38, l. 80, RGASPI.

75 'Chicherin to Litvinov', 20 January 1924, f. 04, op. 4, p. 27, d. 391, l. 3, AVP RF.

76 Noel Thompson, 'Wise, Edward Frank', *ODNB*; Struthers, *Edward*, pp. 46, 48.

77 'Rakovsky to Litvinov', 11 January 1924, f. 325, op. 2, d. 38, l. 91, RGASPI.

78 'Chicherin to Rakovsky', 18 January 1924, f. 04, op. 4, p. 27, d. 390, l. 2, AVP RF; 'Chicherin to Litvinov', 20 January 1924, f. 04, op. 4, p. 27, d. 391, ll. 3–4, AVP RF.

79 Churchill Archives Centre, The Papers of Lady Adeline Hankey, AHKY 1/1/33, 3 February 1924.

80 The Council was the supreme governing body of the Russian and other Soviet republics between 1917 and 1936.

81 4 February 1924, p. 1, conclusion 9(24), minute 1, TNA CAB 23/47. Diplomatic ties resumed on 8 February with Rakovsky's appointment as Chargé d'Affaires, a post he held until 14 November 1925. Keeble, *Britain*, p. 364.

82 'CID Meeting 180', 4 February 1924, p. 2, TNA CAB 2/4.

83 27 February 1924, f. 028, op. 1, p. 101, d. 59444, l. 29, AVP RF. From 1921 to 1925, British industrial output rose by 41.5% and exports by 50%, but exports were still 25% lower than in 1913. By 1924, 1.3 million Britons were still out of work. Aldcroft, *From*, pp. 111–12; Garside, *British*, p. 5, Table 2.

84 27 February 1924, f. 028, op. 1, p. 101, d. 59444, ll. 31–2, AVP RF.

85 7 March 1924, f. 028, op. 1, p. 101, d. 59441, ll. 54–5, AVP RF.

86 The conference (14 April–8 August) aimed to formalise ties, with the USSR keen on British credit but not wanting to commit to settling public and private compensation claims. Both countries signed two draft documents, subject to ratification (a general treaty, and a commerce and navigation treaty). The general agreement clarified earlier treaties, established fishing rights and settled the status of outstanding reparation claims (on this last issue, the treaty was little more than an agreement to agree). The second document gave each country most-favoured-nation trading status. Keeble, *Britain*, pp. 98–9; Parliamentary Papers, 'General Treaty between Great Britain and Northern Ireland and the [USSR]', Cmd 2260 (1924), and 'Treaty of Commerce and Navigation between Great Britain and Northern Ireland and the [USSR]', Cmd 2261 (1924).

87 'Farbman to Rakovsky', 6 May 1924, f. 028, op. 1, p. 101, d. 59441, ll. 174–6, AVP RF.

[The] official Moscow telephone directory does not support contention that Soviet ... Government and Comintern have nothing in common and that Zinoviev is not an official of the former ... page 251 gives the telephone numbers of the various offices of the Sovnarkom and the Council of Labour and Defence. Among them figures: 'No. 900 – train of Comrade Zinoviev, President of the Comintern.' Dated 14 April 1924.

'Speech by M. Zinoviev', 28 April 1924, p. 8 minutes, TNA FO 371/10484 (N3640).

88 'Rakovsky to Chicherin', 6 May 1924, f. 028, op. 1, p. 101, d. 59441, ll. 2–4, AVP RF.

89 'Soviet Espionage on Foreign Missions', 14 June 1924, p. 104 minutes, TNA FO 371/10495 (N4868).

90 'Situation in Leningrad', 23 June 1924, p. 51, TNA FO 371/10484 (N5261).

91 'Soviet Attitude towards Foreign Missions', 17 July 1924, p. 118 minutes, TNA FO 371/10495 (N5948).

92 'Hodgson to MacDonald', 22 August 1924, 'Soviet Espionage on Foreign Missions at Moscow', 30 August 1924, p. 144, TNA FO 371/10495 (N6941).

93 'Lakey', 7 September 1928, p. 2, serial 77a, TNA KV 2/989. However, see also Dale's diary in TNA KV 2/999.

94 Bennett, *A Most* is the definitive account, supplemented by idem, *Churchill*, pp. 79–87. See also Jeffery, *MI6*, pp. 214–22; Andrew, *The Defence*, pp. 148–51; and Smith, *Six*, ch. 17.

95 'Chicherin to Politburo', 24 October 1924, f. 69, op. 8, p. 15, d. 47, l. 5, AVP RF.

96 Rakovsky, London–NKID, Moscow; 24 October 1924–018495; 10 November 1924, TNA HW 12/64.

97 France was Russia's largest creditor by 1914, with £317.5 million in loans. See Michael Jabara Carley, 'Episodes from the Early Cold War: Franco-Soviet Relations, 1917–27', *Europe-Asia Studies* 52:7 (2000), 1275–305.

98 'Litvinov to Rakovsky', 27 October 1924, f. 69, op. 8, p. 15, d. 47, ll. 11–12, AVP RF.

99 'Litvinov to Rakovsky', 31 October 1924, f. 69, op. 8, p. 15, d. 47, l. 14, AVP RF.

100 This special committee comprised MacDonald, Lord Parmoor (Lord President of the Council), Viscount Haldane (Lord Chancellor) and Arthur Henderson (Foreign Secretary). October 1924, conclusion 57(24), minute 231, TNA CAB 23/48.

101 See 'Trebitsch-Lincoln', Appendix.

102 'Chicherin to Litvinov', 1 November 1924, f. 69, op. 8, p. 15, d. 47, l. 19, AVP RF.

103 This result was counter-intuitive to contemporary and subsequent perceptions, exemplified by the Chester-Fay-Young thesis, that the letter was a forgery leaked to ruin Labour's electoral prospects on 29 October.

Lewis Chester, Stephen Fay and Hugo Young, *The Zinoviev Letter* (London, 1967).

104 Clarke, *Hope*, pp. 119–20.

105 3 November 1924, f. 028, op. 1, p. 101, d. 59438, l. 97, AVP RF.

106 'Chairman of ABCR Executive Committee to Stanley Baldwin', 3 November 1924, p. 86, TNA FO 371/10495 (N8411). See also David Jarvis, 'British Conservatism and Class Politics in the 1920s', *The English Historical Review* 111:440 (1996), 59–84.

107 One early sign was Cabinet's refusal to approve a Vickers Ltd request to supply military equipment worth £7.5 million to Moscow; it would be 'inconsistent with the attitude ... by members of the present Government during the recent ... Election' to sanction equipping Soviet Russia 'with arms and ammunition of British manufacture'. 12 November 1924, p. 10, conclusion 59(24), minute 9, TNA CAB 23/49.

108 'Chicherin to Zinoviev', 12 November 1924, f. 69, op. 8, p. 15, d. 47, l. 27, AVP RF. On 15 December, Foreign Secretary Austen Chamberlain cited an intercepted letter from Arthur MacManus stating Zinoviev had been in Moscow in mid-September. 'Chicherin to Rothstein' (copied to Zinoviev, Radek and the NKID Collegium), 25 December 1924, f. 69, op. 8, p. 15, d. 47, l. 56, AVP RF. On Moscow's initial surprise over the Zinoviev affair, however, Russian archival material is clear.

109 Euphemism for another Soviet security/intelligence organ. "Friends" were security/intelligence services of friendly nations, while "special contacts" were sources in those services.

110 Rakovsky, London–NKID, Moscow; 18 November 1924–018844; 5 December 1924, TNA HW 12/65.

111 'Litvinov to NKID Collegium', 22 November 1924, f. 69, op. 8, p. 15, d. 47, ll. 36–7, AVP RF.

112 'Chicherin to Politburo', 24 November 1924, f. 69, op. 8, p. 15, d. 47, l. 35, AVP RF.

113 12 November 1924, f. 17, op. 3, d. 481, l. 1, protocol 1e, RGASPI. Britain most likely meant a Soviet undertaking not to pursue or assassinate "M" overseas, if he indeed existed.

114 'Chicherin to Zinoviev', 15 November 1924, f. 69, op. 8, p. 15, d. 47, l. 28, AVP RF.

115 Rakovsky, London–NKID, Moscow; 12 December 1924–019009; 17 December 1924, TNA HW 12/65. Rakovsky's cable is perplexing since no such ministerial statement appears in the Parliamentary record, *Hansard*.

116 'Chicherin to Politburo' (copied to OGPU and NKID Collegium), 15 December 1924, f. 69, op. 8, p. 15, d. 47, l. 55, AVP RF.

117 'Ewer', September 1949, p. 2, serial 1101, TNA KV 2/1016. See also Andrew, *The Defence*, p. 152.

118 On Churchill's complex attitude towards Party politics, see Stuart Ball, 'Churchill and the Conservative Party', *Transactions of the Royal Historical Society* (Sixth Series) 11 (2001), 307–30. Because he looked for a consistent anti-socialist platform, in his mind Churchill used Socialism to justify changing parties. The result was a more strident position over time. Private correspondence.

CHAPTER 6
The Strike

1 'ROSTA' [Russian Telegraph Agency], 22 June 1925, serial 23ª, TNA KV 2/1109.

2 'Federated Press of America, Supplementary', 19 January 1925, p. 9, TNA KV 2/1432.

3 'Aspects of the General Strike, May 1926', Part V, p. 3, TNA KV 4/282.

4 Sinclair made these comments on 2 March 1925. 'Secret Service Committee Minutes, 1925', TNA FO 1093/68. Warren Fisher chaired the Committee. Also attending were Eyre Crowe and Maurice Hankey. 'Secret Service Committee, Miscellaneous Papers: 1924–26: Baldwin Letter', 10 February 1925, TNA FO 1093/67; 'Secret Service, 1925', 10 February 1925, TNA CAB 127/365. See Bennett, *Churchill*, pp. 86–94, on proceedings, and idem, *A Most*, Annex E, on the intelligence community.

5 12 February 1925, pp. 101–2, D.3. (Labour), vol. 11, D.3.1. (Labour: Sundries), Stanley Baldwin MSS, Cambridge University Library.

6 Burke, *The Spy*, pp. 65–7. See 'Norwood', Appendix.

7 8 April 1925, p. 3, conclusion 20(25), minute 3, TNA CAB 23/49.

8 13 May 1925, p. 3, conclusion 25(25), minute 3, TNA CAB 23/50. Cabinet agreed 'the Home Secretary should decide whether and when ... publication of ... material [regarding] the proposed [CPGB] activities in this country ... should take place'.

9 Bennett, *Churchill*, chs 3–5.

10 26 May 1925, scrap book (blue paper), vol. 1, 81/091, Sinclair MSS; Andrew, *The Defence*, p. 125.

11 A typical report:

> [On] the night of 22 May, the offices of the local Glasgow Communist Party

Committee were broken into and considerable damage was done to papers, etc.: a Constable apprehended a man … Joseph McCall, as he was leaving … and he admitted having done the damage. McCall states … he joined the Party … two months ago as a Fascist spy: in McCall's possession were [*sic*] found a register of names and addresses.

'Report 306' (UK), 28 May 1925, p. 6, CHAR 22/81, Winston Churchill MSS.

12 1 September 1925, p. 377, D.1. (Defence), vol. 2, D.1.6. (STO), Baldwin MSS.

13 Ibid., p. 378.

14 8 July 1925, p. 3, conclusion 36(25), minute 3, TNA CAB 23/50:

> [H]e felt … the proper course was to keep … formal relations as distant as possible; but … not to yield to the demand in some quarters for an early breaking off … to avoid action which [*sic*] might assist the Extremists in this country at the expense of … moderate elements in … opposition parties … opposed to Bolshevism.

15 'Funds Devoted to MI5 by the Foreign Office, vol. 1', 27 July 1925, serial 3A, TNA KV 4/198: 'I am … asking you to increase our allotment for the … year by £1,500, making the total … for 1925/6 … £16,500 [2011: £5.7 million]'. With this, 'I will be able … to deal with the [communists'] increased activities'.

16 'Examples of Seditious Literature, 1919', Part 1, TNA HO 144/1579.

17 'Anglo-Soviet Relations', 23 February 1927, p. 161, TNA FO 371/12589 (N791).

18 Subversion: 'the action of subverting or state of being subverted; overthrow, ruin of a law, rule, system, condition, faculty, character, etc.; of persons, countries, peoples, or their lives and fortunes'. Sedition: 'a concerted movement to overthrow an established government; a revolt, rebellion, mutiny; conduct or language inciting to rebellion against the constituted authority in a State'. *Oxford English Dictionary*. Legally, sedition refers to 'practices which [*sic*] disturb the internal tranquillity of the State' although they 'are not accompanied by overt or direct use of violence'. There is 'no specific offence of sedition', only seditious libel and seditious conspiracy. R. J. Spjut, 'Defining Subversion', *British Journal of Law and Society* 6:2 (1979), 254–61: pp. 256–7.

19 15 November 1927, p. 3, file 516527/1, TNA HO 45/25955; Roy Haines, *King Edward II: His Life, His Reign, and its Aftermath, 1284–1330* (Montréal, 2003), chs 5–7.

20 Parliamentary Papers, *Report from the Secret Committee on the Post Office*, No. 582 (1844), p. 95.

21 Gerald Bray, 'The Act of Supremacy, 1534', *Documents of the English Reformation, 1526–1701* (Cambridge, 2004), pp. 113–14; Spjut, 'Defining', pp. 254–5.

22 Derek Wilson, *Sir Francis Walsingham: A Courtier in an Age of Terror* (London, 2007), pp. 50–1, 57, 219–29, 93–5, 142, 151, 180–7, 236. Walsingham's

> sources … included 'honest gentlemen in all the Shires, cities, and principal towns'; diplomats; merchants, mariners, and others whose work took them abroad; Huguenots and other Protestant friends; foreign courtiers who could be bribed to be [his] eyes and ears; as well as a handful of trained agents placed strategically in over forty centres throughout Europe…. As well as the agents, [he] had to pay a large staff of clerks and scribes, some of whom were linguists or codifiers…. Privy Seal warrants suggest a steady increase in payments from £5753 in 1582 [2011: £415 million] to £13,260 in 1588 [2011: £797 million]. (pp. 100–1)

23 Asa Briggs and Peter Burke, *A Social History of the Media: From Gutenberg to the Internet* (London, 2005), pp. 79–83. See also Simon Burrows, 'Police and Political Pamphleteering in Pre-Revolutionary France', in *Print and Power in France and England, 1500–1800*, ed. David Adams and Adrian Armstrong (Aldershot, 2006), 99–112.

24 Revolution, argued Edmund Burke, was 'the degenerate choice of a vitiated mind' that would end civilisation. *Reflections on the Revolution in France*, ed. J. G. A. Pocock (Indianapolis, IN, 1987), p. 59. He saw it as a new 'dreadful pestilence' and worried the Revolution might inspire English subversives. Louis Gottschalk, 'Reflections on Burke's *Reflections on the French Revolution*', *Proceedings of the American Philosophical Society* 100:5 (1956), 417–29: p. 426 n. 54–5, p. 422. See James Billington, *Fire in the Minds of Men: Origins of the Revolutionary Faith* (London, 1980), ch. 16, on the concept of moral and physical purity in revolutionary Russia.

25 Spjut, 'Defining', pp. 261, 255.

26 *Parliamentary Debates*, Lords, 26 February 1975, vol. 357, column 947. See also Michael Head, *Crimes against the State: From Treason to Terrorism* (Farnham, 2011), pp. 29–32, 100, 108–9, 127–41, and ch. 6; Andrew, *The Defence*, p. 591.

27 Peter Gill, *Policing Politics: Security Intel-*

ligence and the Liberal Democratic State,
Studies in Intelligence (London, 1994), pp.
120–1.

28 Spjut, 'Defining', pp. 254–6.

29 Gill, *Policing*, pp. 121–2; idem and Mark
Phythian, *Intelligence in an Insecure World*
(Cambridge, 2006), p. 68.

30 Mitrokhin, ed., *KGB*, pp. 99, 199.

31 'Law on Sedition', 9 October 1925, p. 2, CP
420(25), TNA CAB 24/175.

32 Ibid., pp. 4, 7.

33 Andrew, *Her Majesty*, p. 318.

34 See Jeffery and Hennessy, *States*, ch. 5;
Richard Maguire, '"The Fascists … are …
to be depended upon." The British Government, Fascists, and Strike-Breaking during
1925 and 1926', in *British Fascism, the Labour
Movement, and the State*, ed. Nigel Copsey
(Basingstoke, 2005), 6–26. When the STO was
brought into action

[I]t was largely from the [BEU], the
National Citizens' Union … and similar
groups that volunteers and Special
Constables were recruited. Indeed, it
was precisely to resolve the problems of
recruiting such people for the [STO] that
the [BEU] – and in particular Sir George
Makgill – the National Citizens' Union
… and other bodies helped establish the
Organisation for the Maintenance of
Supplies [OMS] in early 1925.

John Hope, 'Fascism, the Security Service, and
the Curious Careers of Maxwell Knight and
James McGuirk Hughes', *Lobster* 22 (1991),
1–5: p. 2.

35 Andrew, *Her Majesty*, p. 320.

36 Ibid; Curry, *The Security*, p. 93. For seized
documents, see TNA KV 3/18–/33, and Parliamentary Papers, *Communist Papers. Documents Selected from those Obtained on the
Arrest of the Communist Leaders on 14 and 21
October, 1925*, Cmd 2682 (1926).

37 Andrew, *Her Majesty*, p. 320. See also John
Callaghan and Mark Phythian, 'State Surveil-
lance of the CPGB Leadership: 1920s–1950s',
Labour History Review 69:1 (2004), 19–33.

38 'Slocombe', photographs, TNA KV 2/485;
'Fanny Karlinsky', serial 22A, TNA KV 2/2379.

39 'Sheridan', precautionary index, TNA KV
2/1033. The Embassy was at Chesham House,
Belgrave Square.

40 Ibid., Major Joseph Ball, 24 November
1925, minute 27.

41 Ibid., p. 4.

42 Stafford, *Churchill*, pp. 121–9, 155, 174.

43 Ibid., pp. 126–9.

44 'Ewer', September 1949, pp. 2–3, serial 1101,
TNA KV 2/1016.

45 'Lakey', p. 2, serial after serial 62A, TNA
KV 2/989.

46 He lived at 9, rue Duhesme (18ᵉ *arron-
dissement*) but in March 1929 moved office
from 19, rue d'Antin to 12, rue Vivienne.
'Karlinsky', 10 July 1927, police report, TNA
KV 2/2379; 'Slocombe', 31 July 1930, TNA KV
2/485.

47 'Ewer', September 1949, pp. 2–3, serial 1101,
TNA KV 2/1016.

48 Ibid., p. 4, serial 809a; 'Lakey', 4 July 1928,
serial 72A, TNA KV 2/989.

49 Ibid., pp. 6–7, serial 66a; 24 July 1928, p. 3,
serial 63A; 27 June 1928, p. 2, serial 2A; p. 2,
unnumbered serial between serials 2A and 1A;
'Ewer', September 1949, p. 4, serial 1101, TNA
KV 2/1016.

50 Ibid., pp. 10–11, serial 809a.

51 Jeffery, *MI6*, p. 231.

52 'Lakey', pp. 6–7, serial 66a; 24 July 1928,
pp. 3–4, serial 63A; 27 June 1928, p. 2, serial
2A, TNA KV 2/989; 'Ewer', September 1949,
p. 4, serial 1101, TNA KV 2/1016; Jeffery, *MI6*,
p. 225. Moon worked at Melbury Road until
1926. 'Lakey', 20 August 1928, p. 5, serial 72A,
TNA KV 2/989.

53 Diary, 1 July 1940, Holt-Wilson MSS.

54 'Lakey', 20 August 1928, pp. 4–5, serial
72A, TNA KV 2/989.

55 'Lakey', 29 April 1929, p. 2, serial 105a,
TNA KV 2/990; 'Lakey', 20 August 1928, p. 6,
serial 72A; p. 5, serial 69A, TNA KV 2/989.

56 Ibid., 20 August 1928, serial 72A; pp. 1–2,
serial 71A; p. 4, serial 69A; pp. 6–7, serial 66a;
24 July 1928, p. 3, serial 63A; 27 June 1928,
p. 2, serial 2A; 'Ewer', September 1949, p. 4,
serial 1101, TNA KV 2/1016. See also West and
Tsarev, *The Crown*, p. 11.

57 See 'Willert', Appendix.

58 'Ewer', September 1949, pp. 6–7, serial 1101,
TNA KV 2/1016; 'Lakey', 27 June 1928, p. 3,
serial 2A, TNA KV 2/989; West and Tsarev,
The Crown, pp. 11–12.

59 Ibid., p. 12.

60 Records suggest the actual birthplace was
nearby Ashton & Oldham.

61 Renowned for textiles and cotton spinning
until the 1870s, when it switched mainly to
making paper.

62 'GCCS', 1919–22', p. 7, Appendix, TNA FO
1093/104; 'Edith Lunn', serial 21A, TNA KV
2/2317; 'Edith Lunn', pp. 1–2, TNA KV 2/2318;
'Lunn', 13 August 1925, p. 2, serials 21A and
11A, TNA KV 2/2317; 'Balashikha', *Ency-*

clopædia Britannica Online, www.britannica.
com; 'Our City Balashikha', www.balashiha.ru;
1841, 1871 and 1902 England Censuses, www.
ancestry.co.uk.

63 The closest match is a "Miguel Lunn"
(born around 1852) who arrived in Mexico
on 31 August 1887. 'GCCS, 1919–22', p. 7,
Appendix, TNA FO 1093/104; 'Lunn', serial
21A, TNA KV 2/2317; 'Lunn', pp. 1–2, TNA
KV 2/2318; 'Lunn', 13 August 1925, p. 2, serials
21A and 11A, TNA KV 2/2317; 1841, 1871
and 1901 England Censuses; 'UK Incoming
Passengers Lists, 1878–1960' and 'England,
Alien Arrivals, 1810–11, 1826–1869'; 'New
Orleans, Passenger Lists, 1820–1945', www.
ancestry.co.uk. A Michael Lunn born around
1852 (likely Lunn Jr; records are unclear) died
in Halifax, Yorkshire, on 5 July 1910. Barring a
census error, this raises the possibility his wife
may have later either remarried or lived with
a common law partner since MI5 files clearly
referred to a father in summer 1925. 'England
& Wales, FreeBMD Death Index: 1837–1915',
www.ancestry.co.uk.

64 67 York Mansions, Prince of Wales Road,
Battersea, London. Curiously, Milicent Bagot
– arguably MI5's leading expert on communist
subversion and espionage well into the Cold
War – was born in 1907 at 68 York Mansions,
where she grew up. Bagot began her career
at Special Branch but moved to MI5 in 1931,
after disclosures in 1929 that Soviet intelligence had infiltrated Scotland Yard. Nigel
West, 'Bagot, Milicent Jessie Eleanor', *ODNB*.

65 'Lunn', 3 November 1925, minute 32 and
serial 21A; 25 March 1921, minute 1, TNA KV
2/2317. She died in September 1982, in Ealing,
Middlesex. 'England & Wales, Death Index:
1916–2006', www.ancestry.co.uk.

66 57 (MI5 officers possibly meant 67) York
Mansions, Prince of Wales Road, Battersea,
London.

67 'GCCS, 1919–22', p. 19, Appendix, TNA FO
1093/104; 'Lunn', 25 March 1921, serial 21A,
minute 1, and 5 August 1925, serial 3A, TNA
KV 2/2317. Permanent appointment dates did
not accurately reflect length of service.
Records suggest that as early as 29 October
1919, Helen either already worked as a 'Lady
Translator' or was at least earmarked for such
work at GCCS. Occleshaw, *Dances*, p. 94;
'GCCS, 1919–22', TNA FO 1093/104.

68 Requisitioned site near BP's entrance.
School occupants at various times included
the Commercial Section, Illicit Signals Knox
(ISK) and Illicit Signals Oliver Strachey
(ISOS). The last two attacked ENIGMA and
manually-encoded German *Abwehr* signals,
respectively. 'BP Roll of Honour Notes', p. 2,
www.bletchleypark.org.uk. See also section on
Ernst Vetterlein, Chapter 2.

69 'L: Lunn, H. C.'. 'BP Roll of Honour', p.
17, www.bletchleypark.org.uk; 'Appendix II
to H. Q. War Orders – Part II: G. C. & C. S.
Billeting List – Women, Second Wave and
Later Arrivals', 12 July 1939, TNA HW 3/1.
She died on 12 December 1948, in Chelsea,
London. 'England & Wales, Death Index:
1916–2006'. BP records also list an RAF Flying
Officer J. S. Lunn from 1942 on. He may have
been Helen's brother John Septimus Lunn,
formerly a Captain in the South Lancashire
Regiment. TNA WO 372/12/166702.

70 'Lunn', 5 August 1925, serial 3A; green
Home Office warrant sheet, August 1925; 25
November 1920 extract form, TNA KV 2/2317;
'GCCS, 1919–22', p. 7, Appendix, TNA FO
1093/104; 'Lunn', 26 January 1926, minute 43;
30 October 1925, minute 31; 4 February 1926,
minute 48, TNA KV 2/2317. Lansbury wrote:

> There is also a young woman here who
> formerly lived in Moscow. She is a
> middle-class woman and her people were
> pretty well off, but, of course, they lost
> their money in the Revolution. She has
> not, however, become bitter and soured
> towards ... the Bolsheviks. Her name
> is Lunn. I met her first in Helsingfors
> where she was working in the British
> Embassy. She ... very much wants to get
> back to Russia when peace is signed and
> would like to work for you. I believe she
> is thoroughly straightforward. She is very
> well educated and can speak two or three
> languages. ... I should say she was rather
> an exceptional person altogether.

She died in December 1990 in Northum-
berland. 'England & Wales, Death Index:
1916–2006'.

71 100 Parliament Hill Mansions, London
NW5.

72 'Lunn', 3 November 1925, minute 32; 25
March 1921, minute 1; 30 October 1925,
minute 31; August 1925, green Home Office
warrant sheet; 26 January 1926, minute 43,
serial 21A; 5 August 1925, serial 3A; 13 August
1925, p. 2, serial 11A, TNA KV 2/2317.

73 'England & Wales, Marriage Index: 1916–
2005', www.ancestry.co.uk. Records suggest
she died on 1 March 1959 in Leeds. 'England &
Wales, Death Index: 1916–2006'.

74 'Lunn', 4 February 1926, minute 48, TNA
KV 2/2317.

75 Ibid., 19 March 1926, minute 51.

76 Margaret may have possibly been a long-

term British asset seeking to reassure Moscow of its COMSEC. Content and tone of official British correspondence in the 1920s, though, make this unlikely.

77 'Andrey Rotshteyn', 7 May 1925, p. 2, serial 298A, TNA KV 2/1576.

78 The Presidium of the Comintern Executive Committee appointed Rothstein and Arthur MacManus on 10 January 1923. David Burke has stated Rothstein was from 1924 on also a member of the Comintern International Liaison Service (*The Spy*, p. 61), the OMS, though some doubt remains. Private correspondence.

79 Fanny Karlinsky, ARCOS cipher clerk and sister-in-law of George Slocombe, said she knew Edith 'through work but did not associate privately'. 'Karlinski', 10 July 1927, police report, TNA KV 2/2379.

80 'Lunn', 2 December 1925, serial 38A, TNA KV 2/2317.

81 TREST sought to infiltrate and destroy White groups abroad while SINDIKAT (in two stages) aimed to capture leading counter-revolutionary Boris Savinkov. Andrew and Gordievsky, *KGB*, pp. 68–78; Andrew and Mitrokhin, *The Mitrokhin*, pp. 43–6.

82 Private correspondence.

83 Garside, *British*, p. 5, Table 2. Boosted by the General Strike, unemployment exceeded 14% in May 1926. 'Special Report on Unemployment – Report 129', May 1926, CP 249(26), TNA CAB 24/180.

84 Aldcroft, *From*, p. 96; Dimsdale, 'British', pp. 308–9. Wage linkage to the Retail Price Index to measure cost of living was especially tricky after April 1925:

> [Wage reductions] had been greater in … depressed staple export industries than in … sheltered trades serving the home market [printing, furniture, etc.].… [Restoring] competitiveness required further wage cuts in … unsheltered industries, which workers were unwilling to accept because of previous concessions.… Between 1925 and 1929 … retail prices fell by 7%.

Ibid., p. 318.

85 29 January 1926, p. 6, conclusion 2(26), minute 6, TNA CAB 23/52.

86 Between 1917 and 1929, union membership peaked at 8.35 million in the 1919–20 boom. By 1926, the figure had dropped by 37.5% to 5.22 million. Leo Wolman, 'Union Membership in Great Britain and the United States', *National Bureau of Economic Research Bulletin* 68, 27 December 1937, 1–16: p. 2,

Table 1. CPGB membership rose from 4900 in January 1926 to 12,000 in October that year. Thorpe, 'The Membership', p. 781, Table 1.

87 See Linehan, *British*, particularly ch. 2.

88 28 April 1926, conclusion 19(26), minute 6q, TNA CAB 23/52.

89 Taylor, *English*, p. 240.

90 Clarke, *Hope*, p. 139.

91 Parliamentary Papers, *Report of the Royal Commission on the Coal Industry (1925). Vol. I*, Cmd 2600 (1926).

92 Taylor, *English*, p. 243.

93 Clarke, *Hope*, p. 140; Taylor, *English*, p. 244; Henry Pelling, *A History of British Trade Unionism* (London, 1992), pp. 173–80; Alastair Reid, *United We Stand: A History of Britain's Trade Unions* (London, 2004), chs 14–15; Patrick Renshaw, 'The Depression Years, 1918–31', in *Trade Unions in British Politics: The First 250 Years*, ed. Ben Pimlott and Chris Cook, (London, 1991), 88–108: pp. 97–100.

94 Andrew, *Her Majesty*, p. 321.

95 *Parliamentary Debates*, Commons, 3 May 1926, vol. 195, column 124.

96 4 March 1926, f. 17, op. 162, d. 3 (*osobaia papka*), l. 29, protocol 13, no. 19, RGASPI. In 1926, £1 equalled $4.86 and $1 equalled RR 1.94 so a million roubles was around £106,000. Archive of the Central Bank of the Russian Federation, http://cbr.ru. See also the January 2014 TNA release of files on Soviet funding for the 1984–85 British miners' strike.

97 Andrew, *Her Majesty*, p. 323.

98 Clarke, *Hope*, p. 141.

99 Andrew, *Her Majesty*, p. 323.

100 5 May 1926, f. 17, op. 162, d. 3 (*osobaia papka*), ll. 61–3, protocol 24, RGASPI. See also 14 May (protocol 26), 15 May (protocol 27) and 31 May (protocol 29). Private correspondence.

101 4 May 1926, f. 17, op. 162, d. 3 (*osobaia papka*), l. 57, protocol 23, RGASPI.

102 Ibid., l. 58.

103 7 May 1926, f. 17, op. 162, d. 3 (*osobaia papka*), l. 65, protocol 25, RGASPI.

104 8 May 1926, f. 495, op. 100, d. 299, ll. 15–27, RGASPI.

105 'General Strike: Daily Bulletins, 3–12 May', files 449000/59 and 449000/59A, TNA HO 144/6116.

106 Miller, *A Century*, p. 17.

107 The Government's *British Gazette* and the TUC's *British Worker* did not appear until 5 May since printers had also downed tools. 'The country first learned from the BBC that

there was a strike ... [and] that the strike was over.' Asa Briggs, *The History of Broadcasting in the United Kingdom, vol. 1: The Birth of Broadcasting* (Oxford, 1991), pp. 335–6; see pp. 329–51 on the BBC during the Strike.

108 7 May 1926, conclusion 26(26), minute 2, TNA CAB 23/52. Overall coverage was impartial but with no attempt to show 'realities of working-class life, the sense of solidarity, struggle, and occasional triumph ... the strikers felt', due to a 'certain natural bias towards ... Government'. Briggs, *The History*, pp. 339, 342. In 1926, there were nine million British households, of which a quarter had a radio; by 1939, 80% of households did. That on 1 January 1927 the BBC became a State Corporation shows its perceived worth to government in times of crisis.

109 'The BBC and the Emergency', 6 May 1926, p. 5, D.3. (Labour), vol. 23, General Strike (Sundry Correspondence: 1926), Baldwin MSS.

110 John Reith, *Into the Wind* (London, 1949), p. 109. On reading a draft speech, John Colin Davidson (Deputy Chief Civil Commissioner for Government Publicity, tasked with overseeing Churchill and the *Gazette*) urged Reith not to air the appeal 'lest this give Churchill and his followers an excuse to take over the BBC'. Briggs, *The History*, p. 346; Ball, 'Davidson', *ODNB*.

111 As the Strike loomed, executives from the main British dailies announced they could neither publish their newspapers nor combine efforts to publish one, but would help His Majesty's Stationery Office print anything. *The Morning Post* offered its printing plant and two men, later aided by three others from the *Daily Express* and seven from the *Daily Mail*. University undergraduates provided the remaining manpower. 11 May 1926, p. 5, conclusion 29(26), minute 1, TNA CAB 23/52.

112 Clarke, *Hope*, p. 140.

113 James, ed., *Winston, vol. 4*, p. 3953.

114 Ibid., pp. 3954–5.

115 *Parliamentary Debates*, Commons, 10 May 1926, vol. 195, column 712.

116 A week after the General Strike ended, Churchill estimated in Parliament the gross cost at around £22,000, with an estimated £14,000 in receipts. In any case, 'the total net cost will not exceed £10,000'. James, ed., *Winston, vol. 4*, pp. 3959–60. Circulation cited in Jeffery and Hennessy, *States*, p. 117.

117 'Summary of Events and Action taken by ... MI5', 1–18 April 1921, p. 2, TNA KV 4/246.

118 Ibid., pp. 2–4.

119 Ibid., pp. 5–6, and p. 1, Appendix I. Among MI5 staff were Lieutenant-Colonel Eric Holt-Wilson, and Captains A. Tomlins and Herbert Boddington. They managed respectively the 1921 Emergency Regulations policy, the military secret service and liaison with Special Branch.

120 'Funds Devoted to MI5 by the Foreign Office: Vernon Kell to Nevile Bland', 24 June 1926, TNA KV 4/198.

121 '1926–27 Estimated Expenditure', ibid.

122 'Summary', 3 May, Appendix 7, extracts from MI(B) diary, TNA KV 4/246; 'Metropolitan Police Constabulary Reserve: Emergency', 26 May 1926, p. 2, serial 1A, TNA MEPO 2/1838; 'General Strike, May 1926: Expenses of Special Police', 26 June 1926, TNA MEPO 5/135; 'Disturbances: General Strike, 1926 – Additional Expenditure by Metropolitan Police', 25 May 1927, TNA HO 45/13389.

123 'The Industrial Position', 7 May 1926, pp. 2–3, CP 188(26), TNA CAB 24/179. Cecil was Chancellor of the Duchy of Lancaster, a Cabinet minister without portfolio.

124 8 May 1926, conclusion 27(26) and Appendix, TNA CAB 23/52.

125 H. A. Millis, 'The British Trade Disputes and Trade Unions Act, 1927', *The Journal of Political Economy* 36:3 (1928), 305–29: p. 305.

126 Clarke, *Hope*, p. 141.

127 19 May 1926, p. 15, conclusion 33(26), minute 15, TNA CAB 23/53.

128 26 May 1926, f. 324, op. 2, d. 8, ll. 61–2, RGASPI.

129 Ibid., ll. 62–4.

130 Ibid., l. 65.

131 2 June 1926, f. 324, op. 2, d. 8, ll. 72–3, RGASPI.

132 5 July 1926, f. 324, op. 1, d. 509, ll. 40–4, RGASPI.

133 In June 1926 journalist George Armstrong wrote to Bolton Eyres-Monsell (Treasury Parliamentary Secretary and Chief Conservative Whip) on the upcoming secret USSR trip by Lord Inverforth, the noted industrialist and former Munitions Minister:

[A] result of his mission, if successful, will be the entire re-organisation of ARCOS, and its activities – if indeed ... permitted to exist – controlled by an Anglo-Russian committee presided over by Inverforth (or his British successor) who will hold the casting vote. The [Soviets] are fully aware that ARCOS offices contain a swarm of undesirables, but the task of cleaning out that Augean stable is, for political reasons, a difficult one.

9 June 1926, p. 127, F.2. (Foreign Affairs), Series "B", vol. 115, Foreign Affairs (1926–28), Baldwin MSS. Four Conservative MPs undertook a much more controversial trip from 17 April to 5 May. When Cabinet realised the trip report not only praised aspects of the Soviet system but also criticised some British policies, the four MPs came under great pressure to change their findings. The fear was the original wording might damage government when the report became public. Roger Schinness, 'An Early Pilgrimage to Soviet Russia: Four Conservative MPs Challenge Tory Party Policy', *THJ* 18:3 (1975), 623–31.

134 9 June 1926, p. 5, conclusion 37(26), minute 5, TNA CAB 23/53.

135 11 June 1926, pp. 1–10, CP 236(26), TNA CAB 24/180.

136 16 June 1926, p. 9, conclusion 39(26), minute 7, TNA CAB 23/53.

137 16 June 1926, CP 250(26) [N2811/1687/38], TNA CAB 24/180. British exports to the USSR as a percentage of total annual exports in 1926 were around 0.8% (£6 million). Cmd 3737 (1930), Table 1, pp. 34–41, Table 8.

138 16 June 1926, CP 250(26) [N2811/1687/38], TNA CAB 24/180.

139 Ibid.

140 16 June 1926, conclusion 40(26), minute 5, TNA CAB 23/53.

141 'Secret Service Blue Notes, 1913–37, Civil Estimates, Class I., 21 (Main Note A)', August 1937, p. 2, TNA T 165/445; Parliamentary Papers, 'Estimates for the Civil Services, 1922: Paper 32', Microfiche 129.146, TNA; 'Estimates for the Year ending 31 March 1926: Paper 27', Microfiche 134.183, TNA; and 'Estimates for the Year ending 31 March 1932: Paper 63', Microfiche 139.228, TNA.

142 The estimated vote in years for which information was not available (n/a) was £180,000.

143 'CID Minutes: Meeting 215', 22 July 1926, paragraph 5, TNA CAB 2/4.

144 Three concerns underpinned London's postwar dealings with Washington: the naval balance of power, the extent of US support for Irish Republicans and US policy on British war debts. Roberta Dayer has written:

the [Coalition] Government believed … cooperation with the [USA] on Far Eastern questions might, by fostering … good will, lead either to outright cancellation or, at … least … a scaling down of … war debts…. [E]vidence [suggests] … American

leaders encouraged … English counterparts to indulge … such hopes until the Washington conference of 1921–2 was concluded and the Anglo-Japanese Alliance destroyed.

'The British War Debts to the United States and the Anglo-Japanese Alliance, 1920–3', *The Pacific Historical Review* 45:4 (1976), 569–95: p. 569. See also Ira Klein, 'Whitehall, Washington, and the Anglo-Japanese Alliance, 1919–21', *The Pacific Historical Review* 41:4 (1972), 460–83.

145 26 July 1926, pp. 1–3, CP 303(26), TNA CAB 24/181.

146 'Anglo-Soviet Relations: 19 August 1926', pp. 34–5, signed "A. Gascoigne", 20 August 1926, TNA FO 371/11787 (N3832). Present at the Albert Hall were, among others: the National Citizens' Union, BEU, British Fascists, Society of Officers, ABCR and the Legion of Frontiersmen.

147 'Russia', 21 October 1926, pp. 81–3, TNA FO 371/11787 (N4881).

148 'Russia', 3 September 1926, pp. 49–52, TNA FO 371/11787 (N4251).

149 Ibid.

150 'Russia', 4 December 1926, pp. 100–1, TNA FO 371/11787 (N5425/G).

CHAPTER 7

The Raids

1 1 June 1927, p. 1, conclusion 35(27), minute 1, TNA CAB 23/55.

2 29 September 1927, p. 3, file 865/1924, Part 1, P 5149 [N 4827/309/38], © British Library Board L/P&S/10/1108.

3 'Ewer', 22 August 1930, serial 892a, TNA KV 2/1016. Harker was MI5's Assistant Director of Security ("B" Branch), responsible for investigations, defence and civil security. He joined on 20 November 1920. Andrew, *The Defence*, pp. 127–8; 'Security Intelligence Policy & Organisation: Notes by Holt-Wilson (1920 Onwards)', piece 41 ('Draft Organisation for Amalgamation of Civil with Defence Security Work'), pp. 3–4, TNA KV 4/416–/417.

4 'Soviet Espionage on Foreign Missions', 10 April 1925, p. 158, TNA FO 371/11026 (N2190).

5 17 January 1927, p. 1, conclusion 2(27), TNA CAB 23/54; 'Russia', 18 January 1927, p. 12, TNA FO 371/12589 (N229).

6 Christine White, *British and American Commercial Relations with Soviet Russia, 1918–24* (Chapel Hill, NC, 1992), pp. 9–10.

7 Sinyagina-Woodruff, 'Russia', p. 522. In the

first quarter of 1937, the trade deficit with Moscow was £3 million (2011: nearly £850 million). For all of 1960 it was £21 million (2011: over £1.2 billion); for 1977, £433 million (2011: nearly £4.5 billion); and for 1979, £480 million (2011: over £3.6 billion). 'Anglo-Soviet Trade Balance', 21 May 1938, p. 14, *The Glasgow Herald* digital archive; 'Anglo-Soviet Trade', *Parliamentary Debates*, Commons, 27 July 1961, vol. 645, columns 595–6; Lords, 6 July 1978, vol. 394, columns 1166–71; Commons, 12 May 1980, vol. 984, columns 819–31. Key imports from the USSR included energy and grain. See Starr, 'The Framework', pp. 455–6.

8 'Diplomatic Relations with the [USSR]', 24 January 1927, pp. 2–3, CP 25(27), TNA CAB 24/187.

9 'Anglo-Russian Committee Meeting', 14 June 1929, p. 9, TNA PRO 30/69/266; Cmd 3737 (1930), p. 10, Table 1, and pp. 34–41, Table 8.

10 Eric Phipps (N355), 26 January 1927, p. 76, TNA FO 371/12589 (N590G).

11 'Some Facts from the History of Eesti Pank and Estonian Finance', www.eestipank.ee; Derek H. Aldcroft, 'Currency Stabilisation in the 1920s: Success or Failure?' *Economic Issues* 7:2 (2002), 83–102: Table 2. Area countries depended 'heavily ... on the British market ... did most of their trade in sterling, fixed their own currencies ... to the pound, and held some or all ... reserves in sterling'. T. O. Lloyd, *The British Empire, 1558–1995* (Oxford, 1996), pp. 302–3.

12 (N553), 27 January 1927, pp. 82–4, TNA FO 371/12589 (N590G). Estonia, Finland, Latvia, Lithuania (1920); Afghanistan, Persia, Poland, Turkey (1921); Germany (1922); Austria, Britain, China, Denmark, France, Greece, Italy, Mexico, Norway, Sweden (1924); Japan (1925); Uruguay (1926) recognised Moscow *de jure*; and Czechoslovakia (1922); Switzerland (1927) *de facto*. 'Russia', 7 April 1927, p. 112, TNA FO 371/12601 (N1606).

13 (N553), 27 January 1927, pp. 84–6, TNA FO 371/12589 (N590G).

14 'George Clerk (N550)', 2 February 1927, p. 70, TNA FO 371/12589 (N590G).

15 Ibid., pp. 73–4.

16 'Ronald Lindsay (N551)', 3 February 1927, pp. 65–6, TNA FO 371/12589 (N590G).

17 'Ronald Graham (N552)', 4 February 1927, pp. 67–8, TNA FO 371/12589 (N590G).

18 Ibid., p. 68.

19 'William Muller', 9 February 1927, pp. 127–33, TNA FO 371/12589 (N682G).

20 MacGregor Knox, *Common Destiny: Dictatorship, Foreign Policy, and War in Fascist Italy and Nazi Germany* (Cambridge, 2000), pp. 124–5. See also John Gooch, *Mussolini and His Generals: The Armed Forces and Fascist Foreign Policy, 1922–1940* (Cambridge, 2007), pp. 11–12; Pierre Broué, *The German Revolution, 1917–1923*, Historical Materialism, ed. Ian Birchall and Brian Pearce (Leiden, 2005), p. 689.

21 Soviet–Polish non-aggression negotiations were suspended after a White exile assassinated Soviet representative Pyotr L. Voykov in Warsaw on 7 June 1927. Erickson, *The Soviet*, p. 284; private correspondence. Moscow had long viewed Paris as incidental anyway, except when it came to the Whites. France 'is important for us because: 1. it remains almost the only base for counter-revolution; 2. to stop the gold blockade'. 'Krasin to Chicherin', 29 December 1920, f. 04, op. 4, p. 19, d. 261, l. 13, AVP RF.

22 'Robert Hodgson', 23 February 1927, pp. 158–9, TNA FO 371/12589 (N791).

23 Ibid., pp. 159–61.

24 Ibid., pp. 161–2.

25 Ibid., pp. 162–3.

26 Ibid., p. 163.

27 Ibid., pp. 164–5.

28 Ibid., p. 165. Hodgson later wrote to Gregory: 'I feel strongly the necessity of showing the Soviet Government and its Party' not as 'a peril to ... Civilisation, but as ... a damned nuisance', and 'admissible to ... normal international comity only when it abandons its meddling propensities'. 2 March 1927, p. 237, F.2. (Foreign Affairs), Series "B", vol. 115, Foreign Affairs (1926–28), Baldwin MSS.

29 16 February 1927, p. 7, conclusion 10(27), minute 5, TNA CAB 23/54.

30 Soviet Representative, London–NKID, Moscow; 15 February 1927–025481; 6 February 1927, TNA HW 12/91. This source may or may not have been the same identified in London *rezidentura* files (1927) and by MI5 informant Albert Allen (1928). Still, Soviet intelligence had at least one source in the Foreign Office in the 1920s.

31 Andrew and Mitrokhin, *The Mitrokhin*, p. 48.

32 Samuelson, *Plans*, pp. 34–6.

33 'W. Turner, Acting Consul', 29 May 1927, pp. 2–4, 12, TNA FO 228/3607; *Parliamentary Debates*, Commons, 11 April 1927, vol. 205, columns 5–9; Bruce Elleman, *Moscow and the Emergence of Communist Power in China 1925–30: The Nanchang Rising and the Birth*

of the Red Army (Abingdon, 2009), p. 75. See 'Military Attaché Report 27', 3 June 1927, p. 20, TNA FO 228/3607, on documents returned to Britain.

34 Chernykh, Peking–NKID, Moscow; 25 June 1927–027201; 6 April 1927, TNA HW 12/95.

35 Despite longstanding international practices, the principle of diplomatic immunity was not formally enshrined in law until the 1961 Vienna Convention on Diplomatic Relations, complemented in 1963 by a similar treaty on consular relations. United Nations, *Treaty Series*, vol. 500, p. 95; idem, vol. 596, p. 261.

36 Soviet Representative, Peking–NKID, Moscow; 12 September 1927–028098; 7 April 1927, TNA HW 12/98. See McKnight, *Espionage*, ch. 4, and 'W. Turner, Acting Consul', 29 May 1927, pp. 2–4, TNA FO 228/3607, on Comintern activities in the Far East.

37 Chernykh, Peking–NKID, Moscow; [illegible] September 1927–027956; 8 April 1927, TNA HW 12/98.

38 See Bruce Elleman, *Diplomacy and Deception: The Secret History of Sino-Soviet Diplomatic Relations, 1917–27* (London, 1997).

39 Soviet Representative, London–NKID, Moscow; 13 May 1927–026748; 13 April 1927, TNA HW 12/94.

40 J. H. F. McEwen, 'Lindley, Sir Francis Oswald', *ODNB*.

41 'Lindley to Chamberlain', 19 April 1927, pp. 481–4, TNA FO 800/260.

42 'Foreign Secret Service Expenditure', 6 December 1929, p. 5, TNA CAB 127/367. One source puts the 1925 military intelligence budget alone at ten million gold roubles. Pierre de Villemarest and Clifford Kiracoff, *GRU: Le Plus Secret des Services Soviétiques, 1918–88* (Paris, 1988), p. 121. In 1925, £1 equalled RR 9.428 and one gold rouble was pegged at ten Treasury roubles. Ten million gold roubles was around £1,060,700 (2011: nearly £53.5 million). Archive, http://cbr.ru.

43 Bennett, *Churchill*, p. 96. French intelligence reports named three men in Berlin overseeing intelligence work against Britain, consisting of: funding Party organs; preparing and deploying agents; spreading Bolshevik literature; reviewing military and political documents arriving from Britain; and recruiting agents among British and US Consulate employees in Berlin, and former British military personnel. 'Communisme', 13 May 1927, p. 44, carton 353, dossier 1208, *Fonds Moscou*. From 1927, Bertold K. Ilk in Berlin directed INO work against Britain. Andrew and Mitrokhin, *The Mitrokhin*, p. 50;

West and Tsarev, *The Crown*, pp. 45–51, 53–60; private correspondence.

44 Bennett, *Churchill*, pp. 96–7. This is the best examination of the raid (pp. 94–106). As with the October 1924 Zinoviev Letter, government concerns up to and during the raid centred on subversion of the armed forces. The Committee of Imperial Defence and military intelligence chiefs were far more influential with Cabinet than the heads of the secret agencies. These, in fact, for a long time reported to Cabinet through the military departments. Bennett's findings on both events drew on privileged access to SIS archives.

45 Ibid., p. 98. "Y" received £50 (2011: about £2450) for the information and moved into a public house 'almost immediately' after the raid. 'Lakey', p. 10, serial 72A, TNA KV 2/989.

46 Bennett, *Churchill*, p. 98.

47 'Severance of Diplomatic Relations', TNA KV 3/34; 'City of London Police', 15 May 1927, Part I, pp. 2–3, file 509413/23, TNA HO 144/8403.

48 'ARCOS Raid', 22 May 1927, p. 2, serial 1A, TNA MEPO 38/71. Another Soviet allegation was British police searched female ARCOS employees, something cipher clerk Fanny Karlinsky denied. 'Karlinski', 10 July 1927, police report, TNA KV 2/2379.

49 Rosengolz, London–Litvinov, Moscow; 13 May 1927–026756; 13 May 1927, TNA HW 12/94; Soviet Representative, London–NKID, Moscow; 20 May 1927–026824; 16 May 1927, TNA HW 12/94:

> The rules, instructions, second copies of the re-enciphering tables, one copy of the second code WDK, and the State Bank ciphers were destroyed by us before we received your instructions of the 13th/14th. On the 15th the remainder were [sic] destroyed in accordance with your telegram. On the 16th May we are holding: 1 copy of the key of WDK; the table of check groups and code [sic]; re-enciphering tables WDK-G; 1 copy of the spare tables Western-Q; 1 copy each of INO-Q and Amerika-V; also the Central [?Committee's] cipher…. We have taken all precautions in the event of a raid on the Embassy. Yakovlev

ARCOS listed an "L. Yakovlev" as a clerk. 'Severance of Diplomatic Relations between Russia and the United Kingdom in 1927', undated, TNA KV 3/34. This cable was a reply to one from the NKID Cipher Section on whether ciphers or 'other especially secret documents' were left in the trade delegation, and if at any point such documents had been moved from the embassy to the delegation. NKID, Moscow–Soviet Representative, London; 20 May 1927–026918; 17 May 1927, TNA HW 12/94.

50 'ARCOS', TNA KV 3/15–/16 and /35; Parliamentary Papers, *Documents Illustrating the Hostile Activities of the Soviet Government and Third International against Great Britain*, Cmd 2874 (1927). Special Branch Constable Dore (or Doré), described as 'a fluent Russian scholar', is the only publicly identified member of the raiding party who knew the language. The group consisted of thirty Special Branch officers, nine interpreters and an unspecified number of City of London officers. 'ARCOS', Part 1, file 509413/14, Part 2, file 509413/45, TNA HO 144/8403.

51 Bennett, *Churchill*, p. 94; Parliamentary Papers, *Selection of Papers dealing with the Relations between His Majesty's Government and the Soviet Government*, Cmd 2895 (1927), pp. 69–72.

52 Bennett, *Churchill*, pp. 94–106; 19 May 1927, p. 3, conclusion 32(27), minute 2, TNA CAB 23/55.

53 'Lakey', 20 August 1928, p. 1, serial 72A, TNA KV 2/989.

54 The instruction was: 'Burn all political archives in your possession at once and send a signed and witnessed statement to Moscow that this has been done'. Rothstein, Moscow–Soviet Representative, London; 31 May 1927–026932; 21 May 1927, TNA HW 12/94. See 13 May 1927, f. 17, op. 162, d. 5, ll. 7–8, protocol 102, RGASPI, for the Politburo reaction. Paragraph 1 of the protocol claimed 'British Conservatives decided to follow the example of Zhang Zuolin in their attempt to break relations with the [USSR]'.

55 For a few weeks, 'all political work by Russia was at a standstill'. By July, with fears of war running high, Moscow reportedly ordered preparations for civil war in Britain should it attack the USSR. Authorities noted that by October 1927, Soviet and British agitators had resumed meetings. MI5 assessed the ARCOS Technical Inspection and Engineering Departments as the most active in espionage. 'Revolutionary Propaganda in the UK', 'Activities of Russian Soviet Institutions in the [UK] since the ARCOS Raid', pp. 1–3, and Appendix, p. 2, TNA KV 3/328.

56 Andrew, *The Defence*, p. 155.

57 Tiltman, 'Experiences', p. 7; Andrew, *Her Majesty*, p. 332; see third and fourth meetings, 24 and 30 June 1927, 'Secret Service Committee, 1927', TNA FO 1093/71, and

'Secret Service Committee, 1927: Miscellaneous', TNA FO 1093/73. The Committee did not reach a satisfactory solution until 1931. See Bennett, *Churchill*, pp. 131–4.

58 Bennett, *Churchill*, p. 95.

59 Ibid., pp. 104–6.

60 'ARCOS Raid: Eustace Percy to Austen Chamberlain', 19 May 1927, pp. 556–7, TNA FO 800/260. Lord Percy, an MP and President of the Board of Education, felt a 'break of diplomatic relations, as distinguished from the dismissal of individual diplomats' was really 'an introduction to a state of war, and I have the profoundest misgivings as to the desirability of any such action on our side in present circumstances'.

61 23 May 1927, p. 2, conclusion 33(27), TNA CAB 23/55.

62 After the Second World War, Britain was again the first Western nation to sign a trade agreement with the USSR, on 24 May 1959. Starr, 'The Framework', pp. 453–6.

63 In the literal sense, MI5 alone needed an additional £500 (2011: nearly £164,000). 'Funds Devoted to [MI5] by the Foreign Office, vol. 1: Vernon Kell to Nevile Bland', June 1927, p. 38, TNA KV 4/198.

64 24 May 1927, p. 5, conclusion 33(27), TNA CAB 23/55.

65 25 May 1927, p. 1, conclusion 34(27), minute 1, TNA CAB 23/55.

66 'Conversation between Parenty and Childs', 25 May 1927, pp. 464–6, carton 229, dossier 1548, *Fonds Moscou*. Parenty reported to General Ambroise Després, the French Military Attaché in London, who in turn informed French military intelligence (*Deuxième*, or 2ᵉ, *Bureau*) and the War Minister (former Prime Minister Paul Painlevé).

67 'Military Attaché (London) to War Minister', 26 May 1927, pp. 462–3, carton 229, dossier 1548, *Fonds Moscou*.

68 Ibid., p. 463.

69 'Communist Activities', TNA HO 144/22388, especially files 505663/7, 505663/8, 505663/10, 505663/20, 505663/41 and 505663/79.

70 'Communist Activities', 7 May 1927, p. 3, file 505663/10, TNA HO 144/22388.

71 Ibid., 10 May 1927, p. 3.

72 Ibid., 9 May 1927, p. 3.

73 Ibid., 10 May 1927, p. 3.

74 Ibid., 20 May 1927, pp. 1–3.

75 Ibid., 30 May 1927, p. 1.

76 Ross McKibbin, *The Ideologies of Class:*

Social Relations in Britain, 1880–1950 (Oxford, 1994), ch. 1.

77 15 September 1927, f. 04, op. 4, p. 38, d. 535, l. 58, Appendix 1 of item 2 in Politburo protocol 124, AVP RF: 'We should constantly use the British Press that is benevolent to us.'

78 See 'Saklatvala', TNA KV 2/611–/615.

79 'British Secretariat Meeting: Minutes', 27 June 1927, f. 495, op. 72, d. 23, l. 152, RGASPI.

80 See 'Petrovsky', Appendix.

81 Undated, f. 495, op. 72, d. 23, l. 59, RGASPI.

82 In November 1927, Cabinet approved the sale to Moscow of fifty Gloster Gorcock fighters, an experimental model rejected by the Air Ministry. With limited range and of a defensive nature, these machines posed no threat to the Empire but never actually went into production. 2 November 1927, p. 6, conclusion 53(27), minute 6, TNA CAB 23/55. The following month, however, Cabinet refused to approve the sale of a civilian version of an RAF bomber. 21 December 1927, p. 13, conclusion 63(27), minute 13, TNA CAB 23/55. A year later, Cabinet approved a Soviet order for a hundred Vickers Vixen aircraft, valued at £500,000 (2011: £26 million): 'In favour of granting permission was the magnitude of the order' and the benefit of keeping 1100 men employed for a year. 23 January 1929, p. 3, conclusion 2(29), minute 3, TNA CAB 23/60. The aircraft never saw Soviet service.

83 The fullest examination of the Macartney affair is Bennett, *Churchill*, pp. 107–16. See also 'Macartney', TNA KV 2/647–/648 and 'Hansen', TNA KV 2/649–/656.

84 Wilfred Macartney, *Walls Have Mouths: A Record of Ten Years' Penal Servitude* (London, 1936), pp. 10–11. See 'Macartney', Appendix.

85 In January 1933 the novelist Mackenzie pleaded guilty to violating the Official Secrets Act (OSA) and was fined £200 (2011: £11,600) plus costs for revealing details of intelligence work in his 1932 book *Greek Memories*. Upset, Mackenzie satirised British intelligence in his 1933 novel *Water on the Brain*. Formerly Chief Intelligence Officer for the Middle East and Macartney's superior, Mackenzie wrote a provocative foreword and chapter introductions for *Walls Have Mouths*, blank spaces showing where lawyers again censored him. 'Official Secrets Divulged', 13 January 1933, p. 9, and 'Novelist's War Experiences: Withdrawn Book', 17 November 1932, p. 9, *The Times* digital archive; Andrew, *Her Majesty*, p. 351. See Jeffery, *MI6*, pp. 126–9, on the Aegean Intelligence Service.

86 Bennett, *Churchill*, p. 107.

87 Ibid.

88 Ibid., pp. 108–9. Monkland was 'a British Russian' who never fully explained how he and Macartney met. 'Macartney', pink race form and serial 1054a, TNA KV 2/648.

89 Bennett, *Churchill*, p. 109; 'Hansen', 5 December 1927, serial 38B, TNA KV 2/649.

90 Bennett, *Churchill*, p. 110.

91 Ibid., p. 111.

92 Ibid.

93 Macartney obtained a false passport, likely with help from someone at the Passport Office since on inspection, the file folder labelled with Macartney's alias ("W. Frank Hudson") turned out to be empty. 'Macartney', serial 441a, TNA KV 2/647; see also serial 422a on an MI5 interview of Office personnel concerning the empty folder.

94 Bennett, *Churchill*, pp. 111–15. The jury reached a verdict in fifteen minutes. 'Russia', 19 January 1928, p. 213, TNA FO 371/13316 (N308).

95 'Hansen', Kell letters, 30 December 1931, serial 508a; 11 January 1932, serial 523a, TNA KV 2/655.

96 'Lakey', p. 2, serial 112a, TNA KV 2/990.

97 See 'Reckitt', Appendix.

98 'Ewer', September 1949, pp. 7–8, serial 1101, TNA KV 2/1016.

99 A CPGB offshoot created in 1924 comprising militant members from trade unions. The NMM sought to reduce union bureaucracy and remove those deemed to collaborate with owners, ultimately giving workers control of industry. 'NMM', www.marxists.org.

100 'Lakey', 7 September 1928, p. 1, serial 77a; p. 4, serial 84 [illegible], TNA KV 2/989. See also 'Albert Inkpin', TNA KV 2/1532–/1537.

101 See 'Holmes', Appendix.

102 Rose Cohen frequently travelled to Moscow in the 1920s. 'Ewer', Part II (Cohen), pp. 3–4, TNA KV 2/1016.

103 'Communist Biographies: Arnot, Robin Page', www.grahamstevenson.me.uk; 'Labour Research Department', TNA KV 5/75–/79.

104 'Lakey', 7 September 1928, pp. 1–2, serial 77a, TNA KV 2/989.

105 'Ewer', September 1949, pp. 7–8, serial 1101, TNA KV 2/1016.

106 'Lakey', 20 August 1928, p. 11, serial 72A, TNA KV 2/989.

107 'Ewer', September 1949, pp. 7–8, serial 1101, TNA KV 2/1016.

108 Likely Peter, since the delegation listed

his brother Anton as a cipher clerk (though Anton worked in intelligence assisting Jacob Kirchenstein, the IV Directorate "illegal" *rezident*). Private correspondence.

109 An MI5 man answered the notice under the alias "D. A. Reinmann". 'Federated Press of America, Supplementary', serial 12a, TNA KV 2/1432; 'Lakey', p. 2, serial 71A, TNA KV 2/989. See also Andrew, *The Defence*, p. 152.

110 'Ewer', 30 January 1950, pp. 3–5, serial 1105a, TNA KV 2/1017.

111 John Ottaway first approached Allen on 25 June 1928 in Wallington, Surrey. Posing as a member of the Anti-Socialist Union, he asked if Allen would consider selling information for money. He did, for £75 (2011: £3700) a meeting. 'Federated Press of America, Supplementary', p. 6, TNA KV 2/1432; 'Lakey', p.1, serial 2A, TNA KV 2/989; Andrew, *The Defence*, pp. 128, 157. Callaghan and Morgan misrepresented Allen's involvement with British authorities and the timing of his decision to sell them information. 'The Open Conspiracy', p. 558. In his original piece 'Moscow's Interwar', Madeira clearly stated Allen only told MI5 about his time with the Federated Press months after he left it in November 1927. By mid-1928, MI5 wanted to learn about the ring's work but mainly before the November 1924 *Daily Herald* advert that first put authorities on to Ewer's group (p. 918). Callaghan and Morgan offer no evidence that Albert Allen 'resumed his work for Scotland Yard from at least 1924' (p. 558).

112 In his MI5 debriefings, Allen stated that from the time he joined the Federated Press in 1919, Ewer seemed to be regularly receiving information from Scotland Yard. MI5's John Ottaway reported the Special Branch sources gave Ewer secrets 'over a period of some eight years'. 'Lakey', p. 3, serial 84 [illegible]; p. 3, serial 69A, TNA KV 2/989.

113 See Bennett, *Churchill*, pp. 127–34, and Curry, *The Security*, pp. 5–7, 98–107, on the 1931 reforms.

114 'Ewer', September 1949, p. 5, serial 1101, TNA KV 2/1016; 'Lakey', p. 4, serial 84 [illegible], TNA KV 2/989; idem, p. 2, serial 109a, TNA KV 2/990. The Federated Press, which gave up its Outer Temple, Strand offices on 31 March 1928, always referred to van Ginhoven as "Fletcher". Idem, p. 2, serial 104a, TNA KV 2/990. See 'van Ginhoven', Appendix, and 'Charles Jane', TNA KV 2/1398.

115 'Lakey', pp. 6–7, serial 66a; 24 July 1928, p. 3, serial 63A; 27 June 1928, p. 2, serial 2A, TNA KV 2/989; 'Ewer', September 1949, p. 4, serial 1101, TNA KV 2/1016; Andrew, *The*

Defence, p. 157. £20 in 1919 was the 2011 equivalent of £750; in 1929, £20 was worth £995 in 2011 values.

116 Andrew, *The Defence*, p. 157.

117 'Ewer', September 1949, p. 5, serial 1101, TNA KV 2/1016; 'Lakey', p. 4, serial 1A, TNA KV 2/989.

118 'Ewer', September 1949, p. 2, serial 867a, TNA KV 2/1016. Ewer was unaware of postal intercept warrants on him because MI5 did not tell Special Branch. 'Lakey', 20 August 1928, MI5 comment, serial 72A, TNA KV 2/989.

119 Idem, 12 April 1929, p. 2, serial 104a, TNA KV 2/990.

120 Ibid., p. 3, serial 104a; p. 1, serial 105a.

121 Ibid.

122 West and Tsarev, *The Crown*, p. 12. The Government document was 'Communist Papers', Cmd 2682 (1926).

123 Wilfred Macartney claimed he (Macartney) had, from a Special Branch clerk. Bennett, *Churchill*, pp. 112–13.

124 Private correspondence.

125 'Lakey', 15 October 1928, p. 2, serial 83a; p. 3, serial 84 [illegible]; p. 3, serial 77a, TNA KV 2/989.

126 'Dale', 3 May 1929, newspaper clipping, pp. 1–2, TNA KV 2/997.

127 'Ewer', p. 3, serial 1105a, TNA KV 2/1017.

128 Idem, September 1949, p. 6, serial 1101, TNA KV 2/1016.

129 Ibid., p. 8. Controversy again broke out in mid-1928 over Moscow's alleged routing of around £28,000 (2011: nearly £1.5 million) for the CPGB through Soviet banks between July 1927 and April 1928. Parliamentary Papers, *Russian Banks and Communist Funds*, Cmd 3125 (1928). This period largely coincided with the post-ARCOS disruption of Federated Press operations, which included laundering and distributing Soviet funds to the British Left.

130 'Ewer', September 1949, p. 6, serial 1101, TNA KV 2/1016; 'Dale', 30 June 1932, TNA KV 2/998; 'Jane', 27 February 1930, serial 32A, extract from PF 147/37 Ginhoven, 2 June 1933; 30 January 1950, serial 1105a, TNA KV 2/1398; 'Lakey', 23 February 1929, serial 93a [? illegible]; 7 August 1934, serial 125a, TNA KV 2/990. In July 1929, Eva Reckitt complained of postal delays, suggesting she was still under surveillance. Her day post was on time but her night post was often seven hours late. 'Eva Reckitt', between serials 152a and 151a, TNA KV 2/1370.

131 Speaking of the unidentified officer (thought to have around four years' service), van Ginhoven said: 'I've left a good chap behind'. 'Lakey', pp. 1–2, 4, serial 109a, TNA KV 2/990.

132 On 21 May 1929, a debriefing MI5 officer (either Ottaway or Harker) wrote: 'There is little doubt in my mind that someone, either here or in Russia, has some hold over Hayes'. 'Lakey', p. 3, serial 109a, TNA KV 2/990.

133 'Ewer', September 1949, p. 6, serial 1101, TNA KV 2/1016; 'Dale', 30 June 1932, TNA KV 2/998; 'Jane', 27 February 1930, serial 32A, extract from PF 147/37 Ginhoven, 2 June 1933; 30 January 1950, serial 1105a, TNA KV 2/1398; 'Lakey', 7 August 1934, serial 125a; p. 2, serial 109a, TNA KV 2/990.

134 In December 1924, the NKID reproached Khristian Rakovsky for his agents' high cost and relative ineffectiveness compared to the Comintern's. That body, said NKID, was often better and more rapidly informed. 22 January 1925, p. 285, carton 229, dossier 1548, *Fonds Moscou*.

135 Markus Wolf, in charge of communist East German foreign intelligence from 1952 to 1986, was devastatingly successful in recruiting clerical staff at the heart of West German government. Markus Wolf with Anne McElvoy, *Man Without a Face: The Autobiography of Communism's Greatest Spymaster* (London, 1997).

136 See 'Grenfell', Appendix.

137 'Harold Grenfell', serial 25a, TNA KV 2/507.

138 Following the May 1927 Anglo-Soviet breach, Special Branch reported an increase in communists looking to join chemical and industrial unions, whose members worked in 'reservoirs of war products'. 'The Activities of Russian Soviet Organisations in Great Britain and Ireland since the ARCOS Raid: May 1927–April 1929', 17 April 1929, p. 5, TNA KV 3/328. The increase likely reflected rising Soviet fears of war with the West during the 1926–27 winter, magnified by the intelligence and diplomatic setbacks of the first half of 1927.

139 Private correspondence.

140 Ibid.

141 'Dale', serial 122B, TNA KV 2/998. A month after van Ginhoven and Jane were fired, Colonel John Carter of Special Branch wrote Kell that Hayes was still 'engaged in political espionage'. 'Dale', 6 June 1929, serial 122a.

142 See Zuckerman, *The Tsarist*, chs 4–6, and Leonard, *Secret*, pp. 1–5, on Tsarist foreign intelligence.

143 Nick Barratt, 'Casebook: Spies Like Us', *Your Family History* 1:1 (2010); Andrew and Mitrokhin, *The Mitrokhin*, pp. 58–64.

144 'ROSTA', p. 6, serial 23A, TNA KV 2/1109; 'Ewer', September 1949, serial 755a (red sheet), TNA KV 2/1016; 'Harold Philby', serials 12a and 9a, TNA KV 2/1118. Ewer was not the only recipient. In 1932, the Foreign Office learned St John Philby 'had stolen secret documents ... as Chief British Representative in Transjordan and given them to King Ibn Saud'. Authorities never properly investigated the evidence. Andrew, 'F. H. Hinsley', pp. 30–1.

145 Kenneth Rose, *Elusive Rothschild: The Life of Victor, Third Baron* (London, 2003), p. 51.

146 'Lakey', 12 April 1929, pp. 1–2, serial 104a, TNA KV 2/990.

147 SIS assessed bilateral ties five months before they resumed: 'In their endeavour to obtain recognition, the Soviets consider as their trump card the baiting of the British industrials and business men by promises of large orders'. 'Revolutionary Propaganda in the UK', 21 May 1929, serial 127b, TNA KV 3/328. The Bolsheviks' approach was the same leading up to the 1921 trade agreement and the 1924 *de jure* recognition by Britain.

148 'The organisation of William Ewer which was closed down after the dismissal of Ginhoven and Jane from [Special Branch] was, we think, purely an INO affair'. 'Organisation & Activities of the Russian Intelligence Services (1930–45)', 'MI5 memorandum to SIS', 12 December 1934, p. 1, serial 46a, TNA KV 3/141.

149 'Ewer', September 1949, p. 12, serial 809a, TNA KV 2/1016.

Conclusion

1 Ed., *KGB*, p. xxv.

2 President John F. Kennedy, inaugural address, 20 January 1961: 'Now the trumpet summons us again ... to bear the burden of a long twilight struggle ... against ... tyranny, poverty, disease, and war itself'. www.jfklibrary.org.

3 President George H. W. Bush, address on the Persian Gulf crisis, 11 September 1990: 'Out of these troubled times ... a new world order ... can emerge ... freer from the threat of terror, stronger in the pursuit of justice, and more secure in the quest for peace'. www.bushlibrary.tamu.edu.

4 Andrew, *The Defence*, p. 780.

5 Francis Fukuyama, *Our Posthuman Future* (London, 2002).

6 Dr James Carafano of The Heritage Foundation coined the term on 8 September 2003. President George W. Bush later made the expression the preferred way to describe America's foreign interventions after 11 September 2001: 'Our own generation is in a long war against a determined enemy – a war that will be fought by Presidents of both parties.' 'State of the Union Address', 31 January 2006. www.georgewbush-whitehouse.archives.gov.

7 Robert Kagan, *The Return of History and the End of Dreams* (London, 2008).

8 In 1913, Britain accounted for about 13.5% of global manufacturing output (a 40% decline since 1880). In 1970, the figure was just over 4% and by 2010, not even 2.5%. Torbjørn L. Knutsen, *The Rise and Fall of World Orders* (Manchester, 1999), p. 105, Table 12; Adam Mellows-Facer and Lucinda Maer, 'International Comparisons of Manufacturing Output' (Standard Note SN/EP/5809, House of Commons Library, London, 2012), pp. 1, 4, Table 2.

9 In a 1982 Commons debate, former Foreign Office Minister Edward Rowlands (Labour) argued the Falklands invasion could not have surprised Prime Minister Margaret Thatcher since Britain had 'for many years' been decrypting Argentine communications. *Parliamentary Debates*, Commons, 3 April 1982, vol. 21, column 650. In a radio interview in 2004, nine months after resigning Cabinet over the Iraq invasion, former International Development Secretary Clare Short (Labour) claimed GCHQ eavesdropped on United Nations communications ahead of critical Security Council resolution votes. Idem, Commons, 26 February 2004, vol. 418, columns 427–40; Lords, 26 February 2004, vol. 658, columns 338–51. Neither politician faced charges for violating the OSA.

10 August 1920, September 1920 (twice), May 1923 (twice) and May 1927 (twice).

11 Andrew, *Her Majesty*, pp. 60–1.

12 For instance, using right-wing groups as proxies to disrupt legitimate political gatherings, physically assault socialist and communist activists, and break into leftist premises either to burgle or destroy them.

Appendix: Biographies

America, Federated Press of (1919–1956)

In October 1919, thirty-two union news editors, shocked that 'the US press carried so little news' of ongoing steel strikes, conceived this 'cooperative, non-profit news service solely to cover union activities'. Established on 25 November 'as a news agency, initially a twice-weekly mail service for affiliated journals, [informing them] of labour and left-wing news', by January 1921 the Federated Press served '110 member newspapers, including 22 dailies (many foreign language newspapers), representing a broad spectrum ... including socialist, communist, and trade union opinion'. Detroit journalist and 'self-styled anti-capitalist' Carl Haessler, a Rhodes Scholar at Oxford from 1911 to 1914, ran the Federated Press from 1922. Not long after it was created in 1919, it 'began to toe the Socialist and later the Communist Party line, [employing] many Communist editors and correspondents'.[1]

Baldwin, Stanley (1867–1947)

Educated at Harrow and Trinity, Cambridge, Baldwin came from a prominent industrialist family in the Midlands where he first made a name for himself before entering politics in 1908. In 1917, he joined the Coalition Government as Treasury Financial Secretary. Two years later, he gave away a fifth of his wealth after appealing anonymously in *The Times* to wealthy Britons for help in reducing the war debt. In 1921, Baldwin became Board of Trade President but was a leading rebel at the October 1922 Carlton Club meeting that pushed David Lloyd George out. In Andrew Bonar Law's Cabinet, Baldwin served as Chancellor of the Exchequer until assuming the premiership in May 1923.[2]

Berens, Yevgeny A. (1876–1928)

In May 1923, Karl Radek mentioned having met a 'Berens', 'Mikhalsky' and the 'head of intelligence' (presumably the *rezident*) in Berlin. Admiral Yevgeny A. Berens (sometimes written Behrens) was the Imperial officer who defected to the Bolsheviks in 1917 and eventually commanded their navy. His brother,

1 Jon Bekken, 'Federated Press: An Independent Labour News Service', quoted in Callaghan and Morgan, 'The Open', pp. 558–9; 'Federated's End', 24 December 1956, *Time* digital archive; 'Federated Press Records', http://microformguides.gale.com; 'The Carl Haessler Collection', www.reuther.wayne.edu.
2 'Stanley Baldwin', www.number10.gov.uk.

Admiral Mikhail A. Berens, commanded White naval forces (including in exile) until 1924. Yevgeny Berens was Naval Attaché in Germany before the First World War; from 1920, he served as naval expert with Bolshevik delegations at various conferences (including Genoa and Lausanne).

In 1924–25, he was Naval Attaché in Britain. Avgust Guralsky, the Comintern OMS representative in Berlin from 1922 to December 1923, may have used the "Alexander Mikhalsky" alias and had every chance of meeting Radek at the time of Curzon's note. Artur K. Stashevsky (alias "Verkhovsky") was the first *rezident* (1921–24) of the amalgamated INO-RU station in Berlin, operating under cover of Secretary of the trade delegation.[3]

Carter, John (1882–1944)

Educated at Wellington College public school and then Sandhurst, Carter received his commission in 1901 to serve in India. In 1914, he joined MI5 and three years later spent eighteen months in Italy working with Sir Samuel Hoare. By early 1919, Carter was one of several people considered to head the Home Office Directorate of Intelligence. He lost out to Basil Thomson but joined him in mid-1919 as Assistant Director. Carter took on partial responsibility for Special Branch following Thomson's dismissal in late 1921 (see Chapter 4), and was promoted Deputy Assistant Commissioner under Thomson's replacement, Wyndham Childs. In 1928, Carter took over all Special Branch work. In November 1938, he was promoted Assistant Commissioner but resigned in September 1940.[4]

Chamberlain, Austen (1863–1937)

One biographer wrote:

> [I]n a broader context the Chamberlain who emerged from the war was a subtly different figure from the politician of 1914. He was more conscious than most of his contemporaries that the political environment of Edwardian England could never be recreated. Gone was the somewhat reluctant radical of the pre-war era, replaced by someone

---

[3] Erickson, The *Soviet*, p. 255; private correspondence; 27 February 1923, f. 359, op. 1, d. 5, l. 37, and 11 February 1923, f. 359, op. 1, d. 5, l. 51, RGASPI.

[4] 'Assistant Commissioner of Police', 'Deaths: Carter', 'Obituary–Personal Tributes: Lieutenant-Colonel John Carter': 9 September 1940, p. 9; 17 July 1944, pp. 1, 6, *The Times* digital archive; 'John Carter', 17 January 1902, 5 October 1909, 1 November 1938, www.gazettes-online.co.uk; Part I (Political and Other Correspondence), file 2, pieces 38 (5 March 1919) and 39 (10 March 1919), Templewood MSS; 'Secret Service Committee: Ninth Meeting', 31 March 1925, p. 8, TNA FO 1093/68; Bennett, *Churchill*, pp. 128, 339 n. 42.

who was determined to preserve the existing fabric of ordered society against what he saw as the new threat of Socialism, and ready to abandon some of his earlier beliefs to secure this greater end.[5]

Childs, Wyndham (1876–1946)

A lawyer by training, Major-General Sir Wyndham Childs became Assistant Commissioner for Special Branch on 5 December 1921, taking over the Criminal Investigation Department on 1 April 1922. Childs was retired in October 1928 for being considered 'somewhat imbalanced'. Sir Trevor Bigham succeeded him.[6]

Ewer, William (1885–1976)

Ewer was born on 22 October 1885 in London to silk merchant William Thomas Ewer and his wife Julia Stone. He attended Merchant Taylors' public school and Trinity, Cambridge, attaining Firsts in the Maths (1907) and History (1908) Triposes [examinations].[7]

Grenfell, Harold (1870–1948)

In 1904–05, Grenfell served in the Admiralty Intelligence Department. From 1907 to 1908, he was Governor of Hong Kong Naval Prison. In 1910–11, Grenfell worked in the Admiralty War Staff, followed by an appointment as Naval Attaché to the British Embassy in St Petersburg/Petrograd between April 1912 and November 1917. He then headed the Naval Mission to Finland between December 1918 and June 1919, retiring from the RN in 1920 as a Captain.[8]

Hayes, John (1887–1941)

Born into a police family in Wolverhampton (his brother Charles served as a Metropolitan Police constable and their father became a Chief Inspector), Hayes joined the Metropolitan Police in 1909 and became a sergeant within four years. After the 1919 strike and the end of NUPPO, he went into politics and became a Labour MP for Liverpool in 1923. Hayes held several posts, including Parliamentary Private Secretary to the Pensions Minister and Whip

5   D. Dutton, 'Chamberlain, Sir (Joseph) Austen', *ODNB*.
6   'Obituary: Sir Wyndham Childs', 30 November 1946, p. 7; 'Sir Wyndham Childs: Resignation of Police Post', 8 October 1928, p. 13; 'CID again under One Chief', 11 March 1922, p. 7; and 10 December 1934, p. 11: *The Times* digital archive; Bennett, *Churchill*, p. 339 n. 42; O'Halpin, 'Sir', p. 925.
7   Beavan, 'Ewer', *ODNB*.
8   US Congress, *National Republic of Georgia: Hearings before the Committee on Foreign Affairs, House of Representatives, 69th Congress, First Session, on H. J. Res. 195*, 1–2 April 1926, p. 15.

roles from 1925. The latter included Vice-Chamberlain of the Royal Household from his re-election in 1929 until 1931.[9]

Holmes, Walter (1892–1973)

A CPGB founding member, Holmes left the *Daily Herald* in 1928 to replace William Paul as Editor of the *Sunday Worker*. Upon the 1930 launch of the *Daily Worker* (the CPGB organ that in 1966 became the *Morning Star*), Holmes became its roving correspondent. In this capacity, he visited the USSR and Manchuria.[10]

Holt-Wilson, Eric (1875–1950)

Captain (later Sir) Eric Holt-Wilson joined MI5 on 20 December 1912 and was its founding Deputy Director for nine years, until choosing to retire with Director Sir Vernon Kell in June 1940. Described as 'a man of almost genius for intricate organisation', Holt-Wilson largely ran MI5 for nearly three decades.[11]

Kirchenstein, Jacob (1891–1937)

Also known as "Johnny Walker", he was actually Rudolf M. Kirchenstein, a Latvian born on 7 May 1891. He joined the Red Army in 1918, and finished *Registrupr* courses in 1920 and IV Directorate officer courses in 1930. In 1935, Kirchenstein graduated from the Frunze Military Academy. He operated in Britain between 1924 and 1927, overseeing a clandestine courier service for 'secret correspondence, documents, and funds dealing with both political and espionage matters'. In 1929, as "Frank Kleges", he operated in New York but left for Paris in early 1930. From July that year until 1931, Kirchenstein served as "illegal" *rezident* for Britain, codenamed KNYAZ (Prince).[12]

Klyshko, Nikolai K. (1880–1937)

Born in Vilnius, Lithuania, where he studied at the *lycée moderne*, Klyshko was an engineer by training. The Tsarist regime exiled this member of the Russian Social-Democratic Labour Party, first to Vologda and later to London

---

[9]   Sam Davies, 'Hayes, John Henry', *ODNB*; 'Dale', 1 June 1929, serial 122b, TNA KV 2/998; Reynolds and Judge, *The Night*, p. 109.

[10] 'Holmes, Walter', www.grahamstevenson.me.uk; 'Ewer', Part II (Holmes), p. 7, TNA KV 2/1016. See also 'Walter Holmes', TNA KV 2/1000–/1002.

[11] 'Security Intelligence Policy & Organisation: Notes by Holt-Wilson (1920 Onwards)', piece 41 ('Draft Organisation for Amalgamation of Civil with Defence Security Work'), p. 4, TNA KV 4/416–/417; diary, p. 9, Holt-Wilson MSS; PP/MCR/120, pp. 136–7, Kell MSS.

[12] Private correspondence; Curry, *The Security*, p. 96; Bennett, *Churchill*, pp. 94–106; Volodarsky, *Stalin*, ch. 7; Lurie and Kochik, *GRU*, p. 158. See also 'Jacob Kirchenstein', TNA KV 2/1391–/1392, TNA KV 3/17. For MI5's view, see 'Kirchenstein', biographical sheet, 'Report on the Russian Trade Delegation', 7 December 1925, pp. 1–2, after serial 92a; and pp. 70–3, after serial 98a, TNA KV 2/1391.

from 1907 to 1918. There, he belonged to the local Party committee headed by Maxim Litvinov, a future Foreign Commissar. Britain deported both men in August 1918 and the Bolsheviks appointed Klyshko Assistant Director of the State Publishing Department.

In January 1920, he became Secretary of the peace delegation to Estonia, and in May 1920 was appointed Secretary of the Russian trade delegation in London. He was Political Head of Mission but facilitated Bolshevik intelligence operations. French records suggest his duties included monitoring Leonid Krasin and other delegation members.[13]

Lloyd George, David (1863–1945)

Irish Republican leader Michael Collins once wrote of Lloyd George: 'Born poor is therefore shrewd. Was lawyer therefore crafty.' Raised in a Welsh nonconformist household by his shoe-cobbler (and Baptist minister) uncle, Lloyd George left school at fourteen to study Law. Growing up he was 'acutely aware ... of the class system which helped to shape his local society'. He was heavily involved in local politics in the 1880s, becoming a County Councillor in 1889 and, aged twenty-seven, a Liberal MP in 1890 for Caernarvon Boroughs.[14]

Long, Walter (1854–1924)

Commenting on the postwar coalition, Long wrote: 'The Government spokesman talked about a land fit for heroes to live in', only to be 'answered by ... opponents that a man certainly required to be a hero to live in it'. Fellow Conservative Lord Balcarres said of Long: 'he is the most paradoxical and ill-balanced person I know'. One day 'he delivers a speech of sturdy and uncompromising Toryism ... the next ... he larks off ... to deliver ... an address in which he tries to go one better than the Socialists'.[15]

Macartney, Wilfred (1899–1970)

In 1914, aged sixteen, Macartney enlisted in the 3rd Gordons and in 1915 obtained a commission from the 7th Royal Scots Regiment. In 1916, he served as Assistant Chief Censor in Egypt, later moving to a special organisation under Compton Mackenzie. Late that year, Macartney re-joined his regiment,

---

13 'Note sur la Composition de la Mission Commerciale Soviétique et de la Délégation des Cooperatives Russes "Arcos" à Londres' [Note on the Composition of the Soviet Commercial Mission and the ARCOS Delegation in London], 13 June 1922 [or 1923; illegible], carton 353, dossier 1208, p. 437, *Fonds Moscou*; 'Who's Who in Soviet Russia', 9 April 1923, p. 81, TNA FO 371/9365 (N3179). See also 'Klyshko', TNA KV 2/1410–/1416.

14 Quoted in Toye, *Lloyd George*, p. 222; Grigg, 'Lloyd', p. 20; Morgan, *David*, pp. 10–11, 13.

15 Petrie, *Walter*, p. 216; quoted in Jackson, 'Long, Walter Hume', *ODNB*.

was wounded in France, taken prisoner and escaped to Holland. Transferred to Constantinople as a staff officer because of his languages, he left the military in June 1919.[16]

Makgill, George (1868–1926)

A Scottish aristocrat, Makgill was better known before 1914 as a writer and novelist. He became prominent in wartime anti-socialist circles as Secretary of the Anti-German Union and the British Empire Union. Makgill was a close friend of Vernon Kell (MI5) and Desmond Morton (SIS), and had extraordinary access to political and intelligence circles. Makgill and Morton, for instance, belonged to the same London club.[17]

Morton, Desmond (1891–1971)

He performed important duties within SIS in the period this book covers. As Head of Production, Morton oversaw operations overseas and, informally, domestically, through a network of agents known as the "Casuals" (originally from Makgill's Industrial Intelligence Bureau). Morton was also active in Section V (counter-intelligence and counter-communism) and Section VI (economic/industrial intelligence).[18]

Münzenberg, Willi (1889–1940)

A German communist, by 1921 he was already a pioneer setting up front organisations for the Comintern OMS. 'His magic word was solidarity – at the beginning solidarity with the starving Russians, then with the proletariat of the whole world.' By replacing 'solidarity for charity Münzenberg found the key to the heart of many intellectuals.'[19]

Norwood, Melita (1912–2005)

In 1933, while helping build up Soviet science and technology intelligence networks in Britain, Andrew Rothstein met Melita Sirnis (later Norwood), a secretary working at the British Non-Ferrous Metals Research Association. Rothstein helped vet her for recruitment, which happened in 1934. From 1945, when the Association became involved in the British atomic weapons

---

[16] 'Macartney', p. 508, TNA KV 2/647.

[17] 'Obituary: Sir George Makgill', 20 October 1926, *The Times* digital archive; Bennett, *Churchill*, p. 71; Hope, 'Surveillance', p. 655; Bennett, *A most*, p. 38; see also Hughes, *Spies*, ch. 3.

[18] Bennett, *Churchill*, pp. 40, 91–2, 117, 36, 136–43.

[19] Babette Gross, *Willi Münzenberg: A Political Biography* (East Lansing, MI, 1974), p. 217. See also 'Wilhelm Munzenberg', TNA KV 2/772–/774, and Sean McMeekin, *The Red Millionaire: A Political Biography of Willy Münzenberg, 1917–1940* (New Haven, CT, 2004), pp. 106, 148, 172, 275.

programme, Norwood supplied intelligence Moscow described as 'of great interest and a valuable contribution'. She retired in 1972, 'on present evidence ... the longest-serving of all Soviet spies in Britain'.[20]

Petrovsky, David (1886–1937)

In 1930, Petrovsky reportedly married Rose Cohen (of the Federated Press) in Moscow. Accused of being a Trotskyite, he was executed in 1937; the Soviets charged Cohen with espionage and executed her too later that year.[21]

Raskolnikov, Fyodor F. (1892–1939)

In 1910, Raskolnikov joined the Bolsheviks as a student in St Petersburg, helping run the newspapers *Zvezda* (Star) and *Pravda* (Truth). From 1914 to 1917, he was a naval cadet, graduating as a Sub-Lieutenant; after the October Revolution, he became Deputy Commissar for Naval Affairs. In December 1918, the RN boarded his warship in the Baltic and took him into custody. British authorities transferred Raskolnikov to Brixton prison until his May 1919 exchange for British servicemen the Bolsheviks had captured. In 1920, he received command of the Baltic Sea Naval Force but was dismissed the following year. Raskolnikov then served as Plenipotentiary Representative to Afghanistan; upon leaving in 1923 (or 1924; see Chapter 5), he was prominent in Soviet literary circles before returning to diplomacy in 1930.[22]

Reade, Arthur (1902–1971)

A barrister and journalist, Reade was an Eton- and Oxford-educated homosexual who joined the CPGB soon after its creation. His Trotskyite views led to his departure and he later ran unsuccessfully for Parliament as a Labour candidate. Early in the Second World War, Reade repeatedly sought to join British intelligence but was blocked by MI5. He eventually joined the Special Operations Executive and the Intelligence Corps, though MI5 again blocked his subsequent move to join the Political Warfare Executive. Near war's end, Reade went on to the Judge Advocate General's Department.[23]

---

20 Burke, *The Spy*, pp. 66, 137; Andrew and Mitrokhin, *The Mitrokhin*, pp. 168, 152; private correspondence.

21 'David Petrovskiy', serial 21a, TNA KV 2/1433; 'Cohen', serial 147B, TNA KV 2/1397; Branko Lazitch and Milorad M. Drachkovitch, *Biographical Dictionary of the Comintern* (Stanford, CA, 1986), p. 361.

22 Mawdsley, 'The Baltic', pp. 513–15; Basov, ed., *Boevoi*, Appendix 2; F. F. Raskolnikov, *Tales of Sub-Lieutenant Ilyin*, translator and ed. Brian Pearce (London, 1982), biographical note, ch. 4.

23 John McIlroy, 'The Young Manhood of Arthur Reade', in *Party People, Communist Lives*, ed. John McIlroy, Kevin Morgan and Alan Campbell (London, 2001), 51–77; 'Reade, Arthur', www.grahamstevenson.me.uk. See also 'Arthur Reade', TNA KV 2/1540–/1541.

Reckitt, Eva (1890–1976)

An heiress and key CPGB financier, Reckitt opened Collets Bookshop in London in 1934.[24]

Rothstein, Andrew F. (1898–1994) (and Theodore A.)

A central figure in British Communism, Andrew Rothstein was born in London on 26 September 1898 to Jewish Russian political immigrants. In many ways, his life mirrored his father's own. Theodore Rothstein (1871–1953) fled Imperial Russia for political reasons and settled in Britain in 1890. Andrew and his father opposed the First World War, though Theodore worked for the Foreign and War Offices as a Russian translator. Andrew studied History at Oxford, served in the British Army from 1917 to 1919 and was a founding CPGB member.

Between 1920 and 1945, he worked as a press officer with the first Bolshevik Mission in Britain, and then as a correspondent for the Telegraph Agency of the Soviet Union (TASS), mainly in London and Geneva. Andrew Rothstein became an authority on Soviet history, economy, institutions and foreign relations. He was President of the Foreign Press Association from 1943 to 1950. From 1946, he also lectured at the University of London School of Slavonic and East European Studies but was dismissed in 1950. He died on 22 September 1994.[25]

Savinsky, Aleksandr A. (1868/72/79–1934)

American cryptographer William Friedman once described 'Savinsky, formerly Russian minister to Stockholm' as having greatly improved the Foreign Ministry cryptographic service and kept 'close watch' over it at beginning of the twentieth century. Savinsky himself had the title of 'Chief of the Russian Cabinet of Foreign Affairs' (essentially the Foreign Minister's Chief of Staff) from 1901 to 1910. However, Dr Tatiana A. Soboleva – the semi-official historian of Russian cryptology and the country's leading expert on the subject – does not mention him, only V. V. Sabanin (see Chapter 2). While Savinsky may have had regular dealings with and even nominal responsibility for the

---

[24] 'Ewer', Part II (Reckitt), p. 5, TNA KV 2/1016. See also 'Reckitt', TNA KV 2/1369–/1375; Matthew Worley, 'Reckitt, Eva Collet', *ODNB*.

[25] 'Rothstein, Andrew (and Theodore)', www.grahamstevenson.me.uk. See also Burke, 'Theodore'; 'Andrey and Teodor Rotshteyn', TNA KV 2/1575–/1584. Unusually, Basil Thomson regarded the decision to allow Theodore – once termed 'the secret agent and alter ego of Litvinoff in England' – to remain at the War Office 'a wise one'. 'Rotshteyn', 19 November 1918, p. 3, TNA KV 2/1575; and 17 May 1922, minute 258, TNA KV 2/1576. Andrew Rothstein was so important to both London and Moscow that one of his MI5 files (TNA KV 2/1578) is the only one containing GCCS intercepts (about him) out of hundreds of such personal files examined.

Ministry's cipher bureau, his rank, roles and travels between 1901 and 1910 (including to Britain in August 1909 with Tsar Nicholas II) made it unlikely he oversaw day-to-day cryptographic work.[26]

Trebitsch-Lincoln, Ignatius (1879–1943)

A Hungarian Jew, Trebitsch was a petty criminal in his youth. In 1897, he escaped to Britain, then Canada, then again Britain, ending up an Anglican curate in 1903. He became a Liberal MP in January 1910 but was out of office by November. In 1914, Britain rejected his offers to spy so he turned to Germany. Trebitsch escaped to the USA but it extradited him to Britain in 1915 on fraud charges, where he was imprisoned until 1919. By spring 1920, he was criss-crossing Eastern Europe, conspiring with European and Russian counter-revolutionaries plotting to overthrow Bolshevism known as the White International. Entrusted with its archives, Trebitsch sold them to various intelligence services. Charged with but acquitted of treason in Austria, he was deported in 1922 and headed to China.[27]

Tyrrell, William (1866–1947)

Educated at Bonn and Oxford Universities, the Roman Catholic Tyrrell suspected Bolshevik expansionism and was 'instrumental in protecting this unconventional organisation [the Foreign Office Political Intelligence Department] and in seeing that its product reached the highest level'. After the First World War, Tyrrell chaired an inter-departmental committee on the Red subversive threat. Though he shared Lord Curzon's anti-Bolshevism, Tyrrell – the Foreign Secretary's personal adviser – disliked his leadership style and Francophobia.[28]

[26] NSA Center for Cryptologic History, 'Lecture V', *The Friedman Legacy: A Tribute to William and Elizabeth Friedman*, Sources in Cryptologic History 3, pp. 121–2, www.nsa.gov; Hammant, 'Russian ... I: Some', p. 238; 'Aleksandr Savinskiy', www.rusdiplomats.narod.ru; Soboleva, *Tainopis* (1994) and *Istoriia* (2002); idem, *Istoriia*, p. 277; A. Savinsky, *Recollections of a Russian Diplomat* (London, 1927), title page, pp. 11–178.

[27] Bernard Wasserstein, *The Secret Lives of Trebitsch Lincoln* (New Haven, CT, 1988), chs 1–15; idem, 'On the Trail of Trebitsch Lincoln, Triple Agent', 8 May 1988, *New York Times* digital archive; 'Lincoln & Son', 15 March 1926, 'Fight to the Finish?', 25 December 1939, 'Again, Chao Kung', 1 January 1940, 'Obituary: Ignatius Trebitsch-Lincoln', 18 October 1943, *Time* digital archive; Matthew Parris, 'He was an Author, Fraudster, MP, Fantasist, Charmer ... but He did not Go to Belmarsh', 28 July 2001, *The Spectator* digital archive; Eliezer Segal, 'The Treacherous Mr. Trebisch', *The Jewish Free Press* (Calgary, 2004), p. 10.

[28] Erik Goldstein, 'Tyrrell, William George, Baron Tyrrell', *ODNB*; John Fisher, 'The Interdepartmental Committee on Eastern Unrest and British Responses to Bolshevik and other Intrigues against the Empire during the 1920s', *Journal of Asian History* 34:1 (2000): 1–34, pp. 2–3; Neilson and Otte, *The Permanent*, ch. 10.

van Ginhoven, Hubert (1882–unknown)

Born in 1882 in Alfen on Rhine, Zuid-Holland Province, van Ginhoven became a naturalised Briton in 1905. A gardener by trade, he wanted to join the London Metropolitan Police and despite irregularities with his application (including not fulfilling the residence requirements), authorities granted him citizenship.[29]

Vetterlein, Pavel K. (1882–1961)

Pavel Karlovich's son (see below) believed his father joined the Air Ministry's 'new cryptographic unit' in the 'late 1930s' thanks to a recommendation from his brother Ernst. This was most likely AI4 (the SIGINT branch the Ministry's Air Intelligence Directorate set up in 1934), although the son may have been thinking of GCCS Air Section instead, set up in 1936. During the Second World War, Vetterlein was a Foreign Office civilian at Bletchley Park (and likely Berkeley Street, London; see Chapter 2) from 1939 to 1945. He was in the first wave of male GCCS staff billeted at BP, appearing in Air Section lists of 2 December 1940. For his wartime work, Vetterlein was made Officer, Order of the British Empire (OBE) in June 1950.

Records put him at various BP locations during the war. One was the Mansion itself (offices of senior staff but also occupied by certain sections before Huts and Blocks appeared). Another location was Hut 10, which housed the Air (spring 1940–August 1942), SIS Codes (August 1942–March 1945) and the Japanese Forces (JAFO, March–August 1945) Sections. Vetterlein also worked in Block A, occupied by the Naval (August 1942 to 1945) and Air (August 1942–June 1943; top floor only) Sections. He likely also worked in the Diplomatic Section.

At GCCS, first in the Military and then the Air Sections, Vetterlein reportedly dealt with Soviet traffic Estonia intercepted until 1940 (though this was not only of a military nature). Tallinn intercepted such traffic as early as the 1918–20 Independence War. The bilateral exchange with Britain dated back to 1933: in return for radio interception and direction-finding equipment, Tallinn gave London copies of all intercepts and any cryptographic solutions.[30]

---

[29] 'van Ginhoven, Huibert Cornelis', 'Certificate of Naturalisation', TNA HO 334/40/15207; 'Hubert van Ginhoven', minutes and naturalisation memorial, TNA HO 144/780/125718.

[30] 'Supplement to the *London Gazette*', 8 June 1950, p. 2787, www.london-gazette.co.uk; private correspondence; 'Fetterlein, Paul', 'BP Roll of Honour', 'BP Roll of Honour Notes', pp. 2–5, www.bletchleypark.org.uk; 'Vetterlein', IWM, sections 1–4, 6; McKay, 'British', pp. 6–7; Juurvee, 'Estonian', p. 124; 'Appendix I to H. Q. War Orders–Part II: G. C. & C. S. Billeting List–Men, First Wave', 12 July 1939, 'Test of War Site Communications: List of Personnel in Sections', 27 July 1939, TNA HW 3/1; 'GC and CS Personnel', 2 December 1940, TNA

Vetterlein, Pavel P. (1907–2004)

Before his time at BP, Vetterlein had been in touch with GCCS through his uncle Ernst though 'nothing definite' ever came of it. Called up in 1942 for military service, Vetterlein volunteered for the RAF where he was a clerk. He was sent to Gloucestershire but underwent no aptitude testing and was again classified as a clerk. His uncle urged Vetterlein to have a language assessment before his BP posting but that was the extent of the testing: 'I think they assumed that my uncle was good at it, my father was good at it, that I would be good at it but I wasn't, really.' Vetterlein went on to BP – he initially assumed because of his languages – serving there from 1942 to 1945. Records put him at various BP locations during the war.

He started at Hut 8 (the section processing and decrypting German naval ENIGMA traffic from February 1940) but 'moved two or three times depending on requirements.' He also worked in Block A (see 'Vetterlein, P. K.' above) and Block F. This facility housed: the Air Section (September 1943 to 1945; see Chapter 2); the Newmanry (developing and applying machine cryptanalytical methods; November 1943 to 1945); the Testery (using hand decryption to break the German High Command TUNNY traffic; September 1943 to 1945); and the Military Section (May 1944 to 1945). In the Air Section, Vetterlein worked on the German target.

Late in the war, he spent around two months at a BP station 'in southern England' that intercepted Soviet messages. There, Vetterlein worked against a secure Baudot radio-teletype (i.e. enciphered telephone/telegraph devices or secure teletypes) the Russians called BODO. The station may have been Ivy Farm, Kent, which had since mid-1942 attacked German teleprinter traffic (see Chapter 2). After the war, Vetterlein transferred to the Russian Section.

Following demobilisation, he moved from BP to Eastcote, in north-west London. Intercepting Soviet messages meant 'the intelligence angle had to be explored at more or less the same time as breaking of the cipher.' Vetterlein stayed at Eastcote until GCHQ moved to Cheltenham in 1952–53. His work there depended on which section/department he was in, and he moved as needed. Some of his early work looked at Soviet help to developing countries and involved writing intelligence reports on the subject after reading Russian messages.[31]

HW 14/9; West, *Historical*, p. 13. The first GCCS move to BP was on 18 September 1938. TNA HW 3/33.

[31] 'Fetterlein, P. V.', 'BP Roll of Honour', and 'BP Roll of Honour Notes', pp. 2–5, www.bletchleypark.org.uk; 'Vetterlein', IWM, sections 1–6; David M. Glantz and Harold S. Orenstein, translators and ed., *Belorussia 1944: The Soviet General Staff Study* (Abingdon,

Voigt, Frederick (1892–1957)

In 1919, Voigt joined the *Manchester Guardian*, going to Berlin in 1920 to assist J. G. Hamilton. Voigt replaced him that year as Berlin correspondent, a role he performed until 1933. Excellent contacts in the German Left enabled him to make sensational revelations in December 1926 about secret defence and security collaboration between Germany and the USSR.[32]

Wilkinson, John (unknown)

William Ewer and other Federated Press members knew Wilkinson well, a scientist who worked on chemical warfare at Woolwich Arsenal between 1914 and 1939. In 1925, his name appeared in a card index belonging to a CPGB member. By 1950, as MI5 wound down the Federated Press investigation, Wilkinson was a Senior Scientist at the Ministry of Supply. If not an outright communist himself, Wilkinson probably supported the cause.[33]

Willert, Arthur (1882–1973)

Chief US correspondent for *The Times* from 1910 to 1920, Willert also served as Secretary of the British War Mission in Washington in 1917–18. From 1921 to 1934 he was a member of several British delegations to international conferences, including as Head of the Foreign Office News Department between 1931 and 1934 (see also Chapter 6).[34]

Wise, Edward (1885–1933)

In 1918, Wise was Second Secretary in the Food Ministry. In 1929, he was elected Labour MP for Leicester East.[35] Anthony Struthers is currently writing a biography provisionally entitled *Edward Frank Wise 1885–1933: A Memoir*.

2004), p. 33; David Glantz, *Barbarossa Derailed: The Battle for Smolensk, 10 July–10 September 1941, vol. 1* (Solihull, 2010), p. 325; idem with Jonathan M. House, *To the Gates of Stalingrad: Soviet-German Combat Operations, April–August 1942* (Lawrence, KS, 2009), p. 97.

[32] Markus Huttner, 'Voigt, Frederick Augustus', *ODNB*.

[33] 'Ewer', September 1949, p. 3, serial 755a, TNA KV 2/1016; 'Ewer', serial 1109, minutes, TNA KV 2/1017.

[34] 'Pullen's Lane, The Croft (Sir Arthur Willert, KBE)', www.headington.org.uk; 'Willert, Sir Arthur', www.library.yale.edu. If he 'leaked information, it was likely ... deliberate'. Private correspondence. Probable though this was (given Willert's experience as a publicist and propagandist) the reported existence of a Bolshevik agent close to him remains the unresolved matter. For his views on propaganda and Russia, see Arthur Willert, 'Publicity and Propaganda in International Affairs', *International Affairs (Royal Institute of International Affairs 1931–1939)* 17:6 (1938), 809–26; idem, *Aspects of British Foreign Policy* (New Haven, CT, 1928), ch. 6.

[35] Noel Thompson, 'Wise, Edward Frank', *ODNB*.

Woollcombe, Malcolm (1880/92–1946)

Having joined SIS from the War Office in February 1921, Woollcombe headed the Political Section within six months, doing so until retiring in 1944.[36]

[36] Bennett, *Churchill*, p. 56; Jeffery, *MI6*, p. 167.

Bibliography

Primary Sources

France
Army Historical Service, Vincennes
Fonds Moscou   Deuxième (2ᵉ) Bureau Records, Army General Staff

Russian Federation
Foreign Policy Archive of the Russian Federation (AVP RF), Moscow
Fond 04   Georgi Chicherin Collection
Fond 028   Khristian Rakovsky Collection
Fond 69   "Zinoviev Letter" Collection

Russian State Archive of Socio-Political History (RGASPI), Moscow
Fond 17   Protocols, Politburo of the Central Committee, Communist Party of
               the Soviet Union
Fond 324   Grigori Zinoviev Collection
Fond 325   Leon Trotsky Collection
Fond 359   Maxim Litvinov Collection
Fond 495   Presidium, Executive Committee, Comintern

United Kingdom
British Library (Asia, Pacific & Africa Collections), London
L/P&S/10   Government of India: Political & Secret Subjects
L/P&S/11   Government of India: Political & Secret Files
MSS Eur F 112 Curzon (George Nathaniel) MSS

Caird Archive & Library, National Maritime Museum, Greenwich
Lloyd's List – Overseas Shipping Intelligence (Microfilm)
Lloyd's Register
Hugh Sinclair MSS

Cambridge University Library
Stanley Baldwin MSS
Samuel Hoare (Templewood) MSS
Eric Holt-Wilson MSS

Churchill Archives Centre, Churchill College, Cambridge
Winston Churchill (Chartwell) MSS
Adeline Hankey MSS
Maurice Hankey MSS
James Headlam-Morley MSS

Imperial War Museum, London
Vernon Kell MSS
Pavel Vetterlein Memoirs

Parliamentary Archives, London
John Colin Davidson MSS
David Lloyd George MSS

Special Collections Centre, University of Aberdeen
Malcolm Hay MSS

The National Archives, Kew

ADM 116	Admiralty: Record Office, Cases
ADM 137	Admiralty: Historical Section, Records Used for Official History, First World War
ADM 223	Admiralty: Naval Intelligence Division & Operational Intelligence Centre: Intelligence Reports & Papers
CAB 1	Cabinet Office: Miscellaneous Records
CAB 2	Committee of Imperial Defence Minutes
CAB 21	Cabinet Office & Predecessors: Registered Files, 1916–65
CAB 23	Cabinet Minutes & Conclusions
CAB 24	Cabinet Memoranda
CAB 27	War Cabinet & Cabinet: Miscellaneous Committees, Records (General Series)
CAB 63	War Cabinet & Cabinet Office: Lord Hankey, Papers (Microfilm)
CAB 127	Cabinet Office: Private Collections of Ministers' & Officials' Papers
FO 228	Foreign Office: Consulates & Legation, China: General Correspondence, Series I
FO 366	Foreign Office: Chief Clerk's Department & Successors
FO 371	Foreign Office: Political Departments, General Correspondence from 1906
FO 800	Foreign Office: Private Offices: Various Ministers' & Officials' Papers
FO 1093	Foreign Office: Permanent Under-Secretary's Department: Miscellaneous Unregistered Papers
HD 3	Foreign Office: Permanent Under-Secretary's Department: Correspondence & Papers (Records Created or Inherited by the Secret Intelligence Service)
HO 45	Home Office: Registered Papers
HO 144	Home Office: Registered Papers, Supplementary
HO 334	Home Office: Immigration & Nationality Department: Duplicate Certificates of Naturalisation, Declarations of British Nationality & Declarations of Alienage
House of Commons	Parliamentary Papers: 1922 (Microfiche)
House of Commons	Parliamentary Papers: 1926 (Microfiche)
House of Commons	Parliamentary Papers: 1932 (Microfiche)
HW 3	Government Code & Cipher School & Predecessors: Personal Papers, Unofficial Histories, Foreign Office X Files, & Miscellaneous Records, 1914–45
HW 12	Government Code & Cipher School: Diplomatic Section &

	Predecessors: Decrypts of Intercepted Diplomatic Communications (BJ Series)
HW 14	Government Code & Cipher School: Directorate: Second World War Policy Papers
KV 1	MI5: First World War Historical Reports & Other Papers
KV 2	MI5: Personal (PF Series) Files
KV 3	MI5: Subject (SF Series) Files
KV 4	MI5: Policy (Pol F Series) Files
KV 5	MI5: Organisation (OF Series) Files
MEPO 2	Office of the Commissioner: Correspondence & Papers
MEPO 5	Office of the Receiver: Correspondence & Papers
MEPO 38	Metropolitan Police: Special Branch: Registered Files
PRO 30/69	Ramsay MacDonald & Predecessors & Successors: Papers
T 165	Treasury: Blue Notes
WO 32	War Office & Successors: Registered Files (General Series)
WO 372	War Office: Service Medal & Award Rolls Index, First World War

Wren Library, Trinity College, Cambridge
Maurice Dobb MSS
Edwin Montagu MSS

Wiltshire & Swindon Archives, Chippenham
Walter Long MSS

Printed Primary Sources

United Kingdom. Parliament. *Report from the Secret Committee on the Post Office.* No. 582. 1844.

United Kingdom. Parliament. *Annual Statement of Trade of the UK with Foreign Countries and British Possessions. 1917 Compared with the Four Preceding Years.* Cmd 9127. 1918.

United Kingdom. Parliament. *Annual Statement of Trade of the UK with Foreign Countries and British Possessions. 1917 Compared with the Four Preceding Years.* Cmd 9136. 1918.

United Kingdom. Parliament. *Annual Statement of Trade of the UK with Foreign Countries and British Possessions. 1920 Compared with the Years 1913 and 1919.* Cmd 1503. 1920.

United Kingdom. Parliament. *Annual Statement of Trade of the UK with Foreign Countries and British Possessions. 1920 Compared with the Years 1913 and 1919.* Cmd 1506. 1920.

United Kingdom. Parliament. *Parliamentary Debates.* Commons, vol. 138 (1921).

United Kingdom. Parliament. *Correspondence with the Russian Soviet Government respecting the Imprisonment of Mrs. Stan Harding in Russia.* Cmd 1602. 1922.

United Kingdom. Parliament. *Correspondence between His Majesty's Government and the Soviet Government respecting the Murder of Mr. C. F. Davison in January 1920.* Cmd 1846. 1923.

United Kingdom. Parliament. *Correspondence between His Majesty's Government and the Soviet Government respecting the Relations between the Two Governments.* Cmd 1869. 1923.

United Kingdom. Parliament. *Reply of Soviet Government to His Majesty's Government respecting the Relations between the Two Governments.* Cmd 1874. 1923.

United Kingdom. Parliament. *Further Correspondence between His Majesty's Government and the Soviet Government respecting the Relations between the Two Governments.* Cmd 1890. 1923.

United Kingdom. Parliament. *Parliamentary Debates.* Commons, vol. 163 (1923).

United Kingdom. Parliament. *General Treaty between Great Britain and Northern Ireland and the Union of Soviet Socialist Republics.* Cmd 2260. 1924.

United Kingdom. Parliament. *Treaty of Commerce and Navigation between Great Britain and Northern Ireland and the Union of Soviet Socialist Republics.* Cmd 2261. 1924.

United Kingdom. Parliament. *Report of the Committee Appointed to Enquire into the Claims of the Men Dismissed from the Police and Prison Services on Account of the Strike of 1919.* Cmd 2297. 1924.

United Kingdom. Parliament. *Parliamentary Debates.* Lords, vol. 60 (1924).

United Kingdom. Parliament. *Report of the Royal Commission on the Coal Industry (1925). Vol. I.* Cmd 2600. 1926.

United Kingdom. Parliament. *Communist Papers. Documents Selected from those Obtained on the Arrest of the Communist Leaders on 14 and 21 October, 1925.* Cmd 2682. 1926.

United Kingdom. Parliament. *Parliamentary Debates.* Commons, vol. 195 (1926).

United Kingdom. Parliament. *Parliamentary Debates.* Commons, vol. 198 (1926).

United Kingdom. Parliament. *Documents Illustrating the Hostile Activities of the Soviet Government and Third International against Great Britain.* Cmd 2874. 1927.

United Kingdom. Parliament. *Selection of Papers dealing with the Relations between His Majesty's Government and the Soviet Government.* Cmd 2895. 1927.

United Kingdom. Parliament. *Parliamentary Debates.* Commons, vol. 205 (1927).

United Kingdom. Parliament. *Russian Banks and Communist Funds.* Cmd 3125. 1928.

United Kingdom. Parliament. *Statistical Tables relating to British Foreign Trade and Industry (1924–30). Part I – General Tables.* Cmd 3737. 1930.

United Kingdom. Parliament. *Parliamentary Debates.* Commons, vol. 252 (1931).

United Kingdom. Parliament. *Parliamentary Debates.* Commons, vol. 645 (1961).

United Kingdom. Parliament. *Parliamentary Debates.* Lords, vol. 357 (1975).

United Kingdom. Parliament. *Parliamentary Debates.* Lords, vol. 394 (1978).

United Kingdom. Parliament. *Parliamentary Debates.* Commons, vol. 984 (1980).

United Kingdom. Parliament. *Parliamentary Debates.* Commons, vol. 21 (1982).

United Kingdom. Parliament. *Intelligence and Security Committee Annual Report, 1997–98.* Cmd 4073. 1998.

United Kingdom. Parliament. *Parliamentary Debates.* Commons, vol. 418 (2004).

United Kingdom. Parliament. *Parliamentary Debates.* Lords, vol. 658 (2004).

United Kingdom. Parliament. *Intelligence and Security Committee Annual Report, 2004–05.* Cmd 6510. 2005.

United Kingdom. Parliament. *Intelligence and Security Committee Annual Report, 2010–11.* Cmd 8114. 2011.

United Kingdom. Parliament. *Intelligence and Security Committee Annual Report, 2011–12.* Cmd 8403. 2012.

United States of America. Congress. House of Representatives. *National Republic of Georgia: Hearings before the Committee on Foreign Affairs, 69th Congress, First Session, on H. J. Res. 195.* 1926.

Secondary Sources

Articles and Chapters

Aldcroft, Derek H. 'Currency Stabilisation in the 1920s: Success or Failure?', *Economic Issues* 7:2 (2002): 83–102.

Alexander, Martin. 'Did the *Deuxième Bureau* Work? The Role of Intelligence in French Defence Policy and Strategy, 1919–39', *INS* 6:2 (1991): 293–333.

Allen, V. L. 'The National Union of Police and Prison Officers', *The Economic History Review* 11:1 (1958–59): 133–43.

Anderson, Julie. 'The *Chekist* Takeover of the Russian State', *IJIC* 19:2 (2006): 237–88.

——. 'The Humint Offensive from Putin's *Chekist* State', *IJIC* 20:2 (2007): 258–316.

Andrew, Christopher. 'British Intelligence and the Breach with Russia in 1927', *THJ* 25:4 (1982): 957–64.

——. 'F. H. Hinsley and the Cambridge Moles: Two Patterns of Intelligence Recruitment.' In *Diplomacy and Intelligence during the Second World War: Essays in Honour of F. H. Hinsley*, edited by Richard Langhorne, 22–40. Cambridge: 1985.

——. 'The British Secret Service and Anglo-Soviet Relations in the 1920s – Part I: From the Trade Negotiations to the Zinoviev Letter', *THJ* 20:3 (1977): 673–706.

——, and Keith Neilson. 'Tsarist Codebreakers and British Codes', *INS* 1:1 (1986): 6–12.

——, and Oleg Gordievsky. 'Ciphers and Counter-Intelligence', Special Issue, *INS* 7:1 (1992): 99–121.

Austin, Brian. 'EWB Gill–Taking Wireless to War', *The Journal of the Royal Signals Institution* 29:2 (2010): 48–56.

Ball, Alan. 'Lenin and the Question of Private Trade in Soviet Russia', *Slavic Review* 43:3 (1984): 399–412.

Ball, Stuart. 'Churchill and the Conservative Party', *Transactions of the Royal Historical Society*, Sixth Series, 11 (2001): 307–30.

Bandera, V. N. 'The New Economic Policy (NEP) as an Economic System', *The Journal of Political Economy* 71:3 (1963): 265–79.

Barratt, Nick. 'Casebook: Spies Like Us', *Your Family History* 1:1 (2010).

Barros, Andrew. 'Le 2ᵉ Bureau dans les Années Vingt: L'Impact de la Guerre Totale sur les Renseignements.' In *Naissance et Evolution du Renseignement dans l'Espace Européen (1870–1940): Entre Démocratie et Totalitarisme: Quatorze Etudes de Cas*, edited by Fréderic Guelton and Abdil Bicer, 189–210. Paris: 2006.

Bean, Ron. 'Police Unrest, Unionisation, and the 1919 Strike in Liverpool', *Journal of Contemporary History* 15:4 (1980): 633–53.

Bennett, G. H. 'Lloyd George, Curzon, and the Control of British Foreign Policy, 1919–22', *Australian Journal of Politics & History* 45:4 (1999): 467–82.

Bennett, Gill. 'The Secret Service Committee, 1919–31', *The Records of the Permanent Under-Secretary's Department Liaison between the Foreign Office and British Secret Intelligence, 1873–1939*. London: 2005.

Borman, Arkady. 'Harold Williams: A British Journalist and Linguist in Russia', *Russian Review* 28:3 (1969): 327–37.

Bowden, Tom. 'Guarding the State: The Police Response to Crisis Politics in Europe', *British Journal of Law and Society* 5:1 (1978): 69–88.

Bremmer, Ian, and Samuel Charap. 'The *Siloviki* in Putin's Russia: Who They Are and What They Want', *The Washington Quarterly* 30:1 (2007): 83–92.

Broadberry, Stephen, and Peter Howlett. 'The United Kingdom during World War I:

Business as Usual?' In *The Economics of World War I*, edited by Stephen Broadberry and Mark Harrison, 206–34. Cambridge: 2005.

Burrows, Simon. 'Police and Political Pamphleteering in Pre-Revolutionary France.' In *Print and Power in France and England, 1500–1800*, edited by David Adams and Adrian Armstrong, 99–112. Aldershot: 2006.

Callaghan, John, and Kevin Morgan. 'The Open Conspiracy of the Communist Party and the Case of William Ewer, Communist and Anti-Communist', *THJ* 49:2 (2006): 549–64.

Callaghan, John, and Mark Phythian. 'State Surveillance of the CPGB Leadership: 1920s–1950s', *Labour History Review* 69:1 (2004): 19–33.

Carley, Michael Jabara. 'Episodes from the Early Cold War: Franco-Soviet Relations, 1917–27', *Europe-Asia Studies* 52:7 (2000): 1275–305.

Champion, Brian. 'Spies (Look) Like Us: The Early Use of Business and Civilian Covers in Covert Operations', *IJIC* 21:3 (2008): 530–64.

Close, David. 'Conservatives and the Coalition after the First World War', *The Journal of Modern History* 45:2 (1973): 240–60.

Cooper Jr, John. 'Command of Gold Reversed: American Loans to Britain, 1915–17', *The Pacific Historical Review* 45:2 (1976): 209–30.

Cowan, Michael J. 'The Breaking of Floradora: The German Diplomatic Cipher', *The Cryptogram* 77:6 (2011): 4–5.

Daniels, Robert. 'The Kronstadt Revolt of 1921: A Study in the Dynamics of Revolution', *American Slavic and East European Review* 10:4 (1951): 241–54.

Davies, Norman. 'Lloyd George and Poland, 1919–20', *Journal of Contemporary History* 6:3 (1971): 132–54.

Davis, Richard. '"We are All Americans Now!" Anglo-American Marriages in the Later Nineteenth Century', *Proceedings of the American Philosophical Society* 135:2 (1991): 140–99.

Dawson, Michael. 'Money and the Real Impact of the Fourth Reform Act', *THJ* 35:2 (1992), 369–81.

Dayer, Roberta. 'The British War Debts to the United States and the Anglo-Japanese Alliance, 1920–3', *The Pacific Historical Review* 45:4 (1976): 569–95.

Debo, Richard. 'Litvinov and Kamenev – Ambassadors Extraordinary: The Problem of Soviet Representation Abroad', *Slavic Review* 34:3 (1975): 463–82.

——. 'Lloyd George and the Copenhagen Conference of 1919–20: The Initiation of Anglo-Soviet Negotiations', *THJ* 24:2 (1981): 429–41.

Denniston, A. G. 'The Government Code and Cypher School between the Wars', *INS* 1:1 (1986): 48–70.

Denniston, Robin. 'Diplomatic Eavesdropping, 1922–44: A New Source Discovered', *INS* 10:3 (1995): 423–48.

Dimsdale, N. H. 'British Monetary Policy and the Exchange Rate, 1920–38', *Oxford Economic Paper* 33 (1981): 306–49. Supplement: The Money Supply and the Exchange Rate.

Drummond, I. 'Britain and the World Economy, 1900–45.' In *The Economic History of Britain since 1700, vol. 2: 1860 to the 1970s*, edited by Roderick Floud and Donald McCloskey, 286–307. Cambridge: 1981.

Ehrman, John. 'What Are We Talking About When We Talk About Counterintelligence?', *Studies in Intelligence* 53:2 (2009): 5–20.

Eichengreen, Barry. 'The British Economy between the Wars.' In *The Cambridge*

Economic History of Modern Britain, vol. 2: Economic Maturity, 1860–1939, edited by Roderick Floud and Paul Johnson, 314–43. Cambridge: 2004.

Emsley, Clive. 'Police Forces and Public Order in England and France during the Interwar Years'. In *Policing Western Europe: Politics, Professionalism, and Public Order, 1850–1940*, edited by Clive Emsley and Barbara Weinberger, 159–86. Contributions in Criminology and Penology. New York: 1991.

Englander, David. 'Troops & Trade Unions, 1919', *History Today* 37 (March 1987): 8–13.

——, and James Osborne. 'Jack, Tommy, and Henry Dubb: The Armed Forces and the Working Class', *THJ* 21:3 (1978): 593–621.

Fair, John. 'The Anglo-Irish Treaty of 1921: Unionist Aspects of the Peace', *The Journal of British Studies* 12:1 (1972): 132–49.

Falkus, M. E. 'Russia and the International Wheat Trade, 1861–1914', *Economica*, New Series, 33:132 (1966): 416–29.

Ferris, John R. '"Far Too Dangerous a Gamble"? British Intelligence and Policy during the Chanak Crisis, September–October 1922'. In *Power and Stability: British Foreign Policy, 1865–1965*, edited by Erik Goldstein and B. J. C. McKercher, 139–84. London: 2003.

——. '"The Greatest Power on Earth": Great Britain in the 1920s', *The International History Review* 13:4 (1991): 726–50.

——. 'The Road to Bletchley Park: The British Experience with Signals Intelligence, 1892–1945', *INS* 17:1 (2002): 53–84.

——. 'Treasury Control, the Ten-Year Rule, and British Service Policies, 1919–24', *THJ* 30:4 (1987): 859–83.

——. 'Whitehall's Black Chamber: British Cryptology and the GCCS, 1919–29', *INS* 2:1 (1987): 54–91.

——, and Uri Bar-Joseph. 'Getting Marlowe to Hold His Tongue: The Conservative Party, the Intelligence Services, and the Zinoviev Letter', *INS* 8:4 (1993): 100–37.

Filby, P. William. 'Bletchley Park and Berkeley Street', *INS* 3:2 (1988): 272–84.

——. 'Floradora and a Unique Break into One-Time Pad Ciphers', *INS* 10:3 (1995): 408–22.

Fisher, John. 'The Interdepartmental Committee on Eastern Unrest and British Responses to Bolshevik and Other Intrigues against the Empire during the 1920s', *Journal of Asian History* 34:1 (2000): 1–34.

Freeman, Peter. 'MI1$_{(b)}$ and the Origins of British Diplomatic Cryptanalysis', *INS* 22:2 (2007): 206–28.

Fukuyama, Francis. 'The End of History?', *The National Interest* (summer 1989): 1–17.

Garthoff, Raymond. 'Foreign Intelligence and the Historiography of the Cold War', *Journal of Cold War Studies* 6:2 (2004): 21–56.

Gatrell, Peter. 'Poor Russia, Poor Show: Mobilising a Backward Economy for War, 1914–17'. In *The Economics of World War I*, edited by Stephen Broadberry and Mark Harrison, 235–75. Cambridge: 2005.

Gay, Jules. 'Anglo-Russian Economic Relations', *The Economic Journal* 27:106 (1917): 213–37.

Geyer, Michael. 'The Militarisation of Europe, 1914–45'. In *The Militarisation of the Western World*, edited by John Gillis, 65–102. New Brunswick, NJ: 1989.

Gilbert, Bentley. 'David Lloyd George and the Great Marconi Scandal', *Historical Research: The Bulletin of the Institute of Historical Research* 62:149 (1989): 295–317.

Glenny, M. V. 'The Anglo-Soviet Trade Agreement, March 1921', *Journal of Contemporary History* 5:2 (1970): 63–82.

Goldstein, Erik. 'The Foreign Office and Political Intelligence, 1918–20', *Review of International Studies* 14 (1988): 275–88.

Goodlad, Graham. 'Ditching the Goat: The Fall of Lloyd George', *Modern History Review* 10:4 (1999): 5–8.

Gottschalk, Louis. 'Reflections on Burke's *Reflections on the French Revolution*', *Proceedings of the American Philosophical Society* 100:5 (1956): 417–29.

Graubard, Stephen. 'Military Demobilisation in Great Britain following the First World War', *The Journal of Modern History* 19:4 (1947): 297–311.

Grew, Joseph. 'The Peace Conference of Lausanne, 1922–3', *Proceedings of the American Philosophical Society* 98:1 (1954): 1–10.

Grigg, John. 'Lloyd George: Crusader or Crook?', *Modern History Review* 1:1 (1989): 20–3.

Hamilton, Earl. 'Origin and Growth of the National Debt in Western Europe', *The American Economic Review* 37:2 (1947): 118–30.

Hammant, Thomas R. 'Russian and Soviet Cryptology I: Some Communications Intelligence in Tsarist Russia', *Cryptologia* 24:3 (2000): 235–49.

——. 'Russian and Soviet Cryptology II: The Magdeburg Incident, the Russian View', *Cryptologia* 24:4 (2000): 333–8.

——. 'Russian and Soviet Cryptology III: Soviet COMINT and the Civil War, 1918–1921', *Cryptologia* 25:1 (2001): 50–60.

Hannant, Larry. 'Interwar Security Screening in Britain, the United States, and Canada', *INS* 6:4 (1991): 711–35.

Hendley, Matthew. 'Anti-Alienism and the Primrose League: The Externalisation of the Post-War Crisis in Great Britain, 1918–32', *Albion: A Quarterly Journal concerned with British Studies* 33:2 (2001): 243–69.

Hennessy, Peter, and Gail Brownfeld. 'Britain's Cold War Security Purge: The Origins of Positive Vetting', *THJ* 25:4 (1982): 965–74.

Heymann Jr, Hans. 'Oil in Soviet-Western Relations in the Interwar Years', *American Slavic and East European Review* 7:4 (1948): 303–16.

Hiley, Nicholas. 'Counter-Espionage and Security in Great Britain during the First World War', *The English Historical Review* 101:400 (1986): 635–70.

——. 'Entering the Lists: MI5's Great Spy Round-Up of August 1914', *INS* 21:1 (2006): 46–76.

——. 'Internal Security in Wartime: The Rise and Fall of PMS2, 1915–17', *INS* 1:3 (1986): 395–415.

——. 'Re-Entering the Lists: MI5's Authorized History and the August 1914 Arrests', *INS* 25:4 (2010): 415–52.

——. 'The Strategic Origins of Room 40', *INS* 2:2 (1987): 245–73.

——, and Julian Putkowski. 'A Postscript on PMS2', *INS* 3:2 (1988): 326–31.

Himmer, Robert. 'The Transition from War Communism to the New Economic Policy: An Analysis of Stalin's Views', *Russian Review* 53:4 (1994): 515–29.

Hobson, C. K. 'The Measurement of the Balance of Trade', *Economica* 2 (1921): 132–46.

——. 'The War in Relation to British Foreign Investments', *The Economic Journal* 25:98 (1915): 244–55.

Holland, Max. 'The Propagation of Power of Communist Security Services *Dezinformatsiya*', *IJIC* 19:1 (2005): 1–31.

Holquist, Peter. '"Information is the Alpha and Omega of Our Work": Bolshevik Surveillance in its Pan-European Context', *The Journal of Modern History* 69 (1997): 415–50.

Hope, John. 'Fascism, the Security Service, and the Curious Careers of Maxwell Knight and James McGuirk Hughes', *Lobster* 22 (1991): 1–5.

——. 'Surveillance or Collusion? Maxwell Knight, MI5, and the British Fascisti', *INS* 9:4 (1994): 651–75.

Howson, Susan. 'Slump and Unemployment'. In *The Economic History of Britain since 1700, vol. 2: 1860 to the 1970s*, edited by Roderick Floud and Donald McCloskey, 265–85. Cambridge: 1981.

Huber, Peter. 'Structure of the Moscow Apparatus of the Comintern and Decision-Making'. In *International Communism and the Communist International, 1919–43*, edited by Tim Rees and Andrew Thorpe, 41–64. Manchester: 1998.

Jarvis, David. 'British Conservatism and Class Politics in the 1920s', *The English Historical Review* 111:440 (1996): 59–84.

Jeffery, Keith. 'The British Army and Internal Security, 1919–39', *THJ* 24:2 (1981): 377–97.

——, ed. 'The Government Code and Cypher School: A Memorandum by Lord Curzon', *INS* 1:3 (1986): 454–8.

——, and Alan Sharp. 'Lord Curzon and Secret Intelligence'. In *Intelligence and International Relations, 1900–45*, edited by Christopher Andrew and Jeremy Noakes, 103–26. Exeter: 1987.

——. 'Lord Curzon and the Use of Secret Intelligence at the Lausanne Conference: 1922–3', *The Turkish Yearbook of International Relations* XXIII (1993): 79–89.

Jensen, Peter. 'The Greco-Turkish War, 1920–2', *International Journal of Middle East Studies* 10:4 (1979): 553–65.

Johnson, Simon, and Peter Temin. 'The Macroeconomics of NEP', *The Economic History Review*, New Series, 46:4 (1993): 750–67.

Jones, Gareth. 'The British Government and the Oil Companies, 1912–24: The Search for an Oil Policy', *THJ* 20:3 (1977): 647–72.

Juurvee, Ivo. 'Estonian Interwar Radio-Intelligence', *Baltic Defence Review* 10:2 (2003): 123–37.

——. 'Välisministeeriumi Informatsiooniosakond: Kas Maailmasõdadevhelise Eesti Välisluureteenistus?', *Akadeemia* 2007 (10): 2083–119.

Kahn, David, ed. 'Churchill Pleads for the Intercepts', *Cryptologia* 6:1 (1982): 47–9.

——. 'Soviet Comint in the Cold War', *Cryptologia* 22:2 (1998): 1–24.

Kapera, Zdzisław Jan. *The Enigma Bulletin* 2 (1997).

Kaplan, Herbert. 'Commerce, Consumption, and Culture: Hope & Co. and Baring Brothers & Co. and Russia', *Proceedings of the American Philosophical Society* 142:2 (1998): 258–62.

Kipp, Jacob. 'Lenin and Clausewitz: The Militarisation of Marxism', *Military Affairs* 49:4 (1985): 184–91.

Klein, Ira. 'Whitehall, Washington, and the Anglo-Japanese Alliance, 1919–21', *The Pacific Historical Review* 41:4 (1972): 460–83.

Knight, Amy. 'Russian Archives: Opportunities and Obstacles', *IJIC* 12:3 (1999): 325–37.

Kovalev, Sergei. 'Why Putin Wins', *The New York Review of Books* 54:18 (2007): 64–6.

Krypton, Constantine. 'Secret Religious Organisations in the USSR', *Russian Review* 14:2 (1955): 121–7.

Kux, Dennis. 'Soviet Active Measures and Disinformation: Overview and Assessment', *Parameters, Journal of the US Army War College* 15:4 (1985): 19–28.

Lahaie, Olivier. 'Le Renseignement Militaire Français dans l'Allemagne d'Après-Guerre (mai 1919–mars 1920): A la Recherche d'Une Nouvelle Sécurité', *Revue Historique des Armées* 256 (2009): 32–42.

Landon-Lane, John, and Kim Oosterlinck. 'Hope Springs Eternal … French Bond-holders and the Soviet Repudiation (1915–19).' Solvay Business School, Brussels, 2005.

Lauterbach, Albert. 'Economic Demobilisation in Great Britain after the First World War', *Political Science Quarterly* 57:3 (1942): 376–93.

Lawrence, Jon. 'Forging a Peaceable Kingdom: War, Violence, and Fear of Brutalisation in Post-First World War Britain', *The Journal of Modern History* 75:3 (2003): 557–98.

Leonard, Raymond. 'Studying the Kremlin's Secret Soldiers: A Historiographical Essay on the GRU, 1918–45', *The Journal of Military History* 56 (1992): 403–21.

L'Etang, Jacquie. 'Public Relations and Democracy: Historical Reflections and Implications for Practice.' In *Handbook of Corporate Communications and Public Relations: Pure and Applied*, edited by Sandra M. Oliver, 342–55. London: 2004.

Lyman, Richard. 'Ramsay MacDonald and the Leadership of the Labour Party, 1918–22', *The Journal of British Studies* 2:1 (1962): 132–60.

Macfarlane, L. J. 'Hands Off Russia: British Labour and the Russo-Polish War, 1920', *Past and Present* 38 (1967): 126–52.

Macintyre, Stuart. 'British Labour, Marxism, and the Working Class Apathy in the Nineteen Twenties', *THJ* 20:2 (1977): 479–96.

Macrosty, Henry. 'Statistics of British Shipping', *Journal of the Royal Statistical Society* 89:3 (1926): 452–543.

Madeira, Victor. '"Because I Don't Trust Him, We are Friends": Signals Intelligence and the Reluctant Anglo-Soviet Embrace, 1917–24', *INS* 19:1 (2004): 29–51.

——. 'Moscow's Interwar Infiltration of British Intelligence, 1919–29', *THJ* 46:4 (2003): 915–33.

——. '"No Wishful Thinking Allowed": Secret Service Committee and Intelligence Reform in Great Britain, 1919–23', *INS* 18:1 (2003): 1–20.

Maguire, Richard. '"The Fascists … Are … to Be Depended Upon." The British Government, Fascists, and Strike-Breaking during 1925 and 1926.' In *British Fascism, the Labour Movement, and the State*, edited by Nigel Copsey, 6–26. Basingstoke: 2005.

Mangan, J. A. '"The Grit of Our Forefathers": Invented Traditions, Propaganda, and Imperialism.' In *Imperialism and Popular Culture*, edited by John MacKenzie, 113–39. Studies in Imperialism. Manchester: 1986.

Mawdsley, Evan. 'The Baltic Fleet and the Kronstadt Mutiny', *Soviet Studies* 24:4 (1973): 506–21.

McDonald, Andrew. 'The Geddes Committee and the Formulation of Public Expenditure Policy, 1921–2', *THJ* 32:3 (1989): 643–74.

McIlroy, John. 'The Young Manhood of Arthur Reade.' In *Party People, Communist Lives*, edited by John McIlroy, Kevin Morgan and Alan Campbell, 51–77. London: 2001.

McKay, Craig Graham. 'British SIGINT and the Bear, 1919–1941', *Kungl Krigsvetenskaps-Akademiens Handlingar och Tidskrift* [online edition] 2 (1997): 1–15.

Mellows-Facer, Adam, and Lucinda Maer. 'International Comparisons of Manufacturing Output.' Parliament, House of Commons Library. London: 2012.

Millis, H. A. 'The British Trade Disputes and Trade Unions Act, 1927', *The Journal of Political Economy* 36:3 (1928): 305–29.

Montgomery, A. E. 'The Making of the Treaty of Sèvres of 10 August 1920', *THJ* 15:4 (1972): 775–87.

Murphy, Richard. 'Walter Long, the Unionist Ministers, and the Formation of Lloyd George's Government in December 1916', *THJ* 29:3 (1986): 735–45.

Neilson, Keith. '"Joy Rides"? British Intelligence and Propaganda in Russia, 1914–17', *THJ* 24:4 (1981): 885–906.

O'Halpin, Eunan. 'Financing British Intelligence: The Evidence Up to 1945.' In *British and American Approaches to Intelligence*, edited by Ken Robertson, 187–217. Basingstoke: 1987.

——. 'Sir Warren Fisher and the Coalition, 1919–22', *THJ* 24:4 (1981): 907–27.

Oosterlinck, Kim, and Ariane Szafarz. 'One Asset, Two Prices: The Case of the Tsarist Repudiated Bonds.' Solvay Business School, Brussels, 2004.

Parry, Jon. 'From the Thirty-Nine Articles to the Thirty-Nine Steps: Reflections on the Thought of John Buchan.' In *Public and Private Doctrine: Essays in British History Presented to Maurice Cowling*, edited by Michael Bentley, 209–35. Cambridge: 1993.

Patenaude, Bertrand. 'Peasants into Russians: The Utopian Essence of War Communism', *Russian Review* 54:4 (1995): 552–70.

Pearce, Brian. '1921 and All That', *Labour Review* 5:3 (1960): 84–91.

——. 'Top Cop Who Came Unstuck', *The Newsletter* (1958).

Podsoblyaev, Evgenii. 'The Russian Naval General Staff and the Evolution of Naval Policy, 1905–14', *The Journal of Military History* 66:1 (2002): 37–69.

Pringle, Robert. 'The Heritage and Future of the Russian Intelligence Community', *IJIC* 11:2 (1998): 175–84.

Proctor, Tammy. 'Family Ties in the Making of Modern Intelligence', *Journal of Social History* 39:2 (2005): 451–66.

Pugh, Martin. '"Class Traitors": Conservative Recruits to Labour, 1900–30', *The English Historical Review* 113:450 (1998): 38–64.

Rees, Tim, and Andrew Thorpe. 'Introduction.' In *International Communism and the Communist International, 1919–43*, edited by Tim Rees and Andrew Thorpe, 1–11. Manchester: 1998.

Renshaw, Patrick. 'Anti-Labour Politics in Britain, 1918–27', *Journal of Contemporary History* 12:4 (1977): 693–705.

——. 'The Depression Years, 1918–31.' In *Trade Unions in British Politics: The First 250 Years*, edited by Ben Pimlott and Chris Cook, 88–108. London: 1991.

Roi, Michael L. 'German Holidays: Sir Maurice Hankey Meets the "Ultimate Enemy." Nazi Indoctrination and Physical Training and the DRC's Threat Assessment.' In *Incidents and International Relations: People, Power and Personalities*, edited by Gregory C. Kennedy and Keith Neilson, 113–34. Westport, CT: 2002.

Rybachenok, Irina. 'Takiye Raznyye Klyuchi: Shifrovalnaya Ekspeditsiya MID', *Rodina* 9 (2003): 54–6.

Savage, Gail. 'Social Class and Social Policy: The Civil Service and Secondary Education in England during the Interwar Period', *Journal of Contemporary History* 18:2 (1983): 261–80.

Schinness, Roger. 'An Early Pilgrimage to Soviet Russia: Four Conservative MPs Challenge Tory Party Policy', *THJ* 18:3 (1975): 623–31.

Segal, Eliezer. 'The Treacherous Mr. Trebisch', *The Jewish Free Press*. 24 June 2004.

Seyf, Ahmad. 'Commercialisation of Agriculture: Production and Trade of Opium in Persia, 1850–1906', *International Journal of Middle East Studies* 16:2 (1984): 233–50.

Sharp, Alan. 'Some Relevant Historians – The Political Intelligence Department of the Foreign Office', *Australian Journal of Politics & History* 34:3 (1988): 359–68.

Sinyagina-Woodruff, Yulia. 'Russia, Sovereign Default, Reputation and Access to Capital Markets', *Europe-Asia Studies* 55:4 (2003): 521–51.

Smele, J. D. 'White Gold: The Imperial Russian Gold Reserve in the Anti-Bolshevik

East, 1918–? (An Un-concluded Chapter in the History of the Russian Civil War)', *Europe-Asia Studies* 46:8 (1994): 1317–47.

Smith, Arthur. 'The German General Staff and Russia, 1919–26', *Soviet Studies* 8:2 (1956): 125–33.

Smith, Michael. 'The Government Code and Cipher School and the First Cold War.' In *Action This Day: Bletchley Park from the Breaking of the Enigma Code to the Birth of the Modern Computer*, edited by Michael Smith and Ralph Erskine, 15–40. London: 2001.

Sontag, John. 'Tsarist Debts and Tsarist Foreign Policy', *Slavic Review* 27:4 (1968): 529–41.

Spjut, R. J. 'Defining Subversion', *British Journal of Law and Society* 6:2 (1979): 254–61.

Starr, Kenneth. 'The Framework of Anglo-Soviet Commercial Relations: The British View', *Law and Contemporary Problems* 37:3 (1972): 448–64.

Steiner, Zara, and Michael Dockrill. 'The Foreign Office Reforms, 1919–21', *THJ* 17:1 (1974): 131–56.

Sweetman, John. 'Crucial Months for Survival: The Royal Air Force, 1918–19', *Journal of Contemporary History* 19:3 (1984): 529–47.

Thorpe, Andrew. 'The Membership of the CPGB, 1920–45', *THJ* 43:3 (2000): 777–800.

Thurlow, Richard. 'Soviet Spies and British Counter-Intelligence in the 1930s: Espionage in the Woolwich Arsenal and the Foreign Office Communications Department', *INS* 19:4 (2004): 610–31.

——. 'The Historiography and Source Materials in the Study of Internal Security in Modern Britain (1885–1956)', *History Compass* 6:1 (2008): 147–71.

Tomaselli, Phil. 'C's Moscow Station – The Anglo-Russian Trade Mission as Cover for SIS in the Early 1920s', *INS* 17:3 (2002): 173–80.

Turlington, Edgar. 'The Settlement of Lausanne', *The American Journal of International Law* 18:4 (1924): 696–706.

van der Oye, David Schimmelpenninck. 'Tsarist Codebreaking: Some Background and Some Examples', *Cryptologia* 22:4 (1998): 342–53.

von Tunzelmann, N. 'Britain, 1900–45: A Survey.' In *The Economic History of Britain since 1700, vol. 2: 1860 to the 1970s*, edited by Roderick Floud and Donald McCloskey, 239–64. Cambridge: 1981.

Ward, Stephen. 'Intelligence Surveillance of British Ex-Servicemen, 1918–20', *THJ* 16:1 (1973): 179–88.

Watt, D. Cameron. 'Francis Herbert King: A Soviet Source in the Foreign Office', *INS* 3:4 (1988): 62–82.

Weinberger, Barbara. 'Police Perceptions of Labour in the Interwar Period: The Case of the Unemployed and of the Miners on Strike.' In *Labour, Law, and Crime: An Historical Perspective*, edited by Francis Snyder and Douglas Hay, 150–79. London: 1987.

Willan, T. S. 'Trade between England and Russia in the Second Half of the Sixteenth Century', *The English Historical Review* 63:248 (1948): 307–21.

Willert, Arthur. 'Publicity and Propaganda in International Affairs', *International Affairs (Royal Institute of International Affairs 1931–1939)* 17:6 (1938): 809–26.

Williamson, Philip. 'The Doctrinal Politics of Stanley Baldwin.' In *Public and Private Doctrine: Essays in British History Presented to Maurice Cowling*, edited by Michael Bentley, 181–208. Cambridge: 1993.

Wolman, Leo. 'Union Membership in Great Britain and the United States', *National Bureau of Economic Research Bulletin* 68 (27 December 1937): 1–16.

Yonwin, Jessica. 'UK Election Statistics, 1918–2001.' Parliament, House of Commons Library. London: 2004.

Books

Adams, R. J. Q. *Bonar Law*. London: 1999.

Addison, Paul. *Churchill on the Home Front, 1900–55*. London: 1992.

Aldcroft, Derek. *From Versailles to Wall Street, 1919–29*. The Pelican History of World Economy, edited by Wolfram Fischer. Harmondsworth: 1987.

Aldrich, Richard J. *GCHQ: The Uncensored Story of Britain's Most Secret Intelligence Agency*. London: 2010.

Andrew, Christopher. *For the President's Eyes Only: Secret Intelligence and the American Presidency from Washington to Bush*. London: 1996.

——. *Her Majesty's Secret Service: The Making of the British Intelligence Community*. New York: 1986.

——. *The Defence of the Realm: The Authorized History of MI5*. London: 2010.

——, and Oleg Gordievsky. *KGB: The Inside Story of its Foreign Operations from Lenin to Gorbachev*. London: 1990.

Andrew, Christopher, and Vasili Mitrokhin. *The Mitrokhin Archive: The KGB in Europe and the West*. London: 1999.

Arbel, Dan, and Ran Edelist. *Western Intelligence and the Collapse of the Soviet Union, 1980–90*. London: 2003.

Bagley, Tennent H. *Spy Wars: Moles, Mysteries, and Deadly Games*. New Haven, CT: 2007.

Bainton, Roy. *Honoured by Strangers: The Life of Captain Francis Cromie, 1882–1918*. Shrewsbury: 2002.

Bamford, James. *Body of Secrets: How America's NSA and Britain's GCHQ Eavesdrop on the World*. London: 2001.

——. *The Puzzle Palace: Inside the National Security Agency, America's Most Secret Intelligence Organization*. New York: 1983.

Basov, A. V., ed. *Boevoi put Sovetskogo Voenno-Morskogo Flota*. Moskva: 1988.

Bauer, Friedrich L. *Decrypted Secrets: Methods and Maxims of Cryptography*. Berlin: 2007.

BBC. *BBC London Calling, vol. 3–4*. London: 1963.

Beckett, Francis. *Enemy Within: The Rise and Fall of the British Communist Party*. London: 1995.

Beesly, Patrick. *Room 40: British Naval Intelligence, 1914–18*. London: 1982.

Bennett, G. H., and Marion Gibson. *The Later Life of Lord Curzon of Kedleston – Aristocrat, Writer, Politician, Statesman: An Experiment in Political Biography*. Lewiston, NY: 2000.

Bennett, Gill. *'A Most Extraordinary and Mysterious Business': The Zinoviev Letter of 1924*. London: 1999.

——. *Churchill's Man of Mystery: Desmond Morton and the World of Intelligence*. London: 2006.

Billington, James. *Fire in the Minds of Men: Origins of the Revolutionary Faith*. London: 1980.

Blake, Robert. *The Unknown Prime Minister: The Life and Times of Andrew Bonar Law, 1858–1923*. London: 1955.

Boyd, Brian. *Vladimir Nabokov: The Russian Years*. Princeton, NJ: 1993.

Bray, Gerald. *Documents of the English Reformation, 1526–1701*. Cambridge: 2004.

Broadberry, Stephen. *Market Services and the Productivity Race, 1850–2000: British Performance in International Perspective.* Cambridge Studies in Economic History. Cambridge: 2006.

Briggs, Asa. *The Birth of Broadcasting.* The History of Broadcasting in the United Kingdom, vol. 1. Oxford: 1991.

——, and Peter Burke. *A Social History of the Media: From Gutenberg to the Internet.* London: 2005.

Brook-Shepherd, Gordon. *Iron Maze: The Western Secret Services and the Bolsheviks.* London: 1999.

Broué, Pierre. *The German Revolution, 1917–1923.* Historical Materialism, edited by Ian Birchall and Brian Pearce. Leiden: 2005.

Buchan, John. *The Three Hostages.* Oxford: 1995.

Burke, David. *The Lawn Road Flats: Spies, Writers and Artists.* History of British Intelligence. Woodbridge: 2014.

——. *The Spy Who Came in from the Co-Op.* History of British Intelligence. Woodbridge: 2008.

Burke, Edmund. *Reflections on the Revolution in France.* Edited by J. G. A. Pocock. Indianapolis, IN: 1987.

Butler, David, and Gareth Butler. *Twentieth Century British Political Facts, 1900–2000.* Basingstoke: 2000.

Cain, P. J., and A. G. Hopkins. *British Imperialism, 1688–2000.* Harlow: 2002.

Cannadine, David. *Class in Britain.* New Haven, CT: 1998.

——. *The Decline and Fall of the British Aristocracy.* New Haven, CT: 1990.

Challinor, Raymond. *The Origins of British Bolshevism.* London: 1977.

Chester, Lewis, Stephen Fay, and Hugo Young. *The Zinoviev Letter.* London: 1967.

Childs, Wyndham. *Episodes and Reflections.* London: 1930.

Clarke, Peter. *A Question of Leadership: Gladstone to Thatcher.* London: 1991.

——. *Hope and Glory: Britain, 1900–90.* London: 1997.

Coates, W. P., and Zelda K. *Armed Intervention in Russia, 1918–1922.* London: 1935.

Cook, Andrew. *Ace of Spies: The True Story of Sidney Reilly.* Stroud: 2003.

——. *M: MI5's First Spymaster.* Stroud: 2004.

Cradock, Percy. *Know Your Enemy: How the Joint Intelligence Committee Saw the World.* London: 2002.

Curry, John. *The Security Service, 1908–45: The Official History.* Kew: 1999.

Davies, Norman. *White Eagle, Red Star: The Polish-Soviet War, 1919–20.* London: 1972.

Defty, Andrew. *Britain, America and Anti-Communist Propaganda 1945–53: The Information Research Department.* Abingdon: 2004.

Denniston, Robin. *Thirty Secret Years: Alastair Denniston's Work in Signals Intelligence, 1914–44.* Clifton-upon-Teme: 2007.

de Villemarest, Pierre, and Clifford Kiracoff. *GRU: Le Plus Secret des Services Soviétiques, 1918–88.* Paris: 1988.

Dignan, Don. *The Indian Revolutionary Problem in British Diplomacy, 1914–19.* New Delhi: 1983.

Dorril, Stephen. *MI6: Fifty Years of Special Operations.* London: 2001.

Dukes, Paul. *Red Dusk and the Morrow: Adventures and Investigations in Red Russia.* London: 1923.

Eaden, James, and David Renton. *The Communist Party of Great Britain since 1920.* Basingstoke: 2002.

Elleman, Bruce. *Diplomacy and Deception: The Secret History of Sino-Soviet Diplomatic Relations, 1917–27*. London: 1997.

——. *Moscow and the Emergence of Communist Power in China 1925–30: The Nanchang Rising and the Birth of the Red Army*. Abingdon: 2009.

Emsley, Clive. *The English Police: A Political and Social History*. London: 1996.

Erickson, John. *The Soviet High Command: A Military-Political History, 1918–1941*. London: 2001.

Erskine, Ralph, and Michael Smith. *The Bletchley Park Codebreakers*. London: 2011.

Eudin, Xenia Joucoff, and Harold H. Fisher. *Soviet Russia and the West, 1920–1927: A Documentary Survey*. Stanford, CA: 1959.

Fedor, Julie. *Russia and the Cult of State Security: The Chekist Tradition, from Lenin to Putin*. Studies in Intelligence. London: 2011.

Ferguson, Harry. *Operation Kronstadt*. London: 2008.

Ferguson, Niall. *The World's Banker: The History of the House of Rothschild*. London: 1998.

Fisher, John. *Gentleman Spies: Intelligence Agents in the British Empire and Beyond*. Stroud: 2002.

Fukuyama, Francis. *Our Posthuman Future*. London: 2002.

——. *The End of History and the Last Man*. London: 1992.

Gallacher, William. *Revolt on the Clyde: An Autobiography*. London: 1936.

Gareev, Makhmut. *M. Frunze – Military Theorist*. Washington, DC: 1988.

Garside, W. R. *British Unemployment, 1919–39: A Study in Public Policy*. Cambridge: 1990.

George, Roger, and Robert Kline. *Intelligence and the National Security Strategist: Enduring Issues and Challenges*. Lanham, MD: 2006.

Gilbert, Martin. *Prophet of Truth: Winston Churchill, 1922–39*. London: 1990.

——. *World in Torment: Winston Churchill, 1917–22*. London: 1990.

Gill, Peter. *Policing Politics: Security Intelligence and the Liberal Democratic State*. Studies in Intelligence. London: 1994.

——, and Mark Phythian. *Intelligence in an Insecure World*. Cambridge: 2006.

Gilmour, David. *Curzon*. London: 1994.

Glantz, David. *Barbarossa Derailed: The Battle for Smolensk, 10 July–10 September 1941, vol. 1*. Solihull: 2010.

——, and Harold S. Orenstein, translators and ed. *Belorussia 1944: The Soviet General Staff Study*. Abingdon: 2004.

——, with Jonathan M. House. *To the Gates of Stalingrad: Soviet-German Combat Operations, April–August 1942*. Lawrence, KS: 2009.

Gooch, John. *Mussolini and His Generals: The Armed Forces and Fascist Foreign Policy, 1922–1940*. Cambridge: 2007.

Grigg, John. *Lloyd George: From Peace to War, 1912–16*. London: 2002.

——. *Lloyd George: The People's Champion, 1902–11*. London: 2002.

——. *Lloyd George: The Young Lloyd George*. London: 2002.

——. *Lloyd George: War Leader, 1916–18*. London: 2002.

Gross, Babette. *Willi Münzenberg: A Political Biography*. East Lansing, MI: 1974.

Haines, Roy. *King Edward II: His Life, His Reign, and its Aftermath, 1284–1330*. Montréal: 2003.

Hannaford, Ivan. *Race: The History of an Idea in the West*. Washington, DC: 1996.

Harding, Stan. *The Underworld of State*. London: 1925.

Hayes, J. H. *Some Observations on the Police Strikes, 1918 & 1919*. London: 1921.

Head, Michael. *Crimes against the State: From Treason to Terrorism*. Farnham: 2011.

Hennessy, Peter. *The Secret State: Preparing for the Worst, 1945–2010*. London: 2010.

——. *The Secret State: Whitehall and the Cold War*. London: 2003.

Herman, Michael. *Intelligence Power in Peace and War*. Cambridge: 1996.

Heywood, Anthony. *Engineer of Revolutionary Russia: Iurii V. Lomonosov (1876–1952) and the Railways*. Science, Technology and Culture, 1700–1945. Farnham: 2011.

Hinsley, F. H., and C. A. G. Simkins. *British Intelligence in the Second World War, vol. 4: Security and Counter-Intelligence*. London: 1990.

Hoare, Oliver, ed. *British Intelligence in the Twentieth Century – A Missing Dimension?* Special Issue, *INS* 17:1 (2002).

Hoare, Samuel. *The Fourth Seal: The End of a Russian Chapter*. London: 1930.

Holzman, Michael. *James Jesus Angleton, the CIA & the Craft of Counterintelligence*. Amherst, MA: 2008.

Hopkirk, Peter. *Setting the East Ablaze: On Secret Service in Bolshevik Asia*. Oxford: 1986.

Hostettler, John. *Sir Edward Carson: A Dream Too Far*. Chichester: 1997.

Hughes, Mike. *Spies at Work: The Rise and Fall of the Economic League*. Bradford: 1995.

James, Robert, ed. *Winston Churchill – His Complete Speeches: vol. 3, 1914–22*. New York: 1974.

——. *Winston Churchill – His Complete Speeches: vol. 4, 1922–8*. New York: 1974.

James, William. *The Eyes of the Navy: A Biographical Study of Admiral Sir Reginald Hall*. London: 1955.

Jameson, Fredric. *Postmodernism, or, the Cultural Logic of Late Capitalism*. London: 1991.

Jeffery, Keith. *Field Marshal Sir Henry Wilson: A Political Soldier*. Oxford: 2006.

——. *MI6: The History of the Secret Intelligence Service*. London: 2010.

——, and Peter Hennessy. *States of Emergency: British Governments and Strikebreaking since 1919*. London: 1983.

Jellicoe, John Rushworth. *The Crisis of the Naval War*. London: 1920.

Jenkins, Roy. *Baldwin*. London: 1987.

Judd, Alan. *The Quest for C: Mansfield Cumming and the Founding of the Secret Service*. London: 2000.

Kagan, Robert. *The Return of History and the End of Dreams*. London: 2008.

Keeble, Curtis. *Britain, the Soviet Union and Russia*. Basingstoke: 2000.

Kelsall, R. K. *Higher Civil Servants in Britain: From 1870 to the Present Day*. London: 1955.

King, Joseph. *The Development of Modern Police History in the United Kingdom and the United States*. Criminology Studies. Lewiston, NY: 2004.

Kinvig, Clifford. *Churchill's Crusade: The British Invasion of Russia 1918–20*. London: 2006.

Kirk-Smith, Harold. *William Thomson, Archbishop of York: His Life and Times, 1819–90*. London: 1958.

Knight, Amy. *How the Cold War Began: Igor Gouzenko and the Hunt for Soviet Spies*. Toronto: 2005.

Knox, MacGregor. *Common Destiny: Dictatorship, Foreign Policy, and War in Fascist Italy and Nazi Germany*. Cambridge: 2000.

Knutsen, Torbjørn L. *The Rise and Fall of World Orders*. Manchester: 1999.

Kollwitz, Hans, ed., Richard and Clara Winston, translators. *The Diary and Letters of Kaethe Kollwitz*. Evanston, IL: 1988.

Kolpakidi, Aleksandr, and Dmitriy Prokhorov. *Imperiia GRU: Ocherki Istorii Rossiyskoy Voennoy Razvedki*. Moskva: 2000.

Krasin, Lubov. *Leonid Krassin: His Life and Work*. London: 1929.

Lambert, Nicholas A. *Planning Armageddon: British Economic Warfare and the First World War*. Cambridge: 2012.

Laqueur, Walter. *The Fate of the Revolution: Interpretations of Soviet History*. London: 1970.

Laybourn, Keith. *A Century of Labour: A History of the Labour Party, 1900–2000*. Stroud: 2000.

Lazitch, Branko, and Milorad M. Drachkovitch. *Biographical Dictionary of the Comintern*. Stanford, CA: 1986.

Lenin, Vladimir. *The National-Liberation Movement in the East*. Moscow: 1962.

Leonard, Raymond. *Secret Soldiers of the Revolution: Soviet Military Intelligence, 1918–33*. Contributions in Military Studies. Westport, CT: 1999.

Linehan, Thomas. *British Fascism, 1918–39: Parties, Ideology, and Culture*. Manchester: 2000.

Littell, Robert. *The Company: A Novel of the CIA*. London: 2003.

Lloyd, T. O. *The British Empire, 1558–1995*. Oxford: 1996.

Lucas, Edward. *Deception: Spies, Lies and How Russia Dupes the West*. London: 2013.

——. *The New Cold War: How the Kremlin Threatens both Russia and the West*. London: 2008.

Lurie, V. M., and Kochik, V. Ia. *GRU: Dela I Lyudi*. Sankt Peterburg: 2002.

Macartney, Wilfred. *Walls Have Mouths: A Record of Ten Years' Penal Servitude*. London: 1936.

Macready, Nevil. *Annals of an Active Life: vol. 1 and 2*. London: 1924.

Mallet, Charles. *Lord Cave: A Memoir*. London: 1931.

Mangan, J. A. *'Manufactured' Masculinity: Making Imperial Manliness, Morality and Militarism*. London: 2012.

——. *The Games Ethic and Imperialism: Aspects of the Diffusion of an Ideal*. Harmondsworth: 1986.

Marquand, David. *Ramsay MacDonald*. London: 1997.

Martin, David C. *Wilderness of Mirrors*. New York: 1980.

Marwat, Fazal-ur-Rahim Khan. *The Evolution and Growth of Communism in Afghanistan, 1917–79: An Appraisal*. Karachi: 1997.

Massie, Robert K. *Nicholas and Alexandra*. London: 1967.

Masterman, Lucy. *Charles Masterman: A Biography*. London: 1939.

Mawdsley, Evan. *The Russian Civil War*. Edinburgh: 2000.

Mayer, Arno. *Politics and Diplomacy of Peacemaking: Containment and Counterrevolution at Versailles, 1918–19*. London: 1968.

——. *The Furies: Violence and Terror in the French and Russian Revolutions*. Princeton, NJ: 2000.

McCrillis, Neil. *The British Conservative Party in the Age of Universal Suffrage: Popular Conservatism, 1918–29*. Columbus, OH: 1998.

McKibbin, Ross. *Classes and Cultures – England, 1918–51*. Oxford: 1998.

——. *The Ideologies of Class: Social Relations in Britain, 1880–1950*. Oxford: 1994.

McKnight, David. *Espionage and the Roots of the Cold War: The Conspiratorial Heritage*. Studies in Intelligence. London: 2002.

McMahon, Paul. *British Spies and Irish Rebels: British Intelligence and Ireland, 1916–1945*. History of British Intelligence. Woodbridge: 2008.

McMeekin, Sean. *The Red Millionaire: A Political Biography of Willy Münzenberg, 1917–1940*. New Haven, CT: 2004.

Medlicott, William Norton, *et al.*, ed. *DBFP, 1919–39*, First Series, vol. XVIII. London: 1972.

——. *DBFP, 1919–39*, First Series, vol. XIX. London: 1974.

Middlemas, Keith. *Politics in Industrial Society: The Experience of the British System since 1911*. London: 1979.

Miller, David, and William Dinan. *A Century of Spin: How Public Relations Became the Cutting Edge of Corporate Power*. London: 2008.

Millman, Richard. *British Foreign Policy and the Coming of the Franco-Prussian War*. Oxford: 1965.

Milward, Alan. *The Economic Effects of the Two World Wars on Britain*. London: 1984.

Mitrokhin, Vasiliy, ed. *KGB Lexicon: The Soviet Intelligence Officer's Handbook*. London: 2002.

Morgan, Jane. *Conflict and Order: The Police and Labour Disputes in England and Wales, 1900–39*. Oxford: 1987.

Morgan, Kenneth. *David Lloyd George, 1863–1945*. Cardiff: 1981.

Morris, Lydia. *Dangerous Classes: The Underclass and Social Citizenship*. London: 1994.

NATO. *NATO Handbook 2001*.

Neilson, Keith. *Britain, Soviet Russia and the Collapse of the Versailles Order, 1919–1939*. Cambridge: 2006.

——, and T. G. Otte. *The Permanent Under-Secretary for Foreign Affairs, 1854–1946*. British Politics and Society. Abingdon: 2009.

Nollau, Günther. *International Communism and World Revolution: History and Methods*. London: 1961.

Nott-Bower, William. *Fifty-Two Years a Policeman*. London: 1926.

Occleshaw, Michael. *Dances in Deep Shadows: Britain's Clandestine War in Russia, 1917–20*. London: 2006.

O'Connor, Timothy. *Diplomacy and Revolution: Georgi Chicherin and Soviet Foreign Affairs, 1918–30*. Ames, IA: 1988.

Office, War. *Statistics of the Military Effort of the British Empire during the Great War, 1914–20*. London: 1922.

Osmańczyk, Edmund, and Anthony Mango, ed. *Encyclopedia of United Nations & International Agreements*. London: 2003.

Packer, Ian. *Lloyd George*. London: 1998.

Pearce, Brian, translator. *The Military Writings and Speeches of Leon Trotsky, vol. 5: 1921–1923: How the Revolution Armed*. London: 1979.

Pelling, Henry. *A History of British Trade Unionism*. London: 1992.

Petrie, Charles. *Walter Long and His Times*. London: 1936.

Plotke, A. J. *Imperial Spies Invade Russia: The British Intelligence Interventions, 1918*. Contributions in Military Studies. Westport, CT: 1993.

Popplewell, Richard. *Intelligence and Imperial Defence: British Intelligence and the Defence of the Indian Empire, 1904–24*. Studies in Intelligence. London: 1995.

Porter, Bernard. *Plots and Paranoia: A History of Political Espionage in Britain, 1780–1988*. London: 1989.

——. *The Origins of the Vigilant State: The London Metropolitan Police Special Branch Before the First World War*. Woodbridge: 1991.

Pugh, Martin. *The March of the Women: A Revisionist Analysis of the Campaign for Women's Suffrage, 1866–1914*. Oxford: 2000.

——. *The Pankhursts*. London: 2002.

Ramsay, David. *'Blinker' Hall: Spymaster – The Man who Brought America into World War I*. Stroud: 2009.

Raskolnikov, F. F. *Tales of Sub-Lieutenant Ilyin*. Translated and edited by Brian Pearce. London: 1982.

Reid, Alastair. *United We Stand: A History of Britain's Trade Unions*. London: 2004.

Reith, John. *Into the Wind*. London: 1949.

Reynolds, Gerald, and Anthony Judge. *The Night the Police Went on Strike*. London: 1968.

Riasanovsky, Nicholas. *A History of Russia*. Oxford: 2000.

Rickards, E. C. *Zoe Thomson of Bishopthorpe and Her Friends*. London: 1916.

Rigby, T. H. *Lenin's Government: Sovnarkom, 1917–22*. Cambridge: 1979.

Rogers, Ann. *Secrecy and Power in the British State: A History of the Official Secrets Act*. London: 1997.

Rose, Jonathan. *The Intellectual Life of the British Working Classes*. New Haven, CT: 2001.

Rose, Kenneth. *Elusive Rothschild: The Life of Victor, Third Baron*. London: 2003.

Roskill, Stephen. *Hankey: Man of Secrets, vol. 1: 1877–1918*. London: 1970.

Rothstein, Andrew. *The Soldiers' Strikes of 1919*. London: 1980.

Samuelson, Lennart. *Plans for Stalin's War Machine: Tukhachevskii and Military-Economic Planning, 1925–1941*. Studies in Russian and East European History and Society. Basingstoke: 2000.

Savinsky, A. *Recollections of a Russian Diplomat*. London: 1927.

Searle, Geoffrey. *Corruption in British Politics, 1895–1930*. Oxford: 1987.

Seeger, Murray. *Discovering Russia: 200 Years of American Journalism*. Bloomington, IN: 2005.

Self, Robert. *Britain, America and the War Debt Controversy: The Economic Diplomacy of an Unspecial Relationship, 1917–1941*. Abingdon: 2006.

Sellwood, Arthur. *Police Strike, 1919*. London: 1978.

Sewell, Brian. *Outsider II – Almost Always, Never Quite*. London: 2012.

Skinner, Thomas, ed. *The Directory of Directors for [1914, etc.] – A List of Directors of Joint Stock Companies of the UK*. London: 1914–29.

Slocombe, George. *The Tumult and the Shouting: The Memoirs of George Slocombe*. London: 1936.

Smith, Michael. *Six: A History of Britain's Secret Intelligence Service – Part I: Murder and Mayhem 1909–1939*. London: 2010.

——. *Station X: The Code Breakers of Bletchley Park*. London: 2007.

——. *The Spying Game: The Secret History of British Espionage*. London: 2003.

Soboleva, T. A. *Istoriia Shifrovalnogo Dela v Rossii*. Moskva: 2002.

——. *Tainopis v Istorii Rossii: Istoriia Kriptograficheskoi Sluzhby Rossii "XVIII" – nachala "XX" v.* Moskva: 1994.

Soldatov, Andrei, and Irina Borogan. *The New Nobility: The Restoration of Russia's Security State and the Enduring Legacy of the KGB*. New York: 2010.

Stafford, David. *Churchill & Secret Service*. London: 2000.

Steiner, Zara. *The Lights that Failed: European International History, 1919–33*. Oxford: 2005.

Taylor, A. J. P. *English History, 1914–45.* The Oxford History of England, ed. Sir George Clark. Oxford: 2001.

——, ed. *Lloyd George: A Diary.* New York: 1971.

Taylor, H. A. *The Strange Case of Andrew Bonar Law.* London: 1932.

Thatcher, Margaret. *The Downing Street Years.* London: 1993.

Thomson, Basil. *Queer People.* London: 1922.

——. *The Scene Changes.* London: 1939.

Thorpe, Andrew. *A History of the British Labour Party.* Basingstoke: 2008.

Thurlow, Richard. *Fascism in Modern Britain.* London: 2000.

——. *The Secret State: British Internal Security in the Twentieth Century.* Oxford: 1994.

Tomaselli, Phil. *Tracing Your Secret Service Ancestors.* Barnsley: 2009.

Toye, Richard. *Lloyd George and Churchill: Rivals for Greatness.* London: 2007.

Tucker, Spencer C., ed. *The Encyclopedia of World War I: A Political, Social, and Military History.* Santa Barbara, CA: 2005.

Turner, John, ed. *The Larger Idea: Lord Lothian and the Problem of National Sovereignty.* London: 1988.

Tyrkova-Williams, Ariadna. *Cheerful Giver: The Life of Harold Williams.* London: 1935.

Ullman, Richard. *Anglo-Soviet Relations, 1917–21, vol. 3: The Anglo-Soviet Accord.* Princeton, NJ: 1972.

United Nations. *Treaty Series.*

Van Cleave, Michelle K. *Counterintelligence and National Strategy.* Washington, DC: 2007.

Vincent, David. *The Culture of Secrecy: Britain, 1832–1998.* Oxford: 1998.

Volodarsky, Boris. *Stalin's Agent: The Life and Death of Alexander Orlov.* Oxford: 2014.

von Korostowetz, W. K. *Lenin im Hause der Väter.* Berlin: 1928.

Wakeford, John. *The Cloistered Elite: A Sociological Analysis of the English Public Boarding School.* London: 1969.

Waldron, Arthur. *The Great Wall of China: From History to Myth.* Cambridge: 1990.

Wasserstein, Bernard. *The Secret Lives of Trebitsch Lincoln.* New Haven, CT: 1988.

Watts, Duncan. *Ramsay MacDonald: A Labour Tragedy?* London: 1998.

West, Nigel. *Historical Dictionary of Signals Intelligence.* Edited by Jon Woronoff. Lanham, MD: 2012.

——. *The SIGINT Secrets: The Signals Intelligence War, 1900 to Today: Including the Persecution of Gordon Welchman.* London: 1990.

——, and Oleg Tsarev. *The Crown Jewels: The British Secrets Exposed by the KGB Archives.* London: 1999.

White, Christine. *British and American Commercial Relations with Soviet Russia, 1918–24.* Chapel Hill, NC: 1992.

White, Stephen. *Britain and the Bolshevik Revolution: A Study in the Politics of Diplomacy, 1920–4.* London: 1979.

Willert, Arthur. *Aspects of British Foreign Policy.* New Haven, CT: 1928.

Williams, Andrew J. *Trading with the Bolsheviks: The Politics of East–West Trade, 1920–39.* Manchester: 1992.

Williamson, Philip. *Stanley Baldwin: Conservative Leadership and National Values.* Cambridge: 1999.

——, and Edward Baldwin, ed. *Baldwin Papers: Conservative Statesman, 1908–47.* Cambridge: 2004.

Wilson, Derek. *Sir Francis Walsingham: A Courtier in an Age of Terror.* London: 2007.

Wilson, Keith. *A Study in the History and Politics of* The Morning Post, *1905–26.* Studies in British History. Lewiston, NY: 1990.

Winter, J. M. *The Great War and the British People.* Basingstoke: 1987.

Wolf, Markus, with Anne McElvoy. *Man Without a Face: The Autobiography of Communism's Greatest Spymaster.* London: 1997.

Young, Robert. *Colonial Desire: Hybridity in Theory, Culture, and Race.* London: 1995.

Ziegler, Philip. *The Sixth Great Power: Barings, 1762–1929.* London: 1988.

Zuckerman, Fredric. *The Tsarist Secret Police Abroad: Policing Europe in a Modernising World.* Basingstoke: 2003.

Online Reference Works

Ancestry.co.uk. www.ancestry.co.uk.

Bartleby Quotes. www.bartleby.com.

Encyclopædia Britannica Online. www.britannica.com.

Encyclopædia Iranica. www.iranica.com.

Gazettes Online. www.gazettes-online.co.uk.

London Gazette. www.london-gazette.co.uk.

Matthew, Colin, and Brian Harrison, ed. *ODNB.* www.oxforddnb.com.

MeasuringWorth.com. www.measuringworth.com.

Oxford English Dictionary. www.oed.com.

Spravochnik po Istorii Kommunisticheskoy Partii i Sovetskogo Soyuza, 1898–1991. www.knowbysight.info.

The Glasgow Herald digital archive.

The New York Times digital archive.

The Spectator digital archive.

The Times digital archive.

Time digital archive.

Other Online Sources

'Aleksandr Savinskiy.' www.rusdiplomats.narod.ru.

'Archive of the Central Bank of the Russian Federation.' http://cbr.ru.

Babash, A. V., and E. K. Baranova. 'Kriptograficheskiye Metody Obespecheniya Informatsionnoi Bezopasnosti do Pervoi Mirovoi Voiny', *Tekhnologii Tekhnosfernoi Bezopasnosti* 6:34 (2010): 1–11. http://ipb.mos.ru/ttb.

'Best Cure for Bolshevism.' www.britishpathe.com.

Bletchley Park. www.bletchleypark.org.uk.

Bush, George H. W., President. Address on the Persian Gulf Crisis. 11 September 1990. www.bushlibrary.tamu.edu.

Bush, George W., President. State of the Union Address. 31 January 2006. www.georgewbush-whitehouse.archives.gov.

Clabby, John F. *Brigadier John Tiltman: A Giant among Cryptanalysts.* Fort Meade, MD: 2007. www.nsa.gov.

'Communist Biographies.' www.grahamstevenson.me.uk.

Defense, US Department of. *Joint Publication 1–02: Dictionary of Military and Associated Terms.* 2013. www.dtic.mil.

Elkner, Julie. 'Spiritual Security in Putin's Russia.' www.historyandpolicy.org.

'Federated Press Records.' http://microformguides.gale.com.

'His Grace, Bishop Tikhon (Belavin) of Moscow.' www.oca.org.

Imperial Order of Saint Anna. www.saintanna.ru.

'Joint Intelligence Committee.' www.intelligence.gov.uk.

Kennedy, John F., President. Inaugural Address. 20 January 1961. www.jfklibrary.org.

Mereu, Francesca. 'Putin Made Good on Promise to FSB.' *The Moscow Times.* www.cdi.org.

'National Minority Movement.' www.marxists.org.

NSA Center for Cryptologic History. 'Lecture V.' In *The Friedman Legacy: A Tribute to William and Elizabeth Friedman.* Sources in Cryptologic History 3. www.nsa.gov.

'Our City Balashikha.' www.balashiha.ru.

'Pullen's Lane, the Croft (Sir Arthur Willert, KBE).' www.headington.org.uk.

Putin, Vladimir V., President. State of the Nation Address. 25 April 2005. www.fas.org.

Soldatov, Andrei, and Irina Borogan. 'Istoriia Voennoy Razvedki.' www.agentura.ru.

'Some Facts from the History of Eesti Pank and Estonian Finance.' www.eestipank.ee.

'Special Branch Introduction and Summary of Responsibilities.' www.met.police.uk.

'Stanley Baldwin.' www.number10.gov.uk.

Sugarman, Martin. 'Jewish Personnel at Bletchley Park in World War 2.' www.jewish-virtuallibrary.org.

'The Carl Haessler Collection.' www.reuther.wayne.edu.

Tiltman, John H. 'Experiences 1920–1939.' www.nsa.gov.

WarChron. http://warchron.com.

'Willert, Sir Arthur.' www.library.yale.edu.

Unpublished Sources/Theses

Burke, David. 'Theodore Rothstein and Russian Émigrés in the British Labour Movement, 1884–1920.' Ph.D. diss., University of Greenwich, 1997.

Griggs, Catherine M. 'Beyond Boundaries: The Adventurous Life of Marguerite Harrison.' Ph.D. diss., George Washington University, 1996.

Lokhova, Svetlana. 'The Evolution of the *Cheka*, 1917–26.' M.Phil. thesis, University of Cambridge, 2002.

Wilson, Emily. 'The War in the Dark: The Security Service and the *Abwehr*, 1940–44.' Ph.D. diss., University of Cambridge, 2003.

Index